Canada and Africa in the New Millennium

Canada &Africa in the New Millennium

The Politics of Consistent Inconsistency

David R. Black

WILFRID LAURIER
UNIVERSITY PRESS

This book has been published with the help of a grant from the Canadian Federation for the Humanities and Social Sciences, through the Awards to Scholarly Publications Program, using funds provided by the Social Sciences and Humanities Research Council of Canada. Wilfrid Laurier University Press acknowledges the financial support of the Government of Canada through the Canada Book Fund for our publishing activities.

Library and Archives Canada Cataloguing in Publication

Black, David R. (David Ross), 1960–, author
Canada and Africa in the new millennium : the politics of consistent inconsistency / David R. Black.

Includes bibliographical references and index.
Issued in print and electronic formats.
ISBN 978-1-77112-060-9 (pbk.).—ISBN 978-1-77112-062-3 (epub).—ISBN 978-1-77112-061-6 (pdf)

1. Canada—Foreign relations—Africa. 2. Africa—Foreign relations—Canada. 3. Canada—Politics and government—1993–2006. 4. Canada—Politics and government—2006–. I. Title.

FC244.A35B53 2015   327.7106   C2014-905560-9
                                              C2014-905561-7

Cover design by Blakeley Words+Pictures. Front-cover image by The Canadian Press/ Sean Kilpatrick. Text design by James Leahy.

© 2015 Wilfrid Laurier University Press
Waterloo, Ontario, Canada
www.wlupress.wlu.ca

MIX
Paper from
responsible sources
FSC® C004071

This book is printed on FSC® certified recycled paper and is certified Ecologo. It is made from 100% post-consumer fibre, processed chlorine free, and manufactured using biogas energy.

Printed in Canada

Contents

Preface vii

List of Abbreviations xi

Introduction 1

1 Theorizing Canadian Policy toward Africa 15

2 Canada, the G8, and Africa: The Rise and Decline
of a Hegemonic Project 37

3 "Africa" as Serial Morality Tale in Canadian Foreign Policy 61

4 "Iconic Internationalists" and the Representation
of Canada in/through Africa 83

5 Canadian Aid to Africa: The Elusive Search for Purpose 97

6 Canada and Peace Operations in Africa: The Logic
and Limits of Engagement 127

7 Canadian Extractive Companies in Africa: Exposing the
Hegemonic Imperative (*with Malcolm Savage*) 151

8 Conclusion: Africa Policy and the End of
Liberal Internationalism? 183

Appendix A: Canadian Bilateral Aid to
Sub-Saharan Africa 1990–2010 201

Appendix B: United Nations Peace Support
Missions since 1990 205

Appendix C: Key Canadian Contributions to Peace Operations in
Africa since 1990 219

Notes 245

References 261

Index 289

Preface

As this book was being finalized, around the time of the twentieth anniversary of the Rwandan genocide, another acute humanitarian and political crisis was unfolding in another small, landlocked central African country. When this preface was being written, the renewed crisis in the Central African Republic (CAR) had already displaced nearly a million of the country's 4.5 million people and generated an appalling catalogue of atrocity crimes, mainly committed along sectarian lines. African Union (AU) and French forces were already on the ground, but insufficient given the magnitude and complexity of the crisis. The UN Security Council had authorized a nearly 12,000-person peacekeeping force to be deployed by mid-September 2014. Meanwhile in Ottawa in late April, Canadian government representatives expressed their "extreme concern" and condemnation of the atrocities, and asserted that Canada was "pulling its weight" with a C$16 million contribution of humanitarian assistance and C$5 million contribution in support of the AU and French operations, but were evasive about the possibility of any direct involvement in the planned peacekeeping force. At the same time, six CF-18 fighters and accompanying military personnel had been quickly deployed to bolster NATO's presence in the context of the political crisis in the Ukraine, and 500 election observers were being sent to monitor the Ukrainian elections. At this relatively early stage at least, there was a more or less directly proportional mismatch between the human costs of the crisis in the CAR on the one hand, and the economic, human, and security resources deployed to the Ukraine on the other.

We cannot know at the time this is being written how either of these crises will unfold, but the response thus far has been telling—particularly in light of previous Canadian contributions to "peacekeeping" operations in both Rwanda during the genocide, and the Central

African Republic subsequently (MINURCA, 1998–2000). It would be easy to conclude, based on these observations, that there has been a decisive shift in the current Canadian government's approach to African crises and challenges from that of its predecessors. There is considerable truth in this conclusion. At the same time, however, it runs the risk of overstating the differences, as well as the virtues, of previous governments, and of understating the significant ongoing limitations and inconsistencies that have marked Canada's involvement in sub-Saharan Africa over time. It is this broader and more contextualized understanding that this book seeks to foster.

The research and writing of it has taken an inordinately long period of time. The reasons for this are unimportant; what matters is that, as a result of this lengthy process, I have many to thank for enabling me to get to this point. Essential financial assistance was provided by a Standard Research Grant of the Social Sciences and Humanities Research Council of Canada (SSHRC), the Awards to Scholarly Publications Program of the Federation for the Humanities and Social Sciences, and Dalhousie University. I am grateful to them all. In the course of my peripatetic research and writing process, I benefited greatly from the hospitality and insights of hosts in a number of locations: Ulf Engel in Leipzig and Berlin; Mary Breen in Addis Ababa; Oliver Jutersonke, Keith Krause, and Sandra Reimann at the Centre on Conflict, Development, and Peacebuilding in Geneva; and the Department of International Relations at the University of the Witwatersrand.

While this is clearly not an insider's account, various Canadian, German, British, Ethiopian, and African Union practitioners (governmental and non-governmental) and analysts enriched my understanding. Interviewed on a non-attribution basis, they cannot be named but I am enormously grateful to them all for sharing their time and insights. While several dozen were interviewed for this particular project, many others have assisted with previous and related work, both formally and informally, and in doing so have also aided my understanding of the subject. It is my hope that the opportunities for interaction and exchange with public officials that scholars in my field rely on, but which have become constrained of late, will become more open and productive again in future.

Many friends and colleagues have read versions of the chapters that follow, and have provided valuable comments and critiques.

They include: Bruno Charbonneau, Wayne Cox, Bob Edwards, David Hornsby, Chris Kukucha, Heather Smith, Tiffany Steel, and Paul Williams. A special thanks goes to "partners in crime" Stephen Brown and Molly den Heyer, both of whom read large portions of the manuscript (in Molly's case, the whole thing) and provided sage advice, often in tight time frames. I am also grateful to the three anonymous reviewers for WLU Press, whose comments significantly strengthened the final product. Needless to say, any remaining errors of fact and judgment are entirely my own.

Chapter 2 is a revised and updated version of David Black, "Canada, the G8, and Africa: The Rise and Decline of a Hegemonic Project?" in Duane Bratt and Christopher J. Kukucha, eds., *Readings in Canadian Foreign Policy: Classic Debates and New Ideas*, 2nd ed. (Toronto: Oxford University Press Canada, 2011). It is used with the permission of Oxford University Press. Much of Chapter 7 appeared originally in substantially different form in David Black and Malcolm Savage, "Mainstreaming Investment: Foreign and Security Policy Implications of Canadian Extractive Industries in Africa," in Bruno Charbonneau and Wayne S. Cox, eds., *Relocating Global Order: American Power and Canadian Security After 9/11* (Vancouver: UBC Press, 2010). It is used with the permission of UBC Press. Portions of chapters 2 and 5 appeared originally in substantially different form in David Black, "Between Indifference and Idiosyncracy: The Conservatives and Canadian Aid to Africa," in Stephen Brown, ed., *Struggling for Effectiveness: CIDA and Canadian Foreign Aid* (Kingston: McGill-Queen's University Press, 2012).Thanks to the publishers for permission to use this material. Thanks as well to Lisa Quinn at WLU Press for her patience and ongoing confidence in this project.

Many current and former graduate students made indispensable contributions as research assistants and sounding boards. They have included: Jenny Baechler, Emily Colpitts, Sarah Dunphy, Jordan Guthrie, David Morgan, Ben O'Bright, Malcolm Savage (co-author on Chapter 7), and Carla Suarez. Working closely with graduate students has been one of the great, unanticipated pleasures of my job and I am grateful for all they have done to challenge and teach me.

A number of fellow travellers of more and less long-standing have provided ideas, support, and friendship through the long and sometimes lonely process of research and writing. More recently, I have benefited from the support and encouragement of a new generation of scholars deeply interested in Canada's relationship(s) with Africa. They include Edward Akuffo, Bruno Charbonneau, David Hornsby, and Chris Roberts. Long-time friends have been sources of inspiration, encouragement, and good company in too many times and places to be accurately remembered—among them Erin Baines, Audie Klotz, Jane Parpart, Heather Smith, Claire Turenne Sjolander, Jean-Philippe Thérien, Susan Thomson, Rebecca Tiessen, and Janis van der Westhuizen. My earliest and longest companion on this intellectual journey, from Ginger's in Halifax to the WUSC guest house in Gaborone, to Greenmarket Square in Cape Town, to the wilds of Waterloo, Ontario, has been Larry Swatuk. Here's to the next steps in the journey!

Mentorship, for me at least, is a quality that is often unrecognized and underappreciated at first, but that unfolds, enriches, and inspires in enduring and surprising ways. Two Dalhousie mentors among many—Tim Shaw and Denis Stairs—have stood out in stimulating and shaping my ongoing interest in the subject of this book. Two more distant mentors—Cranford Pratt and Doug Anglin—might be surprised by the impact they have had, but continue to serve as inspirations.

Finally, my family has shared the many trials, distractions, and detours of the writing process. Through it all, they have kept me grounded and supported. This book is for Rory, Holly, Elizabeth, and Heather.

Abbreviations

AAP	G8 Africa Action Plan
AE	Analytic Eclecticism
AMIS	African Union Mission in Sudan
APF	Africa Partnership Forum
APSA	African Peace and Security Architecture
AU	African Union
CAR	Central African Republic
CCIC	Canadian Council for International Cooperation
CF	Canadian Forces
CFA	Commission for Africa
CIDA	Canadian International Development Agency
CIDMAA	Centre d'information et de documentation sur le Mozambique et l'Afrique australe
CIFA	Canada Investment Fund for Africa
CIIEID	Canadian International Institute for Extractive Industries and Development
CNCA	Canadian Network on Corporate Accountability
CPA	Comprehensive Peace Agreement
CPF	Country Programming Framework
CPP	Canada Pension Plan
CSO	Civil Society Organization
CSR	Corporate Social Responsibility
CUSO	Canadian University Services Overseas
DFAIT	Department of Foreign Affairs and International Trade
DFATD	Department of Foreign Affairs, Trade and Development
DITF	Darfur Integrated Task Force

DND	Department of National Defence
DRC	Democratic Republic of the Congo
ECOWAS	Economic Community of West African States
EDC	Export Development Canada
EITI	Extractive Industries Transparency Initiative
EU	European Union
G8	Group of Eight
G20	Group of Twenty
GPOP	Global Peace Operations Program
ICISS	International Commission on Intervention and State Sovereignty
IFI	International Financial Institution
IPS	International Policy Statement
ISAF	International Security Assistance Force
MDGS	Millennium Development Goals
MI	Muskoka Initiative
MNCH	Maternal, Newborn and Child Health
MNF	Multinational Force
MINURCA	United Nations Mission in the Central African Republic
MONUC	United Nations Mission in the Democratic Republic of the Congo
MONUSCO	United Nations Stabilization Mission in the Democratic Republic of the Congo
MSF	Médecins Sans Frontières
MTAP	Military Training Assistance Program
MTCP	Military Training Cooperation Program
NATO	North Atlantic Treaty Organization
NDHQ	National Defence Headquarters
NEPAD	New Partnership for Africa's Development
NGDO	non-governmental development organization
NGO	non-governmental organization
NRCAN	Natural Resources Canada
ODA	Official Development Assistance
ODAAA	Official Development Assistance Accountability Act
OECD DAC	Organization for Economic Cooperation and Development—Development Assistance Committee

PBA	Program Based Approaches
PPC	Pearson Peacekeeping Centre
PRSP	Poverty Reduction Strategy Paper
PSO	Peace Support Operation
R2P	Responsibility to Protect
RCAF	Royal Canadian Air Force
SAP	Structural Adjustment Program
SCFAIT	Standing Committee on Foreign Affairs and International Trade
SHIRBRIG	Standby High-Readiness Brigade
START	Stabilization and Reconstruction Task Force
TCLSAC	Toronto Committee for the Liberation of Southern Africa
UDI	Unilateral Declaration of Independence (Rhodesia)
UN	United Nations
UNAMID	African Union–United Nations Mission in Darfur
UNAMIR	United Nations Assistance Mission for Rwanda
UNAMIS	United Nations Advance Mission in Sudan
UNMISS	United Nations Mission in South Sudan
UNAMSIL	United Nations Mission in Sierra Leone
UNCTAD	United Nations Conference on Trade and Development
UNDP	United Nations Development Program
UNITAF	Unified Task Force
UNMEE	United Nations Mission in Ethiopia and Eritrea
UNMIL	United Nations Mission in Liberia
UNMIS	United Nations Mission in the Sudan
UNOCI	United Nations Operation in Côte d'Ivoire
UNOMIL	United Nations Observer Mission in Liberia
UNOSOM	United Nations Operation in Somalia
UNSG	United Nations Secretary-General
UNTAG	United Nations Transition Assistance Group (Namibia)
WEF	World Economic Forum
WEOG	Western European and Other Group
WTO	World Trade Organization

Introduction

Canada has played an important role in bringing African issues onto the global agenda, within the G8 and other forums. We will continue to press forward, in close collaboration with other partners in Africa and with other donors, to support regional initiatives such as NEPAD.

—Government of Canada, *International Policy Statement—A Role of Pride and Influence in the World: Development*, 2005

In the last five years, the Conservatives have walked away from Africa... Canada must return to Africa. We must rejoin the fight against extreme poverty, malaria, HIV/AIDS, and the effects of climate change. And we must empower women—in Africa and across the developing world.

—Michael Ignatieff, "Rebuilding Canada's Leadership on the World Stage," Speech to the Montreal Council on Foreign Relations, 2 November 2010

This year, joining the hundreds in the crowd [for the Africa Day celebration in Ottawa], were two noticeable additions from the past few years: Foreign Affairs Minister John Baird and Trade Minister Ed Fast. Members of the diplomatic corps and observers applauded the attendance of the two ministers, calling it "unprecedented," with one Tory saying they joined the celebrations to drive forward Canada's relations with the continent.

—Sneh Duggal, "Debating the Beginnings of an African Strategy," 6 June 2012

Canada's engagement with post-independence Africa presents a puzzle. On the one hand, much of the country's identity and reputation as a good international citizen has rested on activism toward the continent, through diplomatic initiatives in multilateral organizations,

1

through aid and humanitarian relief, through (more controversially) multilateral "peace operations," and through the leadership of particular Canadian internationalists. Examples have included the roles played by John Diefenbaker and Brian Mulroney in relation to apartheid South Africa; the extraordinary response to the Ethiopian famine of the mid-1980s; Roméo Dallaire's witness, and ongoing response, to the Rwandan genocide; and Jean Chrétien's leadership in orchestrating the G8's 2002 Africa Action Plan. On the other hand, critics have long noted the inconsistencies and contradictions of Canadian involvement in Africa: through erratic aid policies that benefit Canadians and reinforce inequities; through security policies that fail to match normative advocacy of high-minded principles with sufficient resources to realistically support them; and through large extractive industry investments that undermine local environments and human security. How are we to make sense of these inconsistencies and, more broadly, of the place of Africa in the Canadian political imagination? How, more specifically, do we explain a record that, as reflected in the epigraphs above, has oscillated within the past decade between aspirations toward global diplomatic leadership, through transparent indifference, to renewed interest and initiative?

This book seeks to make sense of the puzzle of Canadian involvement in sub-Saharan Africa. Though the focus is primarily on the period since the start of the new millennium, marked by the striking juxtaposition of Jean Chrétien's G8 activism and Stephen Harper's retreat from continental engagement, these comparatively recent trends are part of a longer history of consistent inconsistency, in which the prominent role of African issues in the Canadian political imagination has been in chronic tension with the country's limited and contradictory role in addressing Africa's multiple challenges.

No one interpretive frame can adequately explain this record. Rather, I will argue that three approaches must be combined to account for it. Canada's involvement in Africa reflects, first, genuine instances of activist engagement, reflecting a more cosmopolitan or solidarist tradition of what international society theorists characterize as "good international citizenship." These instances are the necessary foundation for two other, less celebratory theoretical accounts: Canada's role as a benign face of, and key interlocutor for, western hegemonic interests in Africa; and Africa's role as the basis for a resilient narrative concerning Canada's ethical "mission" in the world, and thus a cornerstone of Canadian identity—a story we tell our-selves about ourselves. The question that comes to the fore in light of the Harper government's departure from the post-colonial pattern of Canadian involvement in Africa is whether this most recent phase should be understood as simply the latest oscillation in the historic pattern of consistent inconsistency, or a more fundamental break with—and retreat from—the liberal internationalist narrative of the Cold War and immediate post–Cold War periods? While this ques-tion is impossible to answer definitively, the framework developed in this book provides the basis for a more theoretically grounded account of what the Harper government has sought to change, and why. It also underscores the way in which Africa—though relatively marginal to Canadian interests as traditionally conceived—has served as an important marker of the wider characteristics of Canada's inter-national role.

In order to properly understand Africa's place in Canada's foreign relations, and Canada's role in Africa, it is necessary to provide an account that encompasses the most important dimensions of Can-adian involvement and their cumulative impact. Thus, in contrast to most previous treatments of Canada's involvement in Africa, this book combines a focus on: multilateral, and particularly G8, diplo-macy; foreign aid—the traditional touchstone of Canada's contin-ental role; security assistance through peace operations and training; and the role of Canadian extractive companies, which have become this country's dominant and deeply controversial face in many parts of the continent. While it is impossible for one book to provide a comprehensive account of Canadian involvement in this huge and diverse region, it is essential that we move beyond views that extrapo-late and generalize from isolated cases and issues.

The research for this book thus draws together comparative his-torical and thematic analyses of the key aspects of Canada's African presence, and its place in the forging of Canadian identity. It aims to provide a comprehensive theoretical account of this country's record and role. As well as secondary and journalistic sources, it is based on interviews and documentary research from publicly available sources, drawing on insights from Canadian practitioners and scholars as well as counterparts in the UK, Germany, Ethiopia, and Tanzania. Thus, although my purpose is fundamentally interpretive, I hope that indi-vidual chapters will be sufficiently grounded to provide persuasive contributions to the thematic debates concerning Canada's evolving roles in multilateral diplomacy, development assistance, peace operations, and the extractive sector.

The Contours of Consistent Inconsistency

There are two linked premises that underpin the analysis in this book. The first is that, particularly judged according to traditional Realist theoretical assumptions, sub-Saharan Africa has been and remains marginal to what would be regarded as core Canadian "national interests." The second is that, notwithstanding (indeed partly because of) this apparent marginality, Canadian involvement in Africa has reflected a recurrent pattern of high-level engagement and intense media and popular focus followed, and sometimes accompanied, by a kind of collective amnesia or indifference. It is this pattern that I characterize as consistent inconsistency. Although the chapters that follow elaborate and explore these premises, they require some clarification at this initial stage.

Africa's historic marginality to Canada and Canadians is a familiar theme that can be quickly summarized (see also C. Brown 2001, 195–98). Because Canada was not a colonial power in Africa, and was indeed itself a settler colony of Britain,[1] its historic linkages with Africa's post-colonial governments and societies were limited and shallow, but also relatively untainted by perceptions of neo-colonialism. Closely related to this was the fact that geostrategically, Canadian interests on the continent were limited and largely derivative. From the perspective of Canadian defence and security policy, Canada's core relationships were those formalized through the Western alliances of NATO and NORAD. Thus, for the first several post-decolonization decades, official Canada tended to view sub-Saharan Africa through the prism of the Cold War, and to manifest a particular sensitivity to the interests of its most important Western allies, including the UK, France, and the US. These motivations were both mitigated and facilitated by its dedication to the more inclusive manifestations of the post–Second World War multilateral order, including the United Nations, the Commonwealth, and, belatedly, la Francophonie. Economic linkages—the other critical dimension of what is traditionally construed as the national interest—have been consistently marginal in relative terms. Grant Dawson (2013, 15) has noted that trade with

Africa remained between 1 percent and 1.5 percent of total Canadian trade in 1969, 1979, and 1989, and had declined to 0.5 percent by 1999, reflecting the dire effects of what was widely portrayed as Africa's "lost decade" during the 1990s. Despite a decade of relatively rapid recovery and growth from 2000, marked particularly by the leading role of the Canadian extractive sector (see Chapter 7), Canadian exports to Africa still amounted to less than 1 percent of total exports in 2011, and around 3 percent of total imports (Schorr and Hitschfeld 2013, 139). Trans-societal linkages, through civil society organizations and, more recently, growing immigration and diasporas, were vibrant but secondary from the perspective of most political leaders and government officials. It is not surprising, therefore, that the most robust and consistent foundation for bilateral relations through the bulk of the post-decolonization era was development assistance or foreign aid, with Africa remaining the largest regional recipient of Canadian aid flows.

What *is* surprising, in light of this historical marginality, is the frequency with which Canada's engagements in Africa have been seen as a top priority of Canadian governments, and/or as exemplars of Canada's role and identity in the world. Yet interspersed with these exemplary "moments" were periods of what were widely perceived as disappointment, dereliction, and/or neglect. Both tendencies have been overstated in practice, but their consistent coexistence is at the root of the puzzle this book seeks to understand. In short, this pattern of consistent inconsistency can be identified both *empirically* and *discursively*, in mutually reinforcing ways.

Empirically, the most obvious instances of inconsistency can be located within Canadian aid policy. These have been reflected, above all, in the dramatic, medium-term swings in aid spending—from the major cuts of the mid-1990s, to the substantial reinvestments of the first decade of the twenty-first century, to the renewed cuts of the 2010s. Notably, these spending swings straddled governments of both Liberal and Conservative partisan stripes. Because Africa was, and remains, the most aid-dependent continent, the impact of these swings has been most acute in this region and the relationships it encompasses. But beyond these macro-level trends, there have been other, more routine inconsistencies: of thematic priorities, of country "partnerships," and of administrative modalities (discussed at length in Chapter 5). The insidious impacts of these unstable priorities and practices mean that it is very difficult to arrive at a reasonable assessment of the long-term effects of Canadian aid to Africa—thus helping to fuel the persistent and corrosive debates concerning "aid effectiveness."

Inconsistent practices are not limited to the aid domain however. There has also been inconsistency in Canada's commitments to peace operations and peacekeeping training, most strikingly in the two decades from 1990 (see Chapter 6). Similarly, there has been a consistent inconsistency between expansive rhetoric in support of African human security (as seen, for example, in advocacy of the responsibility to protect and the related emphasis on civilian protection and the rights of children and youth), and the paucity of resources deployed to act on these priorities. Likewise, there has been a gap between various instances of short-term crisis response and the medium- to long-term imperatives of "peacebuilding" (for example, in Sierra Leone or northern Uganda).

Discursively, these practical inconsistencies have combined with inflated self-assessments and expectations to generate what is characterized in Chapter 3 as a kind of serial morality tale. In short, Canadian "leadership" on African issues (for example, apartheid South Africa, the Africa Action Plan adopted by the G8 at the 2002 Kananaskis Summit, or the Muskoka Initiative on Maternal, Newborn and Child Health) is widely portrayed as exemplifying our "normal" or best selves, marked by prominent instances of ethically oriented activism on the global stage. Conversely, these ethical exemplars have been interspersed with what have been widely seen as instances of dereliction or "abandonment"—for example, the peacekeeping failures of Somalia and Rwanda; the abrupt ending of bilateral aid programs; the amoral pursuit of trade and investment relations within and beyond Africa at the expense of commitments to human rights and security; or indeed the mundane indifference to the many acute human security and development challenges that never make it onto the popular and political agenda. Running parallel to this Africa-centric morality tale, meanwhile, has been a persistent alternative narrative within government circles and among some Realist commentators. In this "realist internationalist" view (Boucher 2012), Canadian governments have too often misunderstood or neglected their primary obligations, relationships, and interests by expending precious time and resources on remote and intractable African "causes." The interplay of these alternative narratives has thus placed sub-Saharan Africa at the centre of debates concerning the inconsistencies and contradictions of Canada's ethical role and values in the world.

The core purpose of this book is to understand the origins and repercussions of these inconsistencies.

Alternative Accounts of Canada in Africa

Remarkably, and in contrast to other major world regions (notably Latin America), there were almost no book-length scholarly analyses of Canada's role in sub-Saharan Africa prior to 2012—despite the striking interest and controversy surrounding various manifestations of Canadian involvement since the beginning of African decoloniz- ation over fifty years ago. A handful of older works have provided relatively comprehensive but slim and/or conceptually limited dis- cussions of Canadian policy at earlier stages in its evolution (e.g., Matthews 1976; Schlegel 1978; A. Clark 1991). More typically, previ- ous contributions focused on particular cases or dimensions within Canadian policy, such as longstanding debates concerning Canada's role in relation to apartheid South Africa (e.g., L. Freeman 1997; R. Pratt 1997) or Canadian development assistance (e.g., Pratt 1994; Morrison 1998). In the more recent past, new thematic and/ or case-based studies have emerged to address various African situa- tions, directly or indirectly. For example, Razack (2004) and Daw- son (2007) have provided alternative accounts of Canada's traumatic deployment of a large "peacekeeping" contingent to Somalia in the immediate aftermath of the Cold War. A new cluster of works from critical, materialist scholar-activists have tackled various aspects of Canada's role in the developing world, including the increasingly prominent role of Canadian extractive industries, rising militarism in the context of Canada's protracted deployment to Afghanistan, and the contradictions of non-governmental development organizations (see, e.g., Gordon 2010; Engler 2012; and Barry-Shaw and Jay 2012). These accounts have provided important and provocative insights, but have difficulty accounting for instances of more genuinely soli- daristic activism, and have not been focused on the way in which Canadian identity has been constituted through the narration of our engagement with Africa. Stephen Brown's (2012b) edited collection on Canadian aid policy and the Canadian International Development Agency (CIDA)—the latter folded into the new Department of Foreign Affairs, Trade, and Development (DFATD) as of mid-2013— has re-energized the strong tradition of scholarship in this area, but it is exclusively concerned with aid policy thematically while ranging well beyond Africa geographically.

Two recent books have provided the first full treatments of Canada's relations with, and role in, sub-Saharan Africa.[2] The 2013 edition of the long-running annual *Canada Among Nations* is focused entirely on Canada's involvement in the continent. This wide-ranging collection has the virtue of thematic breadth and timeliness, but the characteristic limitation of such edited works in terms of limited theoretical focus or analytical consistency. The most substantial single-authored monograph to date is Edward Akuffo's 2012 study of *Canadian Foreign Policy in Africa*. This important study was conceived and written in the shadow of the human security era, extending through much of the Chrétien-Martin years of Liberal rule. Its focus on Canadian involvement in African regional peace, security, and development innovations does not, therefore, provide a full account of the degree and logic of the changes to Canadian involvement in Africa under the Harper Conservatives. It is underpinned theoretically by a constructivist, "non-imperial internationalist" framework stressing the degree to which Canada's "moral identity" in Africa is co-constituted through the engagement between Canadian and African policies and officials. This framework has some affinity with both the "good international citizenship" and the post-colonial frames developed in this book. It highlights Canada's lack of a formal imperial role in Africa in shaping both the character of its involvement on the continent, and the relatively benign way it has been perceived by many African counterparts. Yet this focus on what is *distinct* about Canada's African role underplays the degree to which Canadian policy and practice has reflected a concerted Western approach toward the continent. It also does not account for the apparent ease with which key elements of this Canadian moral identity, such as the "human security agenda" and Canadian development assistance "partnerships," can be as easily disrupted or dispensed with as they have been.

Limitations

Any study of this breadth and ambition, thematically and conceptually, is bound to have some significant limitations. Here, I note four in particular. First, in attempting to come to grips with the place of (sub-Saharan) "Africa" in the Canadian political imagination, the book remains at a relatively high level of abstraction. This reflects the fact that in Canada "Africa is often seen as an undifferentiated entity based ... largely on the [Canadian] imagination," to borrow a phrase from Julia Gallagher's study (2011, 22) of Britain's Africa policy under Prime Minister Tony Blair. While I have attempted to mitigate this level of abstraction through frequent references to specific illustrative cases, this approach obviously does not adequately represent the rich and varied characteristics of this remarkable continent. It can be justified, I would argue, because the very fact that Africa is conceived in this relatively abstract and homogeneous way has important consequences for policy and practice, as I will discuss particularly in Chapter 3.

Second, the important francophone African dimension of Canada's role in Africa, while not absent, deserves fuller treatment. One of the most important foundations for Canada's relatively extensive involvement in the continent is this country's bilingual character and identity, and the Canadian government's efforts beginning in the late 1960s to represent it as such (see Gendron 2006; Schlegel 1978). This has both *enabled* more extensive Canadian involvement in Africa than in most other comparably distant regions, and *motivated* this involvement as a result of the ongoing federal(ist) effort to forge an inclusive, bilingual identity and mitigate nationalist/sovereigntist challenges emanating from the Province of Quebec. More careful attention to the "French fact" in Canada-Africa relations than I have been able to provide is therefore warranted.

Third, the focus on extractive industry investment in Africa, while justified by the extraordinary importance of Canadian-based mining companies on the continent (and indeed globally), means that other dimensions of Canada's growing economic interests in Africa are relatively neglected (see, e.g., Schorr and Hitschfield 2013). These include, but are not limited to, trade relations, engineering, transportation, financial and other services, telecommunications, and education. The role and interests of firms and institutions in these sectors will have a significant bearing on the future of the relationship, especially in the context of the growing international emphasis on the emergence of a "Rising Africa" and the growing economic opportunities it is said to embody.

Fourth, in focusing on the most historically salient dimensions of the Canada-Africa relationship, increasingly important trans-societal linkages are relatively neglected. These include both long-standing relationships between civil society and non-governmental organizations in Africa and Canada, and even more significantly, rapidly growing African diaspora communities in Canada (see, e.g., Carment, Nikolko, and Douhaibi 2013; Tettey and Puplampu 2005). It remains to be seen how these trans-societal linkages will affect the broader relationship, particularly as relatively new and insecure African diaspora communities in Canada find their political and economic footing in succeeding generations. In particular, it will be important in future research to assess the degree to which they may mitigate the consistent inconsistency that has marked the policies of the past.

Map of the Book

The first several chapters of this book lay out the conceptual foundations for its argument. Chapter 1 provides an elaboration of the "analytically eclectic" (Katzenstein and Sil 2008) theoretical framework adopted. How do we explain the paradoxical, and cyclical, blend of engagement and retreat at the policy level and the obsession and indifference in public commentary that has characterized the course of Canada's relations with African countries? As noted above, I will argue that three conceptual "frames" are required. The first, drawing on English School thinking concerning international society, is of Canada and Canadians as "good international citizens" responding to multilateral and humanitarian imperatives with comparative efficiency and dedication. The second, "hegemonic middle-powermanship," draws on neo-Gramscian ideas to illuminate Canada's role as a charter member of the Western alliance, seeking to foster and sustain an order that serves the interests of political and economic elites in Canada and its most important allies. The third, "post-colonial" frame, highlights Western portrayals of Africa as a remote and troubled continent—a mysterious locus of poverty and insecurity—that have served as the basis for a persistent narrative of a Canadian identity torn between moral purpose and dereliction. Whether and how these themes continue to resonate in the post-2006 Conservative era of Canadian foreign policy will be a key question animating this study.

The next three chapters elaborate, in different ways, the three theoretical frames outlined in Chapter 1. In Chapter 2, Canada's G8 diplomacy on Africa is explored. Its role as the smallest of the G8 member states has been both symbolically important and controversial, as different groups and analysts have disputed the practical achievements of this forum. In the early years of the new millennium, Prime Minister Jean Chrétien played a pivotal role in entrenching Africa on the G8 agenda through his government's facilitation of the Africa Action Plan (AAP). How do we explain this role, and what does it reveal about the motivations and impact of Canadian leaders in relation to the continent? Canada's G8 activism can be understood from a neo-Gramscian perspective as an effort to facilitate a new "hegemonic bargain" between the world's wealthiest and most powerful states, and the world's poorest continent. In the end, this effort offers key insights concerning the nature and limits of "hegemonic politics," as both Canada's and the G8's ability to sustain this collective effort has faltered.

In Chapter 3, I employ insights from a post-colonial perspective to argue that the debate concerning Canada's Africa policies in the twenty-first century needs to be situated in the context of a longer historical narrative concerning the country's continental role. In this narrative, a distant and dimly understood Africa has served as the basis for a story of Canada's moral role in the world, featuring leadership, dereliction, and redemption. While both radical and conservative critics contest this account, and offer competing counternarratives, it has played a prominent role in the public discourse surrounding Canadian foreign policy for at least a generation, and helps explain the nature of both policy and commentary on African issues. It may, however, be in the process of being supplanted by a new, more hard-edged narrative of Canada's ethical "mission," with Africa relegated to a marginal role.

The resilience of the moral narrative concerning Canadian "good international citizenship" in Africa, juxtaposed with the sharp inconsistencies and deviations that have marked Canada's continental role, raises the question of why this narrative has retained such currency. A partial explanation is offered in Chapter 4, resting on the practical and symbolic role of high profile Canadians who come to serve as "iconic internationalists," embodying our best selves even as they themselves often sharply criticize official Canadian policy. Two such icons—Roméo Dallaire and Stephen Lewis—are the primary subjects of this chapter. Their extraordinary popularity as heroic and tireless champions for the dignity and resilience of Africans has effectively masked the less edifying record of Canadian policy, even as these same public figures eloquently critique this record.

The second half of the book takes these theoretical and conceptual frames and applies them to a series of more concrete themes. Canadian aid policy in Africa—the focus of Chapter 5—has been on a two-decade-long roller coaster. Under the Chrétien government in the mid-1990s, the share of GDP devoted to aid fell sharply as the government leaned heavily on cuts to aid in its deficit-fighting efforts. Africa bore a disproportionate share of these cuts. Then, as the fiscal situation improved and the global climate for development finance became more expansive, the government reversed course and set CIDA on a path toward sustained reinvestment, with Africa as the principle focus and beneficiary. At the same time, aid policy was brought more firmly in line with emerging transnational consensus on "best practices" that was institutionalized in the Paris Principles on Aid Effectiveness. From 2006 onward, however, the new Harper Conservative government orchestrated another course change, de-emphasizing Africa in a policy climate marked by indifference toward multilateral efforts to promote harmonization, alignment, and recipient "ownership" of development policies. While the durability of this latest course change remains to be seen, the consequences of aid policy shifts (in both spending and thematic priorities) for African "partners" have come a distant second to policy considerations of successive Canadian governments' *own* conceptions of aid effectiveness and the domestic audiences they seek to appeal to. In this respect, aid policies in Africa serve (in post-colonial terms) as a narrative *of* and *for* Canadians, with Africa and Africans as the distant and opaque "other" through which this story is told. The Harper government's abrupt decision to integrate CIDA with the Department of Foreign Affairs and International Trade in its March 2013 Federal Budget can be seen, among other things, as evidence for the prevalence of a particular, shallow story of what "works" in development, and a lack of serious engagement with the complex challenges of aid policy and practice.

Along with development assistance, peace operations ("peacekeeping") have been a hallmark of post–Second World War Canadian internationalism and a prominent dimension of Canadian involvement in Africa, as discussed in Chapter 6. The number and challenges of peace operations expanded dramatically with the end of the Cold War in the early 1990s, and many of these new, more complex and challenging operations unfolded in Africa. Canada was a major participant in several of them. The results—in Somalia, Rwanda, and the eastern Democratic Republic of the Congo (DRC) for example—were painful and sobering. During the first decade of the new century, the level of Canadian deployments in Africa fell sharply while a parallel emphasis on capacity building for African peacekeepers ("African solutions to African problems") gathered momentum. The Canadian approach in this regard was largely consistent with other NATO and G8 governments, and it raises important questions about the future of UN peacekeeping in Africa. Under the Harper government, however, even this reduced level of commitment has been brought into question. The trajectory of Canadian involvement in African peace-and-security operations thus reflects the growing influence of a more conservative, pro-Western variant of internationalism that has long been influential within the Canadian defence establishment as well as the Conservative government. But the resilience of the peacekeeping "myth," despite this limited and inconstant role also underscores the durability of the moral narrative that peace operations in Africa have come to represent.

As this country's traditional points of contact with Africa have weakened, the role of the Canadian private sector, and particularly of extractive companies, has risen significantly. Canada's world-class extractive companies—the focus of Chapter 7—have become among the largest and most numerous investors in this important sector for the continent. Canada also strongly supported the liberalized policy environment that has made African countries so hospitable for multinational extractive companies. There is sharp debate about the environmental, developmental, and human security implications of these investments and the record of Canadian companies is deeply controversial, raising concerns about the need to bring their activities in line with the government's professed development and security objectives. Several efforts have been made to establish more robust standards and investigative procedures for the activities of Canadian extractives in Africa and elsewhere in the developing world. The failure of these efforts illustrates the degree to which "good international citizenship" is effectively trumped by the hegemonic interests of key elements within the Canadian state and among its leading corporate citizens. Meanwhile, the prominence of the debate concerning Canadian extractives in Africa (and Latin America) can be explained, at least in part, by the way in which they disrupt the heretofore dominant ethical narrative of Canada's involvement in the continent.

The conclusion confronts directly the degree to which the changes introduced by the Harper government in Canadian policy toward Africa reflect and reinforce the long-term decline of post–Second World War liberal internationalism. Throughout much of the post-decolonization era, Africa policies have served as exemplars of the liberal internationalist orientation, including both its more admirable and contradictory features. The Harper government's relative retreat from Africa, combined with the rising salience of a narrower and harder-edged narrative concerning Canada's interests and moral purpose, raise two important questions. First, are these changes likely to be sustained across partisan boundaries, notwithstanding the discursive protestations of opposition politicians, such as that of Michael Ignatieff captured in the epigraph to this introduction? Second, how are we to think conceptually about these changes? Here, the three frames introduced in Chapter 1 (good international citizenship, hegemonic middlepowermanship, and post-colonial narration) will be used to illuminate both the direction and depth of the changes introduced since 2006. Global structural and institutional trends, combined with important social and cultural changes in the domestic foundations for Canadian policy toward Africa, reinforce the likelihood of a more durable change in approach.

1

Theorizing Canadian Policy toward Africa

One can agree with Edward Akuffo (2012) that there has never been a coherent Canadian policy toward Africa, and still be struck by the regularity with which African issues have figured prominently in post-1960 Canadian foreign policy. From John Diefenbaker's pivotal role in apartheid South Africa's departure from the Commonwealth; through Lester Pearson's Commonwealth diplomacy concerning Rhodesia's Unilateral Declaration of Independence (UDI); through Quebec and Canada's skirmishing in relation to francophone Africa; through the massive popular and governmental response to the Ethiopian famine; through the Mulroney government's engagement with the endgame of apartheid; through the devastating failures of UN and Canadian peacekeeping in Somalia and Rwanda; through the ethical flourishes and repercussions of Lloyd Axworthy's Human Security Agenda; through Jean Chrétien's role in orchestrating the G8's Africa Action Plan; through the "Responsibility to Protect" and the crisis in Darfur; through the heated controversy among the "chattering classes" regarding the Harper government's "retreat" from Africa—there is arguably no region save North America that has more routinely seized the attention of Canadian foreign policy leaders and commentators. This, in relation to a continent that in 2011 accounted for a mere 2 percent of Canada's bilateral trade and that remains firmly at the margins of Canadian geostrategic concerns.

How does one make theoretical sense of this juxtaposition of apparently marginal interests, in the traditional Realist sense, and high-profile engagement, however intermittent? Why, given this regular engagement, has a more comprehensive policy approach never emerged? What logic(s) can be identified to explain the consistent inconsistency of Canadian attitudes toward, and involvement in, African issues?

As noted in the Introduction, my argument is that no one theoretical approach can persuasively explain this pattern of intense, yet shallow and inconsistent, engagement. Rather, three approaches provide partial explanations, and in some key respects work together to provide a more satisfactory account. An International Society (English School) approach, emphasizing the solidarist possibilities of "good international citizenship," can help make sense of instances of prominent ethical, normative, and practical leadership, but it does not account for the way these "moments" relate to the logic of broader Canadian/Western interests in Africa. Here, a Coxian (or neo-Gramscian) approach is helpful in explaining how Canadian ethical leverage has related to efforts to construct a hegemonic policy framework for African issues, both transnationally and within Canada. In other words, Canadian policy efforts can at times be seen to have been both consistent with, and instrumental in, the forging of a "common sense" response to onerous African challenges that attempts to secure a relatively high level of consent from African governments and elites, while promoting the interests of Western elites. Yet such hegemonic initiatives and aspirations are too fitfully pursued to be consistently credible and effective. In this regard a post-colonial approach is illuminating, emphasizing the degree to which a flat, idealized, and dehistoricized image of Africa has served to underpin a dominant (and now a competing) narrative of Canada's role and identity in the world.

Taken together, the combination of these frames reflects a pragmatic approach to theoretical explanation, or what Katzenstein and Sil (2008) have characterized as "Analytic Eclecticism" (AE—see also Sil 2009; and Cornut 2012). The hallmark of this approach to scholarship is a willingness to "trespass deliberately and liberally across competing research traditions with the intention of defining and exploring substantive problems in original, creative ways," thereby contributing to both "a deeper understanding of a critical problem and theoretical progress for international relations" (Katzenstein and Sil 2008, 110). AE does not supplant a paradigmatic approach, but draws on key insights and ideas from different traditions to provide a more complete and compelling interpretation of certain social problems. Such an approach, I will argue, allows us to make sense of the persistent patterns and apparent contradictions of a Canadian encounter with Africa that has at times enjoyed remarkably high levels of prominence and popularity, but has just as regularly faded into obscurity, with deleterious effects for policy effectiveness.

Canada and Canadians as "Good International Citizens"

While it is easy to be cynical about the idea that Canada and Canadians have sought to "do good" in Africa with any degree of sincerity and persistence, such cynicism is unable to adequately explain the tireless advocacy and dedication of a relatively small group of prominent, and not so prominent, Canadian citizens and organizations acting through and/or alongside the Canadian state. A useful way of thinking about these people and organizations is through a lens of "good international citizenship" within an increasingly (though far from completely) solidaristic "international society."

The idea that states form a society is most commonly associated with the so-called English School of International Relations theory.[1] As Tim Dunne (1998) has noted, it is based on two connected claims about the common interests and shared values of states. First, states are presumed to take into account the impact their decisions have on other members of international society. Second, international society reflects and embodies the presence of intricate patterns of social interaction that display the rules of the game for regular, if not exceptional, behaviour.

From this perspective, international society can be understood as the framework of rules, norms, and institutions produced by the ongoing activities of those who act in the name of states, including political leaders, diplomats, and other state officials. An international society is thus qualitatively different from an asocial international system, in which interaction among the world's states is mechanically regulated by the anarchic structure of the system and the distribution of (military) capabilities within it. To use Hedley Bull's (1977, 9–10, 13) popular distinction, a "system of states (or international system) is formed when two or more states have sufficient contact between them, and have sufficient impact on one another's decisions to cause them to behave—at least in some measure—as parts of a whole." A "society of states," on the other hand, "exists when a group of states, conscious of certain common interests and common values, form a society in the sense that they conceive of themselves to be bound by a common set of rules in their relations with one another, and share in the working of common institutions."

Although members of the English School share a preoccupation with the society of states, they differ sharply on its nature and purpose. Is the purpose of international society to maintain interstate order (even if it is unjust), or to provide for the conditions of individual justice everywhere (ultimately the only sustainable basis for a stable order)? Historically, the most common justification for maintaining international society has been to preserve diverse political communities in a highly diverse context of massive disparities of power between its members and no consensus on the principles of justice. This has been the central commitment of the "pluralist" conception of international society. Pluralists like Robert Jackson (2000; see also Bain 1999) are concerned with reducing interstate harm by restricting the legitimate use of force to self-defence and when authorized by the UN Security Council, and by developing "international harm conventions" that place limits on state conduct in both war and peace. In contrast, the "solidarist" conception of international society emphasizes an emerging consensus around the basic tenets of human rights and hence the promotion of individual justice as the soundest basis for ensuring a stable international order. Solidarists such as Nicholas Wheeler (2000) seek to advance this agenda by incorporating "cosmopolitan harm conventions" designed to reduce injury to individual citizens. They also seek to devise rules of conduct for the morally legitimate use of military force in cases that have been characterized as supreme humanitarian emergencies.

These different conceptions of international society are relevant in both *describing* how the world works (when and where the pluralist or solidarist conception most accurately reflects the current nature of international society), and *prescribing* how it *should* work (that is, whether pluralist or solidarist ethics should be promoted). Pluralists and solidarists thus disagree on the type of foreign policy behaviour they favour.

The debate on appropriate state behaviour is pivotal to how one thinks about "good international citizenship." As Linklater and Suganami (2006, 232) have asked, what "principles of foreign policy ... can promote the moral ideal of the unity of humankind without jeopardizing international order"? In the English School's framework, the starting point for thinking about good international citizenship is that most states recognize that they are answerable to what Martin Wight described as three separate moral constituencies: co-nationals, international society, and humanity (Wight 1991; see also Buzan 2004). In any given political episode, state representatives have the difficult task of weighing their obligations to these three constituencies and balancing their national, international, and humanitarian responsibilities. At the more solidarist end of this spectrum, writers such as Tim Dunne and Nicholas Wheeler have argued that in situations of extreme humanitarian emergency, "the good international citizen must be prepared to ask its soldiers to risk and, if necessary, lose their lives to stop crimes against humanity" (Dunne and Wheeler 2001, 184; also Wheeler and Dunne 1998, 869). If necessary, the good international citizen is expected to do this without explicit authorization from the UN Security Council, even if this may weaken the rule of law within the society of states. For writers on the pluralist end of the spectrum, however, such a position is a dangerous recipe for undermining international order and eroding the already fragile foundations on which peace between states has been constructed since the treaties of Westphalia in the mid-seventeenth century.

In light of this long-running debate, Linklater and Suganami (2006, 238–39 and 243–44) have outlined principles of good international citizenship for both the pluralist and solidarist conceptions of international society. For the pluralists such principles include:

- All societies have a right to a separate existence subject to the need to maintain the balance of power.
- Intervention in the internal affairs of member states to promote some vision of human decency or human justice is prohibited.
- Diplomatic efforts to reconcile competing interests should proceed from the assumption that each state is the best judge of its own interests.
- Because of their unique military capabilities the great powers should assume special responsibilities, determined by mutual consent, for preserving international order.

- Force is justified only in self-defence and in response to states that seek preponderant power.

Solidarists' principles, in contrast, include the ideas that:

- Individuals and the various communities and associations to which they belong are the fundamental members of international society.
- Pluralist commitments to sovereignty and sovereign immunity should be replaced by the notion of personal responsibility for infringements of the laws of war.
- Breaches of the laws of war should be punishable in domestic and international courts.
- The sovereignty of the state is conditional on compliance with the international law of human rights.
- States have responsibilities as custodians of human rights everywhere.

Somewhat surprisingly, though with a few exceptions (e.g., Nossal 1998–99; Bain 1999; Keating 2014), the International Society approach has received relatively little explicit attention in the literature on Canadian foreign policy. Implicitly, however, its core assumptions and the related imperatives of good international citizenship have been quite influential—notably in relation to the "dominant idea" of internationalism (Nossal, Roussel, and Paquin 2010) and the post–Second World War embrace of multilateralism (Keating 2013). Nossal's commonsensical characterization of good international citizenship is phrased in the following terms:

It suggests … that a country's diplomacy can be directed towards ameliorating the "common weal" by taking actions explicitly designed to achieve that end. The possibilities for such good international citizenship include contributing faithfully to development assistance programmes; dispatching troops on a peacemaking mission to a country torn by civil war; organizing a coalition of like-minded countries to pursue the liberalization of agricultural trade; spending appropriate sums of money on military equipment in support of an alliance; organizing support for a global ban on anti-personnel landmines; volunteering combat troops to an international coalition; or putting together a collection of votes for a United Nations resolution on mercenary armies. (1998–99, 99–100)

Nossal's description allows for the possibility that both pluralist *and* solidarist impulses may drive specific decisions and actions. Historically, pluralist assumptions were prevalent in Canadian practice, reflecting federal government sensitivities to Canada's intense societal pluralism and the related need to accommodate diversity (e.g., Stairs 1982). Over time, however, solidarist assumptions became more influential—a process that accelerated sharply following the Cold War, from 1990 onwards (e.g., Gecelovsky and Keating 2001; Keating 2014). In short, Canadian foreign policy came to be associated, nowhere more so than in the collective minds of the attentive public in Canada, with efforts to advance and institutionalize more cosmopolitan principles, such as human rights and human security, and with related efforts to enhance the capacity and effectiveness of multilateral organizations. Specifically in relation to Africa, this tendency in Canadian foreign policy is closely related to what Akuffo (2012) has conceptualized as a "non-imperial internationalist" approach and related "moral identity."

There is good reason to be cynical about the self-congratulatory tendencies of this approach and the limits and contradictions embedded therein. It can, however, be understood as "real" in relation to Canada's role in Africa, in at least three senses. The first is the role of a significant number of state officials—diplomatic, developmental, and military—in attempting to take multilateral mandates seriously and enhance the effectiveness of multilateral initiatives, however overmatched they may be by the conditions they confront. These efforts can be both "elite" and "everyday," as in the celebrated efforts of former UN Ambassador Robert Fowler to enhance the effectiveness of UN Security Council sanctions committees in ways widely credited with helping to end the disastrous civil war in Angola (Möllander 2009), and in the efforts of Canadian aid and military officials to enhance the effectiveness and credibility of the AU Mission in Darfur (AMIS) (see Black 2010a). This is not to discount the equally celebrated moral failures associated with Canadian personnel—most strikingly in the immediate post–Cold War "peacekeeping" operation in Somalia.[2] But it is real *enough* to lend credibility to the notion, and narrative, of good international citizenship.

The second reality underpinning this approach is the role of Canadian political leaders and officials in providing "entrepreneurial leadership" on international initiatives that aim to institutionalize norms and practices advancing "solidaristic" objectives. This tendency was particularly striking during the latter half of the 1990s and the first half of the next decade, with the various initiatives associated with the Human Security Agenda promoted by Lloyd Axworthy—almost all of which had, and have, significant ramifications in Africa. Besides the human security approach itself and related efforts to advance new international practices concerning "peacebuilding," the campaigns to ban land mines, to establish the International Criminal Court, to modify the principle of national sovereignty by advancing an international "Responsibility to Protect" (R2P) people at risk of atrocity crimes, and to protect civilians (particularly children) in contexts of violent armed conflict all garnered considerable international attention, reaction, and some real advances in international practice (McRae and Hubert 2001). Moreover, while there was a striking gap between Canadian "entrepreneurial" and "implementation" leadership on these issues (see Riddell-Dixon 2005)—a point to which we return shortly—they went a long way toward reinforcing the image of Canada as good international citizen.

The third reality, stretching but also reinforcing the International Society approach, is the degree to which the image of Canadian good international citizenship has been underpinned by the advocacy and activism of particular Canadian individuals and non-state organizations. On the latter, the role of organizations like Partnership Africa Canada and Project Ploughshares, and of civil society leaders like Ian Smillie and Ernie Regehr, on "conflict diamonds" and small arms and light weapons, respectively, has long been an important source of Canadian "cosmopolitanism" in both image and practice. With regard to the former, the prominent role of certain "iconic internationalists," such as Roméo Dallaire, Stephen Lewis, James Orbinski, or Samantha Nutt, has done much to reinforce an image of Canadian good international citizenship, even (ironically) when these iconic figures have been sharply critical of the actual policy performance of the Canadian state. In short, they come to represent the Canada that *could be* and, through their own work, can be taken as proxies for our own better selves. The significance of these iconic internationalists will be taken up in Chapter 4.

Hence, there is at least some empirical foundation for the image of Canada as good international citizen in Africa.[3] There are, however, at least two reasons why this approach offers, at best, an incomplete conceptualization of Canada's involvement in the continent and, at worst, a seriously distorting one. The first, alluded to above, is that these activist flourishes have been marked by a yawning gap between aspiration and implementation, both within Canada and internationally. Thus, Nossal's seminal articulation of the tradition of good international citizenship in Canadian foreign policy was written in the context of the onset of "Pinchpenny Diplomacy" during the Chrétien era: "seeing how low Canadian expenditures on international affairs can be kept without forfeiting Canada's position in international forums like the G8" (1998–99, 104). Like Riddell-Dixon, Nossal was highlighting the degree to which the "causes" promoted by Canadian entrepreneurial leadership had come to be routinely, sometimes ludicrously, under-supported when it came to being put into practice. Similarly, there has been striking inconstancy in Canada's "solidarist activism," marked for example by the precipitous decline of Canadian aid spending, particularly in Africa, during the mid-1990s and, more recently, the alacrity with which the Harper government has shifted away from its predecessors' rhetorical commitment to the continent and from long-standing bilateral relationships with a number of African governments.

Second, and at least as important, is the degree to which, and the ways in which, Canada's inconstant continental activism has both reflected and reinforced the hegemonic interests and objectives of Canadian and Western transnational elites. Whether deliberately or otherwise, Canada's relatively benign and positive image on the continent has been usefully exploited in the service of hegemonic projects. To understand these dynamics, a neo-Gramscian or Coxian approach provides important insights.

Canada and Western Hegemonic Aspirations in Africa

While Canadian international activism has sometimes been idealized as more or less equidistant from various international blocs—an image which Akuffo (2012, 203–11) identified among some African regional officials in the course of his research—in reality the dominant state-led forms of Canadian internationalism have always been firmly aligned with the centres of Western wealth and power—anchored first in Britain and, since the end of the Second World War, in the United States.

The neo-Gramscian tradition adapted to the study of global politics by Robert Cox, or what James Mittelman (1998) has characterized as "Coxian historicism," takes as a central point of departure the degree to which a given world order can be characterized as hegemonic, and the forces and processes by which such a hegemonic order is sustained, challenged, broken down, and/or transformed. By hegemony, Cox and others in this tradition do not have in mind the neo-realist emphasis on order sustained through preponderant power, or dominance. Rather, inspired by Antonio Gramsci, they are interested in understanding social orders in which there is a relatively high degree of "fit" between material capabilities, ideas, and institutions, resulting in an order marked by a comparatively high level of consensus and widely perceived legitimacy.[4] Such orders invariably reflect and serve the interests of the powerful, in national societies and among the broader transnational networks that are formed between national elites. But their desirability for the powerful rests on the degree to which they are sustained through "common sense" relationships and ideas that secure relatively high levels of societal support among subordinate groups. Coercion is always present in such orders, and is typically more routine and visible at their margins. Moreover, reflecting Cox's historicist orientation, these orders are understood as inevitably impermanent—always subject to, and challenged by, forces of change, albeit over the course of long periods of time. The challenge facing those who are invested in them is to (re)formulate arrangements of ideas and institutions around which a relatively high degree of consensus and stability can be achieved, while their material and security interests are advanced or at least protected. Alternatively, a hegemonic order can be seen to be in crisis when the elements of consensus are increasingly and forcefully challenged, when the requirement for coercion becomes increasingly prevalent, and when the predominant hegemonic power routinely resorts to unilateralism to assert and defend its preferences (Cox 1989, 829).

A world (or at least an international) order can be seen as hegemonic when it reflects and sustains a close fit with the preferences of what Cox calls dominant "state forms" (involving state–civil society relations, or "complexes") and social (or class) forces arising from the predominant production processes of the day. The most obvious, and more or less hegemonic, world orders of the past two centuries have been the post–World War II *Pax Americana* and, prior to that, the *Pax Britannica*. In short, a hegemonic order is typically underpinned by a dominant society that "must be capable of universalizing its own constitutive principles ... [and] be supremely self-confident of its internal strength and expansive potential, before it can become the founder and guarantor of a world order" based on these principles (Cox 1989, 830). In this sense, the dominant state/states and society/societies of the day perform an essential *architectural*, as well as institutional and enforcement, role. But such an order cannot be enacted and sustained without cooperation and support from the broadest possible coalition of other "state forms," including an important role for "middle powers."

This support is necessary both for practical reasons of burden sharing and divisions of labour, and because of the symbolic and political requirement to project a high degree of consensus and participation. Moreover there is, according to Cox, a distinctive order-building *quality* to the middle-power role that can be identified in a range of historical orders. He writes of this role that "commitment to the process of building a more orderly world system is quite different from seeking to impose an ideologically preconceived vision of the ideal world order. [Canadian scholar-diplomat John] Holmes described the process as 'lapidary' in the sense of building from the bottom up, stone upon stone, a structure that grows out of the landscape, not imposing from above some architectonic grand design" (Cox 1989, 827).[5] For Canada's post–Second World War political and economic elites, this middle-power role (or "middlepowermanship") was both appealing and intuitive. As wartime allies of the US, the UK, and other Western/anti-fascist powers, and sharing a diffuse but powerful harmony of views and interests with the dominant Western powers on how best to organize political and economic life, it was virtually inevitable that they would largely embrace the normative and institutional features of the emerging *Pax Americana*. Moreover, having lived through the appalling destruction of two world wars in rapid succession and a global economic depression, they were moved to overcome Canada's pre-war, post-colonial reticence about international engagement and to embrace an active, internationalist, order-building, and order-sustaining foreign policy (see Nossal, Roussel, and Paquin 2010, chap. 5).

As the erstwhile European colonies of Africa rapidly decolonized from the late 1950s onward, often with considerable and well-founded enmity toward the imperial powers that had ruled them, Canada's postwar middle-power role took on a particular kind of significance that helps to explain the otherwise-surprising prominence of African issues in Canadian external relations. Precisely *because* Canada was not a traditional colonial power in Africa, and was indeed a former settler colony of Great Britain, it was well positioned to play a critical, order-sustaining role in ameliorating relations between the newly independent states of Commonwealth Africa and their erstwhile colonial master.[6] It played a somewhat similar, though belated, role—complicated by domestic imperatives of national unity and Quebec assertionism—in relation to francophone Africa.[7] This role was manifested, for example, in Prime Minister Pearson's Commonwealth diplomacy concerning Rhodesia's UDI in the mid-1960s (L. Freeman 1980; Hayes 1982), and in Prime Minister Trudeau's Commonwealth diplomacy over British arms sales to South Africa in 1971 (Redekop 1982). It was, and is, this distinctive positioning vis-à-vis former imperial powers as well as the Cold War superpowers that underpins what Akuffo (2012) has sought to conceptualize as Canada's "non-imperial internationalist moral identity" in Africa.

There is, of course, a materialist, broadly neo-Marxist, tradition in the study of Canadian foreign policy that has long emphasized the interests of "capitalism in Canada" (C. Pratt 2003, 85), and the role of the Canadian state in advancing those interests, to explain some of the most persistent features of Canada's role in post-independence Africa.[8] Among other things, scholars in this tradition have emphasized the degree to which Canada's aid program has been used to benefit Canadian commercial/class interests through historically high levels of "tying" aid expenditures to Canadian goods and services, and the degree to which Canada's traditional resistance to economic sanctions against South Africa reflected a firmly pro-capitalist understanding of Canadian interests. However, at least until the relatively recent surge in Canadian extractive sector investment on the continent (see Chapter 7; Gordon 2010), Canadian commercial interests have been generally far too limited to justify an active, high visibility role in Africa without reinforcing motivations. An emphasis on *Canadian* commercial/class interests also tended to overlook the degree to which such an active role was consistent with broader Western hegemonic aspirations toward the continent—a point emphasized by Neufeld (1995) in relation to Canada's middle-power role and identity more broadly.

Understood from this broader perspective, a number of key developments in Canadian policy become more comprehensible. For example, Canada's celebrated (though typically exaggerated) activism under Progressive Conservative Prime Minister Brian Mulroney in the struggle to end South African apartheid has been interpreted as a reflection of "enlightened capitalist" motivations. Canadian diplomacy, in the company of other "like-minded" governments (such as Australia and the Nordics), international organizations, and some civil society organizations, can be understood as an effort to pressure the South African regime to accept the ending of institutionalized racism in order to forestall an even more bloody and potentially revolutionary transformation that could effectively "lose" South Africa, with its strategic positioning and natural resource wealth, to the West (Saul 1988; L. Freeman 1997; Black 2001b). Similarly, the tendency of Canadian aid policy to conform with, and in some respects contribute to, the successive transnational policy priorities orchestrated through the international aid regime—notably in the form of the Structural Adjustment policies of the 1980s and '90s, and the Paris Declaration Principles on Aid Effectiveness in the following decade—can be seen as both reflecting and contributing to the articulation of hegemonic policy objectives and practices vis-à-vis developing countries. And the Chrétien government's policy leadership in orchestrating the G8 Africa Action Plan, adopted at the Kananaskis Summit in 2002, can be interpreted as a hegemonic project, albeit an incomplete and only partially successful one (as discussed in the next chapter).

Precisely how these initiatives and trends relate to the features of "good international citizenship" discussed in the previous section is ambiguous. Certainly there are cases where "solidaristic" initiatives consistent with the tradition of good international citizenship were also in line with hegemonic interests, in two senses. First, as seen in the case of apartheid South Africa, a policy approach aimed at bringing a relatively orderly, negotiated end to one of the most widely condemned violations of international human rights norms of the twentieth century was also in line with "enlightened" Western hegemonic interests, both politically and economically. More radical scholars such as John Saul would argue that, in successfully orchestrating the negotiated demise of apartheid, these collaborative efforts undermined the cause of transformation and social justice in South Africa—though this perspective must be weighed against the potential costs and uncertain outcomes of a revolutionary alternative. Similarly, the 1990s emphasis on human security–linked priorities such as peacebuilding, a new International Criminal Court, and the Responsibility to Protect, while reflecting a solidarist preoccupation with alleviating human suffering, can also be seen as deflecting attention from Western complicity in the structural conditions that have helped cause the "humanitarian emergencies" these new norms and practices were conceived to address.

Second, however, these more solidaristic initiatives can and have been used to reinforce the legitimacy and symbolic autonomy of the Canadian state, by projecting an ethically oriented identity that could be contrasted with that of its major Western allies—notably the US and, at times, the UK. Yet given the under-resourced nature of the initiatives associated with the Human Security Agenda, and the gap (noted earlier) between entrepreneurial leadership and its implementation, these can also be seen as a comparatively low-cost way to reinforce the hegemonic position of political elites domestically, in part by masking the class character of other, more central priorities of Canadian foreign policy.[9] This understanding in no way diminishes the commitment and dedication of those who have worked on these issues, both through and in collaboration with the Canadian government. What it illustrates, however, is the hegemony-conforming character of much of what we might otherwise regard as manifestations of "good international citizenship."

Only occasionally does a clear choice have to be made between the imperatives of the latter and of the former. One recent instance revolves around the question of how to address evidence of human and environmental rights violations associated with the burgeoning activities of Canadian extractive companies, in Africa and in other parts of the "developing world" (see Gordon 2010, chap. 4). In this case, a clear blueprint for more robust and enforceable standards of behaviour for Canadian "corporate citizens" in developing countries, articulated by the Advisory Group Report of the *National Roundtables on Corporate Social Responsibility and the Canadian Extractive Industry in Developing Countries* (2007), and later by a private member's bill (C-300) with similar objectives, has been sidelined in favour of the voluntary measures and corporate social responsibility initiatives favoured by industry and their state-based allies. This case will be addressed in Chapter 7.

In sum, there is considerable evidence to support a Coxian/ hegemonic interpretation of Canada's role in sub-Saharan Africa. Yet this approach, too, is incomplete. Most strikingly, Canada's involvement in African issues has been marked by sharp inconsistencies and a bedrock shallowness—of financial and bureaucratic resources, of knowledge, of relationships, and of commitment. As discussed in Chapter 2, this consistent inconsistency is most obvious in the alacrity with which the Chrétien government tackled Canadian fiscal woes on the backs of the world's poor, particularly in Africa, by targeting foreign aid for the largest proportionate share of expenditure reductions; and by the Harper government's more recent decision to distance itself from the (renewed) commitment to Africa signalled by the Chrétien and Martin governments through the G8 Africa Action Plan. To illuminate this paradoxical mix of domestically celebrated activism, and shallowness and inconstancy of commitment, a post-colonial frame can provide valuable insights.

Africa Policy as a Story We Tell
Ourselves about Ourselves

It is impossible to summarize the rich vein of post-colonial scholarship, and its encounter with International Relations, in the brief space available here. Inspired largely by the work of Edward Said (e.g., 1993), it draws on post-structural and historicist methodologies, though in a way that takes account of and can be rendered compatible with sophisticated forms of materialist scholarship (see L. MacDonald 1995). The critical point for purposes of this analysis is that this tradition highlights the way in which the Western "self" was, and continues to be, historically constituted through its framing of the non-Western (or Oriental) "other." The result has been, on the one hand, a shallow, mystified, dehistoricized, and decontextualized account of (post-)colonial societies, in which the voices of the "colonized" are largely absent, and, on the other, a stylized, typically celebratory account of the Western "self" that tends to whitewash our own historical complicity in the conditions of material deprivation, inequality, and exploitation in which many post-colonial peoples live.

It is with regard to Africa, argues Achille Mbembe, "that the notion of 'absolute otherness' has been taken farthest... In several respects, Africa still constitutes one of the metaphors through which the West represents the origins of its own norms, develops a self-image, and integrates this image into the set of signifiers asserting what it supposes to be its identity" (Mbembe 2001, 2). He continues: "narrative about Africa is always a pretext for comment about something else, some other place, some other people" (2001, 3). This powerful insight provokes us to consider what narratives "about Africa" have come to signify in various external contexts, and how and why they have come to bear the meanings that they have. How, in other words, are "we" (in the form of the Canadian state and society) constituted by our engagement with "Africa"?

In an illuminating analysis of the UK's highly idealized engagement with Africa under Tony Blair's Labour government between 1997 and 2007, Julia Gallagher builds on this approach to argue that the "New Labour" government led by Blair, and indeed members of parliament from all parties, developed a highly moralized discourse concerning Africa that effectively "evacuated ambiguity" (Gallagher 2009, 441; see also Gallagher 2011). It also posited an unproblematic harmony of interests between the UK and Africa/Africans, and heavily edited Britain's historical record as an exploitative colonial power—a process aided by the Labour government's traditional self-identification with the anti-colonial movement, and the cosmopolitan ideals within which British popular discourses concerning Africa have typically been framed (Gallagher 2009, 445–46). As scholars such as Ian Taylor (2005a) have noted, the effect was a policy that largely obfuscated the contradictions in British policy toward Africa (e.g., concerning arms sales and other commercial interests) through a heavy emphasis on increased aid and debt relief, and rested on a strikingly shallow analysis of African politics and political economy. In the meantime, argues Gallagher, the attention generated by the government's prominent campaigning on Africa, particularly during the 2005 "Year of Africa" when Britain both hosted the G8 Summit and occupied the EU presidency, produced an enhanced sense of British governmental capacity and "goodness" in the face of long-term relative decline. "The recent British fascination with Africa and the idealized ways in which it is viewed," she concludes, "appears to have more to do with a sense of anxiety about the role, function, capacity, [and] potency of the British state than with African needs and development" (2009, 451). Precisely *because* Africa was so distant and thinly understood, it enabled a process of collective ethical resuscitation that the deeply affective, morally fraught, and sharply contested context of the "thick" UK domestic environment made virtually impossible to achieve.

As noted above, the Canadian position in relation to this postcolonial dynamic is historically ambiguous—both because of Canada's settler colonial history and because its own involvement with colonial Africa was limited and indirect, often having been mediated through Christian missionaries (see Wright 1991; Gendron 2006, 64). Canadian politicians and policy-makers have certainly benefited from, and exploited, Canada's "non-imperial" identity in their relations with the developing world. Yet, as Laura MacDonald has argued, "white Australians, Canadians, and New Zealanders were not constructed as the 'Other' in imperialist discourse but as provincial and less sophisticated versions of 'the Self'" (1995, 115). They, like their "Mother Country" counterparts, tended to view Africa through racialist and/or Christian-mission-driven prisms. These prisms were themselves ambiguous—embodying both imperialistic and solidaristic tendencies. They did, however, conform with the broader "Orientalist" tendency toward a simplified, moralized, and dehistoricized view of, and narrative concerning, Africa.

After the Second World War, and with the onset of decolonization, Africa and Africans were most prominently engaged and "constructed" by the Canadian state and its citizens through the prism of Foreign Aid. Of course, other interests—diplomatic and commercial—were always in play, and the motives for Canadian aid to Africa and elsewhere were famously "mixed" (e.g., Nossal 1988; L. Freeman 1985; Dawson 2013). But the continuities between the ethically oriented, postwar "discourse of development" and the colonial-era "missionary enterprise" meant that the former was strongly infused with "the themes of charity, altruism and universalism" associated with the latter (L. MacDonald 1995, 129). A succession of what would later be termed "humanitarian emergencies" (for example, the Biafran War and the Ethiopian famine), and the ongoing solidarity politics of the struggle against white minority rule in southern Africa, reinforced this dominant frame. As in Blair's Britain, "Africa" became the place where the Canadian aspiration to "do good" in the world could be indulged, even if this aspiration was riddled with contradictions. These contractions could be widely overlooked, or successfully transcended, in the dominant narrative precisely *because* Africa was relatively remote, economically, politically, and imaginatively, and was conceived through a resilient post-colonial prism.

Yet the remoteness of Africa, and the related fact that "hard-nosed" political leaders and officials in External Affairs (now Foreign Affairs, Trade, and Development—DFATD),[10] Defence, Finance, and elsewhere took as their mission the promotion of the "national interest" and persisted in seeing the continent as fundamentally peripheral to those interests, meant that Africa has been caught in a cycle of policy inconsistency, and a narrative of moral leadership, dereliction, and redemption. At what was arguably its nadir, following the Somalia Affair in which soldiers of the Canadian Airborne Regiment tortured Somali youth, causing the death of one, the racism that has always been present in the Canadian post-colonial narrative of Africa came to the fore in ways that produced a deep crisis within the Canadian Forces and led to the disbanding of the regiment (see Razack 2004; Dawson 2007). More routinely, the "serial morality tale" of Canada in Africa (discussed in Chapter 3) has had the general effect of inhibiting the building of deep and sustained relationships, knowledge, and policy capacity with regard to the continent, notwithstanding its routine intrusion into prominent public debates.

Again, this point must be qualified in light of the International Society/Good International Citizenship perspective outlined above. There are some Canadians, within the Canadian state and civil society, who have developed a deep and empathetic understanding of African affairs that transcends the distorting simplifications of a post-colonial frame. Their role, I will argue, has to some degree sustained Canada's positive reputation in Africa when the balance of evidence runs against it. The combination of these two frames, then, helps to explain both the periodic resurgence of activist flourishes in Africa, and the ease with which many Canadians accept these flourishes as emblematic of our "normal" or "natural" collective selves.

The post-2006 policy of the Harper Conservative government presents a different kind of challenge to the heretofore dominant, ethically oriented post-colonial framing of Africa. In brief, the Harper Conservatives have seemed largely, if not entirely, indifferent—sometimes even antagonistic—toward this moral narrative and have displayed a striking disregard for long-standing bilateral relationships that, though relatively shallow, have nevertheless both benefitted from and reinforced the resilience of this narrative. On the one hand, the "Harper era" may ultimately come to mark a rupture in the dominant ethical framing of Canada's post-colonial role in Africa—though it could also mark yet another oscillation in Canada's consistently inconsistent orientation toward the continent. On the other hand, however, the Harper government's apparent policy departure is illuminated by one of the core insights of a post-colonial approach—that is, that the (African) "Other" serves principally as the basis for a story we tell ourselves about ourselves. In this case, the Harper government has sought to craft a different narrative, of a "New" Government and a "New," post-Liberal Canada, in which Canada's interest-based identity as a country of the Americas trumps its long-standing "obsession" with Africa, and in which its "core values" are recast to privilege the defence of a relatively small set of "democratic allies" aligned with the West, starting with Israel. We will return to this theme in the concluding chapter.

Conclusion

The aim of this chapter has been to introduce three distinct but overlapping theoretical frames that can help us make sense of the otherwise puzzlingly erratic pattern of Canadian engagement with Africa. My argument is that none of these frames can provide a full explanation of this pattern, but that together they illuminate the persistent tendencies and tensions that have characterized it. The three frames outlined here are summarized in Table 1.1, specifying some of the core assumptions, behavioural expectations, and evidence used to justify each one.

This argument can be developed and illustrated through an analysis of Canada's multi-dimensional role on the continent over the course of the past two decades, in the form of its G8 diplomacy, its evolving role in development assistance, its changing and diminishing involvement in the continent's multiple peace operations, and its response to the increasingly dominant role of Canadian extractive companies in Africa's burgeoning natural resource sector. The next three chapters will amplify and illustrate the interpretive purchase of these three frames, beginning with a neo-Gramscian interpretation of Canada's role in the G8's decade-long encounter with Africa.

Table 1.1
Three theoretical frames for Canada in Africa

Theoretical Frame	International Society/Good International Citizenship	Coxian/hegemonic middle-powermanship	Post-colonial/narrative
Core Assumptions	• states form a society with shared rules and norms of behaviour • societal stability is best secured by respect for norms of sovereignty and non-intervention (pluralist account), or promotion of individual justice (solidarist account)	• world orders marked by varying degrees of hegemony, in which material and institutional power relations are masked and mitigated by prevalence of a high level of consent among subordinate groups • "middle powers" can play an important order-building role by promoting innovation, adaptation, and stabilization of collective institutions, in line with dominant interests	• identities of national "selves" are defined in relation to idealized, depoliticized, and mystified post-colonial "others" • engagements with these "others" form the basis for collective moral narratives (stories we tell ourselves about ourselves) • understanding of post-colonial "others" is stylized, truncated, and infantilized
Behavioural Expectations	• "good international citizenship" defined as policies explicitly aimed at "ameliorating the common weal" • can involve deep respect for sovereignty of other states (pluralist account) or active efforts to promote "cosmopolitan harm conventions" (solidarist account) • either is accompanied by activist and skilled diplomacy	• efforts by Western middle powers to win consent for principles and initiatives conforming with hegemonic interests, with which they are aligned • such states present a benign face of hegemonic coalitions through non-threatening/non-colonial images • concomitantly pursue policies that support interests of their own and transnational economic elites	• policies toward post-colonial "others" are marked by ethical flourishes and contradictory practices • public statements and commentaries present celebratory and stylized accounts of initiatives toward the "developing world," and/or images of "abandonment" and "dereliction" • policy cycles through phases of intense (though shallow) interest and deep indifference

(continued)

Table 1.1, continued

Theoretical Frame	International Society/Good International Citizenship	Coxian/hegemonic middle-powermanship	Post-colonial/ narrative
Examples of Evidence	• efforts to support operational effectiveness of African Union Mission in Darfur (AMIS) • entrepreneurial leadership on cosmopolitan normative and institutional campaigns (e.g., landmines, ICC, Responsibility to Protect) • role of leading individuals in advocacy and innovation (e.g., Stephen Lewis on HIV/AIDS, Romeo Dallaire on child soldiers)	• "enlightened capitalist" advocacy of pressure on apartheid regime in South Africa, in ways designed to secure negotiated, moderate transition • leadership in crafting G8 Africa Action Plan (AAP) as a collective response to African proposal for a New Partnership for Africa's Development (NEPAD) • promotion of voluntary "partnerships" between mining companies and development NGOS	• persistent gap between claims to ethical leadership and sustained allocation of resources in support of such claims • easy abandonment of professed priorities in face of domestic political exigencies—e.g., cuts to bilateral aid to Africa in periods of fiscal austerity • absence of sustained and strategic policy capacity and analysis vis-à-vis African issues

Chapter **2**

Canada, the G8, and Africa: The Rise and Decline of a Hegemonic Project

In 2001–02, the Canadian government led by then Prime Minister Jean Chrétien seized the opening toward Africa created at the 2001 Genoa G8 Summit and, through a sustained and sophisticated diplomatic effort, ensured that Africa took centre stage at the 2002 Kananaskis Summit in Alberta. The resulting G8 Africa Action Plan (AAP), itself a response to the New Partnership for Africa's Development (NEPAD) championed by several of the continent's then new leaders, effectively set this concert of the world's wealthiest capitalist countries on a path of sustained engagement with the challenges of the world's poorest and least secure continent. Canada itself, having made "Africa" a G8 focus, appeared set to build on its lead through ongoing commitments in aid, security, and investment. Yet by the time of the UK-hosted Gleneagles Summit in 2005—an event that effectively overshadowed previous G8 initiatives toward Africa, including Canada's—there were indications that the ardour of the Canadian government was faltering, at least for the elaborate plans framed by British Prime Minister Tony Blair's government. And by the Heiligendamm Summit in 2007, the new Conservative Prime Minister of Canada, Stephen Harper, was signalling a shift in priority from Africa to the Americas (A. Freeman 2007), setting the stage for subsequent commentary on the Conservatives' ostensible "abandonment" of Africa (see Ignatieff 2009).

How are we to make sense of this trajectory, theoretically and historically? What does it reveal about the intra-hegemonic politics of

Africa's erstwhile "new partnership" with the G8, and the possibility of consistent engagement? What, more particularly, does it reveal about the nature and limits of Canada's role as a "middle" or "secondary" power in the world's wealthiest, though now increasingly marginalized club?

In this chapter, I will explore the usefulness, but also the limits, of a neo-Gramscian approach to understanding Canada's Africa policy through the first decade of the twenty-first century. Canada's extraordinary engagement with African issues in the early part of the new millennium can be understood as "hegemonic work" in two senses. First, it can be seen as an attempt to foster a broadly supported consensus on how to more fully integrate the continent "globalization left behind" into the dominant world order. Second, in this process, it can be seen as reinforcing key, post–Second World War legitimizing myths concerning the Canadian state domestically. However, the success and sustainability of this work were compromised by the shallowness and inconstancy of Canadian interest(s) in Africa. While some limited resurgence of Canadian concern with the continent was evident in the run-up to the 2010 G8 and G20 summits hosted by the Canadian government in Huntsville and Toronto, respectively, reflecting the historic pattern of consistent inconsistency in Canadian policy toward Africa, it would be difficult to rebuild the credibility and connections that were disrupted in the second half of the decade, even if there were a will to do so. This point was underscored by Canada's historic failure to win election to a non-permanent seat on the UN Security Council in October 2010—in part at least because of its diminished involvement with Africa.

The chapter begins with an elaboration of Africa policy as "hegemonic work," as introduced in the previous chapter. It then focuses on what was, and was not, achieved at the 2002 Kananaskis Summit and in its aftermath; Canada's ambivalent role in the context of the 2005 Gleneagles Summit, anchoring "the year of Africa"; and the subsequent de-emphasis of the continent under the Harper Conservatives. Finally, it revisits policy developments surrounding the 2010 summit of the now diminished G8, and considers the implications of this analysis for African governments and organizations.

Africa as Hegemonic Work

As noted in the previous chapter, the G8's sustained engagement with Africa over the course of the first decade of the new millennium can be understood as an attempt to forge a hegemonic project,[1] in the neo-Gramscian sense of fostering a relatively stable and widely accepted order based on an "inter-subjective sharing of behavioural expectations" (Cox 1989, 829). This is particularly challenging, if important, in the face of vast inequalities of wealth and power, such as those that had deepened between the members of the G8 and the governments and peoples of Africa during the previous two decades of neo-liberal globalization.[2] In short, a continent that had been relatively and in some respects absolutely diminished, in material and security terms, by its limited and frequently pathological encounter with globalization (see Ferguson 2006, 25–49) posed a particularly acute challenge to the governments that had been the principal carriers and beneficiaries of that order. The need to be seen to respond to this challenge was heightened at the start of the new millennium by the increasing scale and intensity of the anti-globalization protests that had overshadowed G8 and similar meetings, at Genoa (G8), Seattle (Multilateral Agreement on Investment), Quebec City (Summit of the Americas), and beyond.[3]

In the face of this challenge, several of Africa's most prominent leaders, including Presidents Mbeki of South Africa, Obasanjo of Nigeria, and Wade of Senegal, brought a proposal for a "New Africa Initiative" to the Genoa G8 Summit in 2001 as the basis for a comprehensive new "partnership." G8 governments, led by Canada's Chrétien, the UK's Blair, and France's Chirac, responded quickly and positively, agreeing to the appointment of African Personal Representatives to craft a concerted G8 response to what evolved on the African side into the NEPAD. The African overture was attractive not only because of the considerations noted above, but because a central premise of the plan was an acceptance by African governments of their own primary responsibility for the challenges they faced and the solutions to them. This presented G8 leaders with the prospect of a more attractive "bargain" than had been possible in the past, including implied absolution for their countries' historic role(s) in the continent's struggles. The assessment of former British diplomat and veteran G8 analyst Sir Nicholas Bayne reflects this understanding: "This time, Mbeki, Obasanjo, Wade and their colleagues have accepted that Africans are themselves to blame for their problems and that they must take responsibility for their own recovery" (Bayne 2003, 122). Whatever the historical and analytical shortcomings of this understanding, its political appeal for G8 leaders was readily apparent.

Substantively, both the relatively spare Africa Action Plan (2002) that emerged at Kananaskis, and the massive report of the Commission for Africa (2005) that controversially anchored the G8's next "big push" on Africa at Gleneagles in 2005, reflected and reinforced a set of assumptions about the challenges facing the continent and the prescriptions to deal with them. These assumptions rested firmly within the dominant "post–Washington Consensus" (see W. Brown 2006; Williams 2005; Sandbrook 2005). They represented an elaboration and softening of the draconian, market-oriented structural adjustment reforms that had been imposed across the continent since the early 1980s. They included a new emphasis on governance, security, social development, water, agriculture, and "aid effectiveness," without altering the market- and growth-oriented core of the earlier approach. In this sense, they represented an extension of "Third Way" logic to the global level, assuming a pragmatic, post-ideological consensus on the way forward that effectively denied, or at least obscured, the possibility of structural conflict or contradiction (see Coulter 2009; Gallagher 2011, 137–38). The AAP explicitly took its lead from elements of the NEPAD, and in this way reinforced the sense that this was a new and genuine "partnership." It also sought to institutionalize positive reinforcement and create incentives for prescribed reforms, by rewarding governments that conformed to the "Nepad vision" through an emphasis on support for "Enhanced Partnership Countries" that could serve as "a beacon of 'best practices'" for other governments that "still do not understand or accept what must be done to help themselves" (Fowler 2003, 236).

Taking up this project was compelling to the Canadian government for several reasons. First, the consensus that was being advocated reflected the dominant ideological and policy assumptions of the Chrétien government—a Third Way government in practice if less self-consciously so in principle. Second, and of greater interest theoretically, is that this role fit firmly within what Cox, following the Canadian scholar-practitioner John Holmes, has characterized as internationalist middlepowermanship (Cox 1989, 823–36). This role, for which middle-ranking capabilities are a necessary but not sufficient condition, is one that seeks to foster, sustain, and expand the zones of world order. Since the political communities that have played this role, in current and previous historical contexts, generally lack the ability to impose a coherent, order-building vision, their approach has tended to be more pragmatic and process-oriented rather than architectural (though, as discussed in the previous chapter, a certain amount of "norm entrepreneurship" has often been involved). As seen earlier, Cox follows Holmes in characterizing this role as "'lapidary' in the sense of building from the bottom up, stone upon stone, a structure that grows out of the landscape."

Also as noted in the previous chapter, this is a role that post–World War II Canadian governments had played with some, albeit uneven, regularity—or consistent inconsistency. It was attractive to a relatively wealthy but "secondary" state and its elites insofar as it was understood to serve Canadian interests in a relatively secure, rules-based, and economically liberal order. In the specific context of a G8 response/overture to Africa, moreover, the Canadian government was uniquely placed to orchestrate this effort. As a leading member of both the Commonwealth and la Francophonie, it had developed relatively long-standing and comfortable relationships with Africa's post-colonial governments, free from the direct imperial legacies and baggage of the UK and France. Despite Canada's status as a charter member of the NATO alliance, it was perceived as having little strategic interest in Africa, and few means to pursue them. This, combined with its limited trade and investment role on the continent,[4] meant that it enjoyed a relatively benign image that enhanced its ability to serve as an interlocutor between G8 and African governments. Yet its relatively sophisticated and well-resourced diplomatic and aid resources[5] gave it the necessary means to help lead and "sell" such an intensive diplomatic effort, at least in short bursts. The broader point is that, understood in neo-Gramscian terms, efforts to foster relatively consensual hegemonic arrangements have often involved, and may even require, the particular skills and characteristics of secondary or "middle" powers such as Canada.

This effort was also "hegemonic work" for the Canadian government in another, related sense. To be sure, an order-building role that aspired to "humanize" and stabilize globalization by seeking to incorporate Africa served elite Canadian interests, in a relatively diffuse sense at least. In addition, however, it helped reinscribe and stabilize a hegemonic order domestically by reprising a couple of favourite roles and self-images.[6] On the one hand, a perceived leadership role in addressing African poverty, insecurity, and marginality strongly conformed with and reinforced the "humane internationalist" (or "liberal internationalist") self-image that has enjoyed sustained appeal among the Canadian public and Canadian elites (see C. Pratt 1989a; Munton 2002–03). In this sense, it was consistent with the more solidarist conception of good international citizenship outlined in the previous chapter. Although—indeed because—this image has often been contradicted in practice, such apparently enlightened initiatives have enjoyed considerable popularity and even a measure of collective relief when they have been reprised, as if Canadian foreign policy were reverting to its "natural" or at least its better impulses.[7]

On the other hand, at least partly reflecting a more "hard-nosed" or pragmatic variant of Canadian internationalism, Canada's status and participation in the G7/G8 has also enjoyed considerable popularity (see Kirton 2007). While the constraining effects of summit membership on Canada's international role have elicited some limited academic controversy over the years (e.g., Helleiner 1994–95, 106–8), in general the desirability of this status became both an article of faith and a source of anxiety among Canadian political and bureaucratic elites and their attentive publics. Canada's status as the "smallest of the great" (with the world's eleventh largest GDP in a club of eight by 2009, and sliding—see Potter 2009) simultaneously affirmed our importance in the world, and prompted insecurity about the prospect of decline and "demotion." Thus, an initiative such as that taken at Kananaskis, in which the Canadian government could be seen not only to have fully participated in, but in some real sense to have *led* the G8 toward a more generous and enlightened engagement with Africa was doubly compelling. The fact that Prime Minister Chrétien was in the final, "legacy-minding" years of his long political career firmly reinforced this logic.

Leaving aside the question of the viability and desirability of the collective vision for African renewal developed in the AAP, however, this case also illustrates some core problems and limitations of such hegemonic work. First, as we shall see, the potential for sustained concertation was undermined by the corrosive effects of intra-hegemonic differences of approach and "one-upmanship." Second, participants in such initiatives have extraordinary difficulty sustaining the focus, commitment, and resources necessary to see such initiatives through to their logical ends. In this case, a Canada that had apparently set great store in its G8 leadership on this issue had, within five years, signalled a retreat and reorientation. How did this occur, and what are its implications for Canada's and the G8's African "partners"?

The "Conjunctural Moment" of Kananaskis

The Kananaskis conjuncture produced a degree of focus on Africa without precedent in the nearly thirty years of summit history. The long shadow cast by the 2005 Gleneagles Summit in the UK should not obscure the degree to which it emerged out of a process that was "locked in" at the 2002 Summit.

The Canadian government, and particularly its Prime Minister, worked very hard to achieve this focus. As Robert Fowler, Chrétien's chief "Sherpa" for the summit and Personal Representative for Africa, has somewhat hyperbolically put it, "From Genoa, in July 2001, it was crystal clear that Prime Minister Chrétien would insist that the Canadian summit he would host in 2002 would feature an all-encompassing effort to end Africa's exclusion from the rest of the world and reverse the downward-spiraling trend in the quality of life of the vast majority of Africans" (Fowler 2003, 223).[8] Chrétien, whose previous political success had been far more the result of pragmatism and "street smarts" than statesmanship, was strongly supported in this effort by Tony Blair of Britain and Jacques Chirac of France. What unfolded was a concerted, year-long diplomatic effort involving wide-ranging consultations with G8 governments, African leaders, and NEPAD architects. The result was that a full day of the two-day summit (shortened from the three-day format of previous years) was devoted to discussions concerning Africa, and that for the first time non-G8 leaders, specifically from Africa, were direct participants in summit deliberations. The summit resulted in the adoption of the AAP, incorporating "more than 100 specific commitments" reflecting G8 consensus on where and how they should "respond to NEPAD's promise" (Fowler 2003, 228). These commitments spanned the areas of Resource Mobilization, Peace and Security, Governance, Trade and Investment, Health, Agriculture, Water, and Human Resources. As noted above, the AAP placed particular emphasis on channelling support to "Enhanced Partnership Countries" that "demonstrate a political and financial commitment to good governance and the rule of law, investing in their people and pursuing policies that spur economic growth and alleviate poverty" (see Fowler 2003, 239).

How are we to assess the implications of these commitments? In part, this depends on whether one thinks that G8 summits, and the documents they issue, have been more than talking shops and empty rhetoric (for contrasting views, see Kirton 2002, and Elliott 2003). In part, it depends on one's interpretation of both the AAP and the NEPAD, which Fowler characterized as a "realistic" plan "aimed at making African nations full and equal partners in the global economic and trading system and, above all, at attracting significant levels of foreign investment to that continent" (Fowler 2003, 226; see also Taylor 2005b). Particularly when inflected by the new emphasis on rewards to "Enhanced Partnership Countries," this is a scheme that, whatever its specific provisions and strengths, strongly reflected Western hegemonic preferences concerning the political and economic organization of both African countries and world affairs.

For our purposes, however, the evaluation can be reduced to a triple bottom line. First, the governments of the richest countries of the world gave more, and more sympathetic, attention to the challenges and opportunities confronting Africa than ever before. For this, the determined efforts of Jean Chrétien and his government deserve much of the credit.

Second, however, the AAP, for all its "specific commitments," produced virtually no new resources for Africa beyond those already announced at the 2002 UN Monterrey Conference on Financing for Development several months previously. In sum, it produced a qualified commitment to devote half (roughly US$6 billion) of the US$12 billion in new development funding committed at Monterrey to Africa—far short of the US$64 billion that the NEPAD document estimated the program required. This explains the verdict of most NGO and editorial opinion, reflected in such phrases as, "they're offering peanuts to Africa—and recycled peanuts at that," and "Africa let down by the rich" (*Guardian Weekly* 2002a and 2002b). Thus, Canada's best efforts could not bring its G8 partners around to substantially "putting their money where their mouths were." The net result indicates the ability of Canadian policy-makers to shape agendas concerning Africa on the one hand, but their sharply limited ability to shape outcomes on the other. This can be seen as consistent with the "lapidary" rather than architectural role of middle powers in global order building.

Nevertheless, the third bottom line is that Kananaskis initiated a process of G8 engagement with African issues that proved surprisingly durable. The process leading up to, and following on from, the adoption of the AAP was firmly reinforced by the institutionalization of Personal Representatives of Heads of Government for Africa (APRs), which ensured a measure of follow-up and accountability. At the Evian Summit in 2003, this dynamic was deepened by the creation of the African Partnership Forum (APF), including APRs of "G8 partners, 11 additional Organization for Economic Cooperation and Development donors heavily engaged in Africa, the members of the NEPAD Implementation Committee, and selected African and international organizations." The APF subsequently met twice annually, with the stated objective of serving "as a catalyst for cooperation in support of NEPAD and as a forum for information sharing and mutual accountability" (CIDA 2004, 13). At Sea Island in 2004, the American hosts, who had been characteristically unwilling to engage in concerted multilateral efforts, nevertheless contributed significantly to the momentum of the G8 process by orchestrating a more precise and expansive commitment to African capacity building for peace and security, including the training and equipping of 75,000 peacekeepers, mostly African, by 2010 (see Williams 2008, 316; Yamashita 2013). Beyond Gleneagles (addressed below), there was widespread concern that, with Russia's St. Petersburg Summit in 2006, focus and momentum would be lost. Yet to the surprise of some in the German African Studies community (author interviews, May 2007), Chancellor Angela Merkel restored the focus on Africa at the Heiligendamm Summit, and the Japanese and Italian hosts retained it in 2008 and 2009. In short, a focus on Africa was institutionalized, persisting right up to the now-diminished, one-day Camp David (United States) Summit of 2012.

The impacts of this process are analytically complex. Counterfactually, it is reasonable to conclude that considerably *less* would have been done in response to the NEPAD, and on shared policy priorities related to governance, aid, security, and trade for example, in the absence of this ongoing focus and the opportunities for accountability it generated (see, e.g., DATA Reports 2009 and 2013). At one level, this is a profoundly discouraging assessment, given that the main summit "story line" since 2005 was typically the ongoing failure of G8 governments to live up to their aid commitments, and that G8 activities on security and trade negotiations, for example, have been unsuccessful in moving prospects in these areas decisively forward.[9] In another sense, however, the fact that African governments and organizations continued to invest this process, anchored by annual G8 summits, with a degree of legitimacy and credibility, as if it would or at least *could* produce important improvements, suggests that it had some success as a hegemonic project of fostering a plausible political consensus on the way forward for the continent. Moreover, as the DATA report of 2013 shows, despite failures and setbacks in donor performance, real gains toward the achievement of the Millennium Development Goals (MDGs)[10] have in fact been registered, though less robustly in Africa than elsewhere in the Global South.

The Canadian government, for its part, spent considerable time and effort in the years immediately following Kananaskis bringing its policies toward Africa in line with the G8 consensus, and reporting assiduously on its progress in doing so (see CIDA 2004).[11] On aid, following on from the Monterrey and Kananaskis commitments of 2002, the 2005 *International Policy Statement* (IPS) issued by the government of Chrétien's Liberal successor, Paul Martin, confirmed its intent to double aid to Africa between 2003–4 and 2008–9—slightly more quickly than the doubling of the aid program as a whole by 2010. Moreover, in the context of Prime Minister Chrétien's pre-Kananaskis diplomacy, the government had previously announced a C$500 million "Canada Fund for Africa" in its December 2001 budget, which the Canadian International Development Agency (CIDA) candidly described as "a showcase for Canadian leadership in pursuit of effective development through a series of large-scale, flagship initiatives in support of NEPAD and the G8 Africa Action Plan" (CIDA 2002, 26; see CIDA 2003 and 2011a for details). In terms of aid practices and priorities, the government committed to bringing its program into line with the emerging consensus on "Aid Effectiveness" in the international aid regime, involving harmonization with other donors, aligning with recipient country priorities, and respecting developing country "ownership" (see Lalonde 2009; Black 2006a). Finally, and after at least one false start, it moved to focus on "Enhanced Partnership Countries" by announcing in the context of the 2005 IPS a decision to focus two-thirds of its bilateral aid on twenty-five priority "partners," fourteen of which were to be African.[12]

In terms of trade and investment, even as Canada's presence in African extractive industries grew dramatically (see Chapter 7; also Campbell 2009b), the government supplemented its regular trade and investment development windows, such as the Export Development Corporation, with a C$100 million contribution to a "Canada Investment Fund for Africa" (CIFA) drawn from the Canada Fund for Africa, to be co-funded with and managed by private sector investors.[13] CIFA eventually invested in fifteen African projects, although these were heavily concentrated in pockets of relative continental prosperity in South Africa (4), Nigeria (4), and North Africa (3) and were therefore of dubious developmental impact in nurturing "pro-poor growth" where it was most urgently needed.

Finally, in terms of peace and security, the Canadian government made a modest contribution (C$19 million) through the Canada Fund for Africa to capacity building in West Africa (C$15 million) and at the African Union (C$4 million).[14] Even more modest contributions were sustained through the Military Training and Cooperation Program (MTCP) of the Department of National Defence (see Chapter 6). A considerably larger contribution was eventually made, as international attention to the crisis in Darfur mounted, to the functionality of the African Union Mission in Sudan (AMIS; see Black 2010a). Yet given the inadequacy of this force to the challenge it was faced with, it can be argued that the Canadian (along with other G8) contribution(s) did little more than sustain a veneer of respectability for an overmatched force, while diffusing and obfuscating responsibility for dealing with the crisis (see Black 2010a; Nossal 2005).

In short, Canada's follow up to its conspicuous role surrounding the Kananaskis Summit can be interpreted as a case of "*good enough* international citizenship" (Black and Williams 2008)—good enough, that is, to retain credibility in the eyes of its G8 partners and their African interlocutors, but little more. In fact, the record after Gleneagles in 2005 was one of quiet retreat from the expectations generated in 2001–02.

Gleneagles and Beyond

Prior to the 2005 summit hosted by the UK government at Gleneagles, the governments of Canada and the UK had been the two most consistent and concerted proponents of the G8's engagement with Africa. Not surprisingly, therefore, Canadian Finance Minister Ralph Goodale was asked to join Tony Blair's hand-picked seventeen-member Commission for Africa (CFA), whose massive 461-page report, *Our Common Future*, was conceived to give focus and urgency to summit deliberations. Nevertheless, the CFA and Gleneagles processes revealed some significant differences between these two governments and, beyond them, other G8 members. These had ambiguous but corrosive implications for their collective approach.

As noted above, the "Year of Africa" orchestrated by the British government of Tony Blair, highlighted by the Gleneagles Summit in July 2005, effectively overshadowed previous summit efforts and was widely seen as the new benchmark for G8 efforts, notably by Western civil societies. The Blair government's formidable capacity for "spin," combined with the deep personal commitment of Blair and his Chancellor of the Exchequer Gordon Brown, the extraordinary civil society mobilization of the "Make Poverty History" (MPH) campaign orchestrated by a broad coalition of UK NGOs (with hundreds of thousands wearing white wristbands in support), and the "Live 8" pop concerts orchestrated by "celebrity diplomats" Bono and Bob Geldof, combined to give African issues a degree of popular and media attention in British and other Western societies that was without precedent (see A. Payne 2006). This fed into the broad sense periodically expressed by British officials that, in the words of Tony Blair, "I think the (Gleneagles) G8 last year was the first time Africa has come to centre stage for the G8 Summit" (English translation, cited in Vines and Cargill 2006, 138). Such a view was both symptomatic of G8 hosts' penchant for self-promotion, and a predictable irritant for other G8 governments. Nevertheless, there is no gainsaying the scale of the effort and the extraordinary political theatre it generated. The Gleneagles

Declaration was preceded by the year-long effort of the British-sponsored CFA, whose report noted that Africa was falling badly behind on progress toward the MDGs, including halving the number of people living on less than a dollar a day by 2015, such that on current trends the goals would be achieved 135 years late. The commission's analysis called for a doubling of aid to Africa by the end of the decade, entailing a $25 billion increase, and the allocation of another $25 billion by 2015 (Commission for Africa 2005). Prodded by the UK's Blair and Brown, effectively allied with celebrity and civil society activists, the G8 did produce some relatively substantial and "firm" commitments at Gleneagles. These included commitments to double aid to the continent, write off debts of the poorest eighteen African countries, and take new steps toward trade liberalization and support for peace and security and governance reforms (see "G8 Agreement" 2005; *Globe and Mail* 2005; A. Payne 2006).[15]

As subsequent summits demonstrated, there was good reason to be skeptical about the extent of delivery on these commitments. There were also concerns about the shallowness of the CFA's (and UK government's) analysis of African governance (e.g., Sandbrook 2005; Williams 2005; W. Brown 2006); whether the prescriptions would therefore deliver sustainable and equitable development; and (of particular salience from a post-colonial perspective) how Africa and its people were portrayed, as both passive and noble impoverished victims, in the frenzied run-up to the summit (see Bunting 2005; also Gallagher 2009). Nevertheless, the British government was able to deliver a significantly more robust and ambitious package than the Canadian government had mooted three years before. In contrast, Canada was widely portrayed as an also-ran or even a laggard due to its refusal to join the European G8 members in committing to a timetable for reaching the long-standing aid objective of 0.7 percent of GDP, set by the Pearson Commission on International Development in 1969 (e.g., Elliott 2005).

For its part, the Canadian government surely felt somewhat put out by the implicit and explicit discounting of its own role in G8 efforts to date, but also revealed an emerging difference of perspective on the importance of aid as a vehicle for promoting African development. In short, Canada's commitment to development assistance, despite the increases announced at Monterrey and Kananaskis, was increasingly ambivalent as compared with many European governments, and the UK government in particular. It was also skeptical of what it perceived as commitments that were unlikely to be fulfilled. This was reflected in the comment of a former senior diplomat, noting the "voodoo arithmetic" required to arrive at "the $50 billion quantum" of aid advocated in the CFA report and incorporated in the Gleneagles Declaration (confidential interview, March 2007). Finally, the Canadian government shared with some G8 counterparts (notably the Germans) a sense that the Blair government, in orchestrating its *own* process through the establishment of the Commission for Africa for framing the issue and response, had ignored and undermined the collective G8 processes and modalities set in motion at Kananaskis. One can be deeply skeptical about what was likely to be achieved through these processes and modalities, and still acknowledge that the tensions, differences, and frustrations surrounding Gleneagles revealed the challenges of sustaining an effective hegemonic coalition. Paradoxically, the Gleneagles outcome weakened the G8 effort from a political and procedural standpoint, even as it successfully enhanced some of the group's material commitments.

The Heiligendamm Watershed

If the Gleneagles Summit fractured the axis on Africa that had effectively linked the Canadian and British governments prior to that time, the 2007 Heiligendamm Summit marked a clear course change in Ottawa concerning the political effort and resources the government was willing to commit to the G8's "Africa project." This argument needs to be made carefully. In some respects, very little changed in Canada's Africa policies; indeed at the l'Aquila Summit in 2009 the government was able to claim that it had become the first G8 government to meet the objective of doubling its aid to Africa between 2003–04 and 2008–09 (a claim that, while technically valid, requires some parsing, as discussed below). Yet from 2007 on, it became increasingly clear that Africa had been downgraded as a political and foreign policy priority.

A key turning point occurred in January 2006 when the Liberal government of Paul Martin, Chrétien's successor as Prime Minister, was replaced by a Conservative minority government led by Stephen Harper. The new Prime Minister was not experienced in international affairs,[16] and his inclinations were economically conservative, politically "realist," and pro-Western (see Flanagan 2009; Black 2009).

His economic conservatism, rooted in his training as a neo-classical economist, made him deeply skeptical concerning the utility of foreign aid. He and his government were also intensely partisan, even by conventional political standards, and he was suspicious of both non-governmental organizations and "celebrity diplomats."

Initially, Harper's government had little to say on foreign affairs beyond a strong commitment to the NATO operation in Afghanistan, combining a major combat role with an extraordinary infusion of aid (reflecting a "whole of government" approach),[17] as well as other pointers such as a decidedly pro-Israel tilt in the Middle East and an initial (though later reversed) cooling of relations with China. On Africa there was mostly silence, and policy drift. Thus, when the Heiligendamm Summit again shone a spotlight on G8 commitments to Africa, there was much uncertainty and speculation concerning the position Harper would take.

In the event, several noteworthy developments occurred. First, unlike his predecessor and other world leaders, Harper was "too busy" to meet celebrity diplomats Bono and Geldof. Trivial in itself, this could also be seen as a signal that he was not interested in their agenda of expanded aid and debt relief for Africa. Both subsequently accused Harper of working to block wording in the communiqué on clear targets to meet G8 governments' Gleneagles commitments (see *Globe and Mail* 2007)—a charge the prime minister denied. Then a controversy erupted over the value of Canada's Gleneagles commitment to double aid to Africa between 2003–04 and 2008–09. Whereas the 2005 federal budget tabled by the Liberals had projected this increase to run from the estimated expenditures of C$1.38 billion in 2003–04 to C$2.76 billion in 2008–09, the new government argued that since *actual* aid expenditures in Africa in 2003–04 turned out to be only C$1.05 billion, doubling aid would bring the total to only C$2.1 billion. This accounting adjustment thus effectively reduced the value of Canada's commitment by some C$700 million. Finally, as the summit concluded, Harper signalled a new emphasis on the Americas, noting that while Canada will "remain engaged" and "will meet our targets" in Africa, "a focus of our new government is the Americas" (A. Freeman 2007).

It was not until nearly two years later that more specific policy developments emerged to support this rhetorical shift. Nevertheless, some clear signals were sent—for example, the lack of high level ministerial travel to Africa versus the Americas or Afghanistan (see

J. Clark 2007), and the appointment of a high-profile former journal-ist (Peter Kent) as Minister of State for the Americas, with no compar-able appointment for Africa or Asia. Then, in February 2009, the Min-ister for International Cooperation, Bev Oda, abruptly announced a new streamlined list of twenty priority countries for bilateral aid. This list cut in half the number of African priority countries, to seven from fourteen, while increasing the number of priority recipients in the Americas and Asia (Afghanistan had already emerged as the largest bilateral aid program in Canadian history, at C\$280 million in FY 2007–08, with Haiti becoming the second largest. See CCIC 2009, and Chapter 5). Among those dropped were long-standing Com-monwealth and Francophonie partner governments, including Cam-eroon, Kenya, Malawi, Niger, Rwanda, and Zambia.[18] This was the clearest signal to date of a shift in priorities, and cast into doubt the trajectory for Canadian development assistance to Africa beyond the 2008–09 target date for doubling aid, and the end of spending asso-ciated with the Canada Fund for Africa. Indeed, while at l'Aquila in 2009 Canada was credited with being the first G8 government to meet its doubling target (as noted above), total aid spending remained comparatively modest, and considerably below the Organization for Economic Co-operation and Development–Development Assist-ance Committee (OECD-DAC) average, with a projected figure of no more than 0.31 percent of GNI by 2010 (Tomlinson 2008, 279). This was prior to the aid spending cuts in the 2011 and 2012 austerity budgets,[19] with development assistance once again bearing a highly disproportionate share of the government's efforts to restore "fiscal balance." These developments in aid programming were accompan-ied by the closing of several diplomatic missions on the continent, leaving Canada with fewer diplomatic missions in Africa than any G8 government other than Japan. Similarly, as a result of cuts to its trade-related presence on the continent, Canada was left with only 25 Trade Commissioners for Africa's 47 countries by 2009, compared with 68 Trade Commissioners for Latin America's 13 countries, with fewer than half as many inhabitants (CCA 2009; see also Elder 2013).

The government's diminished interest in Africa, and in initiatives of particular relevance to the continent, can be tracked in other ways as well. In the security domain, Canada's "boots on the ground" in UN-led peace operations in Africa totalled less than fifty in 2008, compared with some 2,500 in Afghanistan (see Chapter 6). Similarly, the "Responsibility to Protect," which had been a hallmark of Canadian foreign policy since 2001 and which has more—albeit controversial—relevance for Africa than any other continent (see Williams 2009), was virtually dropped from the lexicon of Canadian foreign policy (see Boucher 2012). And, notwithstanding ongoing investments in health through CIDA programming, the landmark 2003 legislation ("Canada's Access to Medicines Regime"), which had been intended to greatly increase the availability of inexpensive generic AIDS medication for Africans, proved to be an almost completely dead letter, with the government showing no interest in amending it to make it more effective (Caplan 2009).

In short, while it would be a mistake to overstate the degree of change in Canada's approach to Africa as measured in *actual* resource allocations and practices, by mid-2009 there was clear evidence of declining political interest in various ways, both tangible and intangible. Yet in the tradition of consistent inconsistency, this trend was soon being mitigated, if not reversed. And once again, G8 and broader multilateral diplomacy was instrumental in this process.

Huntsville and Beyond

Evidence of some effort to increase Canada's visibility and refurbish the country's image on the continent was apparent by the latter part of 2009 and 2010. Much of this was motivated by the tardy, and ultimately embarrassingly unsuccessful, bid for a non-permanent seat on the UN Security Council for 2011–12. Whereas there was a striking lack of ministerial visits to Africa for the first several years of the Harper era, as noted by Joe Clark (2007), the first four months of 2010 saw three visits in rapid succession—by Foreign Minister Lawrence Cannon to the opening of the Summit of the African Union in Addis Ababa in January; by International Trade Minister Peter Van Loan to Kenya and South Africa in March; and by the Governor-General, Michaëlle Jean, to Senegal, the DRC, Rwanda, and Cape Verde in April. These visits followed fence-mending representations to African missions in Canada, undertaken in the wake of the abrupt February 2009 announcement of new countries of concentration and, by implication, African de-prioritization (e.g., Oda 2009b).

The material foundation for the claim that "Canada's history and friendship with Africa is strong and long-standing," and that "we will make responsible, meaningful commitments and keep them" (Oda 2009b) rested heavily on two foundations. The first was the argument, noted above, that Canada was the first G8 government to meet its commitment to double aid to Africa, a year ahead of the target date of 2009–10. The fact that this resulted in a relatively modest total commitment of $2.1 billion was not dwelt upon (see Johnston 2010). However, the flagship initiative of the Harper government's image makeover, as well a centrepiece of the Muskoka G8 Summit in June of 2010, was the "G8 Muskoka Initiative: Maternal, Newborn and Under-Five Child Health." First fully articulated in Harper's speech to the World Economic Forum (WEF) in January of 2010, the initiative was anchored by a $1.1 billion commitment of new money by the Canadian government announced during the Muskoka Summit. Also at the summit, the G8 together committed to provide a total of $5 billion in "catalytic" funding over the 2010–15 period, with the aim of generating in excess of $10 billion in new funding from all donors for a collective effort to accelerate progress on Millennium Development Goals 4 and 5.[20] By September 2010, the "Muskoka Initiative" (MI) was said to have generated commitments of $7.3 billion in new funding for maternal and child health (Toycen 2010). By November, it was announced that 80 percent of Canada's $1.1 billion contribution would go to seven countries in sub-Saharan Africa, as Canada's own implementation plans were finally articulated (O'Neill 2010).[21]

The full implications of the MI will take time to become fully apparent, and its broader significance will be revisited in Chapter 8. In relation to G8 diplomacy and the Harper government's Africa policy, however, a few preliminary conclusions are warranted. Broadly speaking, it seems uncharitable to criticize an effort to address the initiative's self-evidently praiseworthy objectives. Indeed, the cynic might note that the initiative was targeted to disarm potential critics: who, after all, could *oppose* its (literally motherhood) objectives? Nevertheless, setting this effort in fuller context suggests that it masks as many uncertainties and weaknesses as it addresses. First, and most importantly, the commitment was being formulated at the same time that the March 2010 budget announced:

With the achievement of the $5-billion aid target,[22] future IAE (International Assistance Envelope) spending levels will be capped at 2010–11 levels and will be assessed alongside all other government priorities on a year-by-year basis in the budget. Relative to the planning track in the September 2009 Update of Economic and Fiscal Projections, which assumed automatic ongoing growth for international assistance spending of 8 per cent per annum, this results in savings of $438 million in 2011–12, rising to $1.8 billion in 2014–15. (Department of Finance 2010)

In other words, the Canadian government was "flatlining" overall aid, resulting in a significant real decline in official development assistance (ODA). The 2012 budget went further, making deep cuts to the aid program with the aid-to-GDP ratio declining from 0.34 percent in 2010 to an estimated 0.27 percent in 2014 (see Chapter 5; S. Brown 2014). The problem here is not simply the decision, in a new round of austerity, to target aid yet again for a disproportionate share of cuts, further eroding Canada's already desultory performance. It is that the "targeted" and "focused" effort to make progress on maternal and child health has come, in effect, *at the expense of* a broader commitment toward poverty alleviation, and thus the systemic underpinnings from which both maternal and child-health failures arise, and on which sustainable progress needs to be built. The prime minister's words in introducing this initiative at the WEF in Davos are telling: "Let us close with something where progress is possible, if we are willing. It concerns the link between poverty and the appalling mortality among mothers and small children in the Third World. Did you know that every year over half a million women die in pregnancy and nearly nine million children die before their fifth birthday?" (Harper 2010). In this phrase, the prime minister effectively articulated a choice to address the *effects* of poverty on maternal and child health, rather than the underlying conditions of poverty to which they were explicitly linked. It is to be hoped, of course, that this initiative will save many lives, in Africa and elsewhere. Yet the choice to overlook, and implicitly accept, the underlying conditions raises doubts about sustainability, and where the effects of poverty will be deflected *to* if they are successfully tackled in the area of maternal and child health.

The second point to note is the relatively late and improvised character of this initiative. Here, it is instructive to compare the MI with the Chrétien government's efforts to animate the Africa Action Plan (AAP) at Kananaskis. First, as discussed above, the scope and ambition of the Chrétien government's approach was far broader—coming as it did in response to African leaders' NEPAD initiative—while the diplomatic focus and effort behind it was far more protracted and sustained. In contrast to the carefully orchestrated, year-long efforts of Prime Minister Chrétien and his Sherpa/African Personal Representative Robert Fowler, Prime Minister Harper's initiative on Maternal and Child Health was not spelled out prior to his Davos speech, less than six months before the summits, and does not seem to have been anticipated within CIDA, where staff were left scrambling to bring it to life with minimal information or guidance (interviews, Addis Ababa, Feb. 2010; Pearson 2010). The lack of planning and reflection was soon exposed by controversial mixed messages over whether the government would or would not support contraception and abortion within this initiative—leading to a broad critique among feminist activists and scholars that the initiative reflected a retreat from gender equity as a government priority (see Carrier-Sabourin and Tiessen 2012; Haussman and Mills 2012).[23] The decision on how much money the government would allocate to the initiative was announced just as the G8 summit was beginning, attenuating any prospect of leading by example.[24] The announced commitment of $1.1 billion in new funding over five years was, on the one hand, substantially more than the Chrétien government's $500 million Canada Fund for Africa, but on the other roughly the same as the Harper government's outlay for the three days of the linked G8 and G20 summits in Huntsville and Toronto, putting the relative level of the government's commitment into relief. Plans for how the money would be spent were announced several months later.[25]

The point of this comparison is not to cast the Harper government in an unflattering light by highlighting the virtues of the Liberal record. After all, the Liberal initiative on the AAP was characteristically long on ambition and modest on concrete resource commitments, while coming in the wake of draconian cuts to aid spending in the 1990s under the same leadership. The comparison does however underscore some of the distinctive characteristics of Canadian policy toward Africa under the Harper Conservatives: a lack of sustained attention and consultation, leading to tardy and/or improvised initiatives; and an emphasis on tightly focused, readily "branded" initiatives consistent with the Conservatives' distinctive interpretation of "results" and "accountability." In the meantime, the ability of Canadian policy-makers to actively participate in the larger debates and dynamics of Africa's international relations has continued to decline.

Conclusion: Regime Specific vs. Cyclical Dynamics

A fuller exploration of the meaning of the Harper government's shift of focus away from Africa (and toward Latin America) will be undertaken in subsequent chapters. What needs to be highlighted in this context is the difficulty of sorting out the degree to which this trajectory represents a long-term shift, or merely the latest phase in an ongoing pattern of intensifying and then receding interest in the continent's affairs and prospects.

There are ways in which the Harper government's approach to Africa, and indeed its approach to foreign policy more broadly, represents a qualitative departure from the dominant patterns of post–Second World War Canadian foreign policy (on the latter, see for example, Chapnick 2011–12). Some of these are alluded to above. Beyond the government's initial inexperience in international affairs, the ideas and attitudes that have shaped its approach seem much closer than any of its predecessors, of any major party, to American conservative predilections concerning multilateralism and foreign aid on the one hand (relatively unsympathetic to both), and to a hard-nosed, realist view of the importance of military capabilities and alliances on the other. The latter was manifested, most obviously, in its enthusiastic commitment to the NATO-led mission in Afghanistan, contrasted with its minimalist approach to UN-led operations in Africa (Sudan partially excepted—see Chapter 6). Similarly, the Harper government has demonstrated little enthusiasm and indeed considerable skepticism in relation to those old manifestations of active internationalism and bicultural identity—the Commonwealth and la Francophonie—both of which led previous Canadian governments to be much more engaged in African countries and issues than they would have otherwise been (e.g., Black 2010b).

The logic of a "tilt" toward Latin America was reinforced by similar, rational-utility maximizing and pro-American predispositions: toward the superior commercial opportunities of the Americas and a closer and more sympathetic engagement in a regional zone of particular, historic American interest (see Healy and Katz 2008). Finally, the Harper Conservatives' unusually intense brand of partisanship arguably impelled them toward a Latin American tilt as a means of "brand differentiation" from the ostensibly Africa-fixated Liberals (Owen and Eaves 2007). More substantially, and consistent with the post-colonial frame discussed in the previous chapter, this "tilt" can be seen as yet another instance of Africa being used to narrate a new Canadian "story," as elaborated in Chapter 3.

If one accepts that the seeds of a more durable shift have indeed been sown, it becomes important to consider the ramifications of the Harper Conservatives' May 2011 electoral victory, in which they secured a majority government,[26] while the historic "Natural Governing Party"—the Liberals—were relegated to less than 20 percent of the popular vote and third-party status.[27] To what extent has a more unfettered Conservative government moved decisively to reinforce the directions it had initiated as a minority government vis-à-vis Africa and the developing world more broadly? Alternatively, will the imperatives of Canada's international role, encompassing both the expectations and legitimating myths of Canadians and the external pressures and opportunities associated with its multilateral commitments, ultimately mitigate or even reverse such an emergent shift— perhaps under a future government of a different partisan stripe? This latter question will be revisited in the concluding chapter.

On the other hand, there is another way of reading the Harper government's diminished interest in Africa. It is not only the current Conservatives who have periodically sought to "rebalance" Canadian foreign policy away from Africa. It was, after all, the Chrétien Liberal government that, in the mid-1990s, presided over the deepest cuts to the Canadian aid program in history, with a disproportionate impact on Africa (see NSI 2003, 78). More broadly, as noted in Chapter 1, various political leaders and permanent officials, notably (though not only) in the Departments of National Defence and Foreign Affairs, have more or less continuously taken the view that given Africa's relative marginality to Canada's core interests and values, prudence demands that resource commitments and political exposure be limited (see Matthews 1976; Dawson 2009). From this perspective, the latest shift in emphasis reflects something less permanent yet more persistent: the chronic "yin and yang" of Canadian foreign policy between its more "liberal" or "humane internationalist" impulses toward good international citizenship, and a more pragmatic or "conservative internationalist" tendency (see Munton 2002–03; Boucher 2012).

More broadly, then, what the completed summit cycle from 2002 to 2010 should teach us is that the Canadian government's interest in, and commitment to, Africa lacks depth and durability—a lesson that is reinforced by the inconstancy of Canadian support for Africa through the 1990s. This pattern of inconstancy erodes, in turn, the base of knowledge, resources, and credibility on which an effective Africa policy depends.

Finally, it is worth reconsidering the hegemonic aspirations of the G8's African project, as understood in neo-Gramscian terms and discussed in the previous chapter. What this case illustrates is that these possibilities are undermined not only by the policy limitations of the summits' most powerful member states; they are also compromised by intra-hegemonic differences over tactics, strategy, and optics, as reflected in the politics surrounding the Gleneagles Summit, and by the political exigencies and course changes of "secondary" powers, such as Canada, that undermine the consistency and success of their hegemonic work. In this sense, the history of the AAP, and Canada's role in it, illustrates the instability and contingency of transnational efforts to build a new "common sense" on the way forward for Africa. It remains to be seen how the changing institutional contours and normative frames of a post–Financial Crisis (and post-G8?) world will tackle this challenge. On the other hand, as a means for refreshing the hegemonic status of the Canadian state vis-à-vis its own society by reiterating its "humane internationalist" credentials, Canada's unsustained leadership within the G8 may have served its purpose.[28] In this sense, Canada's Africa policy and similar moments of ethical initiative serve as a basis for sustaining a favourable self-image domestically, even as the ostensible subjects of these initiatives fade from view.

The question is, how has this favourable self-image continued to gain traction domestically, despite the persistent inconsistencies in Canadian performance over the long term and the evident shallowness of Canadian contributions to African development and security? To answer this question a post-colonial frame, stressing the degree to which "Africa" forms the basis for a self-referential narrative, provides insight.

Chapter

"Africa" as Serial Morality Tale in Canadian Foreign Policy

As emphasized in the discussion of the post-colonial frame in Chapter 1, Africa has always borne a heavy burden of narrative images in the colonial and post-colonial imagination. According to Richard Reid, those in Western countries who took up the "cause" of Africa in the first decade of the new millennium "were part of a long tradition stretching back several decades. That tradition involved the continual objectification of "Africa" as a place where horrendous things happened to benighted people, and where the West could display its full panoply of moral and material powers to positive ends" (Reid 2014: 146). In Canada, as in many other "developed" countries, this distant and dimly understood continent has been most commonly associated with extremes—of violence, disease, poverty, corruption, fanaticism, ecological disaster, and the like (e.g., Smith 2005). This truncated and caricatured view is of course deeply problematic. But it has also rendered the African political landscape as a text on which the Canadian "attentive public"—governmental, non-governmental, and journalistic—has been able to narrate and reprise a favourite morality tale concerning our role(s) and identity in the world. By this I mean a simplified and stylized story in which the main characters (in this case "Canada," its citizens and its political leaders) embody moral virtues and vices, but also a story that serves as a source of expectations and a rough guide to action in the face of what are understood principally as moral or humanitarian crises.

There are two main themes to this narrative that have been inter-woven in an ongoing dialectic for much of the post-decolonization era. The first is of Canada, and Canadians, as relatively selfless and compassionate advocates for those people and countries less for-tunate than ourselves, and as leaders in mobilizing international responses to their plight. This narrative strand draws on a long-standing sense of "mission" in Canada's relations with the colonial and post-colonial world (see L. Macdonald 1995; Nossal 2000). The second is of failure to fulfill these aspirations and obligations—a tale of moral dereliction in which we are indifferent to or even complicit in the suffering of African countries and peoples. In other words, (sub-Saharan) Africa becomes the basis for a narrative concerning what we *can be* in the world, and what we *ought to be*. No other con-tinent/region has served so consistently as the basis for a coherent moral narrative concerning "Canada" and its foreign policy.[1]

This chapter extends our analytical gaze beyond the first decade of the new millennium, examined in the previous chapter, to probe these stylized images in an effort to understand the themes and mean-ings that have been "written onto" Canadian responses to a series of African crises and challenges. Applying key insights from the post-colonial frame outlined in Chapter 1, emphasizing the way in which a truncated, dehistoricized, racialized, and mysterious African "other" becomes the basis for a narrative that is fundamentally *about us*, these successive responses can be read, in effect, as chapters or episodes in a larger story of moral leadership, failure, and attempted redemp-tion. This narrative was particularly prominent and influential for a generation, from the mid-1980s to roughly halfway through the first decade of the twenty-first century. In this version of the narra-tive therefore, I will examine four such episodes, in necessarily broad strokes: the anti-apartheid struggle of the 1980s; the Somalia and Rwanda failures of the early 1990s; the Multinational Force deployed in response to the humanitarian crisis in eastern Zaire/Democratic Republic of the Congo of 1996 and the normative campaigns around human security and the Responsibility to Protect that followed in the later 1990s; and a reprise of the G8's engagement with the contin-ent in the early part of the new millennium, including Jean Chré-tien's leadership at the 2002 Kananaskis Summit, followed by the mobilization around Darfur of Paul Martin's prime ministership. I will then analyze the foreign and development policy practices that have been enabled and conditioned by the narratives surrounding these events, with the aim of clarifying their policy repercussions. In short, what are the policy consequences when the dominant focus on Africa becomes very largely *about us* and our ethical self-definition, rather than the ostensible focus of the policy? I will argue that such a self-referential focus has led to policies that, taken together, tend to be inconsistent, shallow, and incoherent. Finally, the chapter will conclude with a brief examination of whether the predominant pattern of relative indifference toward African issues on the part of the current Conservative government since it was first elected in 2006 should be read as representing a decisive break with Canada's heretofore bipartisan Africa narrative.

On this final point, and indeed throughout the historical trajectory of the publicly dominant Canada-Africa narrative that is the focus of this chapter, it is important to note that there have always been influential subordinate and/or counter-narratives in play. Two of these are particularly significant. The first is what Cranford Pratt termed the "counter-consensus" (Pratt 1983–84) of "progressive" and critical internationalist voices in civil society, the labour movement, Canadian churches, and some quarters of the academy. Many of these were, in fact, key participants in the framing of the dominant narrative, though some of the more radical elements of the counter-consensus have taken a decidedly more jaundiced view of the Canadian state and its ethical pretensions. For example, scholars and activists associated with solidarity groups like the Toronto Committee for the Liberation of Southern Africa (TCLSAC) and the *Centre d'information et de documentation sur le Mozambique et l'Afrique australe* (CIDMAA) were forceful critics of Canadian policy during the 1970s and 1980s, and strong advocates of more transformative politics in and with Africa. They had limited direct influence on Canadian policy, but served as an indirect prod toward more self-consciously progressive initiatives (see Black 2012b, 230).

The second sub- or counter-narrative has been propagated among a small group of influential scholars (e.g., Rempel 2006) and important segments of the political and bureaucratic establishment, including the Canadian Forces, who see the world through realist/statist lenses and therefore have been resistant toward the prioritization of Africa in Canadian foreign policy. This counter-narrative has also had important policy consequences, notably under the Harper

Conservatives, who have adopted what Jean-Christophe Boucher (2012) interprets as a more self-interested and normatively conservative "realist internationalism" that is suspicious of cosmopolitan and/ or altruistic argumentation in the conduct of foreign affairs.

Two further caveats should be entered. First, it should not be presumed that the dominant public narrative concerning Canada's role in Africa has had much traction beyond this country's "political class" or "attentive public," concentrated in some quarters of its party-political establishment, public service, civil society, and mass media. This does not mean it has been unimportant. Rather, it has been an important element in the legitimating framework by which these groups understand the relevance of their country and themselves. In this sense, it has performed a similar role to the one Gallagher (2011, 125–44) attributes to New Labour's Africa policy in Britain, enabling the regular refurbishment of the idea of Canada as a "good state" and of Canadians as "sensitive humanitarians" (Razack 2007, 386). Nevertheless, the lack of widespread traction for this narrative beyond the "chattering classes" also helps to explain why the empirical basis for Canada's role in Africa has been so inconstant in practice.

Second, there have of course been many ongoing engagements between Canada/Canadians and Africa/Africans beyond the key episodes or chapters I will outline in the following narrative account. They include, in particular, the development assistance links, peace operations and military training, and trade and investment relationships (notably though not only in the extractive sector) examined in subsequent chapters. Part of the argument here, however, is that the environment within which these connections unfold, and therefore the *way in which* they are understood and pursued, can be substantially influenced by the dominant public narrative(s) that characterizes the relationship. Narratives, Emery Roe (1991, 290) tells us, "help stabilize and underwrite the assumptions needed for decision making." "To the extent that … [they] become naturalized and taken for granted," adds Christopher Browning (2002, 50), "they structure perceptions of the present and rationalize certain courses of action." The Canada-Africa narrative(s) has not only shaped decision-making in moments of urgency and crisis, but also the nature of the relationship between these critical moments and the resources that can be brought to bear when they arise.

Chapter One: "Moral Leadership" on South Africa

There are a number of possibly entry points for an elaboration of the Canada-Africa story. One would be the diplomatic and developmental interventions surrounding white-settler minority rule and decolonization within the Commonwealth (e.g., Hayes 1982). Another would be the emergence of la Francophonie—a story that would emphasize the crucial role of Africa policy in helping give life and credibility to a "bilingual and bicultural" Canadian national identity and, in so doing, counter the increasingly assertive aspirations of Quebec nationalists (see, e.g., Gendron 2006; Sabourin 1976). Yet another compelling point of departure would be the Ethiopian famine of 1984–86, which not only turned African issues into a mass concern, albeit temporarily, but did more than any previous issue or event to frame "Africa" as a principally humanitarian and moral issue area (see D. MacDonald 1986; Smythe 2007). Indeed, this crisis marked the beginning of an elevated and superficially surprising level of interest and engagement with the continent from the Mulroney Progressive Conservative government first elected in 1984, and of the generation-long dominant narrative that I explore in the current chapter.

It is fair to say, however, that the most sustained and celebrated episode in Canada's African engagements remains the role of the Mulroney government in the endgame of apartheid in South Africa during the later 1980s and early 1990s. In Mulroney's own words, "I was resolved from the moment I became prime minister that any government I headed would speak and act in the finest tradition of Canada" on this issue (Mulroney 2007, 398). In this respect, Mulroney's expressed motivation reflected an idealized conceptualization of Canada's international role, which his own subsequent activism served to reinforce. From 1985 onward, the Mulroney government reversed long-standing Canadian opposition to sanctions against the white-settler South African state, first rhetorically and then through its participation in the crafting of a package of partial sanctions measures in the Commonwealth context. At the 1987 Commonwealth Heads of Government Meeting in Vancouver, Mulroney's own image as a stalwart proponent of a forceful stand against apartheid rule was widely cemented by a reportedly "electric" confrontation with British Prime Minister Margaret Thatcher over the issue (Valpy 1988). He was lionized by leaders of the Frontline States neighbouring South

Africa (including the then highly regarded Zimbabwean leader, Robert Mugabe—see Valpy 1987) and other developing country leaders in a way that paid long-term dividends in the UN context.

Mulroney was not alone in this effort. Former Ontario New Democratic Party leader Stephen Lewis rose to international prominence during this time as Canada's ambassador to the UN and a forceful opponent of apartheid in that context (see Chapter 4). More controversially, Foreign Minister Joe Clark, though favouring a more cautious approach on sanctions against the "apartheid regime," was undeniably seized of the issue and spent a great deal of time and effort on it, within and beyond the Commonwealth (see J. Clark 2013, 118–19). Canadian diplomats in Ottawa and in South Africa engaged in and/or underwrote extraordinary "positive measures," including working closely with opposition groups in South Africa and attending trials to act as witnesses to and sources of moral support for opposition leaders (see Adam and Moodley 1992; van Ameringen 2013). In all, these efforts came to be widely perceived among Canadians as key instances of moral leadership in the best tradition (ironically enough, for a Progressive Conservative government) of "Pearsonian internationalism." They came to serve, certainly throughout the 1990s, as a stylized benchmark or shorthand for what Canada at its best could and should do.

This was not an unproblematic and uncontested narrative however. Academics and activists associated with the Canadian "counter-consensus" had concluded by the latter part of 1987 that the high-water mark of Canadian leadership in the campaign against apartheid had passed, and articulated an alternative narrative highlighting Canadian prevarication and "backsliding," especially on the issue of sanctions (see L. Freeman 1997; R. Pratt 1997). I have concluded on the basis of comparative analysis that Canada's role was not nearly as exceptional internationally as it was portrayed within this country (Black 2001b). Yet even much critical commentary, for example from Canadian church and labour groups, was consistent with and reinforced that idea that Canada *could and should* play an important moral leadership role in the world. The essence of the criticism was that Canadian policy-makers were not following through with this "natural" or at least preferable Canadian role.[2]

A full assessment of Canada's involvement in the demise of apartheid is clearly beyond the scope of this chapter. The point from a post-colonial perspective, however, is that this historical "moment" became stylized and mythologized in a way that reinforced widely shared perceptions of Canadian international goodness—perceptions that were enabled by an abridged and simplified account of the struggle against apartheid that, in Julia Gallagher's words, "evacuated ambiguity" (2009, 441). Since the focus was on *Canadian* leadership, a measured assessment of both the relative significance of Canadian efforts, and the importance of these efforts in the undoing of apartheid, was largely occluded in the dominant public narrative. The global outpouring of respect and affection accompanying Mandela's death and funeral in late 2013 generated, in this country, a surge of commentary that both illustrated and firmly reinforced the story of Mulroney's, and Canada's, international "leadership" in the struggle against apartheid, underscoring its ongoing potency (e.g., Kennedy 2013).

Chapter Two: Moral Dereliction in Somalia and Rwanda

If South Africa came to be represented as a high point of Canadian ethical internationalism, the early 1990s brought two moments of widely perceived failure and shame on African terrain. As a post–Cold War "new world order" dawned, the United Nations, led initially by the United States, undertook an ever-growing number of multilateral "peace operations" in increasingly complex and intrusive circumstances. One of the earliest of these was the Somalia operation, instigated by a media-fed impulse to arrest a major humanitarian emergency unfolding in that country (to "do something"). In 1992 and 1993, Canada deployed more than 900 military personnel, along with the HMCS *Preserver* and Hercules transport aircraft, in the context of the UNOSOM I and later the American-led Unified Task Force (UNITAF) operations. Deployed without an adequate understanding of the local context and in an unprecedented operational environment of ongoing conflict, the result was devastating. For the large American contingent, the furor arising from the ambush, deaths, and humiliating images of dead American soldiers in Mogadishu spawned the "Somalia syndrome"—a deep reluctance to risk American lives for "merely" humanitarian purposes, notably in Africa—with tragic subsequent consequences. The Canadian military experienced its own "Somalia syndrome," as word and images spread of members of the Canadian Airborne Regiment's role in the abuse of Somali captives, the shooting death of one (Ahmad Aruush) and the torture and murder of another (Shidane Arone). The subsequent public inquiry highlighted serious leadership failures (see Herold 2004–05) and led to the disbanding of the Airborne Regiment. The "incidents" in Somalia underscored the persistent current of racism in Canadian society and the Canadian Forces (Razack 2004; also Whitworth 2004, chap. 4), and "shook Canadian Forces confidence as well as the confidence of the Canadian public in the Forces" in a manner that took many years to recover from (Dawson 2007, 170). Somalia itself was largely abandoned and continued to exist in the shadows of world affairs as the prototypical "failed state."

In narrative terms, then, Somalia came to be seen as a moment of moral dereliction, starkly at odds with the Canada that ought to be. That this image both failed to get to grips with the deep challenges of race and racism in the Canadian Forces and Canadian society on the one hand, and to take account of the professionalism and accomplishments of many within the Canadian contingent, both military and diplomatic, on the other was largely lost from the public story (see Razack 2004; and Dawson 2007, respectively). An important subtext for the Canadian Forces was that in this unfamiliar, hostile operational terrain lurked manifold dangers, both operational and political. We see here the renewal of a narrative of Africa as a place where Canada's interests are negligible and where the Canadian Forces run grave risks—and therefore a place where exposure should be carefully limited and tightly time-bound.[3]

The Somalia debacle was the direct precursor to the even more tragic failure of international society, Canada included, during the Rwandan genocide. When the United Nations Assistance Mission for Rwanda (UNAMIR) was approved by the Security Council in September 2003, it "was capped at the minimum viable level of 2500 troops. The mission was expected to be 'fast, cheap, and bloodless'. Major western nations, including Canada, refused to send contingents" (Beardsley 2005a, 46). The subsequent tragedy is well known and need not be recapitulated here. Despite repeated warnings of preparations by extremist elements and requests from the force commander, Canadian Brigadier-General Roméo Dallaire, for permission to act pre-emptively and for reinforcements, no such authorizations were given. In April of 2004, the genocide was launched, ultimately costing as many as 800,000 lives before the Rwandan Patriotic Front consolidated its control in July. As the genocide gathered momentum, the UN reduced its force presence to a rump of 454 soldiers, Western governments acted with impressive speed and efficiency to evacuate their own nationals while abandoning Rwandans, and the Security Council spent months prevaricating while studiously avoiding naming the unfolding slaughter as a genocide, lest they feel compelled to act forcefully as a result. This was widely seen by subsequent investigations as a largely "preventable genocide," and Canadian leaders and officials shared in the sense of collective shame that rightly followed this monumental collective failure (see Beardsley 2005a and 2005b; Dallaire 2003; Anglin 2000–01).

In the case of Canada, however, there was one additional dimension that has become very important to the way the genocide has been remembered. This is the role of Roméo Dallaire as force commander. Required to bear virtually impotent witness to the slaughter, Dallaire was subsequently haunted and very nearly destroyed as a person. When he began to recover, he channelled his own ghosts into becoming a tireless critic of Western (and Canadian) indifference to African suffering, and into advocacy of a far more robust, timely, and effective capacity and will to respond to humanitarian emergencies on the continent. Later, becoming a Liberal Party Senator in Canada's Parliament, he continued to speak and write passionately on these themes.[4] The result in terms of the dominant narrative on Canada in Africa has been paradoxical. On the one hand, Dallaire has often been critical of Canadian policy; yet on the other hand he has come to represent for many Canadians the best tradition of Canadian ethical or humane internationalism. Dallaire himself has continued to believe firmly in the idea of Canada "as a leader of the world's middle powers" and "a leading global citizen" (Dallaire 2006b). Thus, Canadians' own sense of themselves and their collective moral failure in Rwanda were at least partially mitigated, indeed transcended, by Dallaire's passionate advocacy (see Razack 2007). Moreover, as a direct result of his personal witness and trauma, Dallaire became a highly visible and influential public voice in Canada with ready and reliable access to major media outlets. In this and other cases, then, impressive internationalist Canadian citizens and organizations have become visible and vocal symbols of what Canada can/ought to be, even as they are often sharply critical of official Canadian policy. The paradoxical significance of such "iconic internationalists" is taken up in the next chapter.

From a post-colonial vantage, there is much about these cases to be probed.[5] Crucially, however, and remarkably, both Somalia and Rwanda came to be widely portrayed and understood as anomalous deviations from the Canada that ought to be. They were widely viewed as a product of tragically "bad apples" and egregious leadership failures (in the case of Somalia), and/or great-power dereliction (in the case of Rwanda), in ways that allowed Canadians to avoid a more penetrating examination of the social and racial assumptions that had created the permissive conditions for these devastating events. The "Rwanda effect" was particularly telling in the dominant Canada-Africa narrative, in part because of Dallaire's role, but also partly, I would argue, because it was so starkly at odds with the sense of moral purpose and potential that has been at the core of this narrative.[6] That Canada, albeit in the company of many others, had so manifestly failed to do what was possible to avert or at least limit the genocide elicited a kind of redemptive reaction for more than a decade to follow. This reaction was manifested both in responses to discrete events, and in broader "norm entrepreneurship" to define and promote principles and practices aimed at forestalling similar tragedies in future. In both cases, however, the reaction rested on and reinforced a flat, simplified, and salvific humanitarian account of the people and states (typically "failed" or "fragile") that were in need of rescue.

Chapter Three: Toward Redemption through "Human Security"

The most obvious and immediate reaction to Rwanda was manifested in Canada's role in the Zaire/Great Lakes crisis of November 1996, a looming humanitarian emergency that was a direct by-product of the Rwandan genocide and that threatened hundreds of thousands of refugees camped near the eastern border of Zaire (now the Democratic Republic of the Congo). On 9 November, the UN Security Council voted to establish a Multinational Force (MNF) to provide security and relief, and enable repatriation of the refugees. Three days later, when it was clear that neither the US nor France was prepared to lead the force, the Canadian government stepped forward, uncharacteristically, to lead the MNF. The decision was an intensely personal one for Prime Minister Chrétien, and one that also reflected the ethical impulses that have underpinned the dominant Canada-Africa narrative. Although the precise dynamics of the decision to participate and then lead are uncertain, it is clear that Chrétien felt compelled to act, influenced in part by some combination of his wife Aline and his nephew, Canada's Ambassador to the United States and the UN Secretary-General's recently appointed Special Envoy to the Great Lakes region, Raymond Chrétien (Cooper 2000, 65–66; Meyer n.d.; Hennessy 2001). In doing so, he was also responding positively to urgent appeals from humanitarian NGOs and acting in conformity with a "humane internationalist" self-image. His public rationale was redolent of the moral impulses and national self-image highlighted by a post-colonial frame: "Canada may not be a superpower but we are a nation that speaks on the international scene with great moral authority ... now is the time to use that moral authority to stop suffering, avert disaster" (Chrétien 1996).

The problem, as various authors have aptly noted, was that the Canadian government and particularly the Canadian Forces (CF) lacked the resources and experience to successfully fulfill the role for which its political masters had volunteered. As Hennessy notes, for example, the CFs' Operational Planning procedures were premised on the assumption that they would be "a dependent receiver of wider campaign planning by some other nation" (2001, 18). They were therefore unequipped to take on the additional demands of leadership. Similarly, inter-departmental planning capacities were underdeveloped and had to be improvised. Throughout, it became starkly clear how dependent Canadian "leadership" was on the support and approval of US elements. In the end, although 354 Canadian military personnel were deployed to the region (never getting beyond their point of arrival in Uganda), the crisis quickly dissipated when the various parties to the regional conflict effectively instigated a mass movement of refugees back to Rwanda without (indeed partly to forestall) international intervention. The MNF was disbanded, with something close to a palpable sigh of relief from the CF.

How this abortive leadership initiative relates to the dominant Canada-Africa narrative is complex. On the one hand, Canadian leaders responded as their attentive public expected, especially in the shadow of Rwanda, with a forthright commitment to take the lead if necessary in multilateral efforts to bring relief to the hundreds of thousands of affected civilians. Moreover, government officials subsequently claimed, not entirely without reason, that the international initiative Canada briefly led helped break the regional impasse and bring an end to the looming crisis (see Cooper 2000, 74–75). Prime Minister Chrétien asserted in Parliament on 18 November that Canada had "won an early battle against moral blindness and self-interest, by galvanizing the world community into action" (Meyer n.d., 3). On the other hand, for humanitarian NGOs, the MNF's rapid demobilization represented an effective abandonment of the thousands of refugees who were still at large and at risk in the forests of eastern Zaire. Thus the international community's precipitous decision to disband the MNF, in which Canada was centrally involved, was seen as another instance of moral dereliction. Finally, for the Canadian Forces, the lessons learned centred primarily on their own limited capacity and external dependence, the fact that an operational fiasco was only narrowly averted, and (once again) that African conflict zones were complex, operationally forbidding, and fraught with risks that should be minimized to the greatest extent possible.

A second, more protracted case providing a platform for redemptive reaction was the government's response to the deeply rights-abusive military regime of General Sani Abacha in Nigeria, especially after its execution of author Ken Saro-Wiwa and eight other Ogoni activists in November 1995. As this issue became a central focus in Commonwealth politics, with Abacha's Nigeria being "suspended from the councils of the Commonwealth" and becoming a focus for debate concerning various sanctions options, Canadian policy-makers arguably came to "read" the crisis as an echo or natural extension of the anti-apartheid politics of the 1980s (Black 2001b). Domestically, it became a means through which, in the dominant public narrative, Canada could recapture its "traditional" moral leadership role and thus, implicitly at least, redeem itself not only for failures in Africa but the failure to take a forthright stand on rights issues elsewhere in the early Chrétien years. A telling, June 1996 editorial in *The Globe and Mail* thus concluded that "the generals in Lagos will not cower before Canada, but that was never the intention. The purpose of imposing sanctions is to lead by example, which was once second nature to this country on issues of conscience. It is to show that morality has returned to Canada's foreign policy, where it belongs" (*Globe and Mail* 1996). From the *Globe's* perspective then, and consistent with post-colonial assumptions, the issue of how to respond to Abacha was predominantly about *us.*

There were, however, two main problems with this type of reaction. The first was that the idea that morality in foreign policy was "second nature" to this country perpetuated a potent but dubious historical myth. The second was that, as it turned out (and not unlike the MNF experience), Canadian efforts to lead by example suffered from a lack of willing followers, particularly among the developing country majority in the Commonwealth context. They were never willing to adopt the sanctions measures advocated by the Canadian government, which was only spared the embarrassment of ongoing, ineffectual advocacy by the death of General Abacha in June 1998. In this respect, the government's limited understanding of and influence with the Commonwealth's post-colonial majority was revealed.

The controversy surrounding international responses to Abacha's Nigeria overlapped with the "Axworthy era" in Canadian foreign policy. Throughout the latter half of the 1990s Lloyd Axworthy served as Canada's Foreign Minister, and much of the public politics of Canadian foreign policy during this period can be read at least partly through a redemptive lens—often masking, as numerous critics have noted, an underlying erosion of means and continuity of practice. For much of Axworthy's tenure, the "Human Security Agenda" became Canada's foreign policy signature and a key element of the Canadian "brand" (see Grayson 2004; Chapnick 2011–12). Much if not most of what came to be prioritized under this agenda—for example, peacebuilding and the protection of civilians (particularly children) in armed conflict—both reflected and reinforced a renewal of official interest in Africa, since the preponderance of the conflict zones on which the Human Security light was shone were in Africa (see C. Brown 2001). In addition, much of this agenda was pursued at the relatively high and abstract diplomatic level of norm entrepreneurship and institution building. Of these efforts, the one that may yet prove most far-reaching in its effects but remains most highly contested and controversial is the Canadian government's sponsorship of the International Commission on Intervention and State Sovereignty (ICISS) and subsequent championing of the commission's signal innovation—the idea of the "Responsibility to Protect" (R2P—see ICISS 2001; Bellamy 2009).

The origins, content, and ramifications of R2P have become deeply and widely debated—a debate it is impossible to engage in this chapter. Suffice it to say that the Canadian government's role in underwriting the commission and then championing its report was crucially motivated by the Rwandan genocide and the desire to give practical effect to the imperative call that the world should "never again" stand by as such a heinous mass crime unfolded. In a number of respects, the championing of R2P achieved some striking diplomatic successes. The principle was ultimately embedded in the UN General Assembly's World Summit outcome document, albeit in diluted form (see Riddell-Dixon 2005, 1077), in part thanks to vigorous lobbying by Chrétien's Liberal successor and rival, Prime Minister Paul Martin. In this respect, it reinforced the central moral leadership frame of the Canada-Africa narrative, and enabled attentive Canadians to feel some measure of relief that the Canada that ought to be had been partially "restored." At the same time, it has become clear that the level of diplomatic consensus around the principle is shallow at best (see Sharma 2010); and, moreover, that the Canadian government's own willingness and ability to *act* in conformity with R2P is sharply limited. This was starkly illustrated by the international and Canadian responses to the Darfur crisis, discussed in the next section.

Chapter Four: "Limits of Leadership" in the G8 and Beyond

As discussed in the previous chapter, the climax of the Canada-Africa narrative, at least to date, can be located in then Prime Minister Chrétien's sustained campaign to focus the G8 on a coherent and concerted plan for Africa, responding in turn to African leaders' "New Partnership for Africa's Development" (NEPAD). Chrétien, working with his Summit Sherpa and Personal Representative for Africa, Robert Fowler, spent the year between the Genoa Summit in 2001 and the Kananskis Summit in 2002 laying the groundwork for the G8's Africa Action Plan, adopted at the summit itself (see Chrétien 2007, 356–64; Fowler 2003). As previously discussed, fully half of the Kananaskis Summit was spent focusing on African issues—remarkable, particularly given that it was the first G8 summit following the traumatic terrorist attacks of 9/11. Another key innovation was that several African leaders were given a prominent place on the Kananaskis agenda. Leaving aside the question of what precisely was achieved through the AAP then, the events leading to and from Kananaskis can and have been constructed as a high point of Canadian leadership in focusing the world's attention on the challenges facing the African continent.

Certainly, the dominant public characterizations of the initiative during the preparations for the summit were largely consistent with this favoured moral story of both Canadian leaders and the country. "Man of action aims to make a difference in Africa," one glowing account of the Prime Minister's extensive preparatory tour of the continent was entitled (*Globe and Mail* 2002a). In a speech concerning Africa before the World Economic Forum plenary in New York in February 2002, Chrétien himself noted: "I am especially pleased and proud that my G-8 colleagues asked Canada to take the lead on this vital issue even before we took the Chair on January 1st. It was a strong vote of international confidence. In our credibility on the world stage. And in the progressive values we project in the world. Values of caring and compassion. And our belief in an equitable sharing of global prosperity and opportunity" (Chrétien 2002). This quote provides a particularly striking illustration of the way in which "initiativemanship" on Africa has been used to nurture and reinscribe the story of Canadian moral leadership in world affairs. As with Mulroney on South(ern) Africa, it provided a means through which Canadian political leaders were able to (re)assert their own moral credentials and/or attempt to cement their political legacies: this was, after all, a kind of valedictory initiative for Chrétien as the end of his long political career approached.

The problem, as noted in the previous chapter, is that this story masks a great deal of inconsistency with the image it projects. For example, in the next line of the same speech, Chrétien pronounces that, "For many years, we have been an innovative international leader in development assistance." This, from the same Prime Minister who presided over the deepest and most disruptive cuts to foreign aid in the history of Canadian aid-giving during the mid-1990s. Moreover, the degree and character of real progress in G8 Africa policies initiated through the AAP and the Kananaskis initiative was limited at best (e.g., A. Payne 2006; Yamashita 2013). While Africa continued to feature prominently on subsequent G8 agendas, these efforts were often portrayed as novel initiatives by subsequent host leaders (notably Tony Blair at Gleneagles and Angela Merkel at Heiligendamm). Collaboration was compromised by the intra-hegemonic politics of G8 leaders. Meanwhile, especially with the transition to the Conservative prime ministership of Stephen Harper, it became increasingly clear that the new Canadian government had little ongoing interest in engaging with African issues in a sustained and determined way—in other words, in finishing what its predecessor started. This is a theme to which I will return in the concluding section below.

The longer-term effects of the dynamic that the Chrétien government sought to instigate in G8-Africa interactions at Kananaskis were addressed in the previous chapter. Here, it is sufficient to note that in much commentary in Canada, what seemed to matter most was the *initiative itself*, and the way in which it was seen to signify a return to Canadian moral leadership on Africa after the dark days of Somalia, Rwanda, and the savaging of the aid budget during the austerity years of the 1990s. The fact that the summit was widely regarded in media and NGO commentary as a substantive disappointment, with other G8 countries being unwilling to agree to firm collective commitments to transfer new resources to Africa, ironically served to buttress the Canadian government's relatively progressive credentials—obscuring the harsh cuts to Canadian aid of the previous decade (*Globe and Mail* 2002b). The fact, moreover, that it was widely portrayed and interpreted from the perspective of what Canada and the West could and should *do for* an agglomerated Africa reflected the way in which Western agency and virtue continued to be defined and renewed through their engagement with the continent.

The final installment of this Canada-Africa chapter came after the transition to the Paul Martin prime ministership in late 2003, with the unfolding of the Darfur crisis. The transition was fraught, given the long rivalry between Chrétien and Martin and the need for the latter to put some political distance between himself and his predecessor. Nevertheless, Martin was a committed if somewhat unfocused internationalist who attempted to articulate foreign policy around a "Responsibilities Agenda" that both strongly endorsed R2P and clearly made a central discursive place for Africa (Martin 2004). Thus, when the Darfur crisis "broke" internationally in 2004, Martin's rhetoric was bold and strong, expressing in unequivocal terms the need for urgent and robust action and Canada's willingness to "do whatever is required ... [W]e cannot simply sit by and watch what is happening in Darfur continue" (cited in Nossal 2005, 1024). Yet, as Kim Nossal has incisively demonstrated, the government's actual response was, for many months, "conservative, limited, and symbolic" (2005, 1025). Indeed, Nossal provocatively argued that what this case most clearly demonstrated was that both Canadian political leaders and citizens had become addicted to "ear candy" on foreign policy, with minimal connection to what was being done or even what was possible (1025). Such an approach becomes comprehensible theoretically if the impetus for policy on African issues is understood to be largely a function of Canadians' own identity projection and expectations, tenuously connected with the complex realities of the continent itself.

While Canadian commitments to humanitarian and developmental efforts in Sudan as a whole, including Darfur, subsequently grew to over C$760 million between 2006 and 2010 (DFAIT website), and while Canada was among the largest donors to the African Union's overmatched force in Darfur (AMIS) and became one of the largest financial backers of the troubled "hybrid" UN-AU force for Darfur (UNAMID), two features of Canada's response to the Darfur crisis are particularly noteworthy in illustrating the limits of Canadian involvement. The first is that Canada was unwilling to offer a substantial troop commitment ("boots on the ground") for UNAMID. The concurrent commitment to Afghanistan was often invoked to justify our "inability" to commit forces in Sudan (whether the Sudanese regime would have allowed Canadian troops to enter in significant numbers is a separate question). The second is that, given the Canadian government's limited capacity and infrastructure in the region prior to the precipitous prioritization of Sudan around 2003–04, there was a high level of improvisation to the formulation of policy and no firm medium- or long-term commitment to peacebuilding in Sudan beyond the transitional process associated with the 2005 Comprehensive Peace Agreement by which the decades-long conflict between Sudan and South Sudan was finally brought to an uneasy end

(Matthews 2005). This clearly reflects the subtext among permanent officials that long-term commitments and exposure in Africa should be limited—a theme that will be further explored in Chapter 6.[7]

Policy Implications

Taken together, the ongoing "morality tale" of Canada in Africa outlined in this chapter reflects the core post-colonial insights that Western—in this case Canadian—engagements with the continent have enabled the ongoing (re)formation and projection of a stylized account of our *own* identity and virtue, in relation to a simplified, remote, and mysterious portrayal of the continent and its various countries and peoples. How and why does this ongoing narrative of Canada in Africa matter in policy terms? I would argue that it has mattered in at least four key ways.

First, the "discursive environment" surrounding Africa has traditionally expected, indeed demanded, bold statements framed in moral terms. Thus, as the statements from both politicians and editorial opinion cited above indicate, there has been a clear expectation that Canadian leaders *should* express willingness to respond ethically and generously to situations of human suffering in Africa, and that it is in our "best tradition" to do so. Hence, there has been a powerful expectation and incentive for political elites to respond to crises in expansive rhetorical terms, and to engage in periodic initiatives that reinscribe these narrative images. This narrative has thus clearly underpinned (in Nossal's terms) the ear candy impulse among the Canadian "political class," and the projection of Canadian moral superiority in relation to both Western great powers (specifically the US, the UK, and France) and the African "other."

Second, the parallel counter-narrative among many officials in the bureaucracy and personnel in the CF—that Africa is a place of limited or discretionary Canadian interests and high risks, and therefore a place where Canadian involvement and exposure should be minimized—has been a constant drag on the inclination of permanent officials to create the long-term basis for engagement in Africa that the dominant narrative has projected and expected. As a result, Canadian efforts have typically lacked the depth of understanding, the established infrastructure (both human and physical), and the personal and institutional connections on which successful initiatives draw. This problem was manifested in both the MNF and Darfurian cases, for example, and arguably compromised the sustainability of the more comprehensive and concerted effort to shape the G8 agenda for and response to Africa. In short, narrative and counter-narrative have contributed to an ongoing mismatch between public aspirations and expectations on the one hand, and long-term will and capacity for effective action, on the other.

Third, because the dominant public narrative on Canada's role in Africa has been largely about us, there has been little domestic political price to be paid for the failure to act effectively and sustainably in Africa. In other words, the *outcomes* or *effects* of Canadian initiatives have been either heavily mythologized (as with South Africa or Kananaskis), or widely overlooked and/or forgotten (as in Somalia—see Razack 2004, esp. 153–66). What matters most, as I have suggested above, are the initiatives themselves, reinscribing a favourite international self-image, rather than their outcomes. Long-term scrutiny and accountability have been weak, and instances of dereliction have been readily transcended by the next redemptive initiative that "restores" Canadian policy to its good and "true" self. What has been harder to know is whether a serious long-term price has been paid for this gap between discursive promise and policy performance in terms of *international* reputation, credibility, and influence. While it seems logical to expect that this would be the case, in practice there has been a higher level of tolerance for such inconsistencies than there should be, in part because of Canada's limited importance internationally.

Fourth and finally, this narrative pattern has effectively worked against serious analysis of, and engagement with, the structural conditions that have helped to entrench Africa's historic global marginality—including Canada's complicity in these conditions. For example, too little attention has been given to the complex effects of unstable aid volumes and erratic priorities, the impacts of large and growing Canadian extractive industry investments, and the effects of the "brain drain" of many of Africa's best and brightest people to this and other developed Western countries. When Africa comes to be principally understood as a landscape of ongoing hardship in which Canada's "moral impulse" is manifested and exercised, there is little incentive to look *beyond* this narrative to identify and act on the requirements to decisively alter this landscape. Moreover Africa's distance from Canadian realities, both physically and metaphorically, has meant that these challenges and contradictions need not be confronted. Finally, it has been all too easy to "write off" the continent as a hopeless cause on which the expenditure of scarce public resources is a largely "wasted effort," and in so doing discount the rich complexity and promise of many parts of the continent. It is this final impulse that helps to explain the Harper Conservative government's de-prioritization of African countries and issues in its foreign policy.

The Final Chapter? Africa in Contemporary Conservative Foreign Policy

While the dominant Canada-Africa narrative as described above has been a decades-long one, a striking feature of the foreign policy of the Harper Conservative government has been its relative disinterest in Africa (see J. Clark 2007; Africa-Canada Forum 2007; Black 2009). As noted in the previous chapter for example, Harper went out of his way at the Heiligendamm G-8 Summit in Germany in June 2007 to emphasize that Canada's priority would shift to the Americas—a priority that was subsequently elaborated and formalized (see Government of Canada 2009), though with slow and limited practical effects. By 2011 Harper had travelled but once to Africa since taking power, for the 2007 Commonwealth Heads of Government meeting in Uganda, and in 2009 the Canadian International Development Agency cut in half the number of core development partners on the continent, from fourteen to seven. Later, after much speculation that Ottawa would take up the UN's invitation to deploy General Andrew Leslie along with a contingent of the CF to lead the peacekeeping mission in the DRC (MONUC) as Canada's combat role in Afghanistan wound down, the government finally, and tellingly, turned down this UN request (*Globe and Mail* 2010). It is hard to imagine either a Mulroney or a Chrétien government, with their reflexive responsiveness to such UN appeals, taking the same decision.

How are we to understand this apparent shift, and how durable is it likely to be? Has the Canada-Africa narrative that has been so prominent in elite political discourse, at least intermittently, run its course?

These questions are taken up in the concluding chapter. At this stage, it will suffice to note that the evidence is ambiguous. In particular, following the re-election of a majority Conservative government in 2011, a new African narrative has risen to prominence both internationally and, tentatively, in Canada. This narrative of a "Rising Africa" (CCA 2013), and of "Canadian companies [being] well placed to take advantage of opportunities in fast-growing Africa" (DFATD 2013b), indicates a renewed level of interest, albeit with a narrowly commercial and self-interested emphasis. In the context of the current discussion, however, one way to think about the fate of the post-decolonization "story" is to consider whether we have been witnessing a decisive realignment in the narrative hierarchy concerning Canada and Africa. In short, are we witnessing the long-term ascendance of the more hard-nosed narrative of Africa as a dangerous quagmire in which commitment and risk should be minimized *except where* clear Canadian self-interests are in play, and the concomitant marginalization of Africa as serial morality tale? Is the former becoming the dominant public narrative concerning the relationship? Are we seeing a decisive turn against the old "humane internationalist" account? Through the "Harper years," there have been signs that the heretofore subordinate/"official" view concerning the marginality of Africa to core Canadian interests and values is no longer confined to relatively conservative/realist quarters of academia, the bureaucracy, and the CF, but is increasingly articulated in the popular and electronic media. Conversely, images of mass human suffering, even when amplified by a popular figure such as former Governor General Michäelle Jean (see Panetta 2010), no longer trigger the breadth or depth of calls to "do something." As the government demonstrated in relation to MONUC and the DRC, and subsequently with its reticent response to the call for contributions to international operations in Mali (C. Clark 2013a), they can and have been rejected or discounted without fear of political repercussions. It remains to be seen whether this narrative realignment will be become entrenched. In the meantime, what is clear is that "Africa" remains a crucial narrative landscape through which "Canada" (re)defines itself.

Chapter

"Iconic Internationalists" and the Representation of Canada in/through Africa

In the previous chapter, I outlined a resilient post-colonial narrative concerning Canada's ethical mission in Africa that tells a story of cases in which our "normal" or "natural" role of moral leadership is successively fulfilled, contradicted, and restored. Despite its waning influence, this narrative has persisted into the Harper era, and has underpinned much of the reaction to the government's professed tilt toward Latin America and its perceived downgrading (sometimes portrayed as "abandonment") of Africa. In a commentary on former Minister of International Cooperation Bev Oda's February 2009 announcement of twenty priority recipients for Canadian bilateral aid for example, in which eight African countries were dropped from this streamlined list, Anthony Halliday of the Canadian International Council's African Study Group asserted: "This new policy abandons Canada's traditional emphasis on reducing poverty in the world's poorest countries, notably in Africa ... Our traditional values dictate we remain engaged with Africa" (Halliday 2009). What is particularly striking about this commentary is that it invokes a "tradition" of commitment to poverty alleviation and of generosity, particularly toward Africa, that decades of scholarship has largely refuted (e.g., L. Freeman 1985; C. Pratt 1994 and 2003; Morrison 1998; S. Brown 2008 and 2012b). Why such an image still resonates so powerfully with many Canadians despite the weight of accumulated evidence is an intriguing question. In short, why does a narrative that assumes the "naturalness" of Canadian moral leadership, particularly as manifested in Africa, continue to enjoy as much traction as it does?

Several factors help to explain our continued attachment to this benign and generous self-image. One is that it has been regularly refurbished by high-profile initiatives from Canadian political leaders that are heralded as marking a "return" to our "true" or at least better collective selves, notwithstanding the routine pursuit of far more narrowly self-interested and/or indifferent behaviour. As highlighted in Chapter 3, this pattern of consistent inconsistency has often been played out on an African stage as, for example, in Brian Mulroney's engagement with South Africa in the mid-1980s, Lloyd Axworthy's attempt to mobilize opposition to the Abacha regime in Nigeria in the mid-1990s, Jean Chrétien's effort to catalyze the G8 to action through the Africa Action Plan in 2002, or indeed Stephen Harper's "Muskoka Initiative" on maternal, newborn, and child health.

A second, more diffuse and commonsensical explanation is simply that Canadians, like members of most other societies, generally prefer not to think ill of themselves. It is far more comforting to routinely re-invoke a sense of ourselves as good, generous, and constructive "international citizens." The fact that Africa and its travails are far removed from our immediate interests and experiences has conveniently enabled us to sustain this self-image through intermittent attention to instances of apparent leadership and generosity, accompanied by widespread inattention to and ignorance of less attractive realities.

A third explanation goes back to the good international citizenship frame introduced in Chapter 1. In short, there have been significant, if irregular, instances in which personnel associated with the Canadian state—whether military or civilian, senior or subordinate—have acted in ways that have enhanced the performance of multilateral initiatives and, in so doing, have made discernible contributions toward the more solidarist aspirations embedded in key international initiatives. To cite just two prominent examples, Robert Fowler's extraordinary role as Chair of the Angola Sanctions Committee while Canadian Ambassador to the UN during Canada's last Security Council term in 1999–2000 was widely credited as being instrumental in ratcheting up the effectiveness of Security Council sanctions against the rebel UNITA movement, thereby hastening the end of the decades-long Angolan civil war (e.g., Mollander 2009, 8–9). At a less elevated level, modest but practical Canadian contributions were instrumental in ensuring that the African Union's AMIS mission in Darfur achieved a modicum of effectiveness in the face of that region's massive humanitarian emergency (see Black 2010a). I will elaborate on this point in subsequent chapters.

A fourth explanation has received less attention however. This is the role of key public figures—or "voices"—often beyond (and meta-phorically above) government who are seen to embody the best of this country in their activism on behalf of those who are neglected, impoverished, and abused. These figures become, in effect, icons of internationalism, widely portrayed as reflecting our *true* or *best* selves, notwithstanding the deviations from these presumed roles perpe-trated by the compromised and compromising political leaders of the day. Once again, the stage on which these iconic voices intervene has frequently been African.

There are a range of examples of such figures, many coming from the world of humanitarianism but building on this background to enter the domains of advocacy and analysis. They are often closely associated with Canadian or international non-governmental and civil society organizations that have made exceptional efforts to pub-licize and alleviate situations of extreme human suffering. We could cite, among others, Craig and Marc Kielburger of the NGO Free the Children; Samantha Nutt, founder of War Child Canada (Nutt 2011); or James Orbinski, former President of the International Council of Médecins sans frontières (MSF) (Orbinski 2008). In this relatively brief chapter, I will focus on two particularly iconic inter-nationalists—arguably the two most prominent and popular of the contemporary era—Roméo Dallaire and Stephen Lewis. These two exemplary Canadians have both become tireless advocates for the human rights of the poor and marginalized of Africa, and for a more generous and activist Canadian foreign policy especially in relation to this poorest and most insecure of continents. Their role, I will argue, is paradoxical. On the one hand, they have often been sharp and forceful critics of Canadian government policies and (in)actions. On the other hand, their core messages have effectively reinscribed the potentiality and "naturalness" or "rightfulness" of a good and generous Canada, operating principally in a reinvigorated and UN-centred multilateral context. More broadly, they themselves have come to embody and symbolize the best of Canada in the world, in ways that occlude a clear-eyed analysis of the country's considerably less admirable record and thus enable many Canadians to continue to believe in this image.

Theoretically, their role is ambiguous. As people who have worked with, and indeed as, servants of the Canadian state, they can be seen as personifying the *possibility* of good international citizenship in Canadian foreign policy, specifically toward Africa. More importantly, however, insofar as they become perceived embodiments of our collective potential for moral leadership, they at least partially absolve us of the need to develop a deeper and fuller understanding of the roots of Africa's development and security challenges, and of our country's contradictory role in relation to them. Thus, they help to explain the persistence and plausibility of the post-colonial narrative outlined in Chapter 3.

This chapter begins by briefly exploring the important role of Africa in the socialization of key segments of the Canadian "political class" in the post-decolonization (post-1960) era. I will then assess the messages—both explicit and embodied—articulated by Roméo Dallaire and Stephen Lewis, respectively, before analyzing the roles these messages have played in sustaining a benign and hegemonic sense of our global selves.

Africa and the Canadian Public/Political Elite

An influential minority of those who came to dominate Canadian public life and political discourse through most of the past two generations had formative experiences in the Africa that emerged from colonial rule in the 1960s, '70s, and '80s. Stephen Lewis was one of these. His prose on the experience is illuminating:

> It must be understood, without any hint of heady romanticism, that Africa in the 1950s and 1960s … was a continent of vitality, growth, and boundless expectation. It got into your blood, your viscera, your heart. The bonds were not just durable, they were unbreakable. There was something intoxicating about an environment of such hope, anticipation, affection, energy, indomitability. The Africa I knew was poor, but it … was absolutely certain that it could triumph over every exigency. (2005, 44)

Lewis has become perhaps the best known of these "Africa-affected" Canadians, but he was hardly alone. Their number include, to cite only a few prominent examples, well known public policy commentator and political organizer Gerald Caplan, former MP Steven

Langdon, *Globe and Mail* columnist Hugh Winsor, former Members of Parliament and Cabinet Ministers David MacDonald and Walter McLean, and the two senior (ex-)diplomats who spent 130 days as captives of an al-Qaeda-linked cell in Mali, Robert Fowler and Louis Guay (see Fowler 2011). They were often volunteers—for example, with Canadian University Service Overseas (CUSO) and other secular or faith-based NGOs that were themselves the inheritors of a considerably older mission tradition (see Wright 1991; Smillie 1985; Brouwer 2014). Others in the English Canadian "intelligentsia," like prominent political scientists Cranford Pratt and Douglas Anglin, played formative roles in Africa's post-decolonization university system: Pratt was the first principal of the University of Dar es Salaam in Tanzania, while Anglin was the first vice-chancellor of the University of Zambia. Still others, like John Saul and Linda Freeman, became pillars of what Cranford Pratt has characterized as "radical internationalism," as scholar-activists based in Canadian universities who were deeply engaged with solidarity politics vis-à-vis Southern Africa. Similarly, the Quebec of the Quiet Revolution and the federal government's parallel efforts to foster bilingualism and biculturalism were shaped externally by the two jurisdictions' often competing efforts to forge relationships with francophone Africa—relationships that built on a long history of Québécois missionary involvement in the continent.[1] To cite just one prominent example, French Canadian Dominicans founded the National University of Rwanda in 1963 and in the following decade the federal government invested more than $50 million in the institution and supplied it with key personnel, with Prime Minister Lester Pearson as a "chief supporter," according to Carol Off (2000, 15; see also Gendron 2006, 86–87). Some of the people affected by these formative encounters stayed closely involved in African and development issues; others did not, or did so only intermittently. But their coming of age alongside an Africa emerging from the bonds of colonialism and imperialism arguably gave African issues and images a particular resonance in Canadian imaginings of internationalism, alongside the much more hard-nosed and muscular internationalism associated with NATO "alliancemanship" (or "realist internationalism" in Boucher's terms). This is so despite—indeed partly because of—the relatively limited and remote character of Canada's security and economic links to the continent, and reflected its status as the single largest focus of Canadian development assistance efforts.[2]

Interestingly enough, the two figures that are the focus of this chapter manifest, at least in part, two distinct faces of Canadian humane
internationalism. Stephen Lewis reflects the welfarist/developmental-
ist/social democratic strand, while Roméo Dallaire, though sharing
many of these values, has remained a military man and loyal soldier,
convinced of the necessity for muscular interventions and supportive
of the Canadian military and its allies in controversial wars such as
those in Kosovo and Afghanistan. Both have been indelibly shaped
and moved by their African experiences, and continue to be tireless
advocates for Africa's peoples. Each has periodically served the Canadian state; indeed Dallaire returned to a formal role in Canadian public life when he was appointed to the Senate (2005–14) as a Liberal
representing Quebec by former Prime Minister Paul Martin. Lewis, for
his part, has been a lifelong member of the social democratic "elite" of
this country, associated with the New Democratic Party (NDP), but also
served as Canada's Ambassador the UN under the government of Progressive Conservative Prime Minister Brian Mulroney. Yet both have
come to command very high levels of public support and admiration
across partisan lines, verging on heroic status.[3] What messages have
they used their platforms and image to project?

Roméo Dallaire

The story of Dallaire's horrifying immersion in Africa has been well
and widely told, not least by Dallaire himself (2003). There is no
need to rehearse the details here. However a few points about his
experience as commander of the "benighted" (Lawson 2005) United
Nations Force in Rwanda (UNAMIR) that was present to bear witness
to the descent into genocide and to attempt, futilely, to ameliorate it
in 1994 are worth emphasizing. First, unlike many of those prominent Canadians noted above, Dallaire had essentially *no* exposure to
Africa prior to being assigned to this command—as reflected in his
immediate response to being offered a leadership role in the mission: "Rwanda, that's somewhere in Africa isn't it?" (Dallaire 2003,
42). Similarly, he had no previous experience in UN "peacekeeping"
missions. In part because of this lack of experience, juxtaposed with
the disastrous failure of the mission, Dallaire himself remains controversial in some circles and some parts of the world—notably in

Belgium, where he was widely viewed as culpable for the deaths of the 10 Belgian paratroopers that prompted the pullout of the most robust component of the UNAMIR force within days of the start of the genocide (Off 2000, 102–14). He has also been a target of more or less *sotto voce* criticism from some within the "profession of arms" in Canada,[4] and more forthright critiques among some who have studied and written about Rwanda and the genocide (e.g., Courtemanche 2005). Indeed he and his mission were, on his own analysis, used and abused by the veto-holding "great powers" on the Security Council, a profoundly risk-averse UN Secretariat, and the principal parties to the conflict in Rwanda itself.

In Canada, however, such critics and critiques have, over time, been driven into the background and Dallaire has widely come to be seen as a hero, despite his explicit and repeated disavowals of this label. This standing rests, in large measure, on the transparent courage and devotion to duty he displayed in Rwanda, including his extraordinary efforts to save those lives he could; the collective witness Canadians bore to his trauma, trials, and breakdown afterwards (including attempted suicide); the resilience he has shown in facing up to his own demons and his personal responsibility for the failure of UNAMIR; and the way he has come to channel his personal trauma into outspoken and tireless advocacy. Writing from the perspective of critical race theory, Sherene Razack argues compellingly that the various popular portrayals of the general's role in Rwanda mean that in this country, the story of the genocide has been largely supplanted by the story of Dallaire himself. As a result, "his goodness becomes our goodness" (2007, 383); through collective identification with Dallaire's story, Canada and Canadians have been able to grant themselves absolution for our government's share of responsibility in the collective international failure to act. Meanwhile, the experience(s) of Rwandans themselves become a tragic, incomprehensible backdrop to this compelling story of Canadian heroism.

Dallaire's "causes" have grown out of his experiences, and fall firmly within the humane internationalist tradition, reaffirming its vitality in the Canadian political imagination. Most fundamentally, he has become a champion of a universalist conception of human rights, passionately defending the equal rights and dignity of all people with explicit emphasis on attacking the real world tendency to treat the rights of Africans less seriously than those of "Western-ers": "We have a responsibility to protect, we do not have the right to assess and to establish a priority within humanity, for all humans are human and not one of us is more human than any other" (Dallaire 2006a). This, and his experience of the UN's failure in Rwanda, has led him to become a champion of the idea of the Responsibility to Protect (ICISS 2001; Bellamy 2009; Chalk et al. 2010) and, in this context, of more robust, timely, and effective responses to "supreme humanitarian emergencies" such as that in Darfur. Haunted by the children of Rwanda, he has become particularly interested in the role of youth and, in this connection, the campaign against the growing use of child soldiers, providing leadership to the Roméo Dallaire Child Soldiers Initiative (www.childsoldiers.org). And, notwithstand-ing (or perhaps in part because of) his long career involvement with NATO during the Cold War, he has become an advocate for nuclear disarmament (Dallaire 2008).

These causes have often led Dallaire to adopt positions sharply critical of the Canadian government. Admittedly, since the election of the Harper Conservatives in 2006 these criticisms from a (now former) Liberal Senator can be seen to have a partisan cast; how-ever, there can be little doubt, given his forthrightness, that he would not spare his own party on any of these (or related) issues.[5] Yet Dal-laire's advocacy and his criticisms are cast within an idealized and patriotic frame of Canada's *true* vocation as a "leading middle power." An intervention on the crisis in Darfur is revealing on this point, and worth quoting at length:

> Canadians need to realize that a large part of Sudan's intransigence can be directly linked to our own government's unwillingness to accept leadership of the UN mission in Darfur ...
>
> It is not only the responsibility of the U.S. and other Security Council members to solve the crisis in Darfur... It now falls to Canada, as a leader of the world's middle powers, to take charge of the mission, prepare for deployment of Canadian Forces and rally other middle powers—such as Japan, Germany, India, Brazil, and the Scandinavian countries—to com-mit the resources and troops needed to stop the slaughter.
>
> Canada's reputation as a leading global citizen, earned through dip-lomacy and our ability to send highly trained soldiers abroad, is at stake.

As we decide our next step toward Darfur, we must resolve to prevent disgracing this tradition. (Dallaire 2006b)

Leaving aside the question of Dallaire's analysis of international politics, and whether, if Canada were to attempt to "rally other middle powers," any would follow, this intervention is revealing in a number of ways. First, it reveals Dallaire as both a deep patriot and a firm believer in and advocate of the widely mythologized conception of Canada as a force for good in the world. It also shows him to be, not surprisingly, a firm advocate of a robust military role in his conception of Canadian internationalism—and of the Canadian Forces as a kind of spearhead for humane internationalism. In short, it underscores Dallaire's profound conviction (like Bono!) that "the world needs more Canada."[6]

Perhaps most amazingly, given his and UNAMIR's treatment at the hands of the UN and the permanent members on the Security Council, Dallaire continues to wed his conception of Canadian internationalism and international responsibility to a firm belief in a UN-centred multilateralism, as for example in his assertion that "I still believe absolutely that the most legitimate body to authorize humanitarian intervention remains the United Nations Security Council" (Dallaire 2007). In short, and in contrast to the deep skepticism toward the UN that inhabits much of the Canadian Forces, Dallaire is not prepared to let his own experience and cynical understanding overwhelm his conviction that the UN framework offers the best, and perhaps only, way toward a more humane and effective response to human suffering. This is a viewpoint profoundly in keeping with the more idealistic or "progressive" wing of Canadian internationalism, and consistent with the solidarist understanding of good international citizenship discussed in Chapter 1.

In short, both in the positions Dallaire has advocated and in the role he embodies, marked by courage, loyalty, dogged advocacy for the most vulnerable and threatened of the world, and perhaps even a little bit of the good-hearted but slightly naive innocent in a world marked by the cynical machinations of the powerful, he can be seen to both reinforce and reflect the popular image of Canada as an agent of ethical or humane internationalism. He can be understood as an embodiment of our "true" or "better" selves, evidence to the contrary notwithstanding.

Stephen Lewis

Stephen Lewis, who was *Maclean's* magazine's "Canadian of the Year" in 2003, presents a somewhat more complex and challenging analytical picture. To begin, he has had a long, varied, and sustained engagement with both Africa and "official" Canada, yet has remained in some respects a temperamental and political outsider on account of his deeply held identity as a democratic socialist whose "ideology is [his] life" (Lewis 2005, 166). He is, in this respect, an "elite of the margins" in Canadian and to some extent international (or at least Western) society(ies).

Lewis has also displayed an indefatigable attachment to public service, both within Canada (as an MPP and Leader of the Official Opposition in Ontario in the 1960s and '70s, and as Canadian Ambassador to the United Nations in the 1980s) and at the UN (as Deputy Executive Director of UNICEF in the 1990s, and as the Secretary-General's Special Envoy for HIV/AIDS in Africa in the new millennium). Yet all this has never prevented him from "speaking truth to power," as he has understood it. Indeed, his sojourns in public service have often been marked toward their end by sharp criticism of his erstwhile political masters—for example, in his criticism of the Canadian government's loss of momentum on sanctions against South Africa in the late 1980s (see Valpy 1988), or his very undiplomatic critiques of institutional members of the "UN family" (particularly, though not only, the World Bank) while still the Secretary-General's Special Envoy, in the context of his 2005 Massey Lectures (Lewis 2005).

He has thus been a harsher and more persistent critic of various Canadian governments than Dallaire, especially on issues related to Africa and to development. This critical stance has been relatively comfortable, indeed habituated, for Lewis because none of these governments has shared his partisan political attachment. In his Massey Lectures, he trained his finely honed rhetorical sights on the G8 governments that had just made much of Africa at the Gleneagles Summit of 2005, and on the Canadian government in particular. He is worth quoting at length:

And then, finally, there's our own country, Canada. Here, for me, the situation is inexplicable. I have heard what the prime minister of Canada [Paul Martin] has said, and he has been good enough to talk to me directly about it. The arguments of financial incapacity are simply not persuasive.

We promised and continue to promise to reach the 0.7 percent (target for ODA to GDP). We are the author of the promise. Everyone knows that. Everyone on the international scene thinks it's the height of hypocrisy to propound the policy and then fail to meet it ...

The prime minister says that there's nothing worse in internationalism than to make promises that are not kept: that's the real immorality, he argues. With respect, he's wrong. The real immorality is for one of the most wealthy and privileged countries in the world to fail to respond adequately to the life and death struggle of hundreds of millions of impoverished people. (2005, 32–33)

What are we to make of this impassioned critique? Lewis is, at one level, a deep and appropriately jaded cynic concerning the likelihood that the Canadian or indeed any other Western government will respond with adequate urgency, commitment, consistency, and generosity to the plight of the vast majority of Africans, including but not limited to the tens of millions who are living with HIV/AIDS and/or dealing with its aftermath.[7] Elsewhere, having sharply criticized G8 governments' rapid retreat from the commitments made at Gleneagles, he writes: "What lies at the heart of all this ... is the sordid realization that the wealthy governments of the Western world simply cannot be trusted to deliver the goods" (2005, 198). In this context, like many in the development community, he tends to place more faith in the non-governmental and advocacy groups that hold their governments' feet to the fire—and chastises these same groups for letting the G8 off the hook, as for example at Gleneagles when they got swept up in what he has characterized as the false "breakthrough" orchestrated by the UK government of Tony Blair.

Yet at another level, Lewis's approach reveals a residual belief (or perhaps more accurately hope) in the possibility that through reason, persuasion, and passion the Canadian and other leading governments' positions can be redeemed. As revealed above, he remains a firm believer in the necessity of more and better foreign aid, as well as debt relief and multilateral trade reform through the WTO process—all measures requiring government leadership and action. Even as he explicitly doubts the likelihood that any of these reforms will be achieved, he continues to advocate tirelessly for them, suggesting that his doubt is leavened by at least some measure of belief in their possibility. A clue to his approach is provided by his rejoinder to those who charge that his proposals—in this case for a major UN specialized agency focusing on women—are unrealistic. He responds, "I'm advancing this broad proposal ... in the hope that somewhere, some country, perhaps one of the Nordics, will run with it. I'm proposing it because sometimes at the United Nations, when you hammer home a position time and again, ad nauseum, a modest variation of that position is embraced" (2005, 154).[8] There is in his words and thought, then, an underlying conviction that despite all the disappointments of experience, both state and interstate institutions (including the government of Canada) can and should become a force for good in the world.

This fundamentally reformist approach extends to the UN system where, as with Dallaire, Lewis has held to the conviction that in the end, it can and must provide the leadership necessary to deal with the world's most pressing challenges (in this case, global poverty). For example, he writes with regard to the need for capacity building on a massive scale that "coordinated leadership is what's missing from any plans to deal with capacity, and I can't but believe that the leadership should come from the United Nations. Not the money, not the person power, not even the plans themselves, but most emphatically the leadership to get the job done" (2005, 176). In this respect too, then, Lewis retains his belief in the redemptive possibilities of formal public institutions—and by extension, the need for governments such as Canada's to put their energy and effort into expanding the capacity and capability of the UN system. He is, in this regard, a multilateralist of the idealist and inclusive variety—and explicitly *not* of elite, pluralist "concerts" such as the G8 or NATO (see Black and Sjolander 1996). This, too, is a view that falls comfortably within the "progressive" tradition of Canadian internationalism, and in line with the solidarist conception of good international citizenship, which remains firmly and often uncritically wedded to a preference for the UN over more elite, plurilateral commitments.

In sum, notwithstanding his persistent criticism of the Canadian and allied governments, Lewis's own analysis and advocacy reveal a bedrock belief or at least hope that the government of Canada (perhaps led at some not entirely incredible future conjuncture by the NDP), at least some other Western governments, and the multilateral bodies of which they have been strong historic supporters have the potential to become more generous and consistent contributors to the needs of the world's poorest and most vulnerable people. On this, however, he remains ambiguous and conflicted. More to the point of this chapter, however, is that he himself has come to serve as an inspirational model of global service, in which many Canadians see reflected the kind of country they wish theirs to be. Insofar as such a person can be embraced and lionized across partisan and ideological lines, in this country and globally, he can and has been interpreted as reflecting Canada at its best. Moreover, insofar as Lewis continues to attract and hold the support of those who might otherwise be inclined toward a more radical challenge to their own government, and to the global order it contributes to and benefits from, he can perhaps be seen to alleviate the possibility of such a challenge and in this sense contribute, paradoxically, to the persistence of the very order he is so eloquently critical of. Either way, he helps to reinscribe an image of Canadian goodness that is, ironically, sharply at odds with the *actual* performance of the Canadian governments he has so persistently criticized.

Conclusion

While it would be a mistake to overstate the influence of these and similar iconic internationalists, it is nevertheless clear that the breadth and depth of their appeal significantly outstrip all Canadian political leaders, serving and retired. In this context, they play a fascinating double role: as prominent public critics on the one hand, and as sources of public inspiration and comforting reassurance on the other. In the final analysis, their prescriptions are for *more and better* Canada, in terms of the volume, quality, consistency, and virtue of its international contributions, rather than for something fundamentally *different*. Moreover they themselves personify the ethics of commitment, service, and solidaristic engagement that many Canadians have liked to associate our country with in the course of the post–World War II era. In this sense they have effectively helped to sustain a benign, humane internationalist collective self-image, even as they have decried the deviations from it by Canadian governments-of-the-day. They help to explain why Canadian "traditions" of commitment to poverty alleviation and human rights, notably in and through Africa, continue to resonate strongly despite deep historical ambiguities and contradictions. In this regard, they help us to understand the way in which post-colonial narratives gain persuasiveness and purchase.

Canadian Aid to Africa:
The Elusive Search for Purpose

Until comparatively recently, the principal basis for Canadian policy links with Africa was its aid program. While diplomatic, security, commercial, trans-societal, and migration links were always present, they were widely perceived as relatively marginal and were overshadowed in both public policy and the Canadian political imaginary by aid-based connections (to which they were often linked). As a result, critics and commentators have long argued that Canada "does not have an overarching policy towards Africa," and that it has typically viewed the continent through a prism of pervasive poverty, aid, and humanitarianism (Akuffo 2012, 213; see also Sabourin 1976, 150; SSCFAIT 2007, 89).

Two general points need to be made regarding this perception. The first is that, given the widely publicized weaknesses of Canadian aid policy and the Canadian International Development Agency (CIDA), particularly since the mid-1990s, Canadian relations with African governments and societies have been underpinned by a weak and shifting policy foundation.[1] Put bluntly, if aid has been the primary foundation for systematic thinking about Canadian relations with Africa, and if aid policy has itself been notoriously inconstant and risk-averse, it stands to reason that Canadian engagement with Africa more broadly has been affected by these same weaknesses. The second point, however, is that through this same period both security and particularly economic interests (most notably through Canada's powerful extractive sector) have grown substantially. Belatedly and reactively, therefore, Canadian policy-makers have begun to discuss, formulate, and implement new policy responses in these key domains. These responses are the focus of the next two chapters.

Nevertheless, one cannot begin to grasp the purposes, effects, and meanings of Canadian involvement in Africa without careful attention to the trajectory of Canadian aid policy. In this chapter, I will interpret Canadian aid policy in Africa through the three theoretical prisms outlined in Chapter 1. In short, aid policy has always been seen as a principal manifestation of "good international citizenship" in Canada and elsewhere, aimed at least in part at "ameliorating the common weal" (Nossal 1998–99, 99) and as reflecting an attachment to values of human rights (broadly understood) and human solidarity. Yet the inconsistency, contradictions, and distortions of aid in practice have substantially limited the applicability of this view.

Canadian aid policy has also reflected the hegemonic interests and priorities of interlinked national and transnational elites, in ways that have softened the hard edges of unequal global economic and political power. For the past couple of decades, this has involved attempts to foster a common-sense understanding of the path to development through a "new aid agenda" featuring a motif of "partnership." The trend toward Canadian participation in an increasingly comprehensive and hegemonic aid agenda was particularly noteworthy in the first half of the decade from 2000, in the late Chrétien and Martin Liberal years.

Since the rise to power of the Harper Conservatives, however, this trend has been largely arrested, both by omission and commission. Canada's diminished interest and role in African development assistance can be seen, on the one hand, as reflecting hard-headed calculations of Canadian self-interest, understood in both security and economic/"dominant class" terms. At another, deeper level, however, it reflects an effort to reframe the dominant ethical narrative of Canada's role in Africa and, by extension, globally—toward a new (or restored) *kind of* Canadian "realist internationalism" (Boucher 2012) with considerably narrower and more conservative normative aspirations.

In order to set the stage for this analysis, we must first review some key features of the pre-2000s trajectory of Canadian aid to Africa, and the debate concerning the "mixed motives" behind Canadian aid policy. This is the focus of the next section.

Canadian Aid to Africa: Growth and Motivations

Canada initiated an external aid program in the context of the Commonwealth's Colombo Plan in 1950, in parallel with the United States' inauguration of external aid. It was therefore a small and natural step to initiate Canadian bilateral aid programs with Commonwealth African states as they decolonized in the late 1950s and 1960s. Beginning with Ghana in 1958, aid programs were initiated in a succession of Commonwealth African states, and total aid spending in Africa grew steadily. A smaller educational assistance program was initiated for francophone African countries in 1961, though its tardiness and relatively paltry amount (C$300,000 annually versus C$3.5 million for Commonwealth African countries since 1959) prompted some criticism in Quebec (Gendron 2006, 75). Later, after a period of reticence borne largely of deference to French preferences in the context of the Cold War, the federal government responded aggressively to the growing national unity challenges emanating from Quebec in the wake of French President de Gaulle's "*vive le Quebec libre*" speech in 1967. It dispatched the Chévrier mission to francophone African governments in 1968 to "begin a new courtship" underpinned by "promises of important aid programmes" (Sabourin 1976, 143; see also Gendron 2006, 134–36; Elder 2013, 27–30). By the mid-1970s, aid to francophone Africa was outstripping aid to Commonwealth Africa on a per capita basis (Matthews 1976, 106). Small programs were also launched in a couple of non-francophone, non-Commonwealth countries—specifically Ethiopia and Liberia (see Matthews 1976, 102–7; Morrison 1998, chaps. 2 and 3). Aid levels to all of Africa remained far below those to South Asia, however, where Colombo Plan aid had initially been concentrated.

As noted in Chapter 1, the growth of Canada's official aid programming in Africa built on the limited but much longer presence of various non-governmental organizations in both francophone and particularly anglophone Africa. Initially, these organizations were largely church/mission-based, and indeed faith-based organizations have continued to be an important part of the non-governmental development community in Canada and Africa (e.g., Paras 2012). By the 1960s and '70s, however, they were joined by a rapidly proliferating range of new, secular non-governmental development organizations (NGDOs) and other non-governmental "partners" (notably

universities), among them CUSO (Canadian University Service Overseas; see Smillie 1985), WUSC (World University Service of Canada),
and Canadian branches of international NGOs like the Red Cross,
Médecins sans frontières (MSF), CARE, and Oxfam. These groups
were eventually connected through the Canadian Council for International Cooperation (CCIC), and became important project implementers, policy advocates, and public educators on development
issues. Indeed their role was relatively *more* significant in Canadian
aid programming, in Africa and elsewhere, than in most other donor
states (see, e.g., Morrison 1998, 21–22)—a theme to which I will
return.

From the outset, "like other donors, but with more alacrity than
most" (Morrison 1998, 19) Canadian aid policy-makers (concentrated from 1968 onward in the newly formed Canadian International
Development Agency) followed the rapidly changing thematic trends
and fashions that have been a chronic and often debilitating feature
of the international aid regime. From their early emphasis on Technical Assistance, including substantial funding for African students
in Canadian universities, Canadian aid programs came to emphasize
physical infrastructure and food and commodity aid, later followed
by "agriculture and social development in the late 1960s; the poorest countries and basic human needs in the 1970s; human resource
development, poverty alleviation, structural adjustment, women and
development, and the environment in the 1980s; and sustainability,
private-sector development, human rights/democracy/good governance, and peace-building in the 1990s" (Morrison 1998, 19). These
thematic priorities have been remarkable not only for the rapidity
with which they have turned over, but the degree to which they have
resurfaced through time—sometimes but not always cloaked in new
"buzzwords" (Cornwall and Brock 2005). Controversially, however,
the "tied" component of Canadian aid was consistently well above
the Organization for Economic Cooperation and Development–
Development Assistance Committee (OECD-DAC) average, linking
roughly 35 percent of all Canadian aid spending to the purchase of
Canadian goods and services through the 1980s (see Morrison 1998,
472–73, notes 50–53; and CIDA 1987, 51–52).

By the early 1990s, aid to Africa had reached approximately 48
percent of Canadian aid expenditures, with the Americas at roughly
18 percent and Asia having declined to under 35 percent (Morrison

1998, 348). This shift in regional spending patterns reflected both the chill in Canada's relations with India following that country's nuclear test in 1974, and the relatively high, and growing, levels of need in Africa. Indeed, Canada's growing emphasis on aid to Africa paralleled the same trend among OECD donors as a group (Black, Thérien, and Clark 1996, 264–66).[2] However, when the Chrétien Liberal government undertook draconian budget cuts beginning in 1994, foreign aid in general, and aid to Africa in particular, proved to be the softest of targets, even by comparative international standards in a recession-driven era of contracting development assistance (see Appendix A). ODA is estimated to have decreased by 33 percent in real terms between 1988–89 and 1997–98, compared with a 22 percent decline in defence spending and cuts of 5 percent to all other programs in the same period (see Morrison 1998, 413). The aid-to-GNP ratio declined from 0.46 percent in 1991–92 to 0.25 percent in 2000, dropping Canada down to sixteenth of twenty-two states in the OECD-DAC "league table."[3] Aid to Africa was hit hardest of all, with proportionate declines in bilateral aid between 1990 and 2000 of 7.2 percent for Africa, 3.5 percent for the Americas, and 5.3 percent for Asia according to one estimate (NSI 2003, 78).[4] These disproportionately severe cuts were telling on several levels. They underscored the weakness of public concern for aid after years of steady growth in spending and apparently high levels of popular support; the political weakness of the "aid constituency" centred in the NGDO community, and its difficulty in mounting a robust defence of development assistance; the marginality of Africa to core political and economic interests, as defined by Canadian policy-makers, when "the chips were down"; and the fragility of the narrative of Canadian ethical leadership through its Africa policy, as discussed in Chapter 3. They also set the stage for the cycle of renewal, stagnation, and decline that marked the first decade of the new millennium.

The underlying motivations for the emergence, growth, and revolving priorities of Canada's aid program were famously mixed.[5] Scholarship on Canadian aid is unanimous that political motivations were critical in providing impetus to the emergence and growth of foreign assistance, in Africa and elsewhere. First, Cold War considerations were pivotal for a firmly aligned "junior partner" in the Western alliance of NATO countries, anxious to provide a compelling Western alternative to the blandishments of the communist bloc (e.g., Matthews 1976, 103; Elder 2013). Closely related to this was a succession of post–Second World War Canadian governments' deep commitment to the adaptation and viability of the "modern," post-colonial Commonwealth—a priority that shaped the emphasis on Commonwealth recipients and was related to Cold War motivations.[6] Third, as noted above, the politics of national unity drove the rapid growth of aid to francophone African recipients. Taken together, the political logic of supporting Commonwealth African countries as they achieved independence and francophone African countries as Canada sought to assert its bilingual and bicultural identity within la Francophonie led to the emergence of a geographically diffuse aid program—a pattern that was widely criticized and set the stage for more recent controversies over narrowing the list of core bilateral partners (or "countries of focus"), but one that also meant Canada's diplomatic, aid-based "reach" in Africa was more extensive than that of most other Western governments. And fourth, with the intensification of the struggle against white-settler minority rule in Angola, Mozambique, Rhodesia/Zimbabwe, Namibia, and finally apartheid South Africa in the 1960s, '70s, and '80s, Canadian (along with other Western) policy-makers dealt with pressure to take a stronger stand against these increasingly illegitimate regimes, in part by expanding aid to the embattled, majority-ruled "Frontline States" that shared the Southern African region with these settler regimes (e.g., Black 1997).

A second, materialist line of analysis stressed the degree to which Canadian aid, however much it might have been *initiated* due to political motives, was increasingly *shaped by* the commercial and class interests of Canada's "capital owning class" and their allies within the Canadian state (e.g., L. Freeman 1982 and 1985; C. Pratt 1983–84 and 2003). Such analyses pointed, for example, to the persistence of tied aid, the rise of "industrial cooperation" programs within CIDA aimed at enabling Canadian commercial involvement in developing countries, the shift to support for (indeed the requirement of) World Bank and IMF-mandated Structural Adjustment Programs (SAPs) in African recipient countries and, in the latter context, the promotion of liberalized foreign investment regimes and mining codes in Africa and elsewhere.

A third, statist line of analysis was most famously articulated by Kim Nossal (1988), who argued that international political and economic/class explanations for Canadian aid policy-making took too little account of the distinctive calculus of state-based policy-makers *per se*. He proposed an "alternative trinity" of motivations for Canadian aid, stressing its role in sustaining prestige among Canadian officials' state-based peers; the imperative of maintaining a large organizational bureaucracy as an end in itself; and the objective of sustaining these interests while spending as little money as reasonably possible and ensuring that as much was spent in Canada as possible.

More recently, much analytical attention has been given to the institutional weaknesses of the Canadian aid policy-making apparatus—particularly but not only CIDA—and what should be done to fix it (e.g., Carin and Smith 2010; Gulrajani 2010). Indeed, the federal government's announcement in its March 2013 Budget that it would be merging CIDA with DFAIT reflects in part the widely held view that CIDA was beset by chronic administrative dysfunction. These weaknesses were arguably deepened by a succession of organizational "shocks," starting with the deep cuts of the 1990s and continuing with the policy uncertainties and course changes that have marked the Harper years. While not unhelpful, these analyses have tended to skip past the underlying *reasons for* the excessively risk-averse, administratively top-heavy, bureaucratically slow and burdensome, and politically opaque approach that came to be widely decried within CIDA.

Finally, however, and ubiquitously, aid policy-making has always been associated with ethical purpose and argumentation: the degree to which the Canadian state, can, does, and/or *should* attempt to "do good" in the world, through the alleviation of poverty and the pursuit of a more just global order. Historically, ethical argumentation was always a prominent feature of debates about aid. For example, a future Minister of External Affairs, Mitchell Sharp, famously wrote in 1961 that: "There is one good and sufficient reason for international aid and that is that there are less fortunate people in the world who need our help ... [I]f the primary purpose of our aid is to help ourselves, rather than to help others, we shall probably receive in return what we deserve and a good deal less than we expect" (cited in Spicer 1966, 6). Similarly, having scrutinized a variety of alternative, political and economic arguments for the provision of aid, Peyton Lyon finally concluded that, "the only really compelling motive is moral, or humanitarian" (1976, xiii).

As the prevalence of more critical interpretations of the *real* motivations for Canadian aid make clear, the idea that aid should be principally motivated by altruistic or ethical objectives has been honoured more in the breach than in the observance. It is also clear that ethical argumentation has become increasingly residual and ritualistic over the past couple of decades (e.g., SSCFAIT 2007, 88), arguably reflecting the ongoing erosion of what Cranford Pratt characterized as the "humane internationalist" tradition in Canadian foreign policy (see Black 2012b).[7] Nevertheless, at least part of the reason for the debilitating weakness of political support for foreign aid is precisely the continued perception that aid *should be* driven by an ethical concern for, and action to empower, the world's poor and marginalized. When it manifestly fails in this regard, it becomes a key point of contention in the ongoing question of the moral purpose of politics and of the Canadian state.[8]

Thus, without discounting the evidence for the various "mixed motives" sketched above, I will focus on the ways in which aid has been part of this broader ethical debate. More particularly, I will focus in turn on how it has (and has not) reflected Canadian "good international citizenship"; how it has been webbed into the broader transnational aid regime, understood in hegemonic terms; and how it has featured in efforts to frame alternative narratives of Canada's moral purpose in the world.

Aid as an Instance of Good International Citizenship

In principle, as implied above, there can be few clearer manifestations of solidarist good international citizenship than a strong foreign aid program. A sincere and consistent commitment to alleviating global poverty and promoting equitable development is as clear a reflection of a desire to ameliorate the "common weal" as it is possible to find. This does not mean that even well-intentioned foreign aid will not produce unanticipated and sometimes counter-productive results. If there is anything that has been learned in sixty years of development assistance, it is that successful and sustainable results require ongoing humility, reflection, and revision. Nevertheless, foreign aid at its best reflects the pursuit of human solidarity and improvement.

Intermittently and inconsistently, Canadian aid to Africa can be understood, in part, as a sincere reflection of good international citizenship.[9] This is seen in humanitarian, thematic, and locally grounded instances of normative, analytical, and practical leadership.

For instance, both Canadian citizens and the Canadian government responded quickly and generously to the mid-1980s Ethiopian famine, in ways that laid the groundwork for a strong tradition of programming on food security in Ethiopia by Canadian governmental and non-governmental organizations in subsequent years, up to the present (see D. MacDonald 1986; Smythe 2007; author interviews, Addis Ababa, Ethiopia, February 2010). Thematically, and based on a recognition of the critical importance of women's development roles and the deleterious impacts of inequitable gender norms, "in both rhetoric and practice, CIDA [became] a leader internationally in women and development and gender analysis" (Morrison 1998, 19). The results of these efforts were subject to ongoing critical scrutiny and revision, but the durability of the commitment added to the depth of Canadian expertise and the relationships that were built with African communities and counterparts. At a more local level, a variety of sustained, well-designed interventions in specific sectors have produced positive developmental results. To cite just one specific case, CIDA maintained a several-decades-long commitment to the improvement of water and sanitation in northern Ghana. In the process, it learned from early mistakes to achieve considerable success, and built on this experience to draw links with efforts to strengthen local governance and promote gender equality (Arthur and Black 2007, 127–28).

Somewhat more controversially, for many years "Canada's leadership in supporting the development efforts of NGOs and NGIs [was] highly acclaimed, and its programming initiatives in this field ... widely copied" (Morrision 1998, 21; see also CIDA 1987, 68–69). This heavy emphasis on NGO/NGI "partnerships" contributed substantially to the projection of Canadian good international citizenship, both because these organizations could be sources of solidaristic innovation, and because their forthrightly ethical self-image provided a moral veneer to a Canadian aid program that often embodied other, more selfish and inequitable characteristics (see Black and Tiessen 2007). To give one substantial example of the innovative role that Canadian NGOs have periodically played in support of solidarist good international citizenship, the small Canadian NGO Partnership Africa Canada commissioned an investigation by a three-person team led by Canadian development analyst and practitioner Ian Smillie, the report of which was instrumental in the conception of the Kimberley Process that made substantial headway in ending the conflict-sustaining trade in "blood diamonds" and later paved the way for the more developmental Diamond Development Initiative (DDI) (see Maclean and Shaw 2001, 26–27; Smillie 2013; www.ddiglobal.org).

Over time, the more paternalistic and "collaborationist" potential of development NGOs drew the attention of critical scholars of development (e.g., Wallace 2003; Barry-Shaw and Jay 2012), while the structural repercussions of their role in developing societies became a focus of critical scrutiny by analysts from a variety of perspectives. In short, the critical question is: what is the structural logic and ramifications of turning to non-governmental actors, many headquartered and funded from outside Africa, for the provision of much-needed social supports on the continent? At the same time, CIDA's relationships with these "civil society organizations" were increasingly strained and constrained, first by the budget cuts of the 1990s and later by the successive aid reforms of the the new millennium. I will return to the implications of this particular trend below.

The more general point, however, is that Canadian aid to Africa has manifested several persistent features that, taken together, severely limit the applicability of the idea of good international citizenship to this policy domain. The first, and most obvious, is that at least since the early 1990s, Canadian aid has been too diffuse and inconsistent, in terms of thematic priorities and volume, to reflect a serious and sustained commitment to good international citizenship.[10] Notwithstanding the periodic achievements of Canadian aid initiatives in specific times and places, the speed and volume of the cuts in the 1990s could not be achieved without serious disruption to ongoing initiatives and relationships, with both Canadian and especially African "partners." Similarly, as will be discussed further below, the abrupt decision to cut eight core African bilateral country partners (of fourteen) in 2009, only four years after they had been announced, and the subsequent decision to cut residual aid spending in several more key states (including Zimbabwe, on the cusp of a crucial electoral contest), reflects a lack of seriousness and commitment to African "partnerships" (see York 2009b and 2012a). The government's decision only five years later to revise this list, adding back two African "countries of focus" that had been cut in 2009 along with several middle-income countries reflecting Canadian commercial and foreign policy priorities (see Table 5.1; Swiss 2014), reinforces the point. Meanwhile, longstanding thematic priorities, including collaborative relationships with NGDOs, and gender and development, have been sharply altered—and diminished—by policy shifts from the Harper government.[11]

Second, the persistent and dogged defence of aid tying by successive Canadian governments reflected a willful constraint on the potential benefits attainable through Canadian development assistance, and was clearly inconsistent with good international citizenship. Indeed, one of the Harper government's signal achievements was the 2008 announcement of its intent to completely untie Canadian bilateral aid by 2013, in line with donor "best practices" elsewhere.

With the passage of Bill C-293 (the ODA Accountability Act [ODAAA] or "Better Aid Bill") in 2008, a concerted effort was made to set Canadian ODA on a more sustained path of good international citizenship. Advocates of higher quality aid, notably among the broad community of NGDOs, had long favoured a clear legislative mandate for ODA that would entrench its poverty-alleviating mission. Bill C-293 was designed for precisely this purpose, requiring in addition that Canadian aid take into account the perspectives of the poor and be consistent with international human rights standards. However, initiated as a private member's bill that eventually passed with all-party support in a minority parliament, the Act has proved largely toothless in practice, with the government arguing (using a very loose interpretation of the Act) that Canadian ODA is already in compliance with it. Moreover, no mention of this legislation was made as Minister Oda and her successors elaborated the government's own vision of "aid effectiveness" with the policy announcements that followed from 2009 onwards (see Brown 2012b, 98–99). Thus, the ODAAA can be seen, thus far at least, as the exception that proves the rule that Canadian aid policy and practice has largely fallen short of a consistent commitment to poverty alleviation.

Finally, focusing on the achievements of particular Canadian aid initiatives in various parts of the continent can occlude analysis of the broader, transnational trends within which Canadian aid is embedded and to which it has contributed. In short Canada, as a middle-sized and relatively weak development policy actor, has always been enmeshed in the broader "aid regime" centred (at least until recently) around the OECD DAC along with European and G8 policy processes, such as those analyzed in Chapter 2. It is necessary, therefore, to analyze the deeper sources and patterns of Canadian aid policies in Africa, and the broader transnational policy thinking they reflect.

Canadian Aid and the Transnational Hegemonic Dynamics of the Aid Regime

As noted above, the history of Canadian aid has always been connected to a Western hegemonic agenda. From the outset, foreign assistance was conceived as a (typically indirect) means of promoting a non-communist and market-conforming model of economic and political development, while burnishing the reputations and fostering goodwill toward the governments that were part of the Western "fold" (see Spicer 1966, 22–42). Canada and other "non-imperial" countries (in relation to the former colonies of the Global South; see Akuffo 2012) were of particular value in this project, since their aid could not be directly attributed to a "neo-colonial" agenda of retaining imperial linkages and advantages. Yet the effectiveness of these hegemonic aspirations, and of individual bilateral aid programs, was chronically compromised by the inevitable diffusion of effort and competition generated by the proliferation of parallel national priorities and aid-funded projects, and the debilitating requirement that recipient governments expend precious time, effort, and human resources negotiating on each of them.

By the early 1990s, therefore, the participants in the international aid regime began to make more sustained and systematic efforts to harmonize their aid programs around a set of "accepted standards of good aid management" (Wood 2007, 235). These efforts were motivated in part by growing skepticism concerning the usefulness of aid, as well as the recession-instigated budget cuts of which CIDA's were an exemplar (see Schmitz 1996). In this context, a concerted effort was made to forge a more harmonized and integrated aid regime, with the OECD DAC (1996) making a decisive intervention in crystallizing and animating this process. Canadian aid policy in general, and CIDA in particular, was strongly affected, with Canadian priorities being increasingly shaped in relation to these broader, regime-wide dynamics. One key manifestation of this, noted above, was the growing share of aid concentrated in Africa (Black, Thérien, and Clark 1996, 264–67).

Beyond the strong correlation in the geographic distribution of aid within the donor community,[12] a variety of thematic priorities were steadily embraced and elaborated. The backdrop to this process was the formulation and imposition of harsh, neo-liberal Structural Adjustment Programs (SAPs), designed by the World Bank and International Monetary Fund (IMF) in response to the economic and developmental crisis of the 1980s (see Biersteker 1992). These draconian liberalizing and marketizing reforms reflected the economic tenor of the times, anchored by the ascendance of the Reagan and Thatcher governments in the US and UK, but were deeply disruptive in socio-political terms and highly unpopular in "adjusting" countries. The resulting deregulation and spending cuts led to extensive job losses in the public sector and the sharp deterioration of public services throughout the continent. By the late 1980s, various UN agencies were already advocating reforms and aid-funded supplements in an effort to humanize, ameliorate, and thus render more tolerable Structural Adjustment conditionalities (e.g., Green and Faber 1994).

In Canada and indeed throughout the donor community, SAPs were a source of controversy and contestation, within the agencies of the state and between the state and groups in civil society (see Burdette 1994). While the Department of Finance, which was responsible for Canadian representation on the IMF and World Bank, was an early proponent of Structural Adjustment from the beginning of the 1980s onward, it was only with the growing focus on ameliorating their social costs that CIDA formally endorsed SAPs later that decade, while explicitly seeking to alleviate their impact on vulnerable groups through its programming (CIDA 1987). Canada's bilateral aid allocations were increasingly linked to recipients having a viable adjustment program in place. Strong adjusters, such as Ghana, received additional aid, while "defectors," such as Zambia for a time, had new program planning suspended. Within the donor community, "techniques were refined to encourage [adherence] to the new system. The new regime emerged under the direction of the World Bank (consultative groups), the UNDP (roundtables), and participants in the Paris Club—ad hoc meetings of creditor governments" (Burdette 1994, 218). Consultation, collaboration, and "burden-sharing" became more routine among donor states and agencies. For example, in the context of the multilateral Special Program of

Assistance for Low-Income Countries in Sub-Saharan Africa (SPA), adopted in 1987, Canada took particular responsibility for two countries—Ghana and Mali—participating in public expenditure reviews and funding case studies on participation and consultation regarding economic policy (Black, Thérien, and Clark 1996, 271).

These growing habits of consultation and cooperation soon extended to other policy areas, such as Women in Development (later Gender and Development—WID and GAD, respectively), the environment, and human rights and democratic governance. As noted above, there were a few instances (like Women/Gender) where Canada was among the leaders, while in others it was more of a policy taker. These issues were, for the most part, important (and contested) in their own right. They were also, however, firmly linked to the bottom-line requirement for acceptance of neo-liberal economic reform, while also in some respects serving to soften or even mask the importance of this core agenda.

As discussed in Chapter 2, this process of regime deepening and widening became considerably more elaborated in the early years of the new millennium, extending to shared aid management modalities and a ubiquitous emphasis on "partnerships"—between donors and recipients, governments and NGOs, and, as the decade wore on, private and public sector actors (see Cornwall and Brock 2005; Black and Tiessen 2007). At the apex of this dynamic of growing policy concertation was the linked G8 and NEPAD processes, with Canada being among its leading proponents, initially at least (see Chapter 2). Running in parallel with this dynamic were efforts to elaborate a new "Aid Effectiveness Agenda" within the international aid regime. These included: the adoption of the Millennium Development Goals by the UN (2000); the Monterrey Consensus on Financing for Development (2002); the introduction of Poverty Reduction Strategy Papers (PRSPs—1999) as ostensibly "country-owned" but International Financial Institution (IFI)–sanctioned strategy documents to which donor support was increasingly linked; the Rome Declaration on Harmonization (2003); the Paris Declaration on Aid Effectiveness (2005); and the Accra Agenda for Action (2008).[13]

Through these processes, and many others broadly associated with them, the new Aid Effectiveness Agenda crystallized around five core principles, as articulated in the Paris Declaration:

1 recipient country *ownership* of their development agendas, including taking the lead in setting priorities and coordinating donor
   contributions;
2 the *alignment* of foreign aid with recipient countries' priorities,
   systems, and procedures;
3 *harmonization* of donor procedures and activities;
4 managing for results; and
5 *mutual accountability* of donor and recipient countries. (See
   Lalonde 2009, 33; Wood et al. 2008, introduction.)

These principles were formally endorsed by numerous "stakeholders," including bilateral and multilateral donor agencies and recipient governments. Taken at face value, there is much to recommend
them. For example, who would not welcome the idea that aid will
be both more effective and sustainable if it is genuinely "owned" by
recipient countries, and reflects the needs and priorities of their
poor citizens? Similarly, who could oppose the reduction of competitive and debilitating processes of interaction with the proliferating
range of donor agencies, through harmonization of their efforts and
alignment with recipient country priorities?

In practice, however, this agenda has faced numerous challenges
and critiques. While a full exploration of these critiques is beyond
the scope of this chapter, several key points can be made in summary. First, effective concertation among donor states (harmonization) remains exceptionally difficult to achieve and sustain, often
remaining at the level of "low hanging fruit." Not only has it added
significantly to the complexity of intra-donor governance structures
in recipient capitals, but the multilateral agreements that *are* reached
can be very difficult for recipient governments to contest, precisely
because the processes by which they are negotiated are so complex
and painstaking. Second, the ostensibly participatory processes by
which national strategies are arrived at, and thus the foundation
for recipient country "ownership," are typically very shallow. The
range and depth of real participation from local communities and
civil society organizations tends be very limited, while the degree
to which national elites are *interested in* more fulsome participation
from their own poor majority is often questionable. Moreover, the
fact that "nationally owned" PRSP's have ended up with remarkably

similar contents and prescriptions, and that each must be vetted and accepted by the IFIS, leads to the likelihood that formal national priorities often reflect "the politics of the mirror," with recipient government "partners" reflecting back what donors want, and expect, to hear (see Arthur and Black 2007, 126–38; Tomlinson and Foster 2004; den Heyer 2012). In short, and consistent with a neo-Gramscian perspective, these "participatory" and "harmonized" processes can be understood as, in effect, placing a normatively appealing gloss on a process that remains, at its core, contingent upon the marketizing and liberalizing reforms that have underpinned the aid regime since the 1980s. The question for those favouring more genuinely "pro-poor" aid is whether the formalized commitment to recipient "ownership" can be leveraged to enable more responsive and effective outcomes?

Particularly in the first years of the 2000s, the Liberal governments of Jean Chrétien and Paul Martin manifested a high level of sensitivity and responsiveness to this deepening donor consensus around the path to Aid Effectiveness. In the late Chrétien period, during the first few years of the new millennium, not only did the government make a sustained reinvestment in CIDA at a rate of 8 percent a year, with particular emphasis on Africa;[14] it also adopted policies that formally endorsed and reflected the key principles and modalities of the new aid consensus. Within CIDA, the attraction of this course was reinforced by the agency's policy weakness, which made attaching itself to the "best practices" endorsed by an emerging multilateral consensus both compelling and reassuring. The most authoritative statement of this prioritization was *Canada Making a Difference in the World: A Policy Statement on Strengthening Aid Effectiveness* (CIDA 2002). It articulated support for a number of core concepts associated with the emerging Aid Effectiveness Agenda, including multidonor, multi-year Program Based Approaches (PBAS), ownership, donor coordination, and policy coherence. A core tension associated with this changing donor dynamic was the degree to which, by requiring donor agency and recipient government concertation, it compromised and limited the scope for "responsive programming" in relation to NGDOS, answering to their more or less autonomously arrived at programming priorities. As noted earlier in this chapter, an emphasis on responsive programming had been a particular strength of CIDA's. The weakening of the agency's relations with these civil society organizations became an ongoing theme over the remainder of the decade.

Chris Brown and Ted Jackson argue that, "if anything, Chrétien's successor, Paul Martin, was even more committed to Africa" (2009, 163).[15] This is a hard claim to substantiate, but in various ways the Martin government sustained and extended the government's renewed interest in Africa, within CIDA and beyond it. At the 2005 Gleneagles G8 Summit, it confirmed that Canada would at least double its ODA between 2001 and 2010, and committed to doubling aid to Africa even more quickly, between 2003–04 and 2008–09, on what was then projected to be a base figure of $2.8 billion. When the Martin government's foreign policy "blueprint," the 2005 *International Policy Statement*, finally emerged, it articulated the statement that serves as one of the epigraphs in the introduction to this book: "Canada has played an important role in bringing African issues onto the global agenda, within the G8 and other forums. We will continue to press forward, in close collaboration with other partners in Africa and other donors, to support regional initiatives such as NEPAD" (CIDA 2005, 23). Controlling for the inevitable hyperbole of such documents, two features of this statement stand out. The first is the degree to which the Martin government was showcasing its ongoing engagement with the politics of African development. Through the first half-decade of the new millennium, "Africa" became a hallmark issue for successive Liberal governments and an exemplar of Canadian ethical leadership. This was an accentuation of, but not a fundamental departure from, the interest in African issues and countries demonstrated by successive Canadian governments of both main partisan stripes (i.e., Liberal and [Progressive] Conservative), as reflected in the cyclical narrative discussed in Chapter 3. The second is the degree to which this engagement was premised on ongoing collaborative structures and processes. These extended beyond the G8 to include the Africa Partnership Forum—the broadly inclusive forum of African leaders and the continent's major multilateral and bilateral donors launched at the Evian Summit in 2003 (see Cargill 2010, 8–10)—and more broadly still, the 2005 Paris Declaration on Aid Effectiveness. Indeed, the IPS reiterated the commitments made in 2002 in *Canada Making a Difference in the World: A Policy Statement on Strengthening Aid Effectiveness*, that "the principles of aid effectiveness—local ownership, greater partnership, donor harmonization, policy coherence and a focus on results—[would be placed] at the core of Canada's development cooperation program" (CIDA 2005, 6).

In view of the wide dispersal of CIDA's bilateral recipients, the IPS went on to announce the concentration of two-thirds of bilateral aid in twenty-five "development partner countries," with bilateral assistance "increasingly concentrated in sub-Saharan Africa" (CIDA 2005, 23). The government subsequently placed fourteen African countries on the twenty-five-country list, with a fifteenth, Sudan, being prioritized under a separate "Failed and Fragile State" window (see Table 5.1).[16] While Denis Stairs (2005) has convincingly demonstrated that this exercise in concentration was largely illusory in significantly reducing the dispersal of Canadian development assistance, it mattered in at least one significant way. Countries designated as core Development Partners became the focus of longer-term planning processes, with increased numbers of CIDA personnel assigned to them both at headquarters and in the field along with somewhat increased budgets. This in turn enabled CIDA officers responsible for these country programs to participate more fully in the collaborative program-based approaches and intra-donor and donor-recipient governance structures that were increasingly prevalent in recipient countries as a result of the Aid Effectiveness Agenda (see, e.g., den Heyer 2012).

Thus, when the Harper minority government took office in January 2006, there was every indication that Canada—and CIDA—was committed to steadily increasing aid budgets, a somewhat more focused aid program (in terms of both bilateral recipients and priority themes),[17] and above all, a growing emphasis on Africa. It was also committed to shaping its aid priorities and management practices to conform with the steadily deepening multilateral consensus of the international aid regime—a trajectory that could be understood as consistent with neo-Gramscian expectations.

Reframing the Narrative of Canada in the World: The Conservatives and Aid to Africa

As discussed in Chapter 3, however, "Africa" (and various specific issues and causes associated with it) has long been embedded in a narrative that oscillates between ethical leadership and dereliction. Consequently, it has proven impossible to sustain a policy approach

Table 5.1
Designated Countries of Bilateral Aid Focus

2005 International Policy Statement	2009 Countries of Focus	2014 Countries of Focus
Africa	Sub-Saharan Africa	Sub-Saharan Africa
Benin	Ethiopia	Benin
Burkina Faso	Ghana	Burkina Faso
Cameroon	Mali	Congo (DRC)
Ethiopia	Mozambique	Ethiopia
Ghana	Senegal	Ghana
Kenya	Sudan and South Sudan	Mali
Malawi	Tanzania	Mozambique
Mali		Senegal
Mozambique		South Sudan
Niger		Tanzania
Rwanda		
Senegal		
Tanzania		
Zambia		
Americas	Americas	Americas
Bolivia	Bolivia	Caribbean Regional
Guyana	Caribbean Regional Program	Program
Honduras	Colombia	Colombia
Nicaragua	Haiti	Haiti
	Honduras	Honduras
	Peru	Peru
Asia	Asia	Asia
Bangladesh	Afghanistan	Afghanistan
Cambodia	Bangladesh	Bangladesh
Indonesia	Indonesia	Burma
Pakistan	Pakistan	Indonesia
Sri Lanka	Vietnam	Mongolia
Vietnam		Philippines
		Vietnam
Europe	Eastern Europe	Eastern Europe
Ukraine	Ukraine	Ukraine
"Failed and Fragile States"*	North Africa and the Middle East	Middle East and North Africa
Afghanistan	West Bank and Gaza	Jordan
Haiti		West Bank and Gaza
Iraq		
Sudan		

Sources: CIDA website: http://www.acdi-cida.gc.ca/acdi-cida/ACDI-CIDA.nsf/eng/ JER-324115437-MU7; http://www.acdi-cida.gc.ca/countriesoffocus; DFATD website: http://www.international.gc.ca/development-developpement/countries-pays/index. aspx?lang=eng#focus.

* Not included among core bilateral "development partners," but designated for long-term programming commitments.

that builds on African engagements and priorities in a coherent manner. More to the point, the dominant ethical (or liberal/humane internationalist) narrative of "Canada in Africa" has always been contested by more conservative groups in Canadian society and within the state that see our interests and obligations converging around a more hard-headed set of priorities, closely aligned with our traditionally closest friends and allies in the Western club of nations. Proponents of this alternative (realist internationalist) world view, or counter-narrative, have been deeply skeptical of inclusive multilateral arrangements, more cosmopolitan or solidarist aspirations and innovations, and the possibility of substantially ameliorating global poverty through foreign aid. The Harper Conservatives were strongly influenced by this counter-narrative and, as the latter half of the first decade of the new millennium unfolded, aid policy became one of the principle markers of this effort to foster a new, post-liberal/humane internationalist identity and approach to world affairs.

Even before the new Conservative government took office in January 2006, an analysis of public attitudes toward development assistance had demonstrated that those Canadians on the partisan political right, including (at the time) both Progressive Conservative and Reform Party supporters, were far less inclined to support development aid than those in the centre or, even more so, on the left. Alain Noël, Jean-Philippe Thérien, and Sébastien Dallaire (2004) noted that in 2000, polls conducted for the Canadian Election Survey showed that only 10 percent of those who considered themselves PC or Reform supporters favoured increased aid spending, compared with 40 percent of those who supported the NDP and 20 percent who self-identified as Liberals. Overall, they argued, support for "humane internationalism" as reflected in foreign aid was much more fragile and divided than had traditionally been thought.

Reflecting these findings, the Harper Conservatives took office with little on the record concerning aid, and nothing that would suggest a more solidaristic commitment to global poverty reduction. Their election platform, for example, said only that a Conservative government would:

- Articulate Canada's core values of freedom, democracy, the rule of law, human rights, free markets, and free trade—and compassion for the less fortunate—on the international stage;

- Advance Canada's interests through foreign aid, while at the same time holding those agencies involved in this area accountable for its distribution and results; and
- Increase spending on Overseas Development Assistance [*sic*][18] beyond the current projected level and move toward the OECD average level. (Conservative Party 2006, 45)

These vague and somewhat contradictory intentions contrasted with the precise and ambitious targets for enhancing the capacity and prestige of the Canadian armed forces in the same manifesto. The combined emphasis on "compassion for the less fortunate," with its intimations of Christian charity, and an interest-based calculus for the deployment of aid suggested a more limited and instrumental approach. Similarly, emphasis on accountability for its distribution and results reflected the deep skepticism of the Conservatives' electoral base concerning the value of aid, and the ability of those agencies responsible for its distribution (notably CIDA) to do so effectively. The third point offered a rationale for aid based on the limited objectives of international burden sharing and respectability among Canada's Western peers.

In sharp contrast to previous Progressive Conservative governments (see J. Clark 2007, 2), the Conservative caucus and cabinet contained no members with a clearly established interest in Africa. Their collective disposition was arguably indifferent.[19] This broad disposition also applied to more inclusive manifestations of multilateralism, including the UN, the Commonwealth, and the large-scale multi-stakeholder processes by which the Paris Principles and Accra Agenda for Action on international "development cooperation" were negotiated; and to much of the traditional non-governmental "development community" in Canada, with whom Conservative party relations were generally remote (see also Smillie 2012).

In the absence of a constituency of any consequence for aid or for Africa, but with a government that had, as Joe Clark put it, "a prudent regard for keeping Canada's word in the G-8" (2007, 3), the result for the first several years of the Harper era was effectively a policy of drift. This was overlaid with periodic portends of more far-reaching changes which, taken together, effectively tied the hands of Canadian aid policy practitioners and limited their ability to participate fully in medium- and long-term aid policy programming, notably involving multi-donor collaboration.

Among the changes that did emerge was the clear—initially obses-sive—prioritization of Canada's military engagement in Afghan-istan. This had profound implications for CIDA and Canadian aid. Although not among the twenty-five priority countries for bilateral aid on the Martin government's IPS list, Afghanistan rapidly became the largest bilateral aid program in Canadian history, reaching over $270 million by 2007–08 (DFATD 2014b). It was supported by a large Afghanistan Task Force that absorbed a disproportionate share of CIDA's human resources, including the unprecedented assignment of a CIDA Vice-President. Yet the agency's performance in the unfamil-iar and inhospitable political and security terrain of Afghanistan was widely criticized and deepened its reputation for ineffectiveness (see S. Brown 2008, 95–98).

Rhetorically, as noted in Chapter 2, the prime minister signalled a shift toward greater emphasis on the Americas while attending the Heiligendamm G8 Summit in June 2007. This was widely interpreted to reflect not only a comparative lack of interest in Africa, but a parti-san desire to distance Canada's "new" Conservative government from the "Liberal brand," which the government associated with an exces-sive focus on Africa. However, neither the ostensible new emphasis on Latin America and the Caribbean, nor a prospective move away from Africa were reflected in substantive aid policy decisions for nearly two more years, reflecting the low priority placed on aid policy across the board by the Harper government.

Indeed, aside from an ill-conceived (and later shelved) Office for Democratic Governance announced in October 2006 (see Gurzu 2011), and the long overdue September 2008 announcement that aid was to be fully untied by 2012–13, there were *no* substantive policy announcements beyond the Afghanistan file for more than three years. Everyone who was concerned with aid to Africa knew that changes were in the works, but very few were consulted, inside or outside CIDA, and those who may have been consulted by the tight circle around then Minister for International Cooperation Bev Oda were clearly not inclined to discuss what was being contemplated. For major bilateral programs, ostensibly guided by multi-year Country Programming Frameworks (CPFs), existing frameworks were either obsolescent or lapsed (see den Heyer 2012).

The results of this policy drift were, as noted above, debilitating for CIDA officers and their governmental and non-governmental partners. In the absence of any clarity concerning future directions, they could not fully commit to, let alone lead within, the inter-donor planning processes associated with the aid effectiveness agenda. Similarly, project planning processes became mired in multiple layers of approval and indecision, behind which lay a lack of clear purpose. The Auditor General of Canada (2009) reported that the average length of time for CIDA project approval was 3.5 years. As a case in point, a project proposal from a consortium of Canadian NGOs for a $20-million food-security project in Ethiopia, which was initially prompted by CIDA officials, was still working its way through the approval process four years later.[20] Taken together, the absence of clarity regarding aid policy priorities reflected a clear lack of urgency concerning Canada's development programming in Africa.

When the Conservatives' policy direction for Canadian aid to Africa finally began to come into focus in the first part of 2009, their conception of aid effectiveness was largely "made in Ottawa," with little discernible reference to or influence from the broader international processes and agreements to which CIDA was formally committed. In this respect, and in sharp contrast to their Liberal predecessors, the Conservatives seemed relatively unconcerned with efforts to orchestrate a concerted, multilateral, hegemonic approach to Africa's developmental challenges.

The first, and most symbolically charged, marker of a new direction was the government's February 2009 announcement that it would concentrate 80 percent of its bilateral aid in a reduced list of twenty "countries of focus." In the process, it dropped eight of fourteen African countries that had been included as priority partners in the Martin government's list of twenty-five, including a number of very long-standing bilateral recipients from both Commonwealth and francophone Africa (see Table 5.1).[21] This new list provided the most tangible evidence to date of the government's announced intention to refocus on the Americas, with the addition of Colombia, Haiti, Peru, and the Caribbean region as new focus "countries." Almost as striking, however, was the damaging way in which the announcement was handled, with no prior consultation of affected countries or other long-standing development "partners" among the donor and NGDO communities. The political impact was, at best, insensitive and unhelpful given the government's forthcoming moment of opportunity as host of the G8 and G20 summits in June 2010, as well as its campaign for a seat on the UN Security Council. The embarrassing failure of this campaign in the fall of 2010 was widely explained as a result, in part, of the government's alienation of erstwhile African supporters. The February 2009 announcement was followed by several efforts at fence-mending and damage control (e.g., Oda 2009b), but the pertinent point for this analysis is that the government was neither attuned to, nor concerned with, the multilateral ramifications of this decision. This tendency persisted with the June 2014 announcement of a revised list of 25 focus countries (see table 5.1), which not only underscores the relative instability of such ostensibly long-term "partnerships" but the degree to which the Conservative government has come to privilege what it defines as Canadian commercial and foreign policy priorities versus either poverty alleviation or collective aid regime imperatives (see DFATD 2014a).[22]

The fullest statement of the government's "New Effective Approach to Canadian Aid" came in a May 2009 speech by Minister Oda at the Munk Centre in Toronto, in which she asserted: "We pledge to make Canada's international assistance program more efficient, more focused, and more accountable. In short, more effective" (2009a).[23] The speech reiterated the steps already taken on untying aid and reducing the number of bilateral countries of focus, while introducing the three priority themes of "increasing food security, stimulating sustainable economic growth, and securing the future of children and youth." In addition, she outlined two "complementary (foreign policy) themes" to which aid resources would also be allocated—promoting democracy and ensuring security and stability. The implications of these themes will be addressed shortly. What is germane at this stage is that in this entire speech, there was not a single mention of the principles and practices of harmonization or alignment (whether using these or comparable terms). In short, there was no mention of the multilateral (as opposed to Canadian) aid effectiveness agenda.

This point needs to be carefully qualified. It was clear within CIDA itself that the broader multilateral aid effectiveness agenda was still the basis for policy, as reflected in "CIDA's Aid Effectiveness Action Plan (2009–12)" issued later in the same year (CIDA 2009).[24] That plan, unlike the Minister's speech, was explicitly anchored in Canadian multilateral commitments to the Millennium Development Goals (2000), the Monterrey Consensus (2002), the Paris Declaration

(2005), and the Accra Agenda for Action (2008). It contained quantifiable commitments to conduct country missions jointly with other donors (33%), and analytic work jointly with other donors (50%) by 2012–13. Similarly, it committed to channelling "at least 50% of funding to the government sector through country systems, or state to the host government the rationale for using any separate systems" by 2012–13 (CIDA 2009, 5). Collectively, these provisions demonstrated continued commitment to the collaborative modalities of the aid regime—though how precisely these commitments are manifested would require careful field-level research.

Yet at the political level of key policy decisions regarding priority countries and themes, the minister and government appeared unconcerned with the implications of their decisions for CIDA's ability to participate within shared multilateral processes. This underscores the degree to which government-CIDA relationships were characterized not only by different approaches to aid policy implementation, but by a high degree of mutual suspicion (see S. Brown 2009; Smillie 2010).

Along with the opaque process by which the new list of countries of focus was arrived at, the government's lack of concern with the multilateral ramifications of its policy approach is illustrated by the decision-making concerning the new thematic foci of children and youth, food security, and sustainable economic growth, along with the vague foreign policy priorities of democracy promotion and ensuring stability and security. How these thematic priorities were arrived at remains unclear to those outside the minister's inner circle. Moreover, there is nothing inherently undesirable about these particular priorities, or inconsistent with those pursued in the broader international aid regime. The key problem was that the *process* by which they were arrived at militated against consultation with key partners, particularly in developing countries themselves. It thus contradicted the principle of country ownership and alignment—and the ability of those implementing CIDA policy to do so in a timely, transparent, or consistent manner. Once again, the priorities were announced without significant discernible consultation inside or outside CIDA. Having announced the priorities, CIDA organized consultative roundtables three months later on how they should be implemented. After many more months of delay, the agency released sparse (6–8 page) strategy documents for each theme. The Food Security Strategy, for example, was released in early 2010; the Sustainable Economic Growth Strategy, which became the default category for CIDA's previous emphasis on governance, was not released until late October of 2010.

While there is much that could be said about this protracted process of thematic priority setting, the point to be emphasized here is the impact it had on those trying to plan, approve, and implement projects and programs on the ground. In short, both the length and opacity of the approval process, and the fetishizing of focus ("focus within focus," as a Canadian aid official in Ethiopia put it) made it extremely difficult for CIDA personnel to engage in longer-term, multi-donor collaborative processes and commitments—hallmarks of the aid effectiveness agenda—and to be both responsive and reliable in their commitments to developing country "partners." The logic of *Canada's* variant of the aid effectiveness agenda was, from the perspective of at least some CIDA program officers, a step backward toward an emphasis on "outputs" instead of "outcomes"—a preoccupation with the tracking of specific results from Canadian aid dollars regardless of (and potentially at the expense of) a broader concern with systemic outcomes to which Canada was one of several contributors. This is consistent with the Conservatives' deep skepticism concerning aid in general, and their emphasis on clearly discernible value for taxpayers' money, regardless of longer-term implications.

In the meantime, Canadian policy-makers were often forced to delay, prevaricate, and in some cases renege on major commitments, while awaiting clarification on what the agency's new priorities would be, and how they would be operationalized. Planning efforts were beset by uncertainties, delays, and multiple layers of approval. By February 2010, for example, the new Ethiopian country strategy to replace the one for the five-year period ending in 2008–09 had been through thirty-two versions (interview with Canadian aid official, Addis Ababa, February 2010). As of early 2013, there was still no publicly available country strategy. These processes, which the government portrayed as reflecting its commitment to "more effective" aid, therefore compromised CIDA's ability to participate in and support the international aid effectiveness agenda.

The disconnect between the government's approach to aid policy-making and the elements of the broader aid effectiveness agenda to which CIDA was still committed through *Canada Making a Difference in the World* (2002) was reflected in the Auditor General's fall

2009 analysis of the agency. The report was critical of CIDA's lack of progress on its 2002 commitments to align with recipient priorities, harmonize its efforts with other donors, and make more extensive and predictable use of program-based approaches. It concluded: "Many of the weaknesses we identified can be traced back to a lack of corporate management processes to guide and monitor the implementation of CIDA's aid effectiveness commitments... it has yet to develop a comprehensive strategy for implementing its commitments" (Auditor General 2009, 3). Without discounting CIDA's own management problems, however, the agency's failure to make good on its aid effectiveness commitments was also largely attributable to a lack of political leadership from successive ministers and governments. This lack of leadership reflects, in part, the slow and opaque process of decision-making concerning new priority countries and themes—and thus the low priority of aid policy—and the obsession with focus and domestic accountability, both of which are very difficult to square with the imperatives of decentralized responsiveness and collaboration that are at the heart of the transnational aid effectiveness agenda.

A related characteristic of Conservative aid policy decision-making was the absence of consultation with long-established development NGOs and NGO coalitions in Canada—notably but by no means only the Canadian Council for International Cooperation (CCIC). This reflected a pattern of growing estrangement between the government and many Canadian civil society organizations concerned with development—a reflection, in turn, of the growing disjuncture between its "vision" for aid and the humane internationalist values that continue to be championed by much of the NGDO community.

This pattern was highlighted by CIDA's abrupt and highly controversial decisions not to approve new funding for the Canadian Church coalition, KAIROS, ending a 35-year funding relationship with the coalition and its predecessors, and later the CCIC, in November 2009 and July 2010, respectively (see Smillie 2012). Further instances of NGO "defunding" were to follow. These decisions were justified with the dubious rationale that the work of these organizations did not fit with CIDA's new thematic priorities. At a deeper level, however, they reflect a trend toward the instrumentalization of aid funding relationships with Civil Society Organizations (CSOs), based on the government's interpretation of its priorities. As discussed in

Chapter 7, this is illustrated by the "fast track" process through which several controversial collaborations between NGOs and Canadian mining companies in Africa and Latin America were approved for funding, on the one hand, and the new, protracted and opaque process by which CIDA's Partnership with Canadians Branch solicited NGO responses to six calls-for-proposals in 2010, on the other (CCIC and ICN 2012; Brown 2012a).

Conclusion: The Montage of Canadian Aid to Africa

The Conservatives' relative indifference and indeed suspicion concerning Canadian aid in Africa, and toward the "humane internationalist" advocates and agents that have championed and delivered it, have been portrayed in part as an effort at partisan "rebranding" (see Owen and Eaves 2007; Black 2009). In the shadow of the Kananaskis G8 Summit, various "human security" initiatives toward the continent and policy statements emphasizing Canadian leadership on African issues, Africa came to be seen by key Conservatives as a "Liberal" issue. Hence, the "tilt" toward Latin America, Afghanistan, and other more "strategic" priorities—though often overstated—could be portrayed not only as reflecting a more hard-nosed calculation of Canadian interests, but as an effort to symbolically distinguish the "new" Conservatives from the "old" Liberals.

There is clearly some truth to this line of analysis. At a deeper level, however, this rebranding effort made sense not only at the shallow level of partisan brand differentiation, but also because it reflected a deeper rejection of the dominant ethical narrative of Canada in Africa, and hence Canada in the world. As discussed in Chapter 3, the Conservatives' preferred narrative of Canadian internationalism placed much greater emphasis on deepened collaboration with our "closest (Western) friends and allies," and was highly skeptical of the collective effort to ameliorate global poverty that aid, at its best, represented in the traditional humane internationalist narrative. In this respect, the Conservatives' new approach toward aid policy in Africa has reflected an effort to reframe the dominant moral narrative concerning Canada's international role. Whether this effort ultimately succeeds will depend, not least, on the electoral longevity of the Conservative government—but the underlying intent is unmistakable.

Thus, Conservative aid policy in Africa can be understood in part through the prism of the post-colonial tradition, in which engagements with the continent become a means of (re)imagining and (re)articulating a particular understanding of the Canadian "self." Also consistent with this tradition was the fact that the political leaders and policy-makers responsible for these engagements seemed largely unconcerned with the preferences and/or consequences of their decisions for their African "beneficiaries." But clearly this does not tell the whole story of Canadian aid to Africa. At other times, and still in CIDA's (now DFATD's) ongoing participation in the international aid regime, Canadian aid is best understood as reflecting and reinforcing efforts to forge a hegemonic consensus on the terms of Africa's engagement with its donor "partners" and with the broader global economy. At still others, the efforts of particular Canadian agents and programs can be seen as manifestations of sincere "good international citizenship." The Muskoka Initiative on Maternal, Newborn, and Child Health, introduced in Chapter 2, reflects this residual tendency—even if the manner in which it was implemented has diminished this potential. This specific example will be explored further in the Conclusion. Taken together, then, Canadian aid policy in Africa manifests not only an elusive search for purpose, but a complex and layered field of interpretation and understanding.

Chapter

6

Canada and Peace Operations in Africa: The Logic and Limits of Engagement

In contrast to the centrality of Africa to Canadian aid policy from decolonization onward, the continent has typically been portrayed as marginal to Canadian security and defence interests. Yet beginning with the *Opération des Nations Unies au Congo* (onuc) mission in the newly independent Congo in 1960–64, during which a total of 1,800 Canadian personnel were ultimately deployed (Spooner 2009), Canada has long been an active and sometimes prominent participant in African peace operations.[1] In the expansive post–Cold War period from 1990 onward this involvement reached unprecedented heights, with several comparatively large deployments and a number of smaller ones. In the new millennium, these operational roles diminished significantly in scale and scope, but notably were accompanied by a renewed emphasis on capacity building and training, reflecting the broader trend toward "regionalization" of peace operations in Africa ("African solutions to African problems").

Taken together, this persistent engagement with African security challenges presents a theoretical enigma. Given the historic weakness of Canada's direct colonial, geopolitical, and material interests[2] on the continent, how do we account for the relatively routine deployment of scarce security resources there, often in situations of considerable risk?

As discussed in previous chapters, there are a variety of historic, social, and political cultural factors that have played a role, particularly in light of Canada's bilingual history and its prominence within both the Commonwealth and la Francophonie (see Black 2004; Akuffo 2012, 49–82). In this chapter, however, the three theoretical frames discussed in Chapter 1 are utilized as explanations for this pattern. The first is the idea that Canada (or rather the Canadian government) has seen itself as a "good international citizen" in the society of states, and that this has led it to respond positively to requests and opportunities for involvement in African crises and their aftermath. The second, more critical view is that Canada's involvement is best understood as motivated by, and instrumental in, efforts to construct and sustain a hegemonic politico-security regime for Africa, in coordination with other G8 member states. The two views are not entirely incompatible, and both have some purchase in explaining the nature and persistence of Canada's involvement with African peace operations and operational capacity. But both are also partially contradicted, or at least weakened, by the sharp and growing limitations on Canadian involvement. In this regard, Canada's role might be better characterized as "*good enough* international citizenship," supporting an emergent security arrangement rooted in systemic subcontracting and "riot control." To understand these limitations, the softness of Canadian political concern for Africa and the deep wariness of Canadian bureaucratic and defence officials toward African entanglements, embedded in the "alternative narrative" concerning Canada's global role discussed in Chapter 1, must be taken into account. Yet in the final analysis, and despite the chequered history and growing limitations of this country's operational roles, Canadians remain strikingly attached to the idea that peacekeeping is "Canada's most positive contribution to the world" (see Paris, 2014, 289–90). Here, the resilient narrative of Canadian humanitarian and moral leadership highlighted by the post-colonial frame can be usefully deployed.

The chapter begins by briefly revisiting the first two theoretical premises I emphasize as providing potential explanations for Canadian involvement in African peace operations. It then maps this involvement, beginning with commitments to a succession of peace operations followed by an outline of some of the capacity-building and training initiatives that emerged. It analyzes the patterns and limits that these policy and operational activities display, and draws out their implications for both a more secure Africa within international society, and a hegemonic "new deal" for the continent. Finally, it concludes by considering why the "peacekeeping myth" has remained so durable in Canada, connecting this durability to the abiding narrative of Canadian moral leadership in Africa, specifically through an extended understanding of peacekeeping.

Africa, Canadian International Citizenship, and a New "Security Architecture"

As discussed in Chapter 1, the idea that most states, taken together, form an international society marked by broadly shared rules, norms, and institutions is the conception of international politics developed by scholars associated with the "English School."[3] Such a society is seen to be (re)produced by the ongoing activities of those who act in the name of states—political leaders, diplomats, and other state officials, including their armed forces. The rules, norms, and institutions they rely on in turn help to generate and shape foreign policy activity. In particular, they are supposed to define good or responsible international conduct. In other words, the society of states in effect defines conceptions of good international citizenship, or "the principles of foreign policy ... [that] can promote the moral ideal of the unity of humankind without jeopardizing international order" (Linklater and Suganami 2006, 232). Also as discussed in Chapter 1, there is considerable variance in how good international citizenship is conceived. More conservative "pluralist" scholars stress diversity within international society, leading them to emphasize the importance of a robust conception of sovereignty and the order-sustaining role of the norm of non-intervention. This is in keeping with the primary emphasis of the UN Charter. On the other hand, those with more "solidarist" leanings emphasize individual human beings and their communities as the fundamental starting point for international society, and therefore that state sovereignty should be conditional on compliance with the international law of human rights (see Linklater and Suganami 2006, 238–45). This orientation is also embedded in the Charter through its invocation of "fundamental human rights" and "the equal rights of men and women and of nations large and small" (UN Charter, Preamble) and reflects the rising salience of the Universal Declaration of Human Rights, the Convention on Genocide, and the extensive human rights regime that has grown from them.

It is not surprising that the government of a country such as Canada that has, for the most part, prospered within international society should be preoccupied with sustaining it and should be drawn toward the pursuit of "good international citizenship" within it. Historically, the predominant interpretation of international society among Canadian foreign policy practitioners was pluralist in orientation (see Stairs 1982). From the mid-1980s onward, however, Canadian governments adopted more solidarist positions. This was manifested, for example, in the Mulroney Progressive Conservatives' policies toward apartheid South Africa and on "good governance" and human rights in the 1980s and early '90s (see Black 2001b; Gecelovsky and Keating 2001), and in the "human security agenda" of Foreign Minister Lloyd Axworthy under the Chrétien Liberals in the 1990s (e.g., McRae and Hubert 2001; Axworthy 2004). Under the rubric of the latter, high profile initiatives such as the Landmines Treaty, the championing of the Responsibility to Protect and the Rome Treaty establishing the International Criminal Court, and advocacy for particular attention to the plight of war-affected civilians and children held particular relevance for a number of African countries and served as visible displays of Canada's putative "good international citizenship."

Within this broad self-image of increasingly solidaristic citizenship, however, Canadian governments have demonstrated a particular sensitivity to the objectives and interests of the Western alliance and its leading member states. Again, this is hardly surprising given the country's historic, geostrategic, and political-economic interpenetration with the United States in particular, and with the member countries of the G8 and the NATO alliance more broadly. In relation to Africa, this was manifested most clearly in the Chrétien Liberal government's initiative to entrench Africa and its challenges on the G8 agenda, beginning with the Africa Action Plan at the Kananaskis Summit in 2002. As discussed in Chapter 2, the plan can be understood as an attempt to orchestrate a hegemonic "new deal" for Africa, insofar as it aspired to forge a transnational response serving both Western interests and the professed aspirations of leading African states and elites.[4] The AAP was multi-dimensional, with eight separate chapters and "over one hundred specific commitments" according to one of its chief architects, Canadian Ambassador Robert Fowler (2003, 228). However the very first chapter focused on "Promoting Peace and Security," and pledged both enhanced direct support from the G8 for peace efforts in some of Africa's most long-standing and intractable conflicts (specifically Angola, the DRC, Sierra Leone, and Sudan), and assistance to enable African countries and organizations to develop their *own* capability to undertake peace operations (AAP 2002). This agenda, which suited both African leaders seeking to enhance their security capacity and Western leaders seeking to diffuse and reduce their own direct exposure in African security crises and peace operations, became a consistent agenda item at subsequent G8 summits and was accompanied by concrete initiatives from major G8 member states, including the US, the UK, and France (e.g., Yamashita 2013).

As both a good international citizen seeking to respond to humanitarian crises, and a committed participant in a hegemonic coalition seeking to develop new security architecture for the world's most insecure continent, Canada played an active and occasionally pivotal role in the G8 process. This underscores the potential importance of key "middle powers" in order-building efforts in this and previous "world orders." At the same time, however, when these lofty designs and objectives had to be translated into concrete responses to specific operational demands and programs on the continent, Canada's role was sharply limited. Indeed, these limits became steadily more intrusive in the aftermath of Canada's "star turn" in catalyzing the G8's unprecedented and ongoing attention to Africa in the new millennium. Remarkably, under the Harper government, Canada's peacekeeping role has shifted from what had long been portrayed as a virtual article of faith (e.g., Razack 2004, 8), to one that is increasingly marginal in both public pronouncements and foreign policy practice.[5] Yet perhaps even more remarkably, Canadians' attachment to the idea that we do, and should, make an important global contribution through peacekeeping remains largely intact (e.g., Paris, 2014). What does Canada's record of policy and operational involvement in African peace support operations (PSOs) reveal?

Mapping the Record:
Canada and Peace Operations in Africa

Appendices B and C lay out the salient facts concerning Canada's PSO deployments from 1990 onward.[6] Importantly, Canada's ability to deploy French-speaking personnel has significantly expanded the potential number and usefulness of its contributions, given the prevalence of conflicts and peace operations in French-speaking African countries and the desire of the French government to "burden share" in its historic sphere of influence, leading it to lean on the Canadian government for involvement in places like the CAR.[7] Throughout the 1990s and into the first years of the new millennium, prior to the adoption of the AAP in June 2002, Canadian forces were deployed in comparatively large numbers to a succession of operations. These included UNTAG in Namibia (literally straddling the fall of the Berlin Wall and involving a total of 357 military and police personnel plus 50 election monitors), UNOSOM in Somalia (900 personnel plus HMCS Preserver); UNAMIR in Rwanda (up to 112 personnel for logistics support along with air transport and field ambulance capacity, plus the Force Commanders); the Multinational Force (MNF) aimed at providing humanitarian relief to refugees in eastern Zaire (never fully deployed, but for which 354 CF personnel were committed); and UNMEE in Ethiopia-Eritrea (to which 450 Canadians—military observers and a mechanized infantry company—were deployed as part of a Dutch-led SHIRBRIG operation).[8] Smaller deployments were made to, among others, MINURCA in the Central African Republic (where Canada's 45 personnel were the only Western contribution) and, beginning at the very end of the decade, UNAMSIL in Sierra Leone (involving a total of 90 Canadian Forces members in rotation, including an air transport contribution).

Although not strictly speaking confined within the post-1990 time frame of this chapter, the UNTAG operation in Namibia is the key point of departure for an analysis of Canadian involvement in post–Cold War peace operations in Africa. This is because its success in enabling a relatively peaceful transition to majority rule in what had been South African–occupied South West Africa led to unwarranted optimism concerning the prospects for the new, more complex and multi-dimensional peace operations that were to follow. In short, while the Namibian operation was successful in fulfilling its primary objective, this success masked what one Canadian diplomat characterized as "a disturbingly high ratio of good luck to good management" (interview, August 1992). Operating within a fundamentally supportive international and regional context (see Black 2001c), it did not adequately prepare either Canadian or UN personnel more broadly for the unprecedented challenges to come.

Indeed, three of the next four largest operations—specifically Somalia, Rwanda, and eastern Zaire—were sobering and in various ways traumatic experiences for the CF. The substantial innovations and accomplishments of the six-month mission to Somalia were dramatically overshadowed by the controversy and scandal surrounding "the involvement of Canadian troops in widely publicized, suspicious Somali civilian deaths" (Dawson 2007, 3), followed by a high-profile commission of inquiry and the disbanding of the Canadian Airborne Regiment. The experience "pitched the armed forces into one of its darkest periods" (Dawson 2007, 3; see also Herold 2004–05; and Razack 2004), with lasting repercussions. The story of UNAMIR Force Commander Romeo Dallaire's traumatic impotence in the face of both the preparations for and the prosecution of the Rwandan genocide has already been touched upon in Chapters 3 and 4. While Canadians in the field conducted themselves with courage and professionalism in the face of this horrifying event, their government's reluctance to support the UN effort in Rwanda was only marginally less pronounced and shameful than that of many other Western governments. Finally, as discussed in Chapter 3, the MNF deployment in the face of a looming humanitarian disaster in eastern Zaire was initiated by Prime Minister Chrétien in the shadow of the Rwandan failure, reflecting a kind of redemptive impulse. Despite the fact that the international decision to deploy played a role in the subsequent dissipation of the crisis, the Canadian mission only narrowly avoided ending in a very public operational fiasco. Taking on a force leadership role for which it was ill-equipped in terms of doctrine, resources, and experience, the Canadian government and the CF could not obtain effective cooperation from its international partners, could barely sustain its own commitment, was exposed as utterly dependent on the US for intelligence and transport, and could not even get from its Ugandan staging area into theatre in the absence of great(er) power and African government cooperation (see Cooper 2000; Appathurai and Lysyshyn 1998; Hennessy 2001).

The UNMEE deployment, in comparison, was a relatively straightforward, traditional interpositional Chapter VI peacekeeping operation in the context of a ceasefire agreement between two belligerents, to which Canada contributed as part of the Dutch-led multinational SHIRBRIG formation that enabled rapid deployment for the initial six months of the operation. While this operation can be seen as relatively successful, therefore, it represented a step away from the more risky leadership roles that Canada had flirted with in its previous African engagements. It was also the only full-scale brigade deployment of the SHIRBRIG formation as such, despite its initial intention to make troop formations of this scale rapidly deployable. SHIRBRIG's subsequent operational deployments were small-scale headquarters contributions to UNOCI in Côte d'Ivoire, UNMIL in Liberia, and UNAMIS and UNMIS in Sudan. While these small-scale deployments were judged to have been valuable contributions to the operational effectiveness of the missions in question, they nevertheless brought the relevance of SHIRBRIG (itself a reaction to collective failure in Rwanda) into question, and with it Canada's direct participation in significantly scaled, multilateral, high-readiness capacities, even of strictly time-limited duration (see Armstrong-Whitworth 2007; Koops and Varwick 2008). The eventual decision to disband SHIRBRIG in mid-2009 can be seen, among other things, as a manifestation of the declining interest of Canada and other heretofore "like-minded" Western peacekeeping leaders in working with and through UN-led operational structures— a point to which I will return.

This cumulatively sobering experience with African PSOs during the 1990s led, broadly speaking, to two different kinds of reaction in Canadian international security policy. At the lofty level of "norm entrepreneurship" and institutional innovation the Chrétien Liberals, with energetic leadership from Lloyd Axworthy (as Foreign Minister from January 2006) as well as a new Global Issues Bureau in the Department of Foreign Affairs, undertook several high-profile initiatives with potentially significant long-term implications. Several of these have been mentioned above: the Landmines Treaty; sponsorship of the International Commission on Intervention and State Sovereignty (ICISS) and the championing of its hallmark idea, the Responsibility to Protect; and efforts in the Security Council and elsewhere to highlight and respond to the plight of civilians and children in armed conflict. To these we could add Canada's efforts to prompt action on the trade in small arms and on micro-disarmament, its active support for the "Kimberley Process" designed to roll back the trade in "conflict diamonds," and its energetic diplomacy in support of the Rome Treaty and the International Criminal Court (see McRae and Hubert 2001; Smillie 2006). These activities were popular at home, refreshing the narrative of Canada as a moral leader in Africa (as discussed in Chapter 3), and scored some notable successes in international diplomatic forums. However, they were typically thinly supported in material terms. For example, the Canadian Peacebuilding

Initiative, launched in October 1996, was allocated only C$10 million annually to support its wide-ranging brief (see Small 2001). These initiatives also generated, in international citizenship terms, solidarist aspirations and expectations that proved difficult to gain broad international support for as efforts moved from "entrepreneurial" to "implementation" leadership (see Riddell-Dixon 2005). Partly for this reason, initiatives of this type (and the human security discourse that underlay them) were largely eschewed by the new Conservative government first elected in January 2006, notwithstanding some lasting results including the institutionalization of the Stabilization and Reconstruction Task Force (START) within DFAIT (now DFATD), and the ongoing Canadian engagement in and prioritization of Sudan and South Sudan (designated as a CIDA "country"—now two—of concentration in the streamlined CIDA list of 2009).[9]

At the "coal face" of individual peace operations, however, the principal trend was toward much smaller deployments of specialized capabilities in subordinate roles. Thus, Canada's involvement in the UNAMSIL operation in Sierra Leone—a country that, for important historical reasons, Canada might have been expected to take a special interest in—was limited to a handful of CF personnel at any given time, with no provision for medium- to long-term peacebuilding or development support to assist this traumatized country through the critical peace-consolidation phase (see Smillie 2006).[10] For the UNMIL operation in neighbouring Liberia, four Canadians were deployed as part of a SHIRBRIG headquarters planning component. For the critical MONUC (from 2010, MONUSCO) operation in the DRC—the UN's largest operation in one of Africa's most brutalized yet pivotal states— between eight and twelve staff officers, assigned to MONUC headquarters, have been deployed. Indeed the MONUC operation was the focus of a symbolically telling decision point when, toward the end of Canada's decade-long combat role in Afghanistan in 2010, the government turned down a request from the UN to provide the operation's Force Commander (General Andrew Leslie), along with a few dozen additional Canadian troops (C. Clark 2010). For a country that had long nurtured an identity as a "peacekeeping nation," this decision represented a clear departure from past practice and expectations.

Canada's most sustained and substantial contribution to African peace operations in the post-Kananaskis period was its dual deployments in Sudan—to UNMIS/UNMISS,[11] charged with securing the North–South "Comprehensive Peace Agreement" (CPA), and to the

African Union Mission (AMIS) in Darfur and subsequently the hybrid UN-AU UNAMID operation there. Yet while Canada was among the largest financial supporters of the multilateral operations deployed to mitigate atrocity crimes in Darfur, and provided important logistical support such as 105 armoured personnel carriers (AVGPs) and leased helicopters for AMIS, its "boots on the ground" in 2008 consisted of 7 CF personnel assigned to UNAMID and 34 to UNMIS (6 and 14, respectively, by 2012).[12] It is also noteworthy that, beginning under the Liberals and carrying on under the Conservatives, Canada played a significant and sustained role in diplomatic and humanitarian efforts to end the protracted conflict and suffering in northern Uganda. This effort did not, however, involve CF personnel and, while it began as a relatively high-profile initiative with strong support and participation from former Foreign Minister Axworthy and UN Ambassador (and former Liberal Cabinet Minister) Allan Rock, it was carried forward under the Harper Conservative government with almost no public profile (see Bradbury, McDonough, and Dewar 2007).

In short, the predominant motif for CF engagements in Africa in the wake of the adoption of the G8 AAP in 2002 was a willingness to "do our share," at least compared with other G8 and Western governments, but in an overall climate of reticence and risk-aversion. True, the sharply downward trajectory of Canada's deployed contributions to UN peacekeeping operations and the concomitant rise in contributions to NATO-led operations (not only in Afghanistan, but later in Libya) has been paralleled by the trajectory of various "Western European and Other" (WEOG) governments, some of them (for example, Denmark, the Netherlands, Norway, and Sweden) also strong traditional supporters of UN peacekeeping (see Bellamy and Williams 2012). The same trend has been evident in major Western powers—the US, UK, and France—with significant security roles in Africa. Moreover, other multilateral dynamics have significantly influenced this trend—notably the emphasis, supported and sponsored by the G8, on the "regionalization" of African peace operations ("African solutions for African problems"—see Williams 2008). Nevertheless, these broader trends, while reinforcing the dramatic change in Canadian peacekeeping practice vis-à-vis Africa, cannot fully *explain* it. I will return to this analytical question later in the chapter.

Capacity Building and Training

Along with the declining deployment of CF personnel in the context of African peace operations, the other significant trend was a growing emphasis on capacity-building and training activities aimed at enhancing African peacekeeping and peacebuilding capabilities. In this regard, the Canadian approach was entirely consistent with the G8 commitment set out in the AAP in 2002, and operationalized with the initiation of the US-government-funded Global Peace Operations Initiative in 2005 (see Yamashita 2013). It was also consistent with policy and institutional developments within the African Union, including the creation of a new African Peace and Security Architecture (APSA), and with a growing international consensus promoted by the UN Secretary-General (UNSG 2004).[13] Thus, Canada's role was both influenced by and, to a small degree at least, instrumental to this larger "project" for reconstituting and enabling African peace-operations capacity.

There is a longer history of Canadian military training assistance in Africa to which the more recent upsurge in activity added a new chapter. Beginning in 1961, and in the face of resistance from the Department of National Defence (DND) based primarily on resource limitations, a small-scale program focused mainly on training officer cadets and senior officers was initiated with a select group of African Commonwealth member states (Ghana, Kenya, Nigeria, Tanzania, Uganda, and Zambia). This involved both the training of Africans at Canadian military establishments and, on a more limited scale, the deployment of CF personnel to African training establishments. The most ambitious element of the program in its early years was a five-year, C$15 million agreement with Tanzania to aid in the planning and organization of its defence force; build, staff, and pay the foreign exchange costs for a military academy; and equip and train an air transport wing for the Tanzanian army. Over its five-year lifespan, the agreement became a source of frustration and discomfort on both sides, and both "were equally glad to see the agreement come to an end" (Matthews 1976, 111; see also Donaghy 1995). Thus, elements of Canadian, and particularly CF, reticence in relation to African military engagements are deeply rooted, and have contributed to the inconsistency of Canada's security assistance to the continent. So too, however, are the larger geostrategic and hegemonic incentives that have influenced it. Specifically, the initiation of Canada's military training assistance to Africa was shaped by Western alliance considerations: "Since the United States was, for obvious reasons, unacceptable as a donor of aid in such a sensitive area as defence, it was left to the smaller member nations of the West like Canada to fill in the vacuum left by the withdrawal of British officers and training facilities. Indeed, Canada was urged by the British and the Americans to provide such assistance to both Ghana (1961) and Tanzania (1964)" (Matthews 1976, 108). Matthews notes, as well, that an additional motivation was Canada's interest in persuading newly independent African governments of the benefits of Commonwealth membership. While the obstacles to US military assistance in Africa have largely (though not completely) dissipated, there are still ways in which Canada, as a smaller, non-threatening NATO and G8 member without a history of African colonization, can play a useful role in advancing larger Western security objectives. As I will discuss below, the Canadian Forces have tended to be responsive to such considerations, notwithstanding their institutional reticence to undertake commitments in what are often "austere and remote" African contexts (see, e.g., Dawson 2012, 114).

In the most recent upsurge of involvement, the focus (in line with broader G8 priorities) was principally on training and capacity building for peace operations, as opposed to the broader "upstream" and "downstream" concerns with conflict prevention and longer-term peacebuilding.[14] As noted in Chapter 2, under the auspices of the C$500 million Canada Fund for Africa, established in the run-up to the Kananskis Summit in 2002 as a five-year "showcase for Canadian leadership in pursuit of effective development through a series of large-scale, flagship initiatives in support of NEPAD and the G8 [AAP]" (CIDA 2002, 26), C$19 million was allocated to building peace-and-security capacity. Of this, roughly C$15 million was allocated to the West Africa Peace and Security initiative to support ECOWAS in West Africa and its member states. The remaining C$4 million was to be allocated over a three-year period to enhance the AU's peace-and-security capacity through, for example, support for the development of rapid response mechanisms and institutional capacity building. Beyond the Canada Fund for Africa, a further C$50 million was to be earmarked for the Global Peace Operations Program (GPOP) of the Global Peace and Security Fund established by the Canadian government in 2005—Canada's contribution to the Global Peace Operations Initiative introduced by the US in the context of the 2004 Sea Island G8 Summit with the stated objective of helping to train and equip 75,000 peacekeepers worldwide, but mostly in Africa (see Williams 2008, 316). However C$20 million was immediately directed toward support for AMIS, and indeed Canada's and broader Western crisis-induced support for AMIS and the Darfur Integrated Task Force (DITF) of the African Union served as an ongoing distraction from, and obstacle to, the longer-term capacity-building needs of the AU's Peace Support Operations Division and Conflict Prevention Unit (interview with Canadian diplomat, Feb. 2007). This problem was exacerbated by the decision to deploy another AU force—AMISOM—in the comparably "wicked" operational context of Somalia.

GPOP funds were dispersed through a number of channels. For example, the Pearson Peacekeeping Centre (PPC) was tasked with implementing C$10.3 million worth of programs under a GPOP program extension announced in April 2008. These funds were to be used to strengthen "the capacity of targeted African countries to contribute more effectively to the civilian police component of peace operations with the United Nations and the African Union," including those deployed with UNAMID in Darfur (a total of C$7.9 million), and to "help increase the number and improve the skills of African personnel in peace missions" through support for African peacekeeping training centres of excellence (C$2.4 million) (DFAIT 2008). More recently, it supported the "African Police for Peace" training program, delivered by the Pearson Centre (as the Pearson Peacekeeping Centre had been re-christened) and launched in 2011; and a Francophonie project supporting training in several francophone African countries, again delivered by the Pearson Centre.[15] Some GPOP resources have been dispersed through the Military Training and Cooperation Program (MTCP—previously the Military Training Assistance Program, or MTAP) of the Department of National Defence—a program that funds training for some sixty-one member countries (sixteen of which are African) with a modest C$20 million annual budget. Among its activities since 2006–07 have been: Canadian officer postings to peacekeeping training centres in Mali and Kenya; participation by some Africans in Junior Command and

Staff Courses; and training for African peacekeeping forces slated for deployment to Darfur and Somalia, conducted in Canada, Ghana, Kenya, and/or Mali (DMTAP 2007; DMTC 2010).

Several observations can be made about these training and capacity-building efforts. First, in part because Canada's direct stake and interest in African security—both historic and contemporary—have been small, there have been ways in which Canadian contributions and contributors are likely to be relatively attractive to their African counterparts. For example, as noted by Kristiana Powell, in contrast to other donor countries, much of Canada's peace-and-security funding to the AU was "unearmarked," which she suggests reflects "a more partnership-oriented rather than paternalistic approach to supporting the AU" (Powell 2005, 24; see also Akuffo 2012). It also reflects, however, less clearly defined *interests* in relation to African peace-and-security issues.

Second, despite the comparative "surge" in activity in the post-Kananaskis period, Canadian contributions have remained strikingly modest, especially in relation to any realistic assessment of the needs and operational demands facing African policy-makers, planners, and implementers of peace operations (see SSCFAIT 2007, 117–21). Indeed, despite the discursive emphasis on Africa that was a feature of the previous Liberal (Chrétien and Martin) governments' foreign policy, these contributions have also been *relatively* modest in relation to commitments to other regions and operational contexts. For example, despite Africa's unhappy status as the region of the world with the highest number of armed conflicts, many of which have been exceptionally protracted and deadly, only 20 percent of the MTAP's total C$16 million budget went to the continent in 2006–07, and 29 percent of C$20 million to "Africa and the Middle East" in 2009–10. Reflecting the domestic bureaucratic environment and incentives to which it responds, the DND Directorate in charge of the program has been at some pains to stress the cost-efficiency of its effort: "MTAP is a modest program with broad benefits: the multifaceted training it offers returns great value for a minimal investment" (DMTAP 2007, 4).

Third, largely as a function of this "modesty," there is a strong tendency (with a handful of exceptions)[16] to focus resources on immediate operational challenges rather than longer-term, and more systemic and sustainable PSO capacity-building efforts, let alone structural conflict prevention and post-conflict peacebuilding needs. As Powell summarizes, there seems to have been "a worrying trend whereby Canada provides substantial support for crisis response in Africa, that is not also matched with meaningful and sustained political, financial, and material assistance to a broader peace and security agenda" (2005, 24). This could be somewhat glibly characterized as a strong tendency toward "fire brigade internationalism."[17]

Analysis: The Limitations of Good International Citizenship and Hegemonic Middlepowermanship

With a handful of important and destabilizing exceptions,[18] Canadians involved in African peace operations have typically conducted themselves with a high level of competence, courage, and professionalism (see also Dallaire 2003; and Dawson 2007). Canadian contributions of *matériel*, transport, and technical assistance, for example in the case of AMIS in Sudan, have also been valuable in enabling PSOs to achieve a degree of operational respectability. In this sense, Canada's contributions to African peace and security have been marked by a high prevalence of "good international citizens"—dedicated individuals working in challenging environments to ensure the highest possible level of operational effectiveness. But do these individual contributions, admirable though they may be, add up to a collective pattern of good international citizenship?

As the foregoing mapping has illustrated, Canadian involvement in African peace operations—both operationally and in terms of capacity building—has been marked by a number of sharp limitations. Almost invariably, this involvement has been reactive and tightly time-bound. Certainly this was true of the larger operations, in Somalia, the MNF, and Ethiopia-Eritrea. Moreover, since these numerical high points, Canadian "boots on the ground" in Africa have been small and declining in number.[19] Canadian military commentators and political leaders will rightly note that with sharply limited numbers as a result of force and budget cuts in the 1990s (reiterated in the latest round of budget cuts since 2010), the government must make hard decisions about where and what to deploy, and can sometimes barely sustain the major operations it has undertaken let alone expand the CF "footprint" in complex African environments (e.g., MacKenzie 2009). But the places the Canadian government *has* chosen to concentrate its limited resources speak volumes. Compare the peace-and-security presence in Africa with the 2,700 troops deployed at any given time in the volatile Kandahar region of Afghanistan in the NATO-led, UN-authorized ISAF operation from 2005 to 2011, or with "the nearly 40,000 members of the Canadian Forces [who] ... contributed to stabilization and reconstruction initiatives in the Balkan region" between 1991 and 2004 (DND 2004). Whereas the latter were portrayed as "vital national interests" aligned with "core Canadian values," African peace operations have typically been viewed as discretionary and a lower order priority, notwithstanding their devastating human and regional ramifications.

This underscores the long-standing, and (during the new millennium) resurgent, preference of the CF to operate in the context and company of its NATO allies, preferably in NATO-*led* operations, and the concomitant decline in its UN peace-operations role.[20] As the brief history of Canada's military training assistance outlined above illustrates, this preference is hardly new. Justin Massie characterizes it as a reflection of the enduring tradition of "soft-balancing Atlanticism" in Canadian strategic culture. Thus, "when Canada had to choose whether to contribute to NATO or UN peace operations in the 1990s, the choice was rather simple: relevance within the alliance has always prevailed over defensive internationalism in Canadian strategic thinking, regardless of the strategic environment" (Massie 2009, 641). This tendency was reinforced, however, by hard—indeed traumatic—experiences with its African operations during the 1990s. Given the fact that the majority of UN operations and peacekeepers are deployed in Africa, this resurgent preference can be seen to reflect both enduring wariness toward the extraordinary challenges of African conflicts, and growing disenchantment with the UN. A paradoxical case in point was the CF's fulsome participation in the 2011 operation in Libya—on the one hand reinforcing the Harper government's preferred national narrative of Canada as "a courageous, principled warrior" (Paris, 2014, 281–86) operating in the company of its closest NATO allies, but on the other hand being the first UN Security Council–sanctioned operation to formally (though controversially) invoke the quintessentially Liberal cause of the Responsibility to Protect (see Williams and Bellamy 2012).

The pattern of operational deployments is mirrored by Canadian contributions to peace-and-security capacity building. As Stephen

Baranyi (in Powell 2005, 22–23) has noted, for example, Canada's capacity building contributions to both the AU and UN have been dwarfed by its contributions to NATO-led operations, specifically in the Balkans and Afghanistan. Moreover almost 50 percent of the MTAP budget for 2006–07 was allocated to European countries associated with NATO's "Partnership for Peace" arrangement for former East Bloc countries in Central and Eastern Europe, as compared with the 20 percent allocated to African countries whose needs are arguably far more pressing. While this ratio had shifted significantly by 2009–10 (to 22 percent of expenditures on European partners versus 29 percent in Africa and the Middle East and 33 percent in Latin America—see DMTC 2010), the volume of support has remained remarkably modest.

Behind these disparities and the operational limits they imply lies a minimal commitment of bureaucratic and policy resources to African issues and operations at National Defence Headquarters (NDHQ). This, in turn, reflects the bedrock weakness of the political priority placed on Africa by Canada's political and foreign-policy leadership. In short, as far as the CF goes, there is virtually no institutional capacity or will to exercise a sustained intellectual leadership role in relation to African peace-and-security operations. The situation has been marginally better in DFAIT (now DFATD), where issues related to African peace-and-security capacity building have continued to be engaged on a small scale through the initiatives of the Global Issues Bureau and more recently the Stabilization and Reconstruction Task Force (START).[21] Here too, however, resource constraints and the weakening of high-level political interest have led to a decrease in the priority and profile of such efforts. As the funding environment for peacekeeping training and capacity building faces new uncertainties (manifested, for example, in the closure of the Pearson Centre for peacekeeping training in October 2013 and the decision to allow the Global Peace and Security Fund to expire), the Canadian commitment even to these modest roles clearly lacks clarity and consistency of purpose.

A further weakness of Canada's involvement with African PSOs is the relative lack of connection, or bridging, between shorter-term crisis and humanitarian responses, such as those in Sudan/Darfur, northern Uganda, or (previously) Sierra Leone, and the emphasis on "good performers" that has come to the fore in the regular bilateral

development assistance programming delivered (until 2013) by
CIDA. The latter emphasis has led to a preoccupation with developing
bilateral "partnerships" in relation to a select group of countries that
are "able to use aid effectively" (see Chapter 5; also Black 2006a,
323–32). The problem, of course, is that the most challenging and
critical phase for countries emerging from conflict is often the protracted peacebuilding period, when the repercussions of conflict are
most pressing and the probability of reversion to conflict is especially
high. It is precisely in this crucial middle range that Canadian policy
has been weakest, with only a limited and highly selective program-
matic basis for supporting countries through this pivotal "moment."[22]
To reiterate one example, despite contributing to the UNAMSIL operation in Sierra Leone, and despite historic Commonwealth and trans-
societal links with this country, by 2006–07 CIDA had "no significant
assistance program" and "no long-term projects" there, expending a
total of only C$3.2 million from all sources in that fiscal year.[23] This
narrow focus has been firmly reinscribed as a result of the Harper
government's 2009 decision to further limit the number of its core
bilateral partners, or "countries of focus" (see Chapter 5). On the
other hand, and to its credit, the government "stayed the course" in
the very difficult post- and peri-conflict terrain of Sudan and South
Sudan, designating it as a country of concentration and dispensing a
total of nearly C$100 million in 2010–11 (CIDA n.d.). This, however,
has been the exception rather than the rule, and has been brought
into question by the disbanding of the interdepartmental Sudan Task
Force in October 2013 (Mackrael 2013), and the resurgence of civil
violence in South Sudan later that year.

A final issue concerns the role of Canadian peace-and-security capacity-building assistance in relation to the broader objective of con-
structing a new peace-and-security "regime" for Africa, premised on
increased regionalization through the AU and African sub-regional
organizations buttressed by Western support. As noted above, Canada contributed to the consensus-building process around this concept (through its leadership in orchestrating the AAP, including its
peace-and-security commitments), and moved to bring its policies
and programs in line with this trend through increased involvement
in capacity building and training. It needs to be said, first of all, that
this emergent design for African peace and security is controversial.
Among supporters, it is seen as reflecting a new pragmatism and division of labour in peace operations that is a realistic and sensible

response to Africa's security challenges (e.g., Piiparinen 2007). More cynically, it has served the interests of Western powers in facilitating a relatively orderly disengagement from direct responsibility for addressing these challenges, and in enabling them to "pretend … that checkbook diplomacy is a reasonable substitute for sustained political engagement" (Williams 2008, 322; see also Bayart 2004). To this should be added the conclusion, articulated by Yamashita (2013, 342–46), that in the decade since the adoption of the AAP, G8 governments have failed to fulfill their own commitments in relation to this new security architecture in several key areas, including a lack of effective logistical cooperation; the quiet dropping of commitments on disarmament, demobilization, and reintegration (DDR); unreliable arrangements for financial support of African operational deployments; and lack of coordination among distinct national training programs. On the other hand, the new peace-and-security architecture has played into the hands of African governments ideologically, both by reinvigorating pan-Africanist aspirations and, more negatively, by "protecting incumbent regimes from external pressure," as in the cases of Zimbabwe and Sudan (Williams 2008, 318).

In sum, for a transnational regime to have a measure of hegemonic stability in the neo-Gramscian sense, it must be able to make a credible claim to effectiveness and plausibility. Thus far, the efforts toward a more regionalized or even hybridized African security regime lack these qualities, based on their record in situations like Darfur and Somalia as well as the structural weaknesses that persist in their emergent institutional foundations. Moreover these efforts have, in the process, helped to diffuse and obfuscate responsibility for tackling the most acute security challenges on the continent (Black and Williams 2010). Canada's strictly limited contributions to this larger peace-and-security project, both materially and intellectually, will do little to alter this condition.

The Cross-Currents of Enduring Narratives Regarding Canadian Peace Operations in Africa

Rather than "good international citizenship," understood in terms of principles of foreign policy that seek to advance the conditions of humanity while safeguarding international order (Linklater and Suganami 2006, 232), the various often admirable contributions of Canadians toward African peace operations and operational effectiveness can be better understood as having operated within a broader policy logic of *good enough* international citizenship. In practice, this means doing enough to be respectable in the eyes of one's international peers, principally within the Western-dominated OECD, G8, and NATO alliance, and enough to ensure that PSOs in Africa are able to sustain a veneer of operational effectiveness (see Black 2010a)—but no more.

Similarly, Canadian involvement in African peace-and-security operations may have helped to facilitate and legitimize the G8's approach in Africa, both by operating in consonance with the priorities of its larger G8 partners and by providing a relatively benign and non-threatening "face" to Western peace-and-security policies and activities (Akuffo 2012: 187–212). Yet its contribution in this regard has been too limited to significantly affect the long-term credibility and viability of this larger design.

In the final analysis, Canadian contributions are constrained by both bureaucratic and political limitations. Many officials in the Departments of National Defence and of Foreign Affairs, Trade, and Development, as well as members of the Canadian Forces, have been deeply hesitant to commit, and risk, scarce resources—human and financial—in the complex terrain of African peace-and-security operations. Especially within the CF, the strong preference has been to operate as seamlessly as possible in integrated, NATO-based operations, typically led by major alliance partners, rather than the complex, over-extended and militarily less-capable UN and/or AU-led missions that are the norm in Africa. The CF will do what is required (and more particularly, what the federal government requires it do) to ensure that "Canada continues to play its rightful part" (DMTAP 2007, 21) in efforts to build security and peace on the continent, but its "rightful part" has typically been understood in strictly limited terms.

In this respect, returning to the post-colonial frame introduced in Chapter 1, the CF and those close to it (analysts, advocates, etc.) arguably remain, with some important exceptions (see, e.g., Chapter 4), adherents of the popularly subordinate but politically influential "realist internationalist" (Boucher 2012) narrative concerning Canada's international role. As discussed in Chapter 3, this is not a "valueless" narrative; rather it is one that sees Canada's core values and interests as lying in nurturing close collaborative relationships and an ongoing sense of shared purpose with this country's traditionally closest "friends and allies," beginning with the US and extending outward to NATO and other Western and Western-aligned governments. It is a narrative that has been suspicious of more solidarist aspirations and pretensions, which are seen as imprudent and irresponsible in putting Canadian lives and resources at risk with limited prospect of substantive success. It has persisted in viewing African entanglements as marginal, fraught, and dangerous (e.g., Granatstein 2010). It is a narrative that has grown in influence under the Harper Conservatives, who have largely shared this view of Africa and its marginal place in the hierarchy of "Canadian" values and interests. Indeed, one way of interpreting the Harper government's approach to foreign relations is that it has undertaken a sustained effort to shift this more conservative/realist narrative from a subordinate one to the new dominant narrative of Canada in the world, with this country's international identity recast as that of a "courageous, principled warrior" as opposed to a compromised and compromising "peacekeeper" (Paris, 2014). This theme will be explored in the concluding chapter.

Canada's political leaders, for their part, have periodically talked expansively about what should be done in Africa (e.g., Nossal 2005). In the face of the deeply embedded conservative/realist narrative, however, they have shown no consistent inclination to equip the country's armed forces, diplomats, or development practitioners with the necessary resources, time, and mandates to play a sustained, let alone leading, role in support of these expansive aspirations. Nor have they been prepared to risk testing public support by explaining why such investments would be justified, whether ethically or on the basis of long-term self-interest. If this was a characteristic of Liberal governments' African security efforts in the first half of the first decade of the 2000s and during the 1990s, the current Conservative government has virtually abandoned any rhetorical aspiration toward such an activist role on sub-Saharan African security issues. This was evident, for example, in both what it *did* in relation to the French-led operation in Mali, and how it *talked about* it (see C. Clark 2013a). The implications of Canada's deployment in Mali are discussed in Chapter 8.

Paradoxically, however, the majority of Canadians, along with many groups in civil and political society, have remained firmly wedded to a view of the country that sees (in the words of a 2012 Environics poll) "Canada's most positive contribution to the world" as peacekeeping. Roland Paris persuasively argues that while this perception is sharply at odds with the decline of traditional interpositional peacekeeping and of Canada's participation in UN-mandated peace operations, it reflects a deep attachment to a more diffuse understanding of the peacekeeping role as one of "diplomatic peace-maker" (see Paris, 2014, 304–5). This view, he shows, varies in intensity across regions, genders, and "new" (recent immigrant) versus "old" Canadians, but holds across all major social cleavages. The persistence of this view, notwithstanding the powerful current of the conservative/realist alternative narrative in policy circles and a concerted effort by the Harper government to recast the traditional "liberal internationalist" narrative featuring peacekeeping and multilateralist emphases, is on its face puzzling. One way of understanding it is through a post-colonial emphasis on the degree to which Canadian engagements with African (and other comparably remote) "humanitarian emergencies" have enabled the persistence of a durable narrative of Canadian moral leadership—even when the "facts on the ground" (as outlined in this chapter) underscore a far more limited and contradictory reality. From this perspective, it is precisely *because* these operational contexts are so imaginatively remote that it becomes possible to sustain such a widely held and persistent image of Canadian "goodness."

Caught between the constraining influence of the conservative/realist narrative on the one hand, and the impetus for action arising from the narrative and expectation of Canadian "moral leadership" on the other, Canadian governments have been unable to sustain the levels of commitment, interest, and resources that would underpin the order-building aspirations associated with both the international society approach and the neo-Gramscian ideas of hegemonic consensus building, despite periodic inclinations to pursue both. In the past, this has led to a pattern of admirably motivated but under-supported and unsustained initiatives. Under the Harper government, such "initiativemanship" has diminished, but the popular expectation for an active and constructive role continues to periodically resurge. The question therefore remains whether the Harper Conservatives' clear reticence toward security assistance through peace operations in Africa will become part of a longer-term transformation of Canada's orientation toward the continent, or yet another oscillation in the consistent inconsistency of the past.

One important trend that undergirds the prospects for a substantial, though controversial, re-engagement in Africa is the rising prominence of Canadian-based, private-sector extractive companies on the continent. It is to this important trend that we now turn.

7

Canadian Extractive Companies in Africa: Exposing the Hegemonic Imperative

(David Black and Malcolm Savage)

As discussed throughout this book, the dominant public debate concerning Canada's role in Africa in the wake of the 2006 election of the Harper Conservatives concerned the degree to which the Canadian government was "walking away from" the continent (Ignatieff 2010).[1] The evidence to support this proposition, discussed in the last two chapters, was drawn principally from the trajectory of Canadian aid policy, supplemented by patterns of diplomatic (dis)engagement and (human) security assistance through peace operations and other forms. Yet throughout the first decade of the new millennium, a very different trend was gathering momentum. Canadian mining companies were becoming a dominant source of foreign investment and exploration on the continent. Between 2001 and 2011, Canadian assets and investment in the mining sector of Africa increased from C\$2.87 billion to a staggering C\$31.6 billion, with most of the increase coming after 2006 (Campbell 2011; Bhushan 2014). This made Canada the single largest source of foreign investment in African mining sectors for much of the decade. Thus, Canadian companies became dominant players in a sector on which the economic prospects of a significant number of African countries increasingly depend,[2] and which has contributed disproportionately to the rapid rates of growth achieved in Africa during the past decade (see York 2012b). In short, Canadian mining companies, with significant support from the Canadian state, became the dominant face of Canada in much of the continent, in ways that had truly significant—and controversial—ramifications for host countries' and communities' development and security prospects.

As this trend became more clearly recognized and understood, a second line of critique emerged, in some ways contradicting and in others complementing the "abandonment" motif, of a Canadian state that had abandoned its "ethical mission" in sub-Saharan Africa to become an aggressive and unapologetic booster of the extractive sector.

In this context, one key theme of this chapter is that there has been an escalating tension in Canada's involvement in Africa between a historic "brand" or identity emphasizing the continent as a site of humanitarian engagement and moral leadership (as outlined in Chapter 3), and official support and assistance for Canadian extractive companies whose activities have often been seen as undermining human security and development. While this tension has been present in Canadian foreign policy throughout the post–Second World War era, the dramatic increase in the tempo of Canadian extractive company investment abroad has led civil society groups and critical scholars to increasingly highlight potential contradictions between Canada's stated humanitarian and developmental objectives, and the negative impacts of extractive industries (see Gordon 2010; Blackwood and Stewart 2012). This tension and the intensifying debate surrounding it can be partly accounted for through a post-colonial frame. With the Canadian government reducing the reach of its aid presence on the continent and becoming less involved in conflict resolution and peace operations, while simultaneously supporting the unprecedented expansion of Canadian mining companies, the traditional moral narrative of Canada in Africa discussed in Chapter 3 has become increasingly tenuous and disputed.

More concretely, this increased publicity, and controversy, has produced novel challenges for Canadian policy-makers, requiring novel policy responses. Among these challenges and changes has been a growing, though contested, role for civil society groups in foreign-policy debates as both stakeholders and as monitors and whistleblowers concerning Canada's involvement in Africa. Similarly, given the increasingly ubiquitous "partnership" motif of foreign, security, and development policy-making, private sector actors have become prominent and active participants in policy processes. These changes can be seen as an example of what John Ruggie has conceptualized as the "new global public domain," in which private (civil society and corporate) as well as public actors have actively engaged in new arenas "of discourse, contestation, and action concerning the production of global public goods" (Ruggie 2004, 504; see also Dashwood 2012).

Moreover, faced with conflicting demands for a coherent response to the development and security ramifications of Canadian mining companies in Africa and elsewhere in the world, the Canadian government has been faced with important choices concerning the approach it wishes to adopt. Traditionally, the government's position has been that economic, development, and security policies complement each other. "Official" Canada has seen economic growth and investment (in this case through the promotion of its extractive industries) as essentially complementary to developmental goals. This assertion is contained within a conception of security that sees economic growth as essential to securing better living conditions and hence more stable societies. However, as this chapter seeks to demonstrate, one of the impacts of the "new global public domain" is that the Canadian state must respond in novel ways in an effort to sustain the credibility of these core premises. Regardless of how elements within the Canadian state have defined the government's policy objectives in relation to human development and security, the images highlighted by national and international civil society organizations of environmental destruction, social dislocation, and human rights abuses associated with extractive industries call into question Canadian efforts to pursue humanitarian and developmental objectives on the continent. In this respect, the Canadian state has been compelled to respond to pressures emanating from civil society, and indeed has sought to incorporate both civil society and corporate actors in key policy processes. While the Canadian state has defined human development and security in essentially neo-liberal terms, presuming the complementarity of liberal economic, political, and security objectives, it must also respond to claims that its policies have effectively undermined human security, as understood in more critical and transformative formulations of the concept.[3]

The *way* it has done this puts into sharp relief the alternatives of solidaristic good international citizenship, on the one hand, and adherence to Canadian/Western hegemonic norms and interests, on the other. In short, between 2007 and 2011, the Canadian government faced a series of decision points between a course of action that would have taken a more transparent and regulated approach to promoting human rights and environmental and social justice in the context of extractive company operations—an approach consistent with the expectations of good international citizenship—and a voluntary and "partnership-based" approach that continues to privilege the preferences of Canadian corporate interests. The fact that it has ultimately opted for the latter course illustrates how, despite the fact that these two different frames are vigorously represented in foreign policy debates in Canada, hegemonic preferences have typically predominated. But the intense controversy and scrutiny surrounding these decisions also reflects the ongoing salience of the Canadian "moral identity" constructed in and through Africa, as highlighted by a post-colonial frame, and the repercussions that result when it is disrupted.

To make this argument, the chapter begins with a discussion of the traditional marginality of Canadian commercial interests in Africa, demonstrating that while there are some signs of change in this regard, overall economic linkages remain stubbornly limited. It then outlines the growing salience of the extractive sector in Africa, highlighting its economic importance and some characteristic costs and risks associated with its development. This is followed by a discussion of how the traditional post-colonial image (or "brand") of Canada as a developmental and humanitarian champion for Africa has been sharply challenged as a result of the escalating presence of Canadian mining companies. The robust and systematic ways in which the Canadian state has supported and protected Canadian corporations, and its comparatively feeble efforts to promote Corporate Social Responsibility (CSR), are then briefly reviewed. The next section scrutinizes the developmental and human security implications of the investments it has encouraged. Finally, we consider several policy responses taken by the federal government, beginning with its response to the March 2007 Advisory Group Report of the multi-stakeholder National Roundtables on Corporate Social Responsibility and the Canadian Extractive Industry in Developing Countries. The potentially far-reaching implications of this report, offering the possibility of transforming Canada's historically weak role in promoting CSR and long-term developmental benefits from extractive industries into a position of leadership, is considered. We conclude by discussing how this and subsequent opportunities have been foregone, in favour of a much weaker, voluntary, and partnership-based response that leaves intact the neo-liberal premises of the post–Structural Adjustment extractive sector in Africa and continues to sharply disrupt the traditional ethical narrative of Canada in Africa.

Canadian Commercial Interests in Africa: Transcending Marginality?

As noted in the Introduction to this book, Canadian trade-and-investment links with sub-Saharan Africa have always been relatively very minor. At their nadir at the end of the 1990s bilateral trade sank to around 0.5 percent of total Canadian trade and, while recovering in the 2000s, remained under 1 percent of total exports and around 3 percent of imports by 2011. Moreover the profile of these trade relations is not propitious: most trade is in relatively low value-added primary products, with 75 percent of imports in oil and petroleum products, followed by gold, gems, cocoa beans, and uranium; and 20 percent of exports in wheat (including food aid), with no other product accounting for more than 10 percent of the total (see Schorr and Hitschfeld 2013, 138–41). Similarly, investment links, though notoriously difficult to track reliably, are very modest and heavily concentrated in a handful of sectors—notably finance and insurance, mining, and oil and gas—and in a single country—South Africa (CIDP 2014).

With strong aggregate rates of economic growth over the course of the past decade, the economies of sub-Saharan Africa have attracted increasing attention from external investors and traders. In this increasingly competitive environment, Schorr and Hitschfeld (2013, 144–48) stress that Canadian producers and investors risk falling further behind as major rising economies make concerted efforts to expand their African connections.[4] Closely related to this is the need to diversify Canada's economic linkages with African countries. They cite electricity, energy, and infrastructure; education; forestry and fishing; and ecotourism as sectors with good prospects (see also Thomas 2013). And indeed, beginning in 2010 the Harper government has appeared increasingly keen on the economic opportunities that commercial lobbies like the Canadian Council on Africa (CCA—www.ccafrica.ca) have been touting for more than a decade (see Chapter 8). However, along with aggressive competition for market share from old and new entrants, the ability of Canadian-based enterprises to expand in Africa has been inhibited by at least two major factors: a relatively limited government support structure (with only nine full-time Canada-based trade commissioners and four locally engaged trade officers for the entire continent—see Elder 2013, 35); and the notorious risk-aversion of most Canadian businesses (Schorr and Hitschfeld 2013, 145).

Historically, the relative marginality of African economic interests had a paradoxically liberating impact on Canadian "initiative-manship" on the continent, particularly during the ascendance of the human security agenda in the late 1990s and early 2000s (see C. Brown 2001, 195–98). This is consistent with the expectations of a post-colonial approach, as the lack of complexity and ambiguity in such limited and socio-economically distant relationships has enabled the pursuit of relatively "pure," ethically defined initiatives, but has made them exceptionally difficult to sustain. In the Harper era, however, in which apart from a few core relationships and priorities often leading to uncompromising confrontation (with Iran, Russia, and Sri Lanka, for example) the overriding priority has become the pursuit of enhanced trade opportunities and relationships (DFATD 2013a), Africa's relative economic marginality has clearly reinforced its diminished foreign-policy salience. The most striking exception to this pattern has been Canada's large and growing role in the pivotal extractive sector. It is to this sector and the relationships arising from it that we next turn.

Mining and Development, Security and the Environment

The importance of extractive industries to the future of many African countries cannot be overstated. The economies of industrialized countries such as Canada, the United States, and Australia have benefited greatly in terms of aggregate growth from resource extraction, and Africa's vast mineral reserves have generated hope for similar contributions. According to one UNCTAD report, "geography has bequeathed the continent an impressive endowment of mineral wealth, including near-global monopolies of platinum, chromium and diamonds; a high proportion of the world's gold, cobalt and manganese reserves; and extensive reserves of bauxite, coal, uranium, copper and nickel" (UNCTAD 2005, 6). Mining and minerals have been leading sectors in the economies of resource-rich African countries, especially in terms of export earnings. Although predating the investment boom of the past decade, Magnus Ericsson's finding that "mineral exports contribute between 25 and 90 percent of annual export earnings of 13 countries: Botswana, Ghana, Guinea, Liberia, Senegal, Mauritania, Namibia, Niger, Central African Republic, Sierra Leone, Zaire, Zambia and Zimbabwe" is indicative (quoted in Campbell 1999). Given the importance of foreign exchange earned through exports for government revenues, balance of payments, and debt servicing, it is not surprising that resource extraction has become a priority sector in many countries. This is especially true in the wake of the aggressive, market-oriented structural adjustment reforms undertaken (often under duress) during the 1980s and 1990s, stressing the importance of exports and comparative advantage.[5]

The sheer size of the continent's extractive sectors in relation to its overall economy has fuelled the neo-liberal common sense that increased extractive industry investment is surely good for Africa. Supporters emphasize that resource extraction has the potential to contribute to economic development by generating government revenues that can be used for development policies and projects, but also the creation of jobs, the development of infrastructure, and spin-off growth through forward and backward linkages in the economy (Di Boscio and Humphreys 2005).[6] Such claims have been strongly contested however. While all relevant controversies cannot be explored in this short section, some key issues should be highlighted.

One set of concerns emphasized through the advocacy of local communities and international NGOs is the environmental and social impacts of mining activities (Tienhaara 2006; Earthworks and Oxfam 2004; Siegel 2013). Resource extraction has long been recognized as imposing harms on the environment due to the destruction of natural surroundings as well as the use of harmful chemicals such as cyanide and mercury that frequently leak into local water sources. The destruction of natural surroundings and arable land has also led to community unrest, destroying livelihoods that depend on the natural environment such as farming and fishing, and dislocating communities living close to mining concessions (Oxfam 2006).

Extractive industries have also been linked to problems concerning governance, transparency, the distribution of resources and security (often captured under the rubric of the "resource curse"). Connected to the enclave nature of resource extraction, problems often arise from the fact that most of the public revenues from extractive industries are provided to the state through taxes and royalties. Once in the hands of government officials, how these revenues are deployed depends on the quality of governance as well as the priorities and probity of state power-holders. Too often, African governments have lacked the capacity to effectively reinvest these funds into productive activities, and in many cases may not intend to use them for the benefit of their citizens. Frequently, the use of revenues generated from extractive industries has been opaque and poorly monitored, although international efforts such as the Extractive Industries Transparency Initiative (EITI) have been seeking to improve this situation.[7] In worst-case scenarios, extractive industries have been linked to profound human insecurity and rights abuses, with resource revenues financing military and paramilitary activities and sustaining protracted conflicts in Sudan, the DRC, Angola, Sierra Leone, and Liberia, among others (Freedman 2006–07; Le Billon 2006–07; Campbell 2006; Arimatsu and Mistry 2012). The ensuing competition between rivals has destabilized countries and/or regions as groups seek to gain access to the rents generated in extractive sectors.

Such issues remain matters of intense debate. While it is true that extractive industries have been a source of conflict, insecurity (both large- and small-scale), social disruption, and environmental degradation, many argue that this need not be the case (Ascher 2005; Pedro 2006). If extractive industries are to play a greater role in development and minimize negative impacts on local communities, however, strategic interventions will be required from national and local governments (see Pedro 2006; Lisk, Besada, and Martin 2013). Yet as Bonnie Campbell (2003 and 2009a) points out, the ability of governments to perform such roles has been sharply constrained due to the restructuring of the state under the neo-liberal principles of Structural Adjustment—precisely the same principles that have fostered the current "mining boom" in many African countries. In short, the potential for extractive industries to negatively affect African countries is very real, while positive and sustainable contributions have been elusive.

Challenging the Traditional Narrative: Canadian Mining Companies in Africa

Although the previous section focused on the developmental and security issues associated with mining activities, the economic, social, and political challenges of the African continent clearly run much deeper than the problems associated with resource extraction. While it is important to recognize the diversity and richness of the African experience, the continent has nevertheless been the locus of some of the worst manifestations of poverty, drought, war, and human suffering in the world. As noted in Chapter 3 and elsewhere, Africa's various challenges have, in turn, formed the backdrop for a persistent moral narrative concerning Canadian foreign policy, and an identity that (at least until recently) stressed Canadian commitments to the promotion of human security and development, while masking a more contradictory reality.

This is partly because, while such historic efforts reflected a degree of genuine concern for the developmental and security challenges facing Africa (as illuminated by the good international citizenship frame), it is clear that these initiatives also serve important political functions, as highlighted by a post-colonial perspective. In particular, they have contributed prominently to the historic "branding" of Canada as a benign and constructive "friend of Africa" in the global political arena. As Kyle Grayson has argued, "Canada is a country that relies heavily on its expertise in public diplomacy in order to cultivate a positive global brand image that greatly contributes to its soft power capabilities" (2006, 480). By cultivating an image as a leader in human security and development, especially in relation to Africa, Canadian governments have been able both to foster a self-idealizing image of Canada as "good state" at home (see Gallagher 2011, 108), thereby appealing to domestic constituencies attracted by humanitarian and global justice causes, and to generate diplomatic currency abroad. That diplomatic currency served a number of purposes, including differentiating Canadian from American foreign policy, assuming leadership roles in multilateral initiatives associated with the G8 and the United Nations, and gaining diplomatic support in such multilateral forums.[8] It has become clear that these purposes do not concern the Harper Conservative government or its core supporters in the way that they have previous Canadian governments.

Nevertheless, they continue to hold considerable popular appeal in Canadian society and in other political parties.

In light of such persistent foreign-policy branding efforts on the part of Canadian governments, drawing on a benign and construct-ive image in relation to Africa, it is no surprise that from the per-spective of the Canadian public Canada's best known links with the continent have been ethically "branded" development assistance and human security efforts. However, as Peter van Ham (2001) notes, the advantage of branding is that cultivating the right brand can surpass the actual "product" of a country's assets; in this case, it can mask the changing reality of Canada's relationships with Africa. To this can be added the post-colonial insight that the very remoteness of African countries and issues, and their characteristically decontext-ualized portrayal, has enabled the persistence of an *idea* of Canada in Africa that is stubbornly resistant to revision. Thus, while the con-ventional narrative highlighted Canada's development and security efforts, such a perception largely ignored the growing investments that Canadian companies were making in the extractive sectors of many African countries, with ambiguous and troubling security and development effects. Understanding the range and scope of Can-adian mining companies' presence is therefore crucial to gaining a more accurate picture of Canada's role in Africa. The attention increasingly focused on this presence in the popular media and else-where demonstrates that this understanding is growing (see E. Payne 2012); while the civil society mobilization and sharp political contro-versies regarding the Canadian extractive sector are explained in part by the degree to which its role disrupts Canadians' benign self-image.

Given Canada's own mineral wealth and extensive experience in resource extraction, it is no surprise that Canadian companies are at the forefront of the global mining industry.[9] Lemieux (2005) notes that in 2005, 155 of the world's 304 larger resource extraction companies (51%) were based in Canada. By 2009, this percentage had increased marginally, to 53 percent (Natural Resources Canada 2011). Furthermore, using figures from 2002, Ericsson (2005) notes that of the twenty-five largest mining companies in the world, six were Canadian, with one (Barrick Gold Corporation) in the top ten. Thus, while Canada is sparsely represented in the top ranks of global companies, Canadian companies of relatively smaller (but still large) size represent a major force on the global market. In 2009, the value of exploration by Canadian companies was 16 percent of the global total—more than any other country's companies (Natural Resources Canada 2011).

In Africa, Canadian companies have also been major players. In terms of exploration, larger Canadian companies planned to spend C$188 million in Africa in 2009, down 52 percent from the year before due to the world financial crisis but still representing nearly 20 percent of all exploration activity on the continent. This placed Canada second only to South Africa, with most of the latter's investment concentrated in its domestic market (Natural Resources Canada 2011, 5.11; also Campbell 1999). Lemieux notes that at the end of 2005 companies of all sizes listed on Canadian stock exchanges held interests in 660 mineral properties located in thirty-two African countries. As noted earlier, total Canadian company investment in Africa surged from C$6 billion in 2005 to more than C$30 billion in 2011.[10] To put these projections in perspective, total Canadian ODA to Africa was estimated at C$2.169 billion in 2010–11 (CIDA 2011d). In terms of geographical concentration, just over 90 percent of Canadian investments were concentrated in eight countries: South Africa (25.6%), the DRC (17.8%), Madagascar (13.8%), Zambia (9.9%), Tanzania (9.5%), Ghana (6.5%), Burkina Faso (4.7%), and Mauritania (3%) (Campbell 2011; also Bhushan 2014). Interestingly enough, only two of these (Tanzania and Ghana) were included in the streamlined list of seven African countries of focus for bilateral aid announced in 2009. In the 2013 *Global Markets Action Plan*, however, South Africa was the only African country identified as an "emerging market with broad Canadian interests" (DFATD 2013a, 7–8), while Burkina Faso and the DRC were added as countries of focus in the revised 2014 list (see Table 5.1). This is consistent with the argument that the Harper government has been steadily bringing its aid policy in line with its commercial priorities. The minerals of greatest interest have been gold, copper, and to a lesser extent diamonds, though Canadian private sector activity spans a range of other resources as well.

This strong presence in Africa can be attributed to two factors. First, Africa's mining industry has experienced a renaissance in recent decades (Martineau 2005). Beginning in the 1980s with the imposition of Structural Adjustment Programs on much of the continent, African countries were strongly encouraged to liberalize their mining codes to attract foreign investment. Canada played an active role in advocating the liberalization of Africa's mining sector. For example, it was common practice for Canada, along with other OECD countries, to make its development assistance contingent on the acceptance of Structural Adjustment packages that required the liberalization of markets, including the extractive sector. With Ghana leading the way in 1984 by implementing a reformed mining code that protected property rights, streamlined concession processes, lowered taxes and royalties, and guaranteed the repatriation of profits, Africa has subsequently experienced an investment boom in this sector. By 2004, US$15 billion was invested in mining, representing 15 percent of the global market, compared with 5 percent in the mid-1980s. In 2012, Africa's share of world exploration investment was 15 percent, reflecting the ongoing global significance of the African mining sector (UNCTAD 2005; FIDH 2007; MEG 2012).

Second, the opening of African markets has been accompanied by a fundamental shift in the structure of the global mining industry, toward consolidation through mergers and acquisitions, but accompanied by the rise of junior exploration companies (Ericsson 2005). Responding to intense competitive pressures in the global market, mining companies have pursued growth through the rationalization of existing assets rather than developing new ones (Humphreys 2005). According to Ericsson, over US$150 billion was spent on mergers and acquisitions between 1995 and 2005. Despite such consolidation, however, the fundamental composition of the mineral industry remains highly fragmented, with larger companies controlling only 25 percent of the market by the middle of the last decade (Ericsson 2005). With very few monopolies in mineral markets, the industry is still highly competitive with companies seeking to increase their size and visibility in the market place. In this respect, it should be noted that as larger companies gain advantages in terms of access to capital for exploration and development, the fact that Canadian companies are poorly represented at the very top of the spectrum (i.e., the top 10) accentuates their vulnerability. This is particularly the case as smaller companies are generally prone to hostile takeover bids (Ericsson 2005)—a trend highlighted by the foreign takeover of Canadian "champions" like INCO, Falconbridge, and Alcan. Such foreign takeovers, while decreasing Canadian control of such companies, only create a greater incentive for Canada to promote the sector, particularly through the activities of Canadian-owned junior exploration companies as discussed below. At the same time, they underscore the difficulty of securing the cooperation of major extractive companies in collaborative, state-based policy-making processes orchestrated by the Canadian government.

More important in explaining Canada's strong presence in the African market, however, is that this period of consolidation and rationalization has been accompanied by a sharp decline in larger company exploration budgets. In particular, between 1997 and 2001, following the Asian financial crisis and the scandal created by Bre-X's fraudulent claims of gold finds, mineral exploration fell by 55 percent (Humphreys 2005). Although exploration recovered thereafter, at least prior to the world financial crisis of 2008–09, such drastic alterations point to the intense competitive pressures faced by mining companies in the global market. Paradoxically, market competition has also placed pressures on mining companies to expand their assets and diversify their risks. As Humphreys (2005) notes, investors in the mineral industry have demanded safer and more reliable returns forcing mining companies to diversify their geographical base by entering new markets, and their product base by mining more than one mineral. However, rather than engage in the risky business of exploration where millions can be spent with little or no return, larger companies have instead preferred to rely increasingly on the activities of junior exploration companies (Ericsson 2005; Campbell 1999). Such companies are generally more creative and entrepreneurial in their exploration activities. They also "tend to be less subject to controls, less prone to apply best practices and [more inclined] to operate in high risk [areas] and at times zones of conflict" (Campbell 2003, 7). When a commercially viable deposit is discovered, larger companies are then able to acquire concessions with known mineral reserves, thus reducing risk in expanding their assets.

It is in the rise of junior exploration companies that Canada has stood out globally. Exploration companies have been extremely successful in raising capital on Canadian stock exchanges.[11] Thus, Canada has become a hotbed for growth in mineral exploration activity in recent years, with important implications for Africa. It is innovative junior exploration companies that first took advantage of the newly liberalized economies of African nations and thus contributed to the boom in mining investment on the continent (Martineau 2005;

Roberts 2013a, 15). Prior to the 1980s, Africa's mineral wealth had remained largely unexplored due to the limited resources of African governments and the unattractive investment climate. This changed with the rise of the juniors—a development in which Canada has been instrumental—in parallel with the implementation of Structural Adjustment reforms (see Campbell 2009b).

While Canada's presence in the African mineral market is strong, it is not necessarily secure. In particular, Canadian companies have faced stiff competition from companies based in developing countries. Latin American companies have greatly increased their presence. Companies from India, and especially from China, are also increasingly prominent competitors in, for example, copper, iron ore, and base metals, as well as the energy sector. While India has been slowly privatizing its state-owned mining companies (Ericsson 2005), there is no such trend among Chinese companies. Thus, these companies remain important instruments of China's foreign policy and have been used extensively to increase its presence in Africa. Furthermore, the competitive pressure from countries such as India and China is heightened when issues of sustainable development are brought into the picture. According to Pring and Siegle, "[one of] the biggest factors to be faced by mining and other economic development efforts is the reorientation of international and national laws and regulatory frameworks to comply with the paradigm of 'sustainable development'" (2005, 129). While Canadian and other Western companies have faced growing pressure to conform to principles of sustainable development and corporate social responsibility, with potentially significant implications for their profit margins, Chinese and Indian companies have remained largely insulated from such demands.

In sum, Canadian extractive industries have become major players in both the global[12] and African mineral markets. Indeed, in contrast to the traditional developmental identity and "branding" efforts of the Canadian government, they are likely to be this country's dominant public face in many areas of the continent (Grayson 2006, 481; SCFAIT 2005). Yet, for most observers, the activities of Canadian and other countries' mining companies remain obscure. While it is *relatively* easy (though far from simple, given the remoteness of their mine sites) to track larger companies which generally attract more publicity and for which official statistics are kept, the activities of

smaller and junior companies are largely left to estimates and speculation. In short, despite growing publicity, scrutiny, and controversy,
particularly generated by civil society groups and academic research-
ers (e.g., *CJDS* 2010; NSI 2014), this crucial site of Canadian involvement in Africa continues to require more sustained and systematic
attention.

Canadian Government Assistance to the Mining Sector in Africa

While the forces of economic globalization, market liberalization,
and intense competition in commodity markets provide the basis
for increased activity of Canadian mining companies in Africa, the
Canadian government has also played a key role in enabling these
companies to secure a leading position in African markets (Campbell 1999; Keenan 2013). Notwithstanding Canada's comparatively
limited "reach" through trade commissioner services, noted above,
there are a number of ways in which agencies of the Canadian state
have provided robust support for Canadian extractive and other
industries in Africa and elsewhere, as well as to related exporters of
mining equipment and services. These include, first and foremost,
Export Development Canada (EDC), which provides a variety of support services including export finance, risk insurance, and market
information and analysis. Historically, the Canadian International
Development Agency provided direct support for the mining sector
in various African countries (notably Zambia and Zimbabwe) in the
context of its support for private sector development—identified as
one of five thematic priorities for the Agency in the 2005 *International
Policy Statement* and retained in the form of "Supporting Sustainable
Economic Growth" in the Conservatives' streamlined 2009 priority list. CIDA support for the extractive sector has been even more
extensive in Latin America, and has recently been amplified through
controversial new initiatives to support joint programs between Canadian development NGOs and extractive companies—initiatives to
which we will return later in the chapter (see Blackwood and Stewart
2012, 227–31). It also provided funding through the Canada Fund
for Africa, announced just prior to the 2002 Kananaskis Summit, for
the establishment of the Canada Investment Fund for Africa (CIFA).
The Fund was launched in April 2005 with a total capital subscription

of C$212 million raised jointly from the federal government and private sector investors. CIFA's stated aim was to provide risk capital for private investments in Africa that generate sustainable growth. Of its initial eight investments, totaling US$35 million, three were in the mining sector and a fourth in energy. By early 2009, CIFA had invested in six extractive sector projects, four of which were operated by Canadian or Canadian-listed companies (DFAIT 2009). Finally, the C$17 billion Canada Pension Plan (CPP) has been a significant investor in Canadian extractive industry operations overseas, including Africa.

In addition to financial and technical support, other federal agencies are very active in supporting the marketing and commercial "branding" efforts of Canadian extractive and mining supplies and equipment companies. For example, Natural Resources Canada (NRCan), DFAIT/DFATD, and the EDC have supported the promotional efforts of large delegations of Canadian firms at major trade shows and on trade missions. EDC and the Government of Canada (through DFAIT/DFATD, NRCan, and CIDA) have also provided both financial and advisory support to the Canadian Council on Africa, an energetic lobby group promoting business links between Canada and Africa.

All of these sources of support and financing for Canadian investors, with the exception of commercial branding efforts, articulate formal commitments to the promotion of CSR principles (although the Canada Pension Plan Investment Board's "Policy on Responsible Investing" was only issued in February 2007). Yet none give clear indications of *how* these commitments are to be discharged, beyond (in the case of CIDA, for example) encouraging compliance with the (voluntary) OECD Guidelines for Multinational Enterprises (see Blackwood 2006, 96; also Advisory Group 2007, 19). Similarly, the EDC is now committed to "working with the Government of Canada and other stakeholders to identify best practices, and to incorporate into its due diligence those practices that are relevant to the mandate of a financial institution" (DFAIT 2009, 13). It now publishes an annual CSR report and, in 2011, appointed a Chief CSR Advisor.[13] These are advances in the incorporation of CSR principles, but remain relatively vague and weak reeds, especially given the lack of transparency surrounding many of their disbursements and the decision making behind them (the EDC, for example, is not required to disclose its disbursements to the public). While legitimate considerations of commercial confidentiality must be taken into account, these practices reflect ongoing official reticence to actively foster, let alone *enforce*, CSR. Historically then, when developmental and security objectives have been threatened or compromised by Canadian commercial interests, the Canadian state has typically prioritized the needs of industry (see L. Freeman 1985).

Particularly in the era of the "competition state" (Cerny 1997), such state-based efforts to champion and "brand" its own globally oriented companies and investors are virtually inevitable. However, as the next section shows, many of these efforts can be linked to mining activities that have impacted negatively on security and development in various African and other localities. Given the lack of robust provisions to foster improved corporate social and environmental behaviour, there is a real danger that the Canadian "brand" is being tarnished in ways that negatively affect its long-term commercial interests. Moreover, the country's broader foreign-policy "brand" is also at risk of being seriously harmed by a lack of action on corporate behaviour that directly contradicts its stated development and security objectives, including those in the 2008 Official Development Assistance Accountability Act discussed in Chapter 5 (see Blackwood and Stewart 2012; Grayson 2006; E. Payne 2012).

Some Key Controversies Surrounding
Canadian Companies in Africa

Despite the lack of clear and reliable information on the conditions surrounding the operations of Canadian mining companies in Africa—indeed partly because of it—these operations have drawn a good deal of controversy and criticism, on human security, environmental, and developmental grounds. One of the defining features of the new global public domain, as articulated by Ruggie (2004), is that new regimes of accountability are emerging, in which various civil society and multi-stakeholder initiatives are more systematically holding private sector actors to account for the social and environmental effects of their activities. Corporations, for their part, are becoming more sensitive and responsive to this broadened conceptualization of their roles and responsibilities. Whether or not the specific controversies highlighted by Canadian civil society organizations are representative of widespread problems, they have increasingly tainted the sector as a whole, both within Canada and in Africa. The controversies sketched below have served as an important prod to multistakeholder efforts to forge a more advanced and robust approach to CSR issues in Canada. These examples also demonstrate the activities of transnationally networked civil society organizations in bringing extractive industry controversies to light, thus threatening Canada's increasingly tenuous security and development brand while exposing the Canadian state's propensity to privilege corporate interests.

By far the most celebrated controversy concerning Canadian resource companies in Africa is the case of Talisman Energy, which owned a 25 percent stake in the Greater Nile Petroleum Operating Company (GNPOC) between 1998 and 2002, along with the state-owned oil companies of China (40%), Malaysia (30%), and Sudan (5%). Although Talisman was operating in the energy sector, the lingering effects of this controversy had a major influence on subsequent debates concerning CSR in all extractive industries. Talisman's role within the GNPOC bears directly on the relationship between extractive industries and conflict, as GNPOC operations were widely seen as effectively helping to fuel the ongoing civil war "both by contributing to conflict over oil fields and by generating, for the Sudanese regime, revenue used to bankroll the war" (Forcese 2001, 41, 43). Indeed the report of the "Harker Commission," appointed by then Foreign Minister Lloyd Axworthy to investigate the situation, concluded in 2000 that: "There has been, and probably still is, major displacement of civilian populations related to oil extraction. Sudan is a place of extraordinary suffering and continuing human rights violations, even though some forward progress can be recorded, and the oil operations in which a Canadian company is involved add more suffering" (Harker 2000, 15). Despite this finding, and an earlier threat by Axworthy to impose economic sanctions "if it becomes evident that oil extraction is exacerbating the conflict" (cited in Drohan 2003, 266), the Canadian government ultimately retreated from this threat and merely exhorted Talisman to "ensure that their operations do not lead to an increase in tensions or otherwise contribute to the conflict" (Forcese 2001, 46; also Blackwood 2006). Craig Forcese argues that two interrelated factors explain the government's retreat. The first was "the potentially damaging (domestic political) consequences for the government of taking on, and possibly wounding, a key Canadian company" (see also Drohan 2003, 267). This political logic was reinforced by a narrow interpretation of the Special Economic Measures Act (SEMA), authorizing economic sanctions only on the basis of a decision by a multilateral organization to which Canada belongs or on the basis of a cabinet decision that the situation in question constitutes a "grave breach of international peace and security," "resulting, actually or prospectively, in a serious international crisis" (Forcese 2001, 51).

In the end, Talisman divested because of a diffuse combination of factors, including sustained negative publicity, a battered share price, and pending legal action under the Alien Torts Claims Act in the United States (for which no analogue exists in Canada, but which has influenced the CSR orientations of Canadian extractive companies because of its extraterritorial application—see Drimmer and Lieberman 2010). But the case highlights several enduring lessons. First, at the level of the Canadian political and bureaucratic establishment, there continue to be powerful disincentives to place meaningful pressure on Canadian corporations, regardless of the government in power. Second, the bases for promoting CSR have been vague and weak, being principally voluntary in nature and hampered by low levels of transparency and the absence of mechanisms for accountability. Third, sustained controversy orchestrated largely by highly motivated civil society organizations and coalitions, such as the Sudan Inter-Agency Reference Group and the Canadian Network on Corporate Accountability (CNCA), has created a political and public relations climate in which major Canadian extractive industries have become considerably more amenable to stronger and more transparent CSR measures, even if their strong preference continues to be for *voluntary* versus legislated ones. More broadly, the Talisman case illustrates how in some instances, Canadian private sector actors may have considerably greater impact on national and regional security prospects than the Canadian state. Particularly where the presence of the Canadian state is weak (as is increasingly the case in much of Africa), Canadian corporations should be understood as key foreign and security policy actors in their own right, interacting with other firms, states, and non-state actors (Stopford and Strange 1991; Dashwood 2012).

Similar conclusions can be reached concerning a second case bearing directly on high-intensity conflict. In 2002, a UN Security Council "Panel of Experts on the illegal exploitation of natural resources and other forms of wealth in the Democratic Republic of the Congo" named eight Canadian companies among eighty-five cited for violating the leading international standard for CSR—the OECD Guidelines for Multinational Enterprises. These and other companies protested vigorously, and their cause was taken up by their governments, who brought pressure to bear on the Security Council. The council then recommended a six-month renewal of the expert panel report to "verify, reinforce, and where necessary, update the Panel's findings, and/or clear parties named in the Panel's previous reports." Most named companies were subsequently taken off the list and the expert panel was stood down. Despite NGO efforts to pressure home governments to carry the investigations forward, the Canadian government disregarded all but one of the eight dossiers brought to its attention (see Freedman 2006–07, 111–14).

It is not possible in this chapter to probe the accusations made against these Canadian companies, operating in the midst of one of the most protracted and costly conflicts in the world. The general point, however, is that there was no clear and robust basis for investigating these allegations and that, in the absence of such provisions, the Canadian government effectively came to the defence of its corporate citizens without any apparent attempt to seriously probe the charges levelled against them. Ironically, the ultimate impression created by this case, of vague but serious allegations and of a government that appeared unwilling to hold its own corporations to account, reinforced the popular notion that wrongdoing is commonplace and that stronger measures are required.

It is not surprising that the lion's share of attention regarding potential corporate misconduct has focused on the most extreme cases, operating in situations of armed conflict (see Drohan 2003; Böge et al. 2006). Yet there are many more "routine" cases that, while less dramatic, bear directly on the controversies concerning the social, developmental, and environmental implications of Canadian extractive industry investments in Africa. Moreover, because these extractive operations are often linked to social and economic polarization, rising criminality, and community disruption and dislocation, they can be seen as undermining human security in its more routine sense, along with the more acute examples noted above.

Several controversial cases have occurred in donor "favourites" and core Canadian development partners, such as Ghana, Tanzania, and Mali. For example, a 2005 report of the Third World Network—Africa Secretariat highlighted several Ghanaian controversies. These included the precipitous liquidation of Bonte Gold Mines in 2004, "leaving behind un-reclaimed degraded land, unpaid compensation, and a debt of about US$18 million" (Darimani 2005, 2). This closure, the report went on, resulted in a triple loss for local communities, through environmental degradation, uncompensated destruction of farms and land, and the failure to engage in any social responsibility projects in the vicinity of the mine. More broadly, the report highlighted the role of Canadian mining companies in successfully lobbying the Ghanaian government to allow surface mining in the country's dwindling forest reserves. And even more broadly, the policy environment that helped foster the country's current mining boom, in which Canadian companies have been major players, has been so liberal and beneficial to the foreign-owned companies that dominate the sector that some analysts argue it has been of no help in addressing poverty at either the community or country-wide level (Amevor 2007; Akabzaa 2009).

Over the past two decades, Tanzania has also experienced a mining boom in which Canadian companies have been major players. It too has sought to advance this boom with the adoption of a highly liberalized mining code incorporating very favourable terms and conditions for foreign-owned companies (Campbell 2003). And it too is the site of controversy, notably surrounding the Bulyanhulu and North Mara Gold Mines, both now owned by one of Canada's largest mining corporations and the world's largest gold producer, Barrick Gold, through its subsidiary, African Barrick. The company's investments have been strongly supported by financing from government agencies. In the case of Bulyanhulu, for example, it received C$173 million in political risk insurance from the Export Development Corporation and C$351 million from the Canada Pension Plan. Under previous owners Sutton Resources (also a Canadian company), artisanal miners were forcibly evicted from the concession area by Tanzanian troops in 1996, and allegations of large numbers of deaths continue to swirl around the initial development of this lucrative mining operation (Halifax Initiative 2006). In the case of North Mara, the development of the mine reportedly resulted in the displacement and relocation of roughly 10,000 families, and displaced thousands of artisanal miners who used to work the area. In their place, so-called "intruders" seek to scavenge gold from the mine's tailings, and chronic skirmishes with local police have resulted in numerous injuries and even deaths (see York 2011).

On a smaller scale, the Sadiola Gold Mine in Mali, owned since 2009 by IAMGOLD Corp. (41%) along with AngloGold Ashanti (41%) and the government of Mali (18%), and supported by a significant (C$38 million) investment from the CPP, resulted in the displacement of two villages with inadequate replacement land, scarce water resources, and environmental degradation from the mine. These costs have been exacerbated by rising social problems (prostitution, alcoholism, drug use, and the spread of HIV/AIDS) related to the arrival of the mine and its workers (Halifax Initiative 2006). Indeed, a thorough report on the impact of the gold mining industry in Mali by the *Fédération Internationale des Ligues des Droits de l'Homme* (FIDH 2007) provided a detailed analysis of how and why, despite the wealth generated by this industry, Mali remains one of the poorest countries in the world, while the impact of the most important mines has been largely detrimental in human rights and environmental terms. These ongoing developmental shortfalls are a crucial part of the backdrop to the growing instability and violence in the country, which in turn prompted the January 2013 French-led international security operation with Royal Canadian Air Force (RCAF) participation (e.g., Siebert 2013; Roberts 2013b).

Finally, the Third World Network—Africa Secretariat report cited above reflects the widely held view that Canadian government representatives in African countries are in effect advocates and facilitators for their country's mining companies, with no mandate and little inclination to investigate claims of corporate misconduct in a determined and even-handed way. The author of the report, Adbulai Darimani, writes: "The foreign missions of the Canadian government are believed to be stop-shops for corporate lobby and it is now an open secret that CIDA has been playing the role of clearinghouse for negotiating investment deals through technical and financial support" (Darimani 2005, 7). As I will discuss in the next section, little has changed since this report was originally published to alter this impression, and indeed some new initiatives firmly reinforce it.

Without much more extensive research and analysis, including systematic and specific case studies, it is impossible to assess conclusively these reports of corporate irresponsibility and government complicity, and to determine how widespread these issues are.[14] But it is precisely the inability or unwillingness to probe such allegations, and hold Canadian mining companies accountable for their social, developmental, and environmental records, that feeds the impression that problems are widespread and that the government as well as many mining companies have something to hide. These examples also demonstrate the historic disconnect between foreign economic policy (i.e., investment and trade promotion) and a putatively human-security-focused development agenda (whether or not the notion of human security is used to describe it). While Canada's official position has been that market-friendly economic development is a key condition for enhancing human security and development, it is hard to see how the examples noted above can be reconciled with the people-centred emphasis of these ideas. In this light, developments in the new global public domain have led to more systematic pressures (mainly from civil society) to address these crucial regulatory and accountability gaps, a more responsive disposition toward these pressures from some leading corporate interests, and a growing willingness on the part of governmental interests to address these non-state instigated trends. Yet the choices made about *how to* address these pressures and issues tell us a great deal about the sources of influence in Canadian policy-making, and the relative explanatory power of the frames introduced in Chapter 1. In particular, they allow us to compare the relative influence of good international citizenship on the one hand, and nationally and transnationally hegemonic interests and ideas on the other.

Addressing Demands for Corporate Social Responsibility: The Limits of Good International Citizenship

Stimulated by the rapidly growing presence of Canadian extractive industries in the developing world and the escalating controversies surrounding their presence, the Canadian Parliament's Standing Committee on Foreign Affairs and International Trade (SCFAIT) issued a short report on *Mining in Developing Countries—Corporate Social Responsibility* in June 2005. Having been exposed through its hearings to various examples of Canadian mining companies' connections with insecurity, environmental destruction, and social disruption in the developing world, the committee's report made a number of recommendations concerning stronger incentives, strengthened monitoring, new legal norms, and enhanced governmental support for improved corporate social responsibility. Predictably, given its historic predisposition on this issue, the Liberal federal government of the day rejected all but one of the Committee's recommendations. This one, however—that the government "put in place a process involving relevant industry associations, non-governmental organizations and experts, which will lead to the strengthening of existing programmes and policies in this area and, where necessary, to the establishment of new ones" (SCFAIT 2005, 2)—contained the seeds of a potentially substantial reorientation of the Canadian approach.

Drawing on this opening, officials within the Department of Foreign Affairs and International Trade moved to establish an Inter-Departmental Steering Committee involving representatives of eight government agencies plus DFAIT as chair.[15] A parallel non-governmental Advisory Group was also created. Its seventeen members included leading representatives of civil society organizations associated with the CNCA, influential representatives of the private sector (including senior executives of the Prospectors and Developers Association of Canada, the Mining Association of Canada, and Talisman Energy), representatives of ethical investment funds, and leading scholars. The Steering Committee then collaborated with the Advisory Group to organize four National Roundtables in Vancouver, Toronto, Calgary, and Montreal (the major centres for extractive companies in Canada) from June through November of 2006. These roundtables focused on five themes arising out of the SCFAIT report: CSR Standards and Best Practices, Incentives for Implementation of CSR Standards, Assistance to Companies to Implement CSR Standards and Best Practices, CSR Monitoring and Dispute Resolution, and Capacity Building for Resource Governance in Developing Countries (Advisory Group 2007, 1). In March of 2007, the Advisory Group (independent of, but with support from, the intra-governmental Steering Committee) issued a Consensus Report—no small feat given the very different interests involved. This report was to form the basis for a memo to Cabinet, jointly submitted by CIDA, International Trade, Natural Resources Canada, and Foreign Affairs, with Cabinet taking the final decision on how to respond to the Advisory Group's recommendations. One of the report's recommendations, that Canada join the Extractive Industries Transparency

Initiative (EITI), was adopted by the government prior to its release, reportedly over the objections of at least one senior official in Natural Resources Canada.[16] There was thus a palpable sense of excitement and momentum surrounding the Advisory Group's report in the weeks after it was issued, though the long ensuing delay in the government's response dampened this.

Substantively, the Consensus Report made a wide range of recommendations that, in the view of the civil society–based Canadian Network on Corporate Accountability, "would establish Canada as a global leader in Corporate Social Responsibility" (CNCA 2007, 1). At its heart was the proposal to establish a Canadian CSR Framework that would: set clear standards and reporting obligations for Canadian companies; reference international human rights standards and provide for the creation of human rights guidelines for the application of CSR standards; create an ombudsman's office, overseen by a tripartite monitoring and advisory group, to receive complaints regarding the operations of Canadian companies and assess corporate compliance with the standards; and include a provision for withholding government services from companies in cases of serious non-compliance. Among the other significant features of the Advisory Group's recommendations were: steps toward greater transparency and fuller disclosure of support for Canadian companies by agents of the Canadian government, such as the CIFA, EDC, and the CPP; support for industry association tools and civil society capacity building, within Canada and in host countries; and initiatives to support contributions of the extractive sector to host government development priorities, through governance and judicial system support and engagement with regional and multinational instruments and initiatives. Finally, the report advocated a process for ongoing study, scrutiny, and refinement through, for example, a proposal to create a Government CSR Centre of Excellence and a Canadian Extractive Sector Advisory Group. In principle then, these proposals would have had the potential to, at least, hold Canadian companies accountable for significant human rights/security abuses arising from their operations and, at most, promote more broadly based, sustainable, and developmentally oriented results from their investments.

Several distinctive features of both the process and outcome of the National Roundtables are noteworthy, analytically and theoretically. First, the process provides a good illustration of what Dashwood, following Ruggie (2004), highlights as the "reconstituted global public domain" shaped by the interaction between civil society actors and multinational corporations, alongside states (Dashwood 2007, 133).[17] The Roundtable process, aimed toward the production of a new public good (enhanced CSR) among both Canadian companies and host governments but also closely attuned to transnational trends and demonstration effects, *required* the full participation of corporate, civil society, and state participants. In this regard, the Roundtable process revealed the emergence of a substantial degree of common ground between at least some larger mining companies and their representatives, and civil society organizations that have been sharply critical of corporate misconduct.[18] While subsequent developments have clearly demonstrated the limits of this common ground, and the degree of apprehension and mistrust that persists, the process revealed significant movement on both sides.[19]

In particular, major mining corporations have increasingly come to an understanding that their own long-term self-interest, including secure access to resources, depends on their ability to demonstrate good corporate conduct: "While there has been a distinct emphasis on minimizing the negative environmental impacts of extractive-sector activities, in recent years the sector has begun addressing social issues. A number of companies have started referring to their need for a 'social license' to operate" (Advisory Group 2007, 7). To some extent, this has resulted from the punishing experiences of negative exposure faced by some firms. It is surely no accident, for example, that a senior Talisman executive was a key participant in the Roundtable process. Moreover, scholars and analysts have noted "an increasing tide of resource nationalism" (Roberts 2013a, 16) within developing countries, in view of the disappointing developmental effects of the mining boom, that has exacerbated the pressure on extractive companies. But their evolving understanding also reflects a longer-term process of dialogue and learning among "mining majors" that has been unfolding, albeit unevenly, among a handful of Canadian mining companies for at least a couple of decades (Dashwood 2005 and 2007).

At the intra-governmental level, the Roundtable process highlighted the old lesson that one needs to pay close attention to the varying interests and orientations of different government agencies, and elements within them, in order to understand both processes and outcomes (L. Freeman 1985). It also highlighted a new willingness among some in government to accept a more expansive conception of the state's responsibility in relation to its corporate citizens. In this case, the initiative was taken by officials within the then Global Issues Bureau of the Department of Foreign Affairs—a particular corner of this department with a strong focus on human security issues and with responsibility for Canadian involvement in the Kimberley Process addressing "conflict diamonds." The other eight government departments and agencies involved in the Roundtable process represented a wide range of perspectives—some quite supportive of a stronger approach to CSR issues, and others (according to first-hand accounts) taking positions that were more recalcitrant than the industry representatives on the Advisory Group. In particular, and predictably, EDC and NRCan tended to take far more skeptical and status quo–oriented positions. However, the fact that the civil society and industry representatives in the group were able to arrive at a consensus position clearly increased the political impact of their report. It also indicated that, consistent with Ruggie's conception of the new public domain, initiative and leadership have in some instances at least increasingly shifted away from state-based institutions toward diverse combinations of non-state actors.

Moreover, it is significant that the Advisory Group recommendations were closely attuned to important transnational trends and instruments. For example, the report recommended that the Government of Canada adopt the International Finance Corporation (IFC) Performance Standards and the Voluntary Principles on Security and Human Rights as its initial framework standards, while developing guidance notes and pursuing the further evolution of principles, guidelines, best practices, and measurable performance criteria in relation to both the Canadian CSR Framework and "international multi-stakeholder initiatives." Similarly, it advocated adopting the non-governmental Global Reporting Initiative (GRI) or "GRI-equivalent reporting" as the Canadian CSR Framework reporting component, while supporting the development of GRI "sector supplements" where necessary—for example, regarding the oil and gas sector and junior exploration companies (Advisory Group 2007, iv–vi). In short, the Canadian process was strongly influenced by, and in turn aspired

to influence, key transnational, multi-stakeholder initiatives to promote and deepen CSR norms, standards, and procedures. In this
sense it can be seen, once again, as firmly nested within the "reconstituted global public domain."

The Roundtable process and Advisory Group Consensus Report
can therefore be seen as innovative and promising. More to the point
of this book, they were consistent with a solidarist conception of good
international citizenship. Taken together, they would have obliged
Canadian "corporate citizens," their owners, and their employees
to bring their practices into conformity with international laws on
human rights and respect for the environment. They would have
established clear standards to which companies and their officials
should be held and a process by which this would happen. While
the proposed process can hardly be described as draconian, it was
underpinned by the prospect of real, material sanctions (loss of government support) as well as the prospect of negative publicity, as a
concrete incentive for improved corporate behaviour. In this manner, deliberate steps would be taken in an effort to directly ensure
that in the course of their operations, Canadian mining companies
did as much as possible to advance the "common weal"—or at least as
little as possible to damage it.

However the government's response, when it finally came some
two years after the report in March 2009, took a different approach.
"Building the Canadian Advantage" (DFAIT 2009) eschewed the
adoption of clear Canadian CSR standards, instead committing only
to promote various international CSR performance guidelines with
Canadian extractive companies operating abroad. Similarly, while
the Advisory Group's proposed accountability process was anchored
by an ombudsman with robust investigative authority, the government's response created a much weaker "Extractive Sector CSR
Counsellor" that "will only undertake reviews with the consent of the
involved parties" (DFAIT 2009, 11; see also CNCA 2009). The overall
approach shifted from one of even-handedly assessing and enhancing the CSR performance of Canadian extractives, to supporting
and facilitating the taken-for-granted "entrepreneurial advantage"
and CSR "leadership" of these companies and their industry associations. In sum, the government strategy marked a clear retreat from
the most important accountability mechanisms recommended in
the Advisory Group Report, and clearly indicated that the default

position for government continued to be to support and enable the international operations of Canadian corporate citizens, enhancing their "competitive advantage" by improving "their ability to manage social and environmental risk" (DFAIT 2009, 4). In this respect, government policy was brought firmly into line with the hegemonic preferences of the majority of private-sector mining companies, and their allies within the state.

Two subsequent decision points reinforced this direction. First, in October 2010, the then-minority House of Commons narrowly defeated a private member's bill (C-300) introduced by Liberal MP John McKay, entitled *An Act Respecting Corporate Accountability for the Activities of Mining, Oil or Gas in Developing Countries.* The Act would have effectively reinstated the standard-setting and accountability measures advocated by the Advisory Group of the National Roundtables (see Keenan 2013; Simons and Macklin 2010). It was defeated by six votes after vigorous lobbying from representatives of the mining industry, and as a result of divisions within the Liberal party and strategic absences by MPs from other parties. The consequence was that the government's soft and voluntary approach to mining company CSR was reconfirmed.

Then, in late 2011, International Cooperation Minister Bev Oda announced several pilot projects through which CIDA would spend C$6.7 million over five and a half years to partner with three Canadian development NGOs (Plan Canada, WUSC, and World Vision) and three of the country's largest mining companies (Barrick Gold, IAMGOLD, and Rio Tinto Alcan) to co-fund skills-training and capacity-building projects in communities near the companies' mine sites. Two of the projects were in Africa (in Ghana and Burkina Faso), while a third was in Peru (CIDA 2011b; Leblanc 2012; Coumans 2012). Introduced against the backdrop of CIDA de-funding of civil society groups that had been critical of government policies, as discussed in Chapter 5, the new projects elicited extensive controversy and were widely seen as further evidence and elaboration of the government's policy bias toward the interests of the extractive sector. By publicly supporting the CSR activities of some of the country's most profitable corporations in ways that could be construed as "buying" local support without ensuring robust accountability, these pilot projects can be seen as further evidence of the hegemonic tilt in government policy toward Canadian mining companies.

Conclusions

The logic and recommendations of the Advisory Group Report and similar initiatives like Bill C-300, redolent of good international citizenship, will continue to be challenged from at least two perspectives. From the right, advocates of market liberalism, in mining and elsewhere, will express doubts about the negative effects of a more intrusive regulatory regime for CSR, whether legislated or not. As Philip Crowson argues for example, "Mining is primarily an economic activity and a form of wealth creation ... Codes of Conduct to regulate how mining companies behave ... might create new problems, stultifying innovation and freezing corporate structures" (2005, 607–8). From the left, scholars in the tradition of radical political economy will be highly skeptical of a framework that holds out the promise of enhancing the social and political legitimacy of foreign-owned mining and energy industries in Africa that, on the historical evidence, have extracted vast wealth from the continent while leaving a legacy of large-scale ecological degradation, social dislocation, and the enrichment of despotic elites (e.g., Bond 2006). From this perspective, initiatives like the Roundtable process should be understood as corporate "bluewash" masking the fundamental continuities in webs of exploitation—particularly so if they serve, in effect, to produce delay and prevarication.

In practice, and historically speaking, the views of those on the right have typically prevailed in policy terms, overriding the consistent operationalization of human-rights-oriented accountability reforms let alone the more radical critiques and prescriptions of critical scholars and activists. In other words, the preferences and imperatives of hegemonic interests have prevailed over a more transparent and accountable approach, within and/or beyond Canada. Yet given the dynamics of the new global public domain, there is no reason to expect the resulting controversies to recede; indeed all evidence points to the contrary. Measures aiming to ensure better corporate conduct and social, environmental, and developmental outcomes in the extractive sector, particularly in fragile and conflict-affected countries, will be exceptionally difficult and will involve a good deal of ongoing experimentation and revision (see Arimatsu and Mistry 2012). The importance of the developmental effects of Canadian mining extractives in Africa suggest that the ongoing

Canadian debate will continue to resonate strongly elsewhere, with important ramifications for the African communities and countries where they work and for the reputation of the Canadian state within which they are domiciled. This is an area where, given the overlap of Canadian investment, development, security, and human rights roles, the Canadian government *should be* exercising leadership. The lesson of the Roundtable process is that, to date, it has retreated from such a role, viewing the interests and preferences of Canadian corporations as its primary concern.

One thing can be reliably anticipated however. Because the role of the Canadian extractive sector in Africa continues to disrupt and challenge the embedded narrative of Canada's ethical orientation in continental affairs (that is, as a comparatively good or virtuous state), it will continue to elicit acute controversy. The heated political and media debates over the relatively small CIDA projects announced in 2011 as joint undertakings between prominent NGOs and major Canadian extractive companies is indicative. It reflected both the deep discomfiture of many Canadians with the jarring combination of Canadian official aid, humanitarian aid organizations, and the CSR activities of some of the country's most profitable corporations, and longer-term concern that these "pilot projects" portended the "recommercialization" and hence corruption of the Canadian aid program more broadly (see S. Brown 2014). These are important concerns, as elaborated in the conclusion. Nevertheless, the breadth and intensity of the reaction in this country also underscored the deep attachment many Canadians retain to an image of our collective role in sub-Saharan Africa that aspires to a purity of purpose that can never be approached in the real world of politics.

Chapter

Conclusion: Africa Policy and the End of Liberal Internationalism?

Throughout this book two key questions have recurred: What is the nature and magnitude of the changes in Africa policies and practices rendered by the Harper Conservative government? And do these changes portend a decisive long-term shift in, and diminution of, Canada's involvement with the continent?

The questions are not easy to answer, for several reasons. First, as emphasized throughout the foregoing analysis, Canada's involvement in Africa has regularly cycled through phases of more and less interest and attention. It is easy in this context to overestimate the degree of change and underestimate the likelihood of reversion to what is portrayed at any given point in this cycle as the *status quo ante*. Indeed, as noted at the beginning of this book, there have been tentative signs for the past several years of a reawakening of high-level political interest in Africa from the Harper government. Moreover, despite the various changes to Canadian aid policy discussed in Chapter 5, data compiled for the 2013 *Canadian International Development Platform* of the North-South Institute shows that, with the precipitous decline in aid to both Afghanistan and Haiti, Ethiopia became the largest recipient of Canadian bilateral aid in 2012 and African "partners" were three of the government's top five recipients.[1] In its share of total aid spending, Africa has never dropped below 38 percent since the Harper government came to office, and it reached 42 percent in 2012. Therefore, charges of "abandonment" need to be carefully parsed.

Second, as Kim Nossal (2012) has emphasized, the government has given analysts very little to work with by way of clearly developed articulations of its foreign, security, and development policy approach. There has been no foreign or development policy white paper, and policy statements and speeches have tended to be (as is their wont) spare, vague, and platitudinous. The policy process has been opaque and secretive, resulting in abrupt announcements of course changes with limited consultative processes typically following rather than preceding them—as seen, for example, in the decision-making on the government's response to the National Roundtables on Corporate Social Responsibility (DFAIT 2009), new CIDA "countries of focus" and thematic priorities, and the March 2013 decision to merge CIDA with DFAIT.

Third, the government has clearly succeeded in placing discursive distance between itself and the old thematic frames and phrases of its Liberal and Progressive Conservative predecessors. As Nossal (2012, 30; also Carrier-Sabourin and Tiessen 2012; and Paris, 2014) notes, touchstones of Canadian liberal internationalism with strong relevance for Africa—human security, the Responsibility to Protect, gender equality, etc.—have been systematically displaced from government statements and sources. The government's approach to "Africa" has served as a key marker of partisan difference, as reflected in major speeches by leaders of both the Liberal and New Democratic Parties (Ignatieff 2010; Mulcair 2013), with opposition politicians excoriating the government for its indifference toward the continent. Yet it remains unclear how much these discursive differences represent, and/or portend, real change in policies on the ground, and an abiding difference in world view that is likely to become entrenched in practice. Certainly, if the statements and speeches of opposition leaders are to be believed, either party would revert to some variant of the mythologized "open and progressive multilateralism that enabled Canada to be such an effective middle power" (Mulcair 2013), including a renewed engagement with Africa. Yet whether such a reversion could be easily and credibly engineered also depends on how firmly entrenched any new approaches have become under the Conservatives. How, then, are we to understand the nature and durability of the changes made during the past seven years?

One way of approaching this question is through the three theoretical frames that have guided this study. In short, to what extent, and in what ways, has the Conservative approach to Africa reflected changes in Canadian aspirations toward good international citizenship, its inclination toward hegemonic middlepowermanship, and the narrative framing of Canada's ethical identity through portrayals of its engagement with Africa?

Africa, the Harper Conservatives, and Good International Citizenship

In a 2009 study entitled *Global Good Samaritans*, Alison Brysk argued that Canada is one of a handful of countries that exemplify "global good citizenship," helping "to construct and expand the international human rights regime, the thin layer of international understandings, institutions, and exchanges that seek to protect individual human dignity from abuses of power" (Brysk 2009, 4). Canada, she argued, was "a stalwart of the United Nations system [that] has also participated enthusiastically in a plethora of regional and functional international institutions" (2009, 67). She summarized by stating that "Canada's humane internationalist potential as a deeply democratic and highly globalized middle power was activated by progressive elites and a supportive civil society, animated by cosmopolitan values and a benign form of liberal nationalism. Canada's international projection has strengthened democracy at home and abroad, and contributed to the construction of the international human rights regime" (2009, 93). While Brysk doesn't use the English School vocabulary of "solidarist good international citizenship," what she conceives as global good citizenship is very close to the essence of this approach. Her identification of the Canadian government as an exemplar of this approach, with strong public and civil society support, helps clarify what has and has not changed under the Harper government.

First, it must be said that Brysk's characterization of Canadian "global good citizenship" captures the rhetoric, but overstates the results of Canadian activism toward Africa during the Axworthy and late Chrétien years. As discussed in Chapter 3, this surge of activism represented a kind of redemptive reaction to the dereliction that had preceded it, and was severely under-supported in terms of the human and material resources required for meaningful sustainability, notably on human security issues and causes like the Responsibility to Protect (see Chapter 6; also Nossal 1998–99).

Second, however, it is clear that the techniques underpinning the Canadian "human rights foreign policy" that Brysk seeks to capture have been largely disavowed by the Harper Conservatives. While the Conservatives have become, if anything, even more vigorous in their human rights rhetoric than their predecessors (e.g., Baird 2012), their "principled foreign policy" is directly linked to a deeply skeptical and limited view of multilateralism, and a wariness of many of the civil society organizations that were key allies in the Axworthy-era promotion of human security. Their approach is much more focused on bilateralism and/or targeted "coalitions of the willing," as exemplified by Foreign Minister John Baird's argument that, "by working with our friends and allies, by building ad hoc coalitions with those who share our end goals and by using multilateral connections, we amplify our values exponentially" (2012).

How does this bear on policies toward Africa? Previous Canadian governments' deep attachment to various manifestations of inclusive multilateralism—notably the UN, the Commonwealth, and la Francophonie—have been vital in creating both motive and opportunity for Canadian engagement with African governments and issues. Since recently decolonized African member states constituted the single largest membership bloc in each of these organizations, a concern with their organizational viability necessitated a concern with the interests, priorities, and aspirations of their African membership. Multilateral forums have also been crucial venues for "entrepreneurial leadership" on institutional and normative innovations bearing particularly (though controversially) on the human security of Africans, such as R2P and the International Criminal Court. Similarly, CIDA's and, to a lesser extent, DFAIT's extensive collaboration with NGOs and CSOs greatly magnified "Canada's" presence and profile on the continent. And it has been through this country's routine participation in UN-sanctioned peace operations that the Canadian Forces have been regularly called upon to exercise what in Chapter 6 was characterized as *good enough* international citizenship. Thus, the Harper government's skeptical, limited, and instrumental approach to both multilateralism and civil society significantly reduces the foundations for exposure to, and engagement with, Africa.

Another factor compounding the Conservatives' diminished inclination toward good international citizenship in Africa is the comparative absence of what in Chapter 4 were characterized as

Africa-oriented "iconic internationalists" in its inner circle. Within the (Progressive) Conservative tradition in Canada, there are certainly a number of figures who could have performed this role in popularizing and naturalizing the narrative of Canadian ethical leadership vis-à-vis Africa—for example, Flora MacDonald, Joe Clark, or even Brian Mulroney. But these and others of the more or less "Red Tory" persuasion have been marginalized within and/or withdrawn from the reinvented Conservatives.

There are a number of ways of explaining the Conservatives' diminished interest in policies associated with good international citizenship in Africa. A first, more theoretical, explanation is that there is a current of thinking within the Conservative government that simply does not accept the idea that the world can, or should, move in a more cosmopolitan, solidaristic direction. In other words, this current is much more inclined to see international society in the pluralist terms outlined in Chapter 1, with states-as-citizens lacking the common values, interests, will, and ability to act on the more cosmopolitan imperatives associated with the ideas of, among others, human security and R2P (see Boucher 2012). From this perspective, the solidarist flourishes associated with the human security agenda, for example, are not merely unrealistic and undesirable, but potentially dangerous (Bain 1999). Closely related to this is the Conservatives' inclination to understand the portion of international society that truly *matters* to Canada—that with which there is a real harmony of interests and world views—in relatively exclusive terms, confined primarily to the circle of Western liberal democracies (in which they pointedly include Israel). This inclination is reflected in Foreign Minister Baird's (2012) preferred conception of multilateralism as working with friends and allies in ad hoc "coalitions of the willing."

A narrower explanation of the Conservatives' retreat from solidarist good international citizenship in Africa is partisan—that is, that they have sought to use foreign policy, notably though not only toward Africa, in an effort to redefine the party political spectrum in Canada with the Conservatives at its centre. From this perspective, policies and principles closely associated with the Liberal "brand," including activism in Africa, have been marginalized as part of a wider effort to displace the erstwhile "natural governing party" (Nossal 2012). Alternatively, and more narrowly still, Adam Chapnick (2011–12) has argued that what the Conservatives most wish to expunge, in foreign policy at least, is not so much the Liberals writ large as Lloyd Axworthy's cosmopolitan, "soft power" agenda. Either way, Africa has been used to reframe the narrative of Canada in the world—a theme to which I will return.

It would be wrong, however, to suggest that the Conservatives have no interest in being perceived as good international citizens, or projecting "their" Canada as a "good state." As Julia Gallagher (2011) has shown, virtually every government has a need to project a sense of moral purpose, both to its own citizens and to the world. Having disavowed many of the touchstones of the old "Liberal internationalist" order (see Paris, 2014), the Harper government has had some difficulty settling on issues with which to achieve this purpose. Beyond its pro-Israel tilt in the Middle East and its categorical stand against Iran—both controversial and divisive, at home and abroad—its long-promised agency for the promotion of democracy has never seen the light of day (Gurzu 2011). The Office of Religious Freedom established in February 2013 could be a means of engaging important, faith-related sources of tension and conciliation in West and Central Africa (in Nigeria and CAR, for example) as well as many other parts of the world, but only if its efforts were coordinated with substantial and sophisticated diplomatic capacities. Since the latter have been severely cut by the government, the Office and its new Ambassador are best understood as an effort to enhance the Conservatives' domestic political appeal among conservative faith-based groups and ethnic minorities (see Simpson 2013; Carment 2013).

By far the most serious and sustained undertaking from the Conservatives aimed at "ameliorating the common weal," primarily though not exclusively in Africa, has been the Muskoka Initiative (MI) on Maternal, Newborn, and Child Health (MNCH), launched as the ethical hallmark of the Muskoka G8 Summit in June 2010.[2] As noted in Chapter 2, the MI committed the government to providing C\$1.1 billion in new funding for MNCH initiatives, as part of a wider international effort that ultimately generated more than C\$7 billion in new funding. Government leaders routinely invoke this initiative as emblematic of its "values-based" foreign policy (e.g., Baird 2012).[3] This was in many respects a good and well-chosen focus, since the maternal and child health improvements targeted in Millennium Development Goals (MDGs) 4 and 5 are of all MDGs the furthest from being achieved,[4] and Canada has the capacity and expertise to provide a necessary infusion of high-level, state-based leadership in these areas. As discussed in Chapter 2, however, the MI was hampered from the outset by a late start and poor preparation, which undermined the government's potential to lead by example. More seriously, the juxtaposition of substantial new investments in MNCH with the freezing, and then cutting, of the aid program as a whole was internally contradictory, since sustained improvements in MNCH outcomes require long-term health system strengthening as well as poverty alleviation, for which high-quality development assistance can be instrumental. Finally, the government's confusion on whether it would support family planning under the initiative, and its refusal to allow MI funding to be used in support of safe, legal abortions, not only placed it at odds with the governments of the US and the UK as well as the weight of public opinion in Canada, but undermined the relevance of the initiative since unsafe abortions and lack of access to family planning are among the main causes of maternal mortality and morbidity (WHO and UNICEF 2012, 19). The fact that the government was applying a different standard to the reproductive health of poor women in developing countries than it was prepared to apply to women in Canada led Carrier-Sabourin and Tiessen to characterize this Initiative as a manifestation of "hypocritical internationalism" (2012). While the MI will provide tangible assistance to many women and children, therefore, the sustainability of its gains are doubtful given its time-limited character and weak integration with the aid program as a whole, as well as the absence of an appropriately gendered analysis of the obstacles to women's reproductive health.[5]

In the final analysis, the recurring instances of Canadian good international citizenship in Africa, though admirable in intent, have always been too limited, too intermittent, and too time-bound to be considered a defining characteristic of this country's presence on the continent. What has *changed* under the Harper Conservatives is the diminished aspiration (or pretension) to play this role, and the government's retreat from some of the principal means of doing so— particularly inclusive multilateralism and a constructive, responsive relationship with a wide range of civil society organizations. Nevertheless, periodic ethically oriented initiatives, like the MI, the campaign for the protection of civilians in armed conflict, and Canada's

support for AMIS in Darfur, have helped to sustain a positive reputation that has been instrumental in the second explanatory frame
deployed in this book.

Africa, the Harper Conservatives, and Hegemonic Middlepowermanship

Throughout the foregoing analysis, we have seen evidence of the various ways in which Canadian policy and practice has both reflected and
contributed, however modestly, to the wider aspirations of hegemonic
order-building in relation to Africa. This tendency can be seen, for
example, in its G8 diplomacy, its contributions to military and peacekeeping training, its responsiveness to transnationally orchestrated
priorities of Structural Adjustment and "Aid Effectiveness" in the international aid regime, and its promotion of liberalized mining codes
and voluntary corporate social responsibility over a more transparent
and enforceable approach to improved extractive industry performance with regard to human and environmental rights. Indeed, I have
argued that Western "secondary" or "middle powers" have had a distinctive role to play in this process of hegemonic order building, given
their relatively benign image and non-directive approach.

The Harper government's involvement in Africa presents a mixed
picture in relation to this frame. With regard to the interface between
the extractive sector and development assistance, it has pursued a
more openly and aggressively self-interested approach, while arguing
for the developmental benefits of this approach in Africa and working to construct a hegemonic frame within which to situate support
for Canadian extractive companies. In the security domain it has, in
contrast, evinced caution and reticence, as reflected in its approach
to the 2013 crisis and intervention in Mali. Yet in both cases, its
behaviour has manifested substantial continuities with past practice,
accompanied by a retreat from the order-building aspirations of previous Canadian governments.

Few of the Conservative government's policy departures bearing
on Africa have sparked more heated controversy than the 2011 decision to provide CIDA funding for three CSR-related pilot projects,
delivered by Canadian NGDOs in collaboration with three of the country's largest mining companies (Barrick, IAMGOLD, and Rio Tinto
Alcan), in communities adjacent to these companies' operations in

Peru, Burkina Faso, and Ghana. These initiatives, "fast-tracked" at a time when traditional, long-standing CIDA-NGO partnerships were withering, provided a clear indication of the government's desire to pursue closer integration between its foreign and trade policy objective of advancing the interests of Canadian extractive companies, and its development assistance policies with key African and Latin American "partners." Since this initial opening, Minister for International Cooperation Julian Fantino[6] signalled the government's intent to deepen and expand this integrated approach (see Fantino 2012 and 2013). Subsequent steps have included, among other activities, a C$25 million contribution to the University of British Columbia and Simon Fraser University to establish the Canadian International Institute for Extractive Industries and Development (CIIEID—www .ciieid.org), and parallel support for a new African Mineral Development Centre of C$15.3 million over five years. These initiatives have sharply divided civil society groups in Canada, between those (typically associated with large multinational NGDOs) characterized by Minister Fantino as "constructive members of the Canadian and local civil society" who have been willing to partner with CIDA and Canadian extractive companies, and those who argue that Canadian taxpayers' aid dollars should not be used to enhance the image of some of Canada's most profitable corporations. Combined with the government's persistent opposition to a more transparent and enforceable approach to oversight of Canadian extractive operations in the developing world, discussed in Chapter 7, these activities can be clearly understood within a neo-Gramscian framework, emphasizing efforts to forge a common sense understanding of the mutual benefits of extractive industry development among a broad coalition of state, private sector, civil society, and community "partners" (see Vervaeke 2013). Consistent with the Coxian emphasis on utilizing foreign policy in an effort to sustain hegemonic orders both at home and abroad (see Neufeld 1995), the Harper government's international approach has firmly reflected and reinforced its domestic emphasis on the virtues of "responsible resource development."

Three qualifications need to be made. First, to argue that this approach represents an effort to forge consensus in the service of elite interests is not to suggest that no good can come of it. Initiatives like the CIIEID have the *potential* to define, elaborate, and promote a more genuinely developmental approach to extractive sector investments, and greater efforts to ensure the widest possible distribution of their benefits. The training that CIDA is funding in communities adjacent to Canadian mining investments should enable some people in these communities to take advantage of new employment opportunities. Nevertheless, they also tend to obfuscate the inevitable costs and disparities associated with these investments, and the importance of robust governance and oversight of extractive operations. As Siegel concludes with reference to extractive-based development, in contemporary circumstances of increased resource scarcity and extractive intensity "win-win solutions are an illusion. Somewhere in the equation, somebody has to give something up" (2013).

Second, as discussed in Chapter 5, harnessing aid funds in the service of Canadian commercial interests is as old as Canadian development assistance. The contemporary controversy over the effort to integrate extractive industry promotion with economic and social development programming echoes historic controversies over tied aid, CIDA's industrial cooperation division "CIDA-INC," food aid, Structural Adjustment, etc. (e.g., Burdette 1994; Gillies 1994; Charlton 1994). In this sense, the Harper government's approach clearly echoes a succession of self-interested distortions of the poverty-focused "ethical mission" of development assistance, under both Liberal and Progressive Conservative governments.

Third, however, the Harper government's initiatives also reflect a narrower and more strategic approach, more tightly integrated with the specific interests of a particularly powerful sector of the Canadian economy, to which the Conservatives have firmly tethered their own mantra of "jobs, growth, and long-term prosperity." They have also stepped away from the broader order-building objectives that were a characteristic feature of hegemonic middlepowermanship, as exemplified by Canadian G8 diplomacy concerning the comprehensive Africa Action Plan, and have taken little heed of ongoing efforts within the international aid regime to operationalize a consensual Aid Effectiveness Agenda anchored by the Paris Declaration Principles.[7] In this respect, they reflect the government's partial disengagement from broader multilateral processes, its more defensive and cautious approach to international relations, and the diminution of its order-building aspirations and objectives. It is this trend that has led critics to be particularly wary of the integration of CIDA within a new Department of Foreign Affairs, Trade, and Development, which they fear will lead to the steady subordination of aid policy to narrower political and economic interests.

This process is also apparent in the security sector. Besides the government's decision to decline a request from the UN to provide the Force Commander and a small contingent of supporting troops to MONUC in the DRC in 2010, noted in Chapter 6, a telling indication of the new Canadian reticence vis-à-vis African peace-and-security operations was its approach to the French-led intervention in Mali in the first part of 2013. Unquestionably, this conflict has complex roots and will require multi-dimensional peacebuilding efforts if it is to be sustainably resolved (see Sears 2010). Yet as Robert Fowler has stressed,[8] there were very good reasons for Canada to support this operation and the Security Council–sanctioned, African-led mission (AFISMA) authorized to replace it (Fowler 2013; see also Roberts 2013b). Despite the complexity of the conflict, it was clear that fundamentalist Islamic groups were aggressively exploiting the weakness of the Malian government and army along with longstanding North–South tensions, threatening to consolidate their control in a wide swath of the continent. This outcome would have profoundly destabilizing implications for regional and Western countries. Canada and its NATO allies had, in fact, helped fuel the conflict as a result of failure to secure stockpiles of weapons that spilled over the Libyan border with the fall of Muammar Gaddafi. Moreover, notwithstanding popular impressions to the contrary, Canada was hardly a stranger to Mali. The country had long been one of Canada's top bilateral aid recipients in Africa, and had remained on the sharply reduced list of African "countries of concentration" after 2009. These long-standing linkages had helped to create and consolidate vital trans-societal links, primarily in Quebec (see Cousineau and Mackrael 2013). While trade relations were very limited, Canadian extractive industry investments, particularly in gold, were in the order of a half-billion dollars. As noted in Chapter 6, Canada had long supported peacekeeping training at the École de maintien de la paix in Bamako, Mali, until the March 2012 coup that displaced the elected government of the country. Finally, Canada was very specifically and directly asked for assistance at the highest levels by a close ally—the government of France (Foster 2013).

Given these multiple connections and motivations, both hegemonic interests at the transnational level and considerations of good international citizenship would lead one to expect a relatively forthright and robust response to the French request for assistance. And indeed, in the end, Canada did make a modest contribution of a CC-177 Globemaster along with an RCAF Flight and Maintenance crew of forty to provide airlift for the operation—though remarkably, the initial commitment (later repeatedly extended) was for one week only, and Ottawa consistently stressed that it would provide no combat forces. Yet the impression created by the government's confused and deeply reticent messaging about its role was that it was being dragged into the operation against its will and better judgment. John Baird warned a parliamentary committee about the risks of becoming mired in "another Afghanisan," while the government's message during the first several weeks of the operation was summarized by Campbell Clark in the following terms: "The Harper government is so obsessed with stressing what it's not going to do in Mali—combat—that it fumbles whenever it talks about what it will do ... What [Stephen Harper] hasn't set out is a clear idea of what the Canadian role should be. His government has hesitated and delayed" (C. Clark 2013a; see also C. Clark 2013b). It was almost as though by not talking about the situation or Canada's role in it, the government hoped it could make it disappear, politically at least.

The government's deeply reticent approach to security-and-peace-operations commitments in sub-Saharan Africa is in striking contrast to its eager and extensive participation in NATO operations against the Gaddafi regime in Libya, up to and including supplying the Force Commander, Lt General Charles Bouchard of the RCAF. Not only did CF air and naval forces participate extensively; the government vigorously publicized Canada's role in this campaign, capped with an extraordinary victory parade in Ottawa (CBC News 2011). The stark contrast in its approach to these two operations in Mali and in Libya, both practically and discursively, highlights the degree to which it has privileged NATO-led operations over those that lack the Alliance's imprimatur; and the pains it takes to avoid portraying sub-Saharan Africa as a region in which Canada has significant security interests or responsibilities.

Discursively, this is strikingly different from the language of its Liberal predecessors, as reflected for example in the latter's vigorous promotion of the "human security agenda" in Africa, and the expansive rhetoric manifested in Canada's approach to the crisis in Darfur (Nossal 2005; Black 2010a). Practically, however, the differences are much less significant. In 2003, for example, a humanitarian crisis in the Ituri region of eastern DRC prompted the UN Secretary-General to issue an urgent call on the "international community" to mobilize an emergency force, which the French offered 1,000 troops to anchor. Canada responded to this call, characterized as a "moral obligation" by then-Prime Minister Chrétien, with two Hercules C-130 transport aircraft. Like the Globemaster in Mali, this contribution was doubtless useful, but fell short of both the expectations generated by its expansive rhetoric on human security, and reasonable expectations of a prosperous and committed "good international citizen" (see Black 2004, 145).

In short, Canada's "hegemonic middlepowermanship" in Africa has been clear enough in the diplomatic and developmental practices of both the Chrétien-Martin Liberals and the Harper Conservatives—albeit with narrowed focus and aspirations under the latter. Yet both its discourse and practice in relation to intra-hegemonic objectives have been shallow and unsustained. In the security domain, it has veered from rhetorically expansive but practically limited under the Liberals, to rhetorically reticent and practically limited under the Conservatives. In neither case, then, has the logic of hegemonic middlepowermanship been consistently applied. This leads to a consideration of the third and final post-colonial frame animating this study—"Africa" as narrative foil for the (re)definition of Canadian collective identity.

Africa as a Story We Tell Ourselves about Ourselves

In Chapter 3, I discussed the way in which African engagements have served as the narrative foundation for a kind of serial morality tale about Canada's collective moral virtue, its dereliction, and efforts at redemption. As illuminated by post-colonial approaches, this narrative role depends upon and consistently reinscribes a flat, dehistoricized and depoliticized portrayal of the African "other." The policy consequences have been several: a chronic mismatch between rhetorical aspirations and bureaucratic capacities or inclinations to fulfill those aspirations; a lack of public scrutiny or concern for the *consequences* of unfulfilled policy objectives; and a shallow understanding of the contextual and historical conditions within which African crises have occurred/recurred.

If much of the post-African-decoloniziation period was marked by the steady elaboration of this moral narrative concerning the Canadian state and its role in the world—Canada's "moral identity," in Akuffo's terms—it is clear that in this as in other foreign policy domains, the Harper government set out to recast the narrative. With regard to Africa, this process has unfolded in two overlapping phases. Initially, the government sought to deprioritize Africa primarily through discursive omission. It had little to say about Africa; with very few exceptions, its ministers did not travel to Africa; and it distanced itself from the multilateral contexts through which it would be required to engage Africa and its varied concerns (see J. Clark 2007; Owen and Eaves 2007). Meanwhile, it signalled its intent to refocus its priorities in the "developing world" with a 2009 strategy document on relations with Latin America (Government of Canada 2009; see also Black 2009)—something no Canadian government had ever undertaken with regard to Africa. When it was announced by CIDA that seven of the fourteen core bilateral partners in Africa, as designated by the 2005 *International Policy Statement*, were to be dropped in the new 2009 list of countries of concentration, none of the affected governments was consulted. Extraordinarily, nineteen African ambassadors subsequently appeared simultaneously before the Parliamentary Foreign Affairs committee to ask why this had occurred. It is hard not to perceive this complete lack of consultation as indifference bordering on contempt.

The paradox was that, these important signals notwithstanding, much of Canada's policy practice in Africa remained relatively unchanged. As noted above, Canada continued to reinvest in aid to Africa, and to allocate the largest share of the International Assistance Envelope to the continent. It continued to be among the more generous donors to peace operations and humanitarian aid in Darfur and Sudan/South Sudan and, as discussed in Chapter 6, to provide modest but well received assistance for peacekeeping training on the continent. Meanwhile, trade and investment, particularly though not only in the extractive sector, grew steadily (except for the first years of the global financial crisis in 2008–09) to unprecedented levels in absolute terms.

Various potential explanations for the Harper government's discursive distancing from Africa have been noted above. These range from raw partisanship—a desire to distinguish the "New" Conservative government from a focus that it saw as too closely associated with the Liberal "brand"—to the more theoretical and substantive argument that many of those thinking about foreign policy within the government took a realist view of the world in which Africa was marginal to Canada's "vital national interests." From the latter perspective, it was simply imprudent to focus scarce Canadian resources and political capital on the continent, since it exposed the government to inordinately high potential risks and offered relatively minimal rewards. The point to be stressed here is that, in reducing its political emphasis and exposure in Africa, the Conservative government was, as discussed in Chapter 3, tapping into and elevating an important counter-narrative concerning Africa to the ethical story that had predominated for the previous generation. Many permanent officials, particularly in Foreign Affairs and the CF, had long viewed the propensity of their political bosses to devote (intermittently at least) high levels of energy, time, and resources to African and/or human security issues as a deviation from the interest-based calculus they should be applying. This current has been present at least since the time when Joe Clark and Brian Mulroney were widely perceived by many of their officials as having become entirely too preoccupied with collective efforts to foster change in apartheid South Africa. The Conservative government was therefore both reflecting and firmly elevating this alternative, "realist internationalist" narrative (Boucher 2012), in line with its more rationalist approach to politics and foreign policy, in which the pursuit of "jobs, economic growth, and sustainable prosperity" in the midst of a dangerous world became the government's professed highest purpose. In doing so, however, it took no account of the diplomatic costs of treating so dismissively a set of ethical preoccupations and diplomatic relationships that had generated a positive if overly generous international profile for the Canadian government. Perhaps the government was, in this respect, captured by its own narrative and theoretical assumption that whatever other states might say publicly, they set very little store by such ethical pretensions in practice, and would therefore hardly notice their decline in the discourse of Canadian foreign policy.

The second phase of the Harper government's new narrative frame for Africa emerged not long after it began a belated process of mending fences with its African counterparts, eyes firmly set on the its forthcoming campaign for a seat on the UN Security Council (see Oda 2009b). In this phase, Conservative ministers began to talk about Africa, visit Africa, and engage with African representatives and lobbies, like the business-oriented Canadian Council on Africa, with increased frequency. Even the prime minister visited Senegal and the DRC in October 2012—his second visit to sub-Saharan Africa—eliciting considerable commentary to the effect that, "after years of apparent neglect, the Harper government has discovered Africa's potential" (York 2012c). This renewed interest still fell well short of its predecessors in terms of high-level emphasis and engagement, however. And when government representatives talked about Africa, it was firmly within the emergent narrative frame of a "new" or "rising Africa."

In 2011 for example, former Trade Minister, Peter Van Loan, told a Toronto conference on "Africa Rising: Entrepreneurship and Innovation Frontiers": "I've seen first hand the opportunities and potential in Africa's economy. Like many Canadian companies, I recognize the potential of this market and I believe that Canada can be a great partner in helping to build the 'new Africa'" (2011). Just over a year later, Van Loan's successor as Trade Minister, Ed Fast, opened the Tenth Anniversary Symposium of the Canadian Council on Africa. In his remarks, Fast noted: "African countries currently number among the world's fastest growing economies. Couple that with healthy commodity prices, steadily increasing foreign investment, the recent embrace of technology and ever-improving political climates, and you'll agree that today's Africa is poised to play a new role on the world's economic stage" (2012). Meanwhile, John Baird preceded the prime minister's October 2012 visit with his own visit to Nigeria, targeted by the government for its market potential, where he signed a foreign investment agreement and launched a new Canada-Nigeria commission (York 2012c). Ed Fast followed up by leading a business delegation to Nigeria and Ghana in early 2013.

This "Africa rising" narrative, both in Canada and more broadly, has the virtue of providing an antidote to the pervasive "Afro-pessimism" that dominated much of the 1980s and 1990s, and extended into the first years of the new millennium. It accurately portrays the extraordinary opportunities that are now available to *some* in sub-Saharan Africa. From the government's perspective, it fits neatly with its "win-win" discourse concerning the presumed complementarities of interest between Canadian extractive companies, African countries and

communities, and Canadian aid policy objectives of poverty alleviation. But it is at least as flat, shallow, ahistorical, and misleading as
the more negative and moralistic portrayals it has superceded (see
Medhora and Samy 2013). It is also much narrower than the policy
frames deriving from the multi-dimensional G8 Africa Action Plan
of the previous decade, which the Chrétien government had such a
significant hand in shaping.

The "Africa rising" narrative of extraordinary mutual opportunity thus leaves virtually no space for an appropriately contextualized
and balanced discursive and policy approach. It helps to explain, in
this regard, why the Harper government was so tongue-tied and flat-
footed in its response to the Malian crisis and French-led intervention. With no interest in resurrecting the discarded human-security
frame, and with no place in the "Africa rising" narrative for the hard,
long-term, and multi-dimensional work of peacemaking and peacebuilding in a chronically poor and deeply divided society, there was
literally no basis upon which to imagine and articulate a coherent
rationale for its involvement.

Conclusion: Retreat or Renewal?

Taken together, the three frames around which the analyses in this
book are structured suggest a mixed answer to the first question posed
at the outset of this conclusion—what is the nature and magnitude of
the changes in Africa policies and practices rendered by the Harper
government? In practice, there have been significant continuities in
the broad strokes of policy practice—partly because the Harper government never actually "walked away from Africa," and partly because
the policy virtues of its predecessors have been (in keeping with the
serial morality tale discussed in Chapter 3) routinely exaggerated and
mythologized. Nevertheless, there is no doubt that the Harper government has presided over a general retreat in the breadth and depth
of Canadian political interest and engagement with Africa. Canadian
presence, profile, and reputation have all diminished, as the government has articulated a narrower, more realist and defensive narrative of Canada's role in the world. In this regard, and consistent with
post-colonial insights, "Africa" has continued to serve as an important
marker of this shift—a means through which the Canadian government has attempted to re-articulate Canada's role and identity in the

world, regardless of the consequences for Africans themselves. There has also been a retreat from the aspirations of both good international citizenship and hegemonic middlepowermanship, with their ethical-activist and order-building connotations, respectively.

The second question posed at the outset—do the changes that have taken place in Africa policy under the Harper government portend a decisive long-term shift in Canada's involvement with the continent?—is of course impossible to answer with certainty. As noted at the outset of this chapter, both major opposition parties have been highly critical of the Conservatives' "retreat" from Africa, implying that they would restore some version of the previous approach—though both have also evinced an exaggerated perception of what that approach was. Yet it is also clear that the Conservatives' have paid a negligible political price at home for their diminished interest and engagement with sub-Saharan Africa. Indeed, much of their political base likely sees this as good, hard-headed, prudent policy—a welcome corrective to the soft-minded moralism of its Liberal predecessors. More broadly, it is striking how easily what had been widely regarded as touchstones of the "humane" or "liberal internationalist" tradition in mainstream Canadian political culture—for example, peacekeeping, multilateralism, the United Nations, and, more recently, human security and the Responsibility to Protect—have been de-emphasized with virtual impunity. It is not that many Canadians do not feel deeply distressed by these trends. It is just that not *enough of them* in the *right places* do to alter the current government's political calculus or the general direction of policy.

Of course, eventually the party-political order can be expected to change. As discussed above, moreover, the Conservative government has itself partially re-engaged the continent, albeit with a narrowly commercial emphasis. But the longer the "new normal" in Canada-Africa relations prevails, the harder it will be to credibly and capably re-engage—bearing in mind that Canada's previous engagements with Africa were already shown to be shallow, inconsistent, and under-resourced. In this respect the historic consistent inconsistency of Canadian involvement with the continent will be amplified. Meanwhile sub-Saharan Africa, despite its physical, social, and political distance from Canada, will continue to serve as an important marker of Canadian identity and its trajectory in world affairs.

Appendix A

Canadian Bilateral Aid to Sub-Saharan Africa, 1990–2010

Year	Total Canadian ODA (in USD millions)	Aid to GNI %	ODA to Sub-Saharan Africa (absolute, in USD millions)	ODA to Sub-Saharan Africa (% of total Canadian ODA)	Top 5 African recipients (ODA total net, in USD millions)
1990	2,469.88	0.44	1,002.15	40.57	1. Cameroon – 151.67 2. Kenya – 112.76 3. Ghana – 94.92 4. Zambia – 87.80 5. Côte d'Ivoire – 80.39
1991	2,603.86	0.45	434.16	16.67	1. Ghana – 39.90 2. Cameroon – 33.11 3. Ethiopia – 31.98 4. Mozambique – 29.76 5. Tanzania – 29.09
1992	2,515.18	0.46	426.81	16.97	1. Ghana – 38.68 2. Tanzania – 31.74 3. Mozambique – 28.61 4. Zimbabwe – 27.20 5. Zambia – 25.96
1993	2,399.64	0.45	298.52	12.44	1. Ghana – 29.21 2. Mozambique – 29.18 3. Tanzania – 20.16 4. Ethiopia – 19.60 5. Senegal – 18.39
1994	2,249.61	0.43	259.99	11.56	1. Mali – 20.31 2. Rwanda – 18.20 3. Mozambique – 17.38 4. Senegal – 17.01 5. Ghana – 16.71
1995	2,066.67	0.38	275.06	13.31	1. Tanzania – 25.37 2. Ghana – 22.68 3. Côte d'Ivoire – 22.22 4. Zambia – 18.74 5. Rwanda – 16.76

(continued)

Year	Total Canadian ODA (in USD millions)	Aid to GNI %	ODA to Sub-Saharan Africa (absolute, in USD millions)	ODA to Sub-Saharan Africa (% of total Canadian ODA)	Top 5 African recipients (ODA total net, in USD millions)
1996	1,795.47	0.32	271.51	15.12	1. Ghana – 20.99 2. Rwanda – 20.37 3. Côte d'Ivoire – 20.22 4. Cameroon – 16.98 5. Senegal – 15.99
1997	2,044.61	0.34	231.44	11.32	1. Rwanda – 21.41 2. Senegal – 15.49 3. Ghana – 14.07 4. Ethiopia – 13.38 5. Zambia – 11.76
1998	1,706.64	0.30	286.70	16.80	1. Côte d'Ivoire – 45.54 2. Cameroon – 39.50 3. Ghana – 17.01 4. Mozambique – 12.87 5. Senegal – 12.27
1999	1,706.29	0.28	225.24	13.20	1. Côte d'Ivoire – 18.76 2. Mali – 18.34 3. Cameroon – 18.13 4. Senegal – 17.50 5. Ethiopia – 14.81
2000	1,743.60	0.25	179.67	10.13	1. Ghana – 16.21 2. Mali – 12.67 3. Tanzania – 11.64 4. Senegal – 11.31 5. Ethiopia – 10.94
2001	1,532.75	0.22	182.31	11.89	1. Mozambique – 13.88 2. Ethiopia – 12.38 3. Ghana – 11.23 4. Malawi – 10.96 5. Mali – 8.97
2002	2,004.16	0.28	356.53	17.79	1. Cameroon – 80.29 2. Côte d'Ivoire – 78.73 3. Nigeria – 18.06 4. Mali – 13.62 5. Ghana – 12.39
2003	2,030.60	0.24	463.47	22.82	1. DRC – 74.49 2. Ethiopia – 38.02 3. Tanzania – 34.33 4. Mozambique – 26.70 5. Mali – 25.20

(continued)

Year	Total Canadian ODA (in USD millions)	Aid to GNI %	ODA to Sub-Saharan Africa (absolute, in USD millions)	ODA to Sub-Saharan Africa (% of total Canadian ODA)	Top 5 African recipients (ODA total net, in USD millions)
2004	2,599.13	0.27	566.58	21.80	1. Ethiopia – 59.48 2. Ghana – 48.54 3. Mali – 44.14 4. Cameroon – 43.19 5. Tanzania – 32.71
2005	3,756.34	0.34	665.44	17.72	1. Ethiopia – 64.93 2. Mozambique – 56.19 3. Ghana – 51.73 4. Zambia – 49.70 5. Mali – 35.50
2006	3,683.16	0.29	834.59	22.66	1. Cameroon – 206.88 2. Sudan – 79.30 3. Ethiopia – 62.48 4. Ghana – 53.85 5. Mozambique – 49.36
2007	4,079.69	0.29	785.59	19.26	1. Ethiopia – 90.52 2. Ghana – 78.57 3. Sudan – 70.78 4. Mozambique – 57.34 5. Tanzania – 56.73
2008	4,794.71	0.33	1,242.11	25.91	1. Ethiopia – 152.55 2. Mali – 99.12 3. Sudan – 83.91 4. Mozambique – 77.23 5. Ghana – 74.01
2009	4,000.07	0.30	1,118.49	27.96	1. Sudan – 105.04 2. Ghana – 99.80 3. Tanzania – 93.98 4. Ethiopia – 87.18 5. Mali – 83.46
2010	5,214.12	0.34	1,381.73	26.5	1. Ethiopia – 140.38 2. Ghana – 114.20 3. Tanzania – 111.55 4. Sudan – 108.27 5. Mali – 96.04

Source: OECD StatExtracts, "Total Flow by Donor," "Aid Disbursements to Countries and Regions" (Paris: Organization for Economic Cooperation and Development, 2014), http://stats.oecd.org.

Note: ODA totals to Sub-Saharan Africa (SSA) exclude multilateral aid and therefore significantly understate total Canadian aid to SSA.

Appendix B

United Nations Peace Support Missions since 1990
(with Canadian contributions in Africa highlighted)

Mission		Start	End	Authorized Maximum Strength and Canadian Contribution
UNTAG	United Nations Transition Assistance Group (Namibia)	Apr. 1989	Mar. 1990	**Authorized maximum strength:** 4,493 all ranks, 1,500 civilian police, and just under 2,000 international and local staff; the mission was strengthened by some 1,000 additional international personnel who came specifically for the elections **Canadian contribution:** Operation MATADOR: 257 logistics personnel, 100 RCMP officers, and 50 election monitors
UNIKOM	United Nations Iraq-Kuwait Observation Mission	Apr. 1991	Oct. 2003	**Authorized maximum strength:** 3,645 all ranks, including 300 military observers **Canadian contribution:** Operation RECORD—at the time of its establishment, Canada contributed a senior staff officer to serve at UNIKOM headquarters, and a contingent of 300 CF personnel primarily from 1 Combat Engineer Regiment, based in Edmonton; CF engineers continued to deploy on Operation RECORD until March 1993, when the Canadian commitment was reduced to five United Nations Military Observers (UNMOS)
MINURSO	United Nations Mission for the Referendum in Western Sahara	Apr. 1991	Present	**Authorized maximum strength:** 237 military personnel and 6 police officers **Canadian contribution:** no contribution listed in UN database
UNAVEM II	United Nations Angola Verification Mission II	June 1991	Feb. 1995	**Authorized maximum strength:** 350 military observers, 126 civilian police, and 14 military medical staff **Canadian contribution:** Canada listed by the UN database as a contributor of military and civilian police personnel

(continued)

Mission		Start	End	Authorized Maximum Strength and Canadian Contribution
ONUSAL	United Nations Observer Mission in El Salvador	July 1991	Feb. 1995	**Authorized maximum strength:** 380 military observers, 8 medical officers, and 631 police observers Canadian contribution: 5 UNMOS
UNAMIC	United Nations Advance Mission in Cambodia	Oct. 1991	Mar. 1992	Authorized maximum strength: 1,090 military personnel **Canadian contribution:** not available via database; UN data indicates Canadian involvement
UNPROFOR	United Nations Protection Force (Croatia, Bosnia Herzegovina)	Feb. 1992	Mar. 1995	**Authorized maximum strength:** 38,599 military personnel, including 684 UNMOS, and 803 civilian police **Canadian contribution:** Operation HARMONY—more than 2,000 CF personnel served in the Balkan region with UNPROFOR and one of its successor missions, the United Nations Peace Forces Headquarters (UNFP); the Canadian contingent comprised two major units and a logistics battalion; it also included UNMOS and staff officers employed in various headquarters Brigadier-General Lewis MacKenzie of the CF served with UNPROFOR as Chief of Staff from February to April 1992, when he was promoted to Major-General; and from May to August 1992 as Commander, Sector Sarajevo Canada also provided the Deputy Theatre Commander, UNPROFOR, from September 1992 to March 1995 and the Deputy Theatre Commander, UNFP, from April 1995 to January 1996.
UNTAC	United Nations Transitional Authority in Cambodia	Mar. 1992	Sep. 1993	**Authorized maximum strength:** 15,547 troops, 893 military observers, and 3,500 civilian police **Canadian contribution:** not available via database; UN data indicates Canadian involvement

(continued)

Mission		Start	End	Authorized Maximum Strength and Canadian Contribution
UNOSOM I	United Nations Operation in Somalia	Apr. 1992	Mar. 1993	**Authorized maximum strength:** 50 military observers, 3,500 security personnel, and up to 719 military support personnel **Canadian contribution:** Operation DELIVERANCE—deployment of a 900-person contingent and of HMCS Preserver and Hercules transport aircraft
ONUMOZ	United Nations Operation in Mozambique	Dec. 1992	Dec. 1994	**Authorized maximum strength:** 6,625 troops and military support personnel, 354 military observers, and 1,144 civilian police **Canadian contribution:** Operation CONSONANCE—14 Canadian officers were in theatre by February 1993; they would each finish one-year tours they had started in other operations; all were employed in the ONUMOZ headquarters, the regional headquarters, and at assembly areas; their main task was to count and then demobilize both guerrilla and government soldiers, and to move weapons taken from these individuals to regional arms depots for safe storage; once demobilized, the ex-fighters would be sent to training centres; the next rotation totalled 15 personnel
UNOSOM II	United Nations Operation in Somalia II	Mar. 1993	Mar. 1995	**Authorized maximum strength:** 28,000 military and civilian police personnel **Canadian contribution:** UN database lists Canada as a contributor of military and civilian police personnel (Operation DELIVERANCE spanned UNOSOM I and II, ending in May 1993)
UNOMUR	United Nations Observer Mission Uganda-Rwanda	June 1993	Sep. 1994	Authorized maximum strength: 81 military observers **Canadian contribution:** Chief Military Observer Brigadier-General Romeo Dallaire, June–October 1993

(continued)

Mission		Start	End	Authorized Maximum Strength and Canadian Contribution
UNOMIG	United Nations Observer Mission in Georgia	Aug. 1993	June 2009	**Authorized maximum strength:** 459 total personnel, including 129 military observers and 16 police officers **Canadian contribution:** no contribution listed in UN database
UNOMIL	United Nations Observer Mission in Liberia	Sep. 1993	Sep. 1997	**Authorized maximum strength:** 303 military observers, 20 military medical personnel, 45 military engineers **Canadian contribution:** no contribution listed in UN database
UNMIH	United Nations Mission in Haiti	Sep. 1993	June 1996	**Authorized maximum strength:** 6,000 troops and military support personnel and 900 civilian police **Canadian contribution:** Police Commissioners Superintendent Jean-Jacques Lemay, October 1993–* (*UNMIH was prevented from deploying at this stage) Chief Superintendent Neil Pouliot, July 1994 to February 1996 Force Commander Brigadier-General J.R.P. Daigle, March to June 1996
UNAMIR	United Nations Assistance Mission for Rwanda	Oct. 1993	Mar. 1996	**Authorized maximum strength:** 2,548 military personnel, including 2,217 formed troops and 331 military observers, and 60 civilian police **Canadian contribution:** Operation SCOTCH—began in April 1994 and involved 312 Hercules C-130 flights to Kigali, Rwanda or to Goma, DRC to deploy 1 Canadian Division Headquarters and Signal Regiment to UNAMIR; the main body of the regiment returned home at the end of January 1995 Operation PASSAGE—deployed 2 Field Ambulances for humanitarian flights for UNHCR or CIDA from April to October 1994; 8 Air Communications and Control Squadron (8ACCS) was deployed at Nairobi and Kigali; on 16 September 1994 the Kigali airport was turned over to civilian control and by 28 September 8ACCS had returned to Canada Force Commanders: Major-General Roméo Dallaire, October 1993 to August 1994; Major-General Guy Tousignant, August 1994 to December 1995

(continued)

Mission		Start	End	Authorized Maximum Strength and Canadian Contribution
UNASOG	United Nations Aouzou Strip Observer Group	May 1994	June 1994	Authorized maximum strength: 9 military observers **Canadian contribution:** no contribution listed in UN database
UNMOT	United Nations Mission of Observers in Tajikistan	Dec. 1994	May 2000	Authorized maximum strength: 120 military observers **Canadian contribution:** no contribution listed in UN database
UNAVEM III	United Nations Angola Verification Mission II	Feb. 1995	June 1997	**Authorized maximum strength:** 350 military observers and 126 civilian police Canadian contribution: 9 UNMOs
UNCRO	United Nations Confidence Restoration Operation in Croatia	May 1995	Jan. 1996	**Authorized maximum strength:** 6,581 troops, 194 military observers, and 296 civilian police **Canadian contribution:** not available via database; UN data indicates Canadian involvement
UNPREDEP	United Nations Preventive Deployment Force (former Yugoslav Republic of Macedonia)	Mar. 1995	Feb. 1999	**Authorized maximum strength:** 1,049 troops, 35 military observers, and 26 civilian police **Canadian contribution:** not available via database; UN data indicates Canadian involvement
UNMIBH	United Nations Mission in Bosnia and Herzegovina	Dec. 1995	Dec. 2002	**Authorized maximum strength:** 2,057 civilian police personnel and 5 military liaison officers **Canadian contribution:** not available via database; UN data indicates Canadian involvement
UNTAES	United Nations Transitional Administration for Eastern Slavonia, Baranja, and Western Sirmium	Jan. 1996	Jan. 1998	**Authorized maximum strength:** 5,000 troops, 100 military observers, and 600 civilian police **Canadian contribution:** not available via database; UN data indicates Canadian involvement

(continued)

Mission		Start	End	Authorized Maximum Strength and Canadian Contribution
UNMOP	United Nations Mission of Observers in Prevlaka	Jan. 1996	Dec. 2002	Authorized maximum strength: 28 military observers **Canadian contribution:** Operation CHAPERON—provided UNMOP with one CF member to serve as a UNMO; this contribution was maintained from 1996 to 2001
UNSMIH	United Nations Support Mission in Haiti	July 1996	July 1997	**Authorized maximum strength:** 1,297 military and 291 civilian police personnel **Canadian contribution:** not available via database; UN data indicates Canadian involvement
MINUGUA	United Nations Verification Mission in Guatemala	Jan. 1997	May 1997	**Authorized maximum strength:** 155 military observers and requisite medical personnel **Canadian contribution:** Operation VISION—staff checks identified 17 Spanish-speaking personnel, of whom 15 were selected to deploy
MONUA	United Nations Mission in Angola	June 1997	Feb. 1999	No data currently available
UNTMIH	United Nations Transition Mission in Haiti	Aug. 1997	Nov. 1997	**Authorized maximum strength:** 250 civilian police personnel and 50 military personnel **Canadian contribution:** Operation CONSTABLE—provided UNTMIH with 650 personnel, the largest contingent, comprised of a small reconnaissance battalion to conduct patrols and other operations in Port-au-Prince and throughout Haiti; a helicopter squadron to provide casualty evacuation services, a 24-hour mission capability, and a medium airlift capability; a military police platoon to provide criminal investigation services; a Military Information Support Team to provide the civilian population with timely, accurate information about UN activities; and a full-scale Logistics Group to provide virtually all the support services required to administer and sustain the Canadian units deployed with the United Nations Support Mission in Haiti (UNSMIH)

(continued)

Mission		Start	End	Authorized Maximum Strength and Canadian Contribution
MIPONUH	United Nations Police Mission in Haiti	Dec. 1997	Mar. 2000	**Authorized maximum strength**: 300 civilian police personnel Canadian contribution: police personnel
MINURCA	United Nations Mission in the Central African Republic	Apr. 1998	Feb. 2000	**Authorized maximum strength**: 1,350 troops and military support personnel and 24 civilian police **Canadian contribution**: Operation PRUDENCE—the initial contribution of 45 personnel deployed in April 1998; the main role was to support the mission's communications system and the Canadian contingent incorporated a communications detachment, support personnel, and staff officers; the contingent was expanded in October 1998 to provide extra signals personnel to support national elections planned for the end of 1998; in total, the contingent comprised a signals troop of 25 CF personnel, 4 staff officers employed at MINURCA headquarters, a command and support element of 22 CF personnel and, during the presidential elections, 32 more Canadian signallers to support remote electoral sites
UNOMSIL	United Nations Observer Mission in Sierra Leone	July 1998	Oct. 1999	**Authorized maximum strength**: 210 military observers, a 15-person medical unit, and 5 civilian police advisors **Canadian contribution**: no contribution listed in UN database
UNMIK	United Nations Interim Administration in Kosovo	June 1999	Present	**Authorized maximum strength**: up to 4,718 police personnel (including formed units and border police) and 38 military liaison officers **Canadian contribution**: no contribution listed in UN database

(continued)

Mission		Start	End	Authorized Maximum Strength and Canadian Contribution
UNAMSIL	United Nations Mission in Sierra Leone	July 1998	Oct. 1999	**Authorized maximum strength:** 17,500 military personnel **Canadian contribution:** Operation SCULPTURE—in November 1999, 5 CF officers arrived in Sierra Leone to serve as UNMOs; they were responsible for monitoring the disarmament of the combatants of the belligerent factions, and their reintegration into civilian live; they also monitored the ceasefire and humanitarian assistance provided by international organizations During May 2000, 437 Transport Squadron from 8 Wing Trenton, Ontario, provided a CC-150 Polaris long-range transport aircraft and 20 personnel to move 300 Indian troops and their equipment from New Delhi to Sierra Leone; the same month, when UNAMSIL's peacekeeping force was increased to 13,000 all ranks, Canada sent more Air Force personnel from 8 Wing Trenton and 17 Wing Winnipeg to the airport in Freetown to help unload cargo; in the two weeks this detachment was on the ground, its 40 members handled more than 2.4 million kilograms of freight and baggage
UNTAET	United Nations Transitional Administration in East Timor	Oct. 1999	May 2002	**Authorized maximum strength:** 9,150 military personnel and 1,640 civilian police **Canadian contribution:** Operation TOUCAN provided a total of 600 CF personnel for six months, including 250 sailors, a 250-strong Company Group, and 100 Air Force personnel; thereafter it provided a small contingent of staff officers and police personnel

(continued)

Mission		Start	End	Authorized Maximum Strength and Canadian Contribution
MONUC	United Nations Organization Mission in the Democratic Republic of the Congo	Nov. 1999	July 2010	**Authorized maximum strength:** 19,815 military personnel, 760 military observers, 391 police, and 1,050 personnel of formed police units **Canadian contribution:** Operation CROCODILE—10 staff officers, with expertise in fields such as law and information operations and training, are employed at MONUC Headquarters in Kinshasa and divisional headquarters in Kisangani Also police personnel
UNMEE-SHIRBRIG	United Nations Mission in Ethiopia and Eritrea—Advance Mission	Dec. 2000	June 2001	SHIRBRIG maximum strength: unclear **Canadian contribution:** Operation ECLIPSE—the 450-strong CF contingent helped establish the mission in a six-month commitment during which the Canadians were integrated with the Dutch contingent to form a Canadian-Dutch battle group
UNMEE	United Nations Mission in Ethiopia and Eritrea	July 2000	July 2008	**Authorized maximum strength:** up to 5,000 military personnel, including 120 military observers, and 1,250 civilian police officers **Canadian contribution:** there is some discrepancy regarding the Canadian contribution (although Canada definitely contributed to the SHIRBRIG mission that launched UNMEE—see above): the CF website indicates an ongoing contribution to UNMEE via Operation ADDITION; however, UN statistics indicate that Canada was not a troop or police contributor to UNMEE
UNMISET	United Nations Mission of Support in East Timor	May 2002	May 2005	**Authorized maximum strength:** up to 5,000 military personnel, including 120 military observers, and 1,250 civilian police officers **Canadian contribution:** not available via database; UN data indicates Canadian involvement

(continued)

Mission		Start	End	Authorized Maximum Strength and Canadian Contribution
UNMIL-SHIRBRIG	United Nations Mission in Liberia—Advance Mission	Sep. 2003	Nov. 2003	**SHIRBRIG maximum strength:** the UN's Department of Peacekeeping Operations (DPKO) requested SHIRBRIG assistance to form the core of UNMIL's interim headquarters in Monrovia, Liberia, during the transition from ECOMIL to UNMIL; SHIRBRIG scheduled to provide 35 personnel across the spectrum of headquarters responsibilities **Canadian contribution:** the CF mission to SHIRBRIG was Operation LIANE—in September 2003, 4 personnel deployed to with the SHIRBRIG headquarters; after conducting in-clearances and mission planning, they deployed to Monrovia, Liberia; 2 officers (a lieutenant-colonel and a captain) filled the positions of G1 and G3 Plans (Administration and Operational Plans) and 2 non-commissioned members provided security assistance
UNMIL	United Nations Mission in Liberia	Sep. 2003	Present	**Authorized maximum strength:** 15,000 military personnel, including 250 observers and 160 staff officers, and 1,115 police officers **Canadian contribution:** no contribution listed in UN database
UNOCI	United Nations Operation in Côte d'Ivoire	Apr. 2004	Present	**Authorized maximum strength:** 8,645 troops and staff officers, 192 military observers, 1,555 police, and 8 customs officers **Canadian contribution:** contributed police personnel from the beginning of the mission in 2004; 9 police officers deployed as of March 2013 to assess and identify the training standards and needs of police officers in Côte d'Ivoire
MINUSTAH	United Nations Stabilization Mission in Haiti	June 2004	Present	**Authorized maximum strength:** up to 8,940 military personnel and up to 4,391 police **Canadian contribution:** Operation HALO—the CF deployed about 500 personnel and 6 CH-146 Griffon helicopters to assist the multinational force in bringing stability to the country

(continued)

Mission		Start	End	Authorized Maximum Strength and Canadian Contribution
ONUB	United Nations Operation in Burundi	June 2004	Dec. 2006	**Authorized maximum strength:** 5,650 military personnel, including 200 military observers, and 120 police personnel **Canadian contribution:** no contribution listed in UN database
UNAMIS-SHIRBRIG	United Nations Advance Mission in Sudan–SHIRBRIG	July 2004	Feb. 2005	**SHIRBRIG maximum strength:** SHIRBRIG deployed 17 members to Sudan as part of UNAMIS, a special political mission mandated by UNSCR 1547; SHIRBRIG provided 14 personnel out of a 27-person military team to help build up and plan the mission **Canadian contribution:** unclear
UNMIS-SHIRBRIG	United Nations Mission in the Sudan–SHIRBRIG	Apr. 2005	Dec. 2005	**SHIRBRIG maximum strength:** SHIRBRIG called to assist the DPKO in planning for the deployment of a UN mission in Sudan; SHIRBRIG was deployed in UNMIS to provide the nucleus of the Force HQ, the Joint Military Coordination Office, and the Integrated Support Services **Canadian contribution:** unclear, though Canadian Brigadier-General Gregory Mitchell, then Commander of SHIRBRIG, served as Deputy Force Commander
UNMIS	United Nations Mission in the Sudan	Mar. 2005	July 2011	**Authorized maximum strength:** up to 10,000 military personnel, including some 750 military observers, and up to 715 police **Canadian contribution:** Operation SAFARI—varied in size, but as of March 2013 Task Force Sudan comprised 20 CF members serving as UNMOs at team sites across southern Sudan, 8 on staff at UNMIS HQ in Khartoum, and 3 with the Canadian support element in Khartoum
UNMIT	United Nations Integrated Mission in Timor-Leste	Aug. 2006	Dec. 2012	**Authorized maximum strength:** 1,608 police personnel and 34 military liaison and staff officers **Canadian contribution:** police personnel

(continued)

Mission		Start	End	Authorized Maximum Strength and Canadian Contribution
UNAMID	African Union/United Nations Hybrid Operation in Darfur	July 2007	Present	**Authorized maximum strength:** 19,555 military personnel and 6,432 police **Canadian contribution:** Operation SATURN—initially comprised of 7 personnel, including 3 logistics experts at UNAMID headquarters and 4 soldiers training UNAMID troops to operate six-wheeled Grizzly and Husky armoured vehicles, general purpose (AVGPs) on loan from the CF (the loan ended in 2009 when Nigeria, Rwanda, and Senegal introduced their own armoured vehicles) The Canadian contingent in Darfur as of March 2013 was comprised of 6 staff officers with substantial experience in operations, intelligence, logistics, administration, and civil-military co-operation (CIMIC); each member of the team is assigned to a position at UNAMID Headquarters in El Fasher, Sudan
MINURCAT	United Nations Mission in the Central African Republic and Chad	Sep. 2007	Dec. 2010	**Authorized maximum strength:** 5,200 military personnel, 25 military liaison officers, and 300 police officers **Canadian contribution:** no contribution listed in UN database
UNIFSA	United Nations Interim Security Force for Abyei	June 2011	Present	**Authorized maximum strength:** 4,200 military personnel and 50 police personnel **Canadian contribution:** no contribution listed in UN database
UNMISS	United Nations Mission in the Republic of South Sudan	June 2011	Present	**Authorized maximum strength:** up to 7,000 military personnel and up to 900 civilian police personnel. **Canadian contribution:** Operation SOPRANO—as of March 2013 consisted of 12 CF personnel to work as staff officers and military liaison officers at UNMISS force headquarters in Juba and at various locations throughout South Sudan; they contribute technical planning and operational expertise

(continued)

Mission		Start	End	Authorized Maximum Strength and Canadian Contribution
AFISMA	African-Led International Support Mission in Mali	Dec. 2012	Present	**Authorized maximum strength**: data currently unavailable **Canadian contribution**: currently consists of one CC-177 Globemaster III heavy-lift transport aircraft and about 40 RCAF personnel, including flight and maintenance crews from 429 Transport Squadron and traffic technicians from 2 Air Movements Squadron, both units of 8 Wing Trenton
MONUSCO	United Nations Organization Stabilization Mission in the Democratic Republic of the Congo	Mar. 2013	Present	**Authorized maximum strength**: 19,815 military personnel, 760 military observers, 391 police, and 1,050 personnel of formed police units **Canadian contribution**: Operation CROCODILE—has continued through the transition from MONUC to MONUSCO; currently it comprises 9 members including 8 staff officers with expertise in fields such as communications, information operations and training, and a senior non-commissioned member who handles all national support tasks; staff officers are divided between MONUSCO HQ in Kinshasa and its eastern sector HQ in Goma.

Sources: United Nations Department of Peacekeeping Operations (http://www.un.org/en/peacekeeping/operations) and Canadian Department of National Defence (http://www.forces.gc.ca/en/index.page). All data current as of March 2013.

Key Canadian Contributions to Peace Operations in Africa since 1990

COUNTRY: SIERRA LEONE

Timeline: November 1999–July 2005

International mission: UNAMSIL

Mandated by the United Nations

On 7 February 2000, the Council revised UNAMSIL's mandate. It also expanded its size, as it did once again on 19 May 2000 and on 30 March 2001.

UNAMSIL successfully completed its mandate in December 2005.

Purpose: to cooperate with the Government and the other parties in implementing the Lome Peace Agreement and to assist in the implementation of the disarmament, demobilization and reintegration plan.[a]

Canadian contribution: Operation Sculpture

CF members began serving with the International Military Assistance Training Team (IMATT) in 2000 and the mission concluded on 15 February 2013.

PEACEKEEPING FORCES: Canadian Contribution	PEACEKEEPING FORCES: Total Contribution by All Partners
In November 1999, 5 CF officers arrived in Sierra Leone to serve as United Nations Military Observers (UNMOs). They were responsible for monitoring the disarmament of the combatants of all the belligerent factions, and their reintegration to civilian life. They also monitored the ceasefire and humanitarian assistance provided by international organizations. In May 2000, 4 of the 5 Canadian observers returned home, having completed their six-month tour of duty; the fifth, a senior officer, remained in Sierra Leone to serve on the staff of the UN force commander.	Authorized maximum strength: 17,500 military personnel, including 260 military observers, and up to 170 police personnel[b] Maximum deployment (31 March 2002): 17,368 military personnel; 87 UN police; 322 international civilians; 552 local civilians Strength as of 30 November 2005: 1,043 total uniformed personnel, including 944 troops, 69 military observers, and 30 police, supported by 216 international civilian personnel, 369 local civilian staff, and 83 UN Volunteers

(continued)

During May 2000, 437 Transport Squadron from 8 Wing Trenton, Ontario, provided a CC-150 Polaris long-range transport aircraft and 20 personnel to move 300 Indian troops and their equipment from New Delhi to Sierra Leone. That same month, when UNAMSIL's peacekeeping force was increased to 13,000 all ranks, Canada sent more Air Force personnel from 8 Wing Trenton and 17 Wing Winnipeg to the airport in Freetown to help unload cargo. In the two weeks this detachment was on the ground, its 40 members handled more than 2.4 million kilograms of freight and baggage.

At the end of June 2000, 4 more CF members were sent to Freetown to serve as observers, bringing the total back up to 5.[c]

In total there were 23 rotations between November 2000 and 15 February 2013. The responsibilities of Task Force Freetown included:

• Providing military advisory and training support to the Sierra Leone Ministry of Defence, Joint Force Command, and various formations and units of the Republic of Sierra Leone Armed Forces (RSLAF)

• providing technical infantry expertise, training and education advice, strategic development and leadership

• supporting the development of the RSLAF Maritime Wing

• sponsoring literacy and numeracy training for RSLAF members

• supporting the preparation of an RSLAF task force for deployment with the Africa Union Mission in Somalia (AMISOM)

• carrying out civil-military co-operation (CIMIC) projects.[d]

Contributors of military personnel: Bangladesh, Bolivia, China, Croatia, Egypt, Gambia, Germany, Ghana, Guinea, India, Indonesia, Jordan, Kenya, Kyrgyzstan, Malawi, Malaysia, Nepal, Nigeria, Norway, Pakistan, Russian Federation, Slovakia, Sweden, Tanzania, Ukraine, United Kingdom, Uruguay, and Zambia

Contributors of police personnel: Australia, Bangladesh, Cameroon, **Canada**, Gambia, Ghana, India, Jordan, Kenya, Malawi, Malaysia, Mauritius, Namibia, Nepal, Niger, Nigeria, Norway, Pakistan, Russia, Senegal, Sri Lanka, Sweden, Tanzania, Turkey, United Kingdom, United States, Zambia, and Zimbabwe

(continued)

FINANCIAL: Canadian contribution	FINANCIAL: Total
During this period, Canada also donated about $860,000 worth of body armour and helmets to outfit two battalions of infantry that had arrived for UN duty without personal protection equipment. Estimated 90 CF members have been in rotation in Sierra Leone (cost of their salaries, living, transport, etc.)	Total estimated expenditures: $2.8 billion[e]

NOTES

a   Department of Peacekeeping Operations (DPKO), "Past Operations—UNAMSIL." (DPKO–United Nations, 2008), http://www.un.org/en/peacekeeping/missions/past/ unamsil/index.html.
b   DPKO, "Sierra Leone—UNASMIL—Facts and Figures" (DPKO–UN, 2008), http://www .un.org/Depts/dpko/missions/unamsil/facts.html.
c   Defence Canada, "National Defence and the Canadian Forces. Backgrounder: Canadian Contribution in Sierra Leone: Operation REPTILE and Operation SCULPTURE" (n.d.), http://www.forces.gc.ca/en/operations-abroad-current/op -sculpture.page.
d   Department of National Defence (DND), "Operation Sculpture" (2012), retrieved on 14 April 2013 from http://www.cjoc.forces.gc.ca/exp/sculpture/index-eng.asp.
e   Ibid.

COUNTRY: LIBERIA

Timelines: September 1993–September 1997 (UNOMIL)
              September 2003–November 2003 (SHIRBRIG)
              September 2003–present (UNMIL)

International Mission:

UNOMIL was established in support of the efforts of the Economic Community of West African States (ECOWAS) and the Liberian National Transitional Government to implement peace agreements; investigate alleged ceasefire violations; assist in maintenance of assembly sites and demobilization of combatants; support humanitarian assistance; investigate human rights violations and assist local human rights groups; observe and verify elections[a]

SHIRBRIG was associated with UNMILSHIRBRIG (Multinational Standby High Readiness Brigade for UN Operations). It was a rapid deployment force, consisting of units from a number of member states, trained to the same standard, using the same operating procedures and inter-operable equipment, and taking part in combined exercises at regular intervals.[b]

(continued)

At the time that UNMIL was created there were 3,500 ECOWAS Mission in Liberia (ECOMIL) troops in Liberia. Composed of soldiers from eight West African countries, ECOMIL was not prepared to run a UN mission of 15,000 troops. SHIRBRIG was requested to provide a headquarters component for UNMIL during the transition from ECOMIL to UNMIL. The SHIRBRIG personnel would augment the UN Interim Headquarters until the main UN force headquarters arrived, which was tentatively scheduled for 1 November 2003. SHIRBRIG would then leave Liberia around 6 November.[c]

Purpose: SHIRBRIG was asked to provide officers to assist with the transition of the ECOWAS Military Mission in Liberia (ECOMIL) elements to UN command and control, before handing over to the main Force Headquarters on 1 November 2003.

Canadian contribution: Operation Liane

Mandate: Four Canadian Forces officers deployed on Operation LIANE, the Canadian contribution to the United Nations (UN) Mission in Liberia (UNMIL), from late September until early November 2003. The officers deployed with the Standby High-Readiness Brigade for UN operations (SHIRBRIG). The four Canada-based officers were non-permanent, or "augmentation" members of the SHIRBRIG headquarters planning staff.[d]

PEACEKEEPING FORCES: Canadian Contribution	PEACEKEEPING FORCES: Total Contribution by All Partners
4 Canadian personnel—2 officers (a lieutenant-colonel and a captain) for administration and operations, and 2 non-commissioned members for security assistance.[e]	UNOMIL authorized strength: *For September 1993–November 1995:* 303 military observers, 20 military medical personnel, 45 military engineers; there was also a provision some 90 international and 136 local civilian staff, and 58 UN Volunteers
	For November 1995–November 1996: 160 military observers, supported by military medical personnel; there was also a provision for some 105 international civilian and 550 local civilian staff, and 120 UN Volunteers
	For November 1996–September 1997: 92 military observers, supported by military medical personnel and international and local civilian staff
	Contributors of military personnel: Austria, Bangladesh, Belgium, Brazil, China, Congo, Czech Republic, Egypt, Guinea-Bissau, Hungary, India, Jordan, Kenya, Malaysia, Nepal, Netherlands, Pakistan, Poland, Russian Federation, Slovak Republic, Sweden, and Uruguay[f]

(continued)

SHIRBRIG deployed 20 members[g]

The UNMIL mission (which followed the SHIRBRIG mission) included:

Initially authorized strength 19 September 2003–13 July 2005: 15,000 military personnel, 250 military observers, 160 staff officers, 1,115 police officers including formed units, and the appropriate civilian component

Currently authorized: On 17 September 2012, the Security Council decided to decrease UNMIL's military strength by about 4,200 personnel, in three phases between August 2012 and July 2015. Mission military strength would be at about 3,750 personnel by July 2015. At the same time, the Council decided to increase the number of UNMIL's authorized formed police units by some 420 personnel for a new authorized ceiling of 1,795 personnel.

Current strength (28 February 2013): 8,142 total uniformed personnel, including 6,668 troops, 128 military observers, and 1,346 police, including formed units; 466 international civilian personnel, 985 local staff, and 226 UN Volunteers

Contributors of military personnel: (Canada not included as troops were contributed only to SHIRBRIG mission) Bangladesh, Benin, Bolivia, Brazil, Bulgaria, China, Croatia, Denmark, Ecuador, Egypt, El Salvador, Ethiopia, Finland, France, Gambia, Ghana, Indonesia, Jordan, Kyrgyzstan, Malaysia, Moldova, Montenegro, Namibia, Nepal, Niger, Nigeria, Pakistan, Paraguay, Peru, Philippines, Poland, Romania, Russian Federation, Senegal, Serbia, Togo, Ukraine, United States, Yemen, Zambia, and Zimbabwe.

(continued)

	Contributors of police personnel: Argentina, Bangladesh, Bosnia and Herzegovina, China, Egypt, El Salvador, Fiji, Gambia, Germany, Ghana, India, Jordan, Kenya, Kyrgyzstan, Namibia, Nepal, Nigeria, Norway, Pakistan, Philippines, Poland, Russian Federation, Rwanda, Serbia, Sri Lanka, Sweden, Switzerland, Turkey, Uganda, Ukraine, United States, Uruguay, Yemen, Zambia, and Zimbabwe.[h]
FINANCIAL: Canadian Contribution	**FINANCIAL:** Total
Since September 2002, CIDA has allocated more than $8.4 million to West Africa, including a humanitarian assistance contribution, announced in July 2003, of $1.75 million for Liberia and neighbouring countries. About $3 million has been earmarked for relief projects in Liberia, with more than $1.3 million designated for Liberian refugees in neighbouring countries.[j]	UNOMIL expenditures: $103.7 million (gross), $99.3 million (net)[i] UNMIL approved budget (1 July 2012–30 June 2013): $518.1 million

NOTES

a   DPKO, "United Nations Observer Mission in Liberia—UNOMIL" (DPKO–UN, n.d.), http://www.un.org/en/peacekeeping/missions/past/unomil.htm.

b   SHIRBRIG, "Introduction" (n.d.), retrieved November 20, 2008 from http://www.shirbrig.dk/html/sb_intro.htm.

c   Defence Canada—Operations Database, "Details/Information for Canadian Forces (CF) Operation LIANE" (2008), http://www.cmp-cpm.forces.gc.ca/dhh-dhp/od-bdo/di-ri-eng.asp?IntlOpId=289&CdnOpId=349.

d   National Defence and the Canadian Forces, "Canadian Forces to Contribute Officers in Liberia" (2008), retrieved 1 December 2008 from http://www.comfec-cefcom.forces.gc.ca/pa-ap/nr-sp/doc-eng.asp?id=1196.

e   Defence Canada—Operations Database, "Details/Information for Canadian Forces (CF) Operation LIANE."

f   DPKO, "United Nations Observer Mission in Liberia—UNOMIL—Facts and Figures" (DPKO–UN, n.d.), http://www.un.org/en/peacekeeping/missions/past/unomil.htm.

g   SHIRBRIG, "UNMIL" (2008), retrieved 27 November 2008 from http://www.shirbrig.dk/html/unmil.htm.

h   DPKO, "United Nations Mission in Liberia—UNMIL—Facts and Figures" (DPKO–UN, 2013), http://www.un.org/en/peacekeeping/missions/unmil/facts.shtml.

i   DPKO, "UN—Completed Peacekeeping Missions. Liberia—Facts and Figures" (DPKO–UN, n.d.), http://www.un.org/Depts/dpko/dpko/co_mission/unomilF.html.

j   Defence Canada, "News Release—Canadian Forces to Contribute Officers to UN
     Mission in Liberia" (23 September 2003), retrieved 20 November 2008 from http://
     www.comfec-cefcom.forces.gc.ca/pa-ap/nr-sp/doc-eng.asp?id=1196.

COUNTRIES: ETHIOPIA AND ERITREA

Timeline: 31 July 2000–31 July 2008

Canada: December 2000–June 2001

International Mission:

SHIRBRIG (associated with UNMEE)

UNMEE (United Nations Mission in Ethiopia and Eritrea)

Purpose:

SHIRBRIG—to monitor the UN-established Temporary Security Zone (TSZ) between Ethiopia and Eritrea, and verify the redeployment of Ethiopian forces in Eritrea from positions taken after 6 February 1999 which were not under that country's control in May 1998.[a]

UNMEE—in June 2000, after two years of fighting in a border dispute, Ethiopia and Eritrea signed a cessation of hostilities agreement following proximity talks led by Algeria and the Organization of African Unity. In July, the Security Council set up UNMEE to maintain liaison with the parties and establish a mechanism for verifying the ceasefire. In September 2000, the Council authorized UNMEE to monitor the cessation of hostilities and to help ensure the observance of security commitments.

Canadian contribution:

SHIRBRIG—Operation Eclipse—tasked to provide military observers and a mechanized infantry company to the Dutch-led peacekeeping effort

UNMEE—Operation Addition

PEACEKEEPING FORCES: Canadian Contribution	PEACEKEEPING FORCES: Total Contribution by All Partners
Operation Eclipse (SHIRBRIG):	UNMEE:
Deployment began in late December 2000, when 450 Canadian soldiers began arriving in east Africa to support UNMEE. The deployment was a joint effort with the Netherlands and Denmark under the auspices of SHIRBRIG, which made its debut with this operation	Authorized maximum strength: 4,200 military personnel, including up to 230 military observers Current strength (31 May 2008): 240 troops, 81 military observers, 151 international civilian personnel, 194 local civilian staff, and 61 UN Volunteers

(continued)

Canada's "Task Force East Africa" (TFEA) comprised the following sub-units:

- an armoured reconnaissance platoon
- a Company Group made up of the following elements:
  - H Company of The Royal Canadian Regiment (three mechanized infantry platoons);
  - an engineer troop;
  - a combat service-support platoon; and
  - a company headquarters,

all supported by a Canadian National Command Element and a National Support Element.[b]

For the rest of their six months in east Africa, the Canadian soldiers monitored compliance with the signed protocol concerning the Eritrean militia, and facilitated the return of Eritrean civil administrators and police to the TSZ. They also carried out "quick-impact" humanitarian projects to help people returning to villages in the Canadian area of operations: they refurbished the Senafe elementary school, and distributed school supplies, clothing, sports equipment and toys. These projects were completed by the Canadian soldiers themselves, with partial funding from CIDA. On 11 June the Canadians handed their responsibilities over to the Indian Battalion, and by the end of June the entire Canadian contingent had returned home.

Operation Addition (UNMEE):

There were four 8-month rotations of 6 UNMOs. On each rotation the senior Canadian officer acted as UNMEE's Chief Operations Officer.

Operation Addition marked the first use by the CF of its newly formed Theatre Activation Team (TAT) concept. Based out of CFB Kingston, Ontario, the TAT assisted in establishing the military

Contributors of military personnel: (Canada not included on DPKO website despite Operation Addition) Algeria, Austria, Bangladesh, Bolivia, Brazil, Bulgaria, China, Croatia, Czech Republic, Denmark, Finland, France, Gambia, Germany, Ghana, Greece, Guatemala, India, Iran, Jordan, Kenya, Kyrgystan, Malaysia, Mongolia, Namibia, Nepal, Nigeria, Norway, Pakistan, Paragyay, Peru, Poland, Romania, Russian Federation, South Africa, Spain, Sri Lanka, Sweden, Tanzania, Tunisia, Ukraine, United States, Uruguay, and Zambia

(continued)

and diplomatic groundwork between the UN, Ethiopian, and Eritrean representatives in Asmara. The team included an advance party of engineering troops.

The Canadian military had also agreed to supply a mechanized infantry company group with engineering and logistics support—approximately 450 personnel—for the six-month rotation.[c]

FINANCIAL: Canadian Contribution	FINANCIAL: Total
Not available	Approved budget for 1 July 2007–30 June 2008: $113.48 million

NOTES

a   Defence Canada—Operations Database, "Canadian Forces (CF) Information (ECLIPSE)" (2008), http://www.cmp-cpm.forces.gc.ca/dhh-dhp/od-bdo/di-ri-eng .asp?IntlOpId=285&CdnOpId=342.

b   National Defence and the Canadian Forces, "Operation ECLIPSE" (2008), retrieved 21 November 2008 from http://www.comfec-cefcom.forces.gc.ca/pa-ap/ops/eclipse -eng.asp.

c   Information regarding Operation Addition is from: National Defence and the Canadian Forces—Operations Database, "Canadian Forces (CF) Information (ECLIPSE)."

COUNTRY: CENTRAL AFRICAN REPUBLIC
Timeline: April 1998–February 2000
Canada: April 1998–October 1999

International Mission:
MINURCA (United Nations Mission in the Central African Republic)

Purpose: to assist in maintaining and enhancing security and stability in Bangui and vicinity; supervise, control storage, and monitor the disposition of weapons retrieved in disarmament exercise; assist in capacity building of national police; provide advice and technical support for legislative elections. Later, MINURCA was also mandated to support the conduct of presidential elections and supervise the destruction of confiscated weapons.[a]

Canadian contribution: Operation Prudence

Mandate was to assist the Government of the Central African Republic to maintain peace, security, and freedom of movement, and to assist in protecting key installations in the capital city of Bangui; to supervise, control storage, and monitor a disarmament program; to ensure freedom of movement for UN personnel and protect UN property; to assist with the training of a national police force, and to support future national elections.[b]

(continued)

PEACEKEEPING FORCES: Canadian Contribution	PEACEKEEPING FORCES: Total Contribution by All Partners
The initial contribution to MINURCA was 45 personnel under the designation Operation Prudence. Deploying on 15 April 1998, the main role was to support the mission's communications system; the contingent incorporated a communications detachment, as well as support personnel and staff officers. The contingent was expanded in October 1998 to provide extra signals personnel to support national elections planned for the end of 1998. By late 1999 MINURCA was deemed to have been successful and the UN peacekeeping contingents began planning their departures from the mission. The Canadian mission was closed out in December 1999.[d] The contingent comprised a signals troop of 25 CF personnel, 4 staff officers employed at MINURCA Headquarters, a command and support element of 22 CF personnel, and, during the presidential elections, 32 more CF signallers to support remote electoral sites.[e]	Maximum authorized strength: 1,350 troops and military support personnel and 24 civilian police, supported by international and local civilian staff. There was also a provision for 114 international civilian staff, 111 local staff, and 13 UN Volunteers. Additional short-term and medium-term UN observers were deployed during the legislative (November–December 1998) and presidential (September 1999) elections.[c] Contributors of military personnel: Benin, Burkina Faso, Cameroon, **Canada**, Chad, Côte d'Ivoire, Egypt, France, Gabon, Mali, Portugal, Senegal, Togo, and Tunisia
FINANCIAL: Canadian Contribution	FINANCIAL: Total
Not available	Expenditures for the period 27 March 1998–30 June 1999: $60.2 million (gross) Appropriation for the period 1 July 1999–30 June 2000: $41.1 million (gross), including costs related to the liquidation of the mission[f]

NOTES

a DPKO, "Completed Peacekeeping Operations—Central African Republic" (DPKO–UN, 2001), http://www.un.org/Depts/DPKO/Missions/car.htm.

b Defence Canada, "Details/Information for Canadian Forces (CF) Operation *PRUDENCE*" (2008), http://www.cmp-cpm.forces.gc.ca/dhh-dhp/od-bdo/di-ri-eng.asp?IntlOpId= 115&CdnOpId=137.

c DPKO, "Completed Peacekeeping Operations—Central African Republic—MINURCA—
   Facts and Figures" (DPKO–UN, 2001), http://www.un.org/Depts/DPKO/Missions/
   minurcaF.html.
d Ibid.
e Defence Canada, "Operation PRUDENCE" (2008), retrieved 28 November 2008 from
   http://www.comfec-cefcom.forces.gc.ca/pa-ap/ops/prudence-eng.asp.
f Ibid.

COUNTRY: SOMALIA

Timelines: April 1992–March 1993 (UNOSOM I)
            March 1993–March 1995 (UNOSOM II)

Canada: April 1992–March 1993

International Missions: UNOSOM I and II

UNOSOM I was established to monitor the ceasefire in Mogadishu and escort deliveries of humanitarian supplies to distribution centres in the city. The mission's mandate and strength were later enlarged to enable it to protect humanitarian convoys and distribution centres throughout Somalia. It later worked with the Unified Task Force in the effort to establish a safe environment for the delivery of humanitarian assistance.[a]

UNOSOM II was established in March 1993 to take appropriate action, including enforcement measures, to establish throughout Somalia a secure environment for humanitarian assistance. To that end, UNOSOM II was to complete, through disarmament and reconciliation, the task begun by the Unified Task Force for the restoration of peace, stability, law, and order. UNOSOM II was withdrawn in early March 1995.[b]

Canadian contribution: Operation Deliverance

(Canadian operations in Somalia are not listed in either the DND Past Operations list or the DND Operations Database.)

PEACEKEEPING FORCES: Canadian Contribution	PEACEKEEPING FORCES: Total Contribution by All Partners
Operation Deliverance—involved deployment of a 900-person contingent, of HMCS *Preserver*, and of Hercules transport aircraft. On 30 May 1993, after six months, the Canadian UNOSOM contingent handed their responsibilities over to UNOSOM II forces from other countries and returned to Canada.[c]	UNOSOM I: Authorized strength: 50 military observers, 3,500 security personnel, and up to 719 military support personnel, supported by international civilian and local staff. Maximum deployment (28 February 1993): 54 military observers and 893 troops and military support personnel, supported by international civilian and local staff

(continued)

	Contributors of military personnel: Australia, Austria, Bangladesh, Belgium, **Canada**, Czechoslovakia, Egypt, Fiji, Finland, Indonesia, Jordan, Morocco, New Zealand, Norway, Pakistan, and Zimbabwe[d]
	UNOSOM II:
	Authorized strength (March 1993–4 February 1994): 28,000 military and civilian police personnel; there was also provision for approximately 2,800 international and local civilian staff
	Authorized strength (4 February–25 August 1994): 22,000 all ranks, supported by international and local civilian staff
	Authorized strength (25 August 1994–2 March 1995: 15,000 all ranks, supported by international and local civilian staff
	Strength at the start of withdrawal (30 November 1994): 14,968 all ranks, supported by international and local civilian staff
	Contributors of military and civilian police personnel: Australia, Bangladesh, Belgium, Botswana, **Canada**, Egypt, France, Germany, Ghana, Greece, India, Indonesia, Ireland, Italy, Kuwait, Malaysia, Morocco, Nepal, Netherlands, New Zealand, Nigeria, Norway, Pakistan, Philippines, Republic of Korea, Romania, Saudi Arabia, Sweden, Tunisia, Turkey, United Arab Emirates, United States, Zambia, and Zimbabwe
FINANCIAL: Canadian Contribution	FINANCIAL: Total
Not available	UNOSOM I: $42.9 million (net)[e] UNOSOM II: $1.6 billion (net)[f]

NOTES

a   DPKO, "Completed Peacekeeping Operations—United Nations Operation in Somalia I" (DPKO–UN, 2003), http://www.un.org/Depts/dpko/dpko/co_mission/unosomi .htm.

b   DPKO, "Completed Peacekeeping Operations—United Nations Operation in Somalia II" (DPKO–UN, 2003), http://www.un.org/Depts/dpko/dpko/co_mission/unosom2 .htm.

c   National Defence and the Canadian Forces, "Communications and Electronics Branch—Annex A—Peacekeeping Missions" (2005), retrieved 1 December 2008 from http://www.commelec.forces.gc.ca/org/his/bh-hb/appendix-annexe-a-eng .asp.

d   DPKO, "Completed Peacekeeping Operations—Somalia—UNOSOM I—Facts and Figures" (DPKO–UN, 2003), http://www.un.org/Depts/dpko/dpko/co_mission/ unosom1facts.html.

e   Ibid.

f   Ibid.

COUNTRY: RWANDA

Timeline:October 1993–March 1996

Canada: October 1993–December 1995

International Mission: UNAMIR

UNAMIR was originally established to help implement the Arusha Peace Agreement signed by the Rwandan parties on 4 August 1993. UNAMIR's mandate and strength were adjusted on a number of occasions in the face of the tragic events of the genocide and the changing situation in the country; its mandate came to an end on 8 March 1996.[a]

Canadian contribution: Operation Scotch and Operation Passage

(Canadian operations in Rwanda are not listed in either the DND Past Operations list or the DND Operations Database.)

PEACEKEEPING FORCES: Canadian Contribution	PEACEKEEPING FORCES: Total Contribution by All Partners
Operation Scotch—began on 11 April 1994 and involved 312 Hercules C-130 flights to Kigali, Rwanda, or to Goma, DRC, to deploy 1 Canadian Division Headquarters and Signal Regiment to UNAMIR. The main body of the Regiment returned home at the end of January 1995. Operation Passage—deployed 2 Field Ambulances for humanitarian flights for UNHCR or CIDA from April–October 1994.	Authorized strength (5 October 1993–20 April 1994): 2,548 military personnel, including 2,217 formed troops and 331 military observers; 60 civilian police; supported by international and locally recruited civilian staff Authorized strength (21 April–16 May 1994): 270 military personnel; supported by international and locally recruited civilian staff Authorized strength (17 May 1994–8 June 1995): approximately 5,200 troops and military support personnel and 320 military observers; and 90 civilian police (in February 1995, the authorized strength of the civilian

(continued)

8 Air Communications and Control Squadron (8ACCS) was deployed at Nairobi, Kenya, and Kigali. On 16 September 1994 the Kigali airport was turned over to civilian control, and by 28 September 8ACCS had returned to Canada.[b]

Force Commanders:
Major-General Romeo A. Dallaire (Canada) October 1993–August 1994
Major-General Guy Tousignant (Canada) August 1994–December 1995

police was increased to 120); supported by international and locally recruited civilian staff

Authorized strength (9 June–8 September 1995): 2,330 troops and military support personnel, 320 military observers, and 120 civilian police; supported by international and locally recruited civilian staff

Authorized strength (9 September–11 December 1995): 1,800 troops and military support personnel, 320 military observers, and 120 civilian police; supported by international and locally recruited civilian staff

Authorized strength (12 December 1995–8 March 1996): 1,200 troops and military support personnel and 200 military observers; supported by international and locally recruited civilian staff

Strength at withdrawal (29 February 1996): 1,252 troops and military support personnel and 146 military observers; approximately 160 international and 160 local civilian staff, and 56 UN Volunteers

Contributors of Military And Civilian Police Personnel: Argentina, Australia, Austria, Bangladesh, Belgium, Brazil, **Canada**, Chad, Congo, Djibouti, Egypt, Ethiopia, Fiji, Germany, Ghana, Guinea, Guinea Bissau, Guyana, India, Jordan, Kenya, Malawi, Mali, Netherlands, Niger, Nigeria, Pakistan, Poland, Romania, Russian Federation, Senegal, Slovak Republic, Spain, Switzerland, Togo, Tunisia, United Kingdom, Uruguay, Zambia, and Zimbabwe[c]

FINANCIAL: Canadian Contribution	FINANCIAL: Total
Not available	$453.9 million (net)—from inception of mission to 30 June 1997, inclusive of administrative closing

NOTES

a DPKO, "Completed Peacekeeping Operations—United Nations Assistance Mission for Rwanda" (DPKO–UN, 2001), http://www.un.org/Depts/dpko/dpko/co_mission/unamir.htm.

b National Defence and the Canadian Forces, "Communications and Electronics Branch—Annex A—Peacekeeping Missions" (2005), http://www.commelec.forces.gc.ca/org/his/bh-hb/appendix-annexe-a-eng.asp.

c DPKO, "Completed Peacekeeping Operations—Rwanda—UNAMIR—Facts and Figures" (DPKO–United Nations, 2003), http://www.un.org/Depts/dpko/dpko/co_mission/unamirF.htm.

COUNTRY: SUDAN/DARFUR

Timeline: 31 July 2007–present

International Mission: UNAMID
A joint African Union/United Nations Hybrid operation in Darfur was authorized by Security Council resolution 1769 of 31 July 2007. The Council, acting under Chapter 7 of the United Nations Charter, authorized UNAMID to take necessary action to support the implementation of the Darfur Peace Agreement, as well as to protect its personnel and civilians, without "prejudice to the responsibility of the Government of Sudan." UNAMID formally began operations on 31 December 2007.
Canadian contribution: Operation Saturn

PEACEKEEPING FORCES: Canadian Contribution	PEACEKEEPING FORCES: Total Contribution by All Partners
CF operations in Sudan began in 2005 with the deployment of the first UNMOs to serve with the United Nations Mission in Sudan. Soon after, 105 Grizzly and Husky AVGPs were delivered to Sudan for use by the Nigerian, Rwandan, and Senegalese contingents deployed with the African Union Mission in Sudan. On 31 December 2007, AMIS stood down and the UN partnered with the AU to launch UNAMID as a follow-on mission. Operation Saturn began on the same date as a follow-on mission to Operation Augural, providing staff officers with expertise in logistics to work at UNAMID Headquarters, and Canadian soldiers expert in handling the Husky	Authorized strength (31 July 2007): up to 19,555 military personnel; 6,432 police, including 3,772 police personnel and 19 formed police units comprising up to 140 personnel each; and a significant civilian component Current authorized strength (31 July 2012): up to 16,200 military personnel; 4,690 police; 2,310 police personnel; and 17 formed police units comprising up to 140 personnel each Current strength (28 February 2013): 20,852 total uniformed personnel, including 15,634 troops, 325 military observers, and 4,893 police (inclusive of formed units); 1,081 international civilian personnel, 2,906 local civilian staff, and 450 UN Volunteers[a]

(continued)

and Grizzly vehicles to train soldiers of the Nigerian, Rwandan, and Senegalese contingents to drive and operate the Canadian AVGPs.

The Husky and Grizzly vehicles remained in service with UNAMID until Nigeria, Rwanda, and Senegal completed the introduction of their own armoured vehicles in 2009. At that time, the Canadian armoured trainers were withdrawn from Task Force Darfur.

Currently, Task Force Darfur, the CF team in UNAMID, has an established strength of 6, all staff officers with substantial experience in operations, intelligence, logistics, administration, and civil-military co-operation (CIMIC). Each member of the team is assigned to a position at UNAMID Headquarters in El Fasher, Sudan.[c]

Contributors of military personnel: Australia, Bangladesh, Bolivia, Burkina Faso, Burundi, **Canada**, China, Egypt, Ethiopia, France, Gambia, Germany, Ghana, Guatemala, Indonesia, Italy, Jordan, Kenya, Malawi, Malaysia, Mali, Mozambique, Namibia, Nepal, Netherlands, Nigeria, Pakistan, Rwanda, Senegal, Sierra Leone, South Africa, Sweden, Tanzania, Thailand, Togo, Turkey, Uganda, United Kingdom, Yemen, Zambia, and Zimbabwe[b]

Contributors of police personnel: Bangladesh, Benin, Burkina Faso, Burundi, Cameroon, Côte d'Ivoire, Djibouti, Egypt, Ethiopia, Gambia, Germany, Ghana, Indonesia, Jamaica, Jordan, Kyrgyzstan, Madagascar, Malawi, Malaysia, Nepal, Niger, Nigeria, Pakistan, Palau, Rwanda, Senegal, Sierra Leone, Tajikistan, Tanzania, Togo, Tunisia, Turkey, Yemen, and Zambia[d]

FINANCIAL:	FINANCIAL:
Canadian Contribution	Total
Not available	Approved budget (1 July 2012–30 June 2013): $1.51 billion

NOTES

a   DPKO, "African Union/United Nations Hybrid Operation in Darfur—UNAMID—Facts and Figures" (DPKO–UN, 2013), http://www.un.org/en/peacekeeping/missions/unamid/facts.shtml.

b   DPKO, "Darfur—UNAMID—Facts and Figures" (DPKO–UN, 2008), retrieved from December 1, 2008 from http://www.un.org/Depts/dpko/missions/unamid/facts.html.

c   DND, "Operation Saturn" (2012), retrieved 14 April 2013 from http://www.cjoc.forces.gc.ca/exp/saturn/index-eng.asp.

d   DPKO, "African Union/United Nations Hybrid Operation in Darfur—UNAMID—Facts and Figures."

COUNTRY: SUDAN

Timeline: 24 March 2005–9 July 2011

International mission: UNMIS

The Security Council, by its resolution 1590 of 24 March 2005, decided to establish the United Nations Mission in the Sudan (UNMIS) to support implementation of the Comprehensive Peace Agreement signed by the Government of Sudan and the Sudan People's Liberation Movement/Army on 9 January 2005; and to perform certain functions relating to humanitarian assistance, and to the protection and promotion of human rights.

The mandate of UNMIS ended on 9 July following the completion of the interim period set up by the Government of Sudan and SPLM during the signing of the Comprehensive Peace Agreement (CPA) on 9 January 2005.

Canadian contribution: Operation Safari

Operation SAFARI was the military component of the Canadian whole-of-government engagement in southern Sudan that also included activities by DFAIT, CIDA, and the RCMP.

PEACEKEEPING FORCES: Canadian Contribution	PEACEKEEPING FORCES: Total Contribution by All Partners
Task Force Sudan was the Canadian Forces contingent in UNMIS. The CF have been active in Sudan and South Sudan since the beginning of Operation Safari on 15 June 2004, when the initial rotation of CF members deployed to serve with the United Nations Advance Mission in Sudan (UNAMIS), the forerunner of UNMIS. Under Operation Safari, 12 rotations of CF members served with UNMIS; most were forward-deployed around the country as UNMOs, and a few served as specialized staff advisors at UNMIS Headquarters in Juba and Khartoum.[a]	Authorized strength: up to 10,000 military personnel, including some 750 military observers; up to 715 police; and an appropriate civilian component
At its peak, Task Force Sudan comprised 30 CF members, including 20 serving as UNMOs at team sites across southern Sudan, 8 on staff at UNMIS Headquarters in Khartoum, and 3 with the Canadian support element in Khartoum.[b]	Strength at maximum deployment: 10,519 total uniformed personnel, including 9,304 troops, 513 military observers, and 702 police officers; 966 international civilian personnel, 2,837 local civilian staff, and 477 UN Volunteers
	Strength at withdrawal (30 June 2011): 10,352 total uniformed personnel, including 9,250 troops, 465 military observers, and 637 police officers; 965 international civilian personnel, 2,803 local civilian staff, and 331 UN Volunteers
	Contributors of military personnel: Australia, Bangladesh, Belgium, Benin, Bolivia, Brazil, Burkina Faso, Cambodia, **Canada**, China, Croatia, Denmark,

(continued)

	Ecuador, Egypt, El Salvador, Fiji, Finland, Germany, Ghana, Greece, Guatemala, Guinea, India, Indonesia, Japan, Jordan, Kenya, Kyrgystan, Malaysia, Mali, Moldova, Mongolia, Namibia, Nepal, Netherlands, New Zealand, Nigeria, Norway, Pakistan, Paraguay, Peru, Philippines, Poland, Republic of Korea, Romania, Russian Federation, Rwanda, Sierra Leone, Sri Lanka, Sweden, Switzerland, Tanzania, Thailand, Turkey, Uganda, Ukraine, United Kingdom, Yemen, and Zambia
	Contributors of police personnel: Argentina, Australia, Bangladesh, Bosnia and Herzegovina, Brazil, **Canada**, China, Egypt, El Salvador, Ethiopia, Fiji, Gambia, Germany, Ghana, India, Indonesia, Jamaica, Jordan, Kenya, Kyrgystan, Malaysia, Mali, Namibia, Nepal, Netherlands, Nigeria, Norway, Pakistan, Philippines, Russian Federation, Rwanda, Samoa, Sri Lanka, Sweden, Turkey, Uganda, Ukraine, United States, Yemen, Zambia, and Zimbabwe[c]
FINANCIAL: Canadian Contribution	**FINANCIAL:** Total
Not available	Total: $5.76 billion (estimated)

NOTES

a   DND, "Operation Soprano" (2012), retrieved 14 April 2013 from http://www.cjoc .forces.gc.ca/exp/soprano/index-eng.asp.

b   DND, "Operation Safari" (2013), retrieved 14 April 2013 from http://www.cjoc.forces .gc.ca/exp/safari/index-eng.asp.

c   DPKO, "United Nations Mission in Sudan—UNAMIS—Facts and Figures" (DPKO–UN, 2013), retrieved 14 April 2013 from http://www.un.org/en/peacekeeping/missions/ unmis/facts.shtml.

COUNTRY: SOUTH SUDAN
Timeline: 9 July 2011–present

International Mission: UNMISS

The Security Council, by resolution 1966 on 8 July 2011 determined that the situation faced by South Sudan continued to constitute a threat to international peace and security in the region. The Security Council established the United Nations Mission in the Republic of South Sudan (UNMISS) for an initial period of one year, starting from 9 July 2011.

UNMISS is on the ground to consolidate peace and security and to help establish conditions for development.

Canadian contribution: Operation Soprano

Operation Soprano is the military component of a "whole-of-government" engagement in South Sudan that also includes the RCMP.

PEACEKEEPING FORCES: Canadian Contribution	PEACEKEEPING FORCES: Total Contribution by All Partners
Task Force South Sudan consists of 12 CF personnel who work as staff officers and military liaison officers at UNMISS Force Headquarters in Juba and at various locations throughout the Republic of South Sudan. Task Force South Sudan members contribute technical planning and operational expertise.[a]	Authorized strength: up to 7,000 military personnel; up to 900 civilian police personnel; and an appropriate civilian component
	Current strength (28 February 2013): 7,176 total uniformed personnel, including 6,478 troops, 144 military liaison officers, and 554 police officers; 852 international civilian personnel, 1,349 local civilian staff, and 397 UN Volunteers
	Contributors of military personnel: Australia, Bangladesh, Benin, Bolivia, Brazil, Cambodia, **Canada**, China, Denmark, Ecuador, Egypt, El Salvador, Fiji, Germany, Ghana, Guatemala, Guinea, India, Indonesia, Japan, Jordan, Kenya, Kyrgyzstan, Mali, Moldova, Mongolia, Namibia, Nepal, Netherlands, New Zealand, Nigeria, Norway, Papua New Guinea, Paraguay, Peru, Philippines, Poland, Republic of Korea, Romania, Russian Federation, Rwanda, Senegal, Sri Lanka, Sweden, Switzerland, Tanzania, Timor-Leste, Uganda, Ukraine, United Kingdom, United States, Yemen, Zambia, and Zimbabwe

(continued)

	Contributors of police personnel: Argentina, Australia, Bangladesh, Bosnia and Herzegovina, Brazil, China, El Salvador, Ethiopia, Fiji, Gambia, Germany, Ghana, India, Indonesia, Kenya, Kyrgyzstan, Malaysia, Namibia, Nepal, Netherlands, Nigeria, Norway, Philippines, Russian Federation, Rwanda, Samoa, Senegal, South Africa, Sri Lanka, Sweden, Switzerland, Turkey, Uganda, Ukraine, United States, Zambia, and Zimbabwe[b]
FINANCIAL: Canadian Contribution	FINANCIAL: Total
Not available	Approved budget (1 July 2012–30 June 2013): $876 million

NOTES

a DND, "Operation Soprano."
b DPKO, "United Nations Mission to South Sudan—UNMISS—Facts and Figures" (DPKO-UN, 2013), http://www.un.org/en/peacekeeping/missions/unmiss/facts.shtml.

COUNTRY: DEMOCRATIC REPUBLIC OF CONGO
Timelines: 30 November 1999–1 July 2010 (MONUC) 1 July 2010–present (MONUSCO)
International mission: MONUC—the Democratic Republic of the Congo (DRC) and five regional states signed the Lusaka Ceasefire Agreement in July 1999. To maintain liaison with the parties and carry out other tasks, the Security Council set up MONUC on 30 November 1999, incorporating UN personnel authorized in earlier resolutions.[a] MONUSCO—took over from MONUC on 1 July 2010 in accordance with Security Council Resolution 1925 of 28 May to reflect the new phase reached in the country. The new mission has been authorized to use all necessary means to carry out its mandate relating, among other things, to the protection of civilians, humanitarian personnel, and human rights defenders under imminent threat of physical violence, and to support the Government of the DRC in its stabilization and peace consolidation efforts.[b]
Canadian contribution: Operation Crocodile

(continued)

PEACEKEEPING FORCES: Canadian Contribution	PEACEKEEPING FORCES: Total Contribution by All Partners
Task Force Democratic Republic of the Congo (TFDRC), the Canadian contingent in MONUSCO, had 9 members as of March 2013, including 8 staff officers with expertise in fields such as communications, information operations and training, and 1 senior noncommissioned member who handles all national support tasks. The staff officers are divided between MONUSCO Headquarters in Kinshasa and its eastern sector headquarters in Goma.[c]	MONUC: Initial authorized strength: 5,537 troops, 500 military observers, and appropriate civilian component
	Maximum authorized strength (31 July 2007): Up to 19,815 military personnel, 760 military observers, 391 police, and 1,050 personnel of formed police units
	Strength as of 30 June 2010: 18,653 troops, 704 military observers, and 1,299 police; 973 international civilian personnel, 2.783 local civilian staff, and 641 UN Volunteers
	Contributors of military personnel: Algeria, Argentina, Bangladesh, Belgium, Benin, Bolivia, Bosnia and Herzegovina, Burkina Faso, Cameroon, **Canada**, Central African Republic, Chad, Chile, China, Côte d'Ivoire, Czech Republic, Denmark, Egypt, El Salvador, France, Ghana, Guatemala, Guinea, India, Indonesia, Ireland, Italy, Jordan, Kenya, Libya, Madagascar, Malawi, Malaysia, Mali, Mongolia, Morocco, Mozambique, Nepal, Netherlands, Niger, Nigeria, Norway, Pakistan, Paraguay, Peru, Portugal, Romania, Russia/Russian Federation, Senegal, Serbia, Serbia and Montenegro, South Africa, Spain, Sri Lanka, Sweden, Switzerland, Tanzania, Togo, Tunisia, Turkey, Ukraine, United Kingdom, United States of America, Uruguay, Vanuatu, Yemen, and Zambia
	Contributors of police personnel: Argentina, Benin, Burkina Faso, Bangladesh, Cameroon, **Canada**, Central African Republic, Chad, Egypt, France, Guinea, India, Italy, Ivory Coast, Jordan, Madagascar, Mali, Morocco, Nepal, Niger, Nigeria, Pakistan, Romania, Russian Federation, Senegal, Spain, Sweden, Switzerland, Togo, Turkey, Ukraine, Uruguay, Vanuatu, and Yemen[d]

(continued)

MONUSCO:

Initial authorized strength: 19,815 military personnel, including 760 military observers; 391 police personnel and 1,050 personnel of formed police units; appropriate civilian, judiciary, and correction component

Additional authorization (28 March 2013): for an initial period of one year and within the authorized troop ceiling of 19,815, include an "Intervention Brigade" consisting *inter alia* of three infantry battalions, one artillery, and one Special Force and Reconnaissance company.

Current strength (28 February, 2013): 19,160 total uniformed personnel, including 17,273 military personnel, 507 military observers, and 1,380 police; 985 international civilian personnel, 2,902 local civilian staff, and 591 UN Volunteers

Contributors of military personnel: Bangladesh, Belgium, Benin, Bolivia, Bosnia and Herzegovina, Burkina Faso, **Canada**, China, Czech Republic, Egypt, France, Ghana, Guatemala, India, Indonesia, Ireland, Jordan, Kenya, Malawi, Malaysia, Mali, Morocco, Nepal, Niger, Nigeria, Norway, Pakistan, Paraguay, Peru, Poland, Romania, Russian Federation, Senegal, Serbia, South Africa, Sri Lanka, Sweden, Switzerland, Tanzania, Tunisia, Ukraine, United Kingdom, United States, Uruguay, Yemen, and Zambia

Contributors of police personnel: Bangladesh, Belgium, Benin, Burkina Faso, Cameroon, Central African Republic, Chad, Côte d'Ivoire, Djibouti, Egypt, France, Guinea, India, Jordan, Madagascar, Mali, Niger, Nigeria, Romania, Russian Federation, Senegal, Sweden, Switzerland, Togo, Turkey, Ukraine, and Yemen.[e]

(continued)

FINANCIAL: Canadian Contribution	FINANCIAL: Total
Not available	MONUC total: $8.73 billion MONUSCO approved budget (1 July 2012–30 June 2013): 1.40 billion (Estimated additional costs with deployment of the intervention brigade: $140 million over a full year)

NOTES

a   DPKO, "MONUC" (DPKO–UN, 2008), retrieved 1 December 2008 from http://www
.un.org/Depts/dpko/missions/monuc.

b   DPKO, "MONUSCO" (DPKO–UN, 2013), http://www.un.org/en/peacekeeping/
missions/monusco/index.shtml.

c   DND, "Operation Crocodile" (2012), retrieved 14 April 2013 from http://www
.cjoc.forces.gc.ca/exp/crocodile/index-eng.asp.

d   DPKO, "United Nations Organization Mission in the Democratic Republic of
Congo—MONUC—Facts and Figures" (DPKO–UN, 2013), retrieved 14 April 2013
from http://www.un.org/en/peacekeeping/missions/monuc/facts.shtml.

e   DPKO, "United Nations Organization Stabilization Mission in the Democratic
Republic of the Congo—MONUSCO—Facts and Figures" (DPKO–United Nations,
2013), http://www.un.org/en/peacekeeping/missions/monusco/facts.shtml.

COUNTRY: CÔTE D'IVOIRE
Timeline: 4 April 2004–present

International Mission: UNOCI

Acting under Chapter 7 of the UN Charter, the Security Council, by resolution 1528 (2004), established the United Nations Operation in Côte d'Ivoire (UNOCI) beginning 4 April 2004 with a mandate to facilitate the implementation by the Ivorian parties of the peace agreement signed by them in January 2003. Following the 2010 presidential election and the ensuing political crisis in Côte d'Ivoire, UNOCI has remained on the ground to protect civilians and support the Ivorian government in disarmament, demobilization, and reintegration (DDR) of former combatants, as well as on security sector reform.

PEACEKEEPING FORCES: Canadian Contribution	PEACEKEEPING FORCES: Total Contribution by All Partners
Canada has supported UNOCI since its creation in 2004. There are currently 9 police officers, mainly from the RCMP who are deployed to UNOCI.[a]	Initial authorized strength (4 April 2004–23 June 2005): 6,910 total uniformed personnel, including 6,240 troops, 200 military observers, 120 staff officers, and 350 police officers

(continued)

The mission mandate calls for non-executive policing duties, which includes a monitoring role. Canadian police officers are responsible for assessing and identifying the current training standards and needs of police officers in Côte d'Ivoire.[b]

Current authorization (26 July 2012): 8,645 troops and staff officers, 192 military observers, 1,563 police officers, and 8 customs officers

Current strength as of 28 February 2013: 11,005 total uniformed personnel, including 9,361 troops, 190 military observers, 1,454 police (including formed units); 417 international civilian personnel, 766 local civilian staff, and 179 UN Volunteers

Contributors of military personnel: Bangladesh, Benin, Bolivia, Brazil, Chad, China, Ecuador, Egypt, El Salvador, Ethiopia, France, Gambia, Ghana, Guatemala, Guinea, India, Ireland, Jordan, Malawi, Moldova, Morocco, Namibia, Nepal, Niger, Nigeria, Pakistan, Paraguay, Peru, Philippines, Poland, Republic of Korea, Romania, Russian Federation, Senegal, Serbia, Tanzania, Togo, Tunisia, Uganda, Uruguay, Yemen, and Zimbabwe.

Contributors of police personnel: Argentina, Bangladesh, Benin, Burkina Faso, Burundi, Cameroon, **Canada**, Central African Republic, Chad, Djibouti, Democratic Republic of the Congo, Egypt, France, Ghana, Guinea, Jordan, Madagascar, Niger, Nigeria, Pakistan, Rwanda, Senegal, Togo, Tunisia, Turkey, Ukraine, Uruguay, and Yemen[c]

FINANCIAL:	FINANCIAL:
Canadian Contribution	Total
Not available	Approved budget (1 July 2012–30 June 2013): $600 million

NOTES

a   Government of Canada, "Canada–Côte d'Ivoire Relations" (Ottawa, March 2013), http://www.canadainternational.gc.ca/cotedivoire/bilateral_relations_bilaterales/ canada_cotedivoire.aspx.

b   Royal Canadian Mounted Police, "International Peace Branch: Current Operations" (2012), http://www.rcmp-grc.gc.ca/po-mp/missions-curr-cour-eng.htm#n2.

c   DPKO, "United Nations Operation in Côte d'Ivoire—UNOCI—Facts and Figures" (DPKO–UN, 2013), http://www.un.org/en/peacekeeping/missions/unoci/facts .shtml.

COUNTRY: MALI	
Timeline: January 2013–present	
International mission: AFISMA The Security Council, acting under Chapter 7, adopted Resolution 2085 on 20 December 2012 to authorize the deployment of an African-led international support mission in Mali (AFISMA) for an initial year-long period. The mandate is to support efforts by national authorities to recover the north.[a] Opération Serval—the French military operation launched on 11 January 2013 at the request of the Malian authorities and the United Nations to support the Malian armed forces. The mandate of the operation is to stop the militants in the north from advancing toward the south and to protect the security of the 5,000 French nationals living in Mali.[b]	
Canadian operation: Air Task Force Mali (in support of Opération Serval)	
PEACEKEEPING FORCES: Canadian Contribution	PEACEKEEPING FORCES: Total Contribution by All Partners
Canada's contribution to French operations in Mali consisted of one CC-177 Globemaster III heavy-lift transport aircraft and about 40 RCAF personnel: flight and maintenance crews from 429 Transport Squadron and traffic technicians from 2 Air Movements Squadron, both units of 8 Wing Trenton, Ontario. The mandate of Air Task Force Mali was limited to airlift, and specifically excludes combat.[e]	There are currently 6,300 AFISMA troops deployed in Mali from Nigeria, Niger, Togo, Burkina Faso, Senegal, Benin, Guinea, Ghana, and Chad.[c] As well, there are currently an estimated 4,000 French soldiers in Mali.[d]
FINANCIAL: Canadian Contribution	FINANCIAL: Total
Not available	Not available

NOTES

a   United Nations. "Security Council Authorizes Deployment of African-Led International Support Mission in Mali for Initial Year-Long Period" (2012), http://www.un.org/News/Press/docs/2012/sc10870.doc.htm.

b   Ministère de la défense, "Mali: lancement de l'opération Serval" (12 January 2013), http://www.defense.gouv.fr/operations/mali/actualite/mali-lancement-de-l -operation-serval.

c   Ministère de la défense, "Mali: arrivée du contingent burkinabé de la MISMA à Tombouctou" (12 April 2013), http://www.defense.gouv.fr/operations/actualites/mali-arrivee-du-contingent-burkinabe-de-la-misma-a-tombouctou.

d   Ministère de la défense, "Opération Serval: point de situation sue les operations du jeudi, 11 avril 2013" (12 April 2013), http://www.defense.gouv.fr/operations/mali/actualite/operation-serval-point-de-situation-sur-les-operations-du-jeudi-11-avril-2013.

e   DND, "Canadian Armed Forces Contribution to Mali" (2013), retrieved 14 April 2013 from http://www.forces.gc.ca/site/feature-vedette/2013/01/index-eng.asp.

Notes

Notes to Introduction

1 With remote colonial residues from pre-revolutionary France.
2 It is perhaps indicative of the ongoing rise, fall, and rise of interest in Africa that this renewed scholarly focus on Canada's involvement in Africa has emerged not only in the context of a new, transnational narrative of "Rising Africa," but following more than five years of relative indifference toward the continent from the Harper government.

Notes to Chapter 1

1 The next several paragraphs draw on Black and Williams (2008). For an excellent, succinct exploration of the International Society/English School approach, see Murray (2013).
2 For contrasting interpretations, see Razack (2004) and Dawson (2007).
3 This perspective is consistent with the motif of "Friend" to Africa outlined by Grant Dawson (2013) in his distinction between Canada as "Partner, Player, and Friend" in relations with the continent's post-colonial regimes.
4 The neo-Gramscian/Coxian tradition has inspired a large number of contributions. For an important compendium of Cox's own thinking, see Cox with Sinclair (1996). The particular description in this paragraph is derived primarily from Cox's 1981 article "Social Forces, States, and World Orders," reproduced in Cox with Sinclair (1996, 85–123). For an excellent review essay on the neo-Gramscian tradition in international relations, see Bieler and Morton (2004).
5 For a fuller exploration of this role, see Black (1997).
6 Obviously, describing the Canadian state as non-imperial requires careful qualification. As many scholars have noted, "Newcomer" (settler) Canada long pursued a colonial relationship with, and approach toward, the First Peoples of the country—a relationship that continues to cause grave difficulties and to undermine Canada's still-relatively benign international image.

7   The fact that Canada's active engagement with francophone Africa
    was belated underscored the historic centrality of the British Empire/
    Commonwealth, and fuelled Quebec nationalist claims that "French
    Canada" could only be properly represented by the Government of
    Quebec given the province's French-speaking majority. The federal
    government's rapid pursuit of expanded ties with francophone Africa
    was, in turn, stimulated largely by its reaction to Quebec's increasingly
    assertive nation-building aspirations and pursuit of international auton-
    omy. Prior to the late 1960s, its approach to francophone Africa had
    reflected a particular sensitivity to France's central role in the affairs of
    its ex-colonies. For an excellent discussion of this three-cornered rela-
    tionship and its manifestation in Canada–Francophone Africa dynam-
    ics, see Gendron (2006).
8   In addition to Cranford Pratt (2003; 1983–84), the most persistent
    though by no means only scholar in this tradition has been Linda Free-
    man (e.g., 1985; 1997).
9   For example, bilateral and Western alliance defence relationships,
    through NATO and NORAD, and the emphasis and resources devoted to
    the negotiation of bilateral free trade agreements from the late 1980s
    onwards. On the "doubly hegemonic" role of Canada's middle-power
    role, see Neufeld (1995).
10 It was announced in the Federal Budget of March 2013 that the then
    Department of Foreign Affairs and International Trade (DFAIT) would
    be merged with CIDA, and renamed the Department of Foreign Affairs,
    Trade, and Development (DFATD). At the time of writing, this merger
    was still a work in progress, and its ramifications for Canadian devel-
    opment and Africa policies remained to be worked out—though they
    appear to have reinforced the trend under the Conservatives toward the
    (re)commercialization of aid. See Goyette (forthcoming).

Notes to Chapter 2

This chapter is revised and updated from Black, "Canada, the G8 and
Africa: the Rise and Decline of a Hegemonic Project?" In D. Bratt and
C. Kukucha, eds., *Readings in Canadian Foreign Policy: Classic Debates and
New Ideas*, 2nd edition. Don Mills: Oxford University Press, 2011.

1   The language of "hegemonic work" in the title of this section is bor-
    rowed from Coulter (2009, 201).
2   Between independence in 1960 and 1995, for example, Africa had the
    slowest growth per capita of all the main "developing" regions (Africa,
    Latin America, Asia), and actually experienced negative GDP growth per
    capita between 1991 and 1995 (see ECA 2012, 60–66).
3   The need to respond to these and similar protests, both procedurally

and substantively, was clearly in the minds of summit planners (see, e.g., Fowler 2003, 225).

4 A point that must be significantly qualified in light of the large and growing role of Canadian extractive companies in the mining and energy sectors of many African countries: see Chapter 7.

5 Another point that must be qualified given Canada's relatively limited and inconstant commitment to aid and diplomacy, as will be elaborated below.

6 For a neo-Gramscian exploration of the interplay between transnational and domestic hegemonic work in Canadian "middle power (or Pearsonian) internationalism," see Neufeld (1995).

7 As reflected in the subtitle of Kananaskis Sherpa and African Personal Representative Robert Fowler's reflection on the Kananaskis process: "Towards a Less Self-Centred Canadian Foreign Policy" (Fowler 2003, 219).

8 Fowler was himself a periodic "Africa hand," as reflected in his comment that "as I approached the end of my career I would have another—this time unique—opportunity to assist Africa, a continent and a people that have held my fascination and deep affection for all of my adult and professional life" (Fowler 2003: 221). He had already achieved some renown for his pivotal role as Chair of the Angola Sanctions Committee, while Canada's UN Ambassador and Security Council representative in 1999–2000, by instigating the creation of an unprecedented Panel of Experts to evaluate how sanctions against UNITA were being violated, and how they could be made more effective. The panel's report caused a furor by "naming names," but also highlighted key features of the Angolan war economy and produced recommendations that helped choke off UNITA's ability to sustain the conflict (see Möllander 2009). Fowler's close association with the continent, and his renown, were further reinforced due to his abduction by al-Qaeda-linked rebels in West Africa for 130 days in the first half of 2009, while on a UN mission in Niger. For his own account of this ordeal, see Fowler (2011).

9 As reflected, for example, in the collapse of the "Doha Development Round" of trade negotiations; the ongoing challenges in pivotal African conflict areas—notably the DRC—to which the G8 AAP formally committed its collective efforts; and the failure to fulfill commitments in support of peacekeeping coordination and funding. On the latter, see Yamashita (2013, 342–46).

10 The eight poverty-focused objectives, and various sub-targets, around which international efforts have been mobilized since the UN Millennium Summit of 2000, with a deadline of 2015. See http://www.un.org/millenniumgoals/poverty.shtml.

11　The theme of accountability for commitments has become a Canadian "signature issue" under the Harper government. This is consistent with the order-building predilections of hegemonic middlepowermanship, since increased credibility of international commitments can be understood as a necessary condition for expanded zones of order.

12　The designated African Development Partners were: Benin, Burkina Faso, Cameroon, Ethiopia, Ghana, Kenya, Malawi, Mali, Mozambique, Niger, Rwanda, Senegal, Tanzania, and Zambia. This list was substantially reduced by the Harper government less than four years later, as discussed in Chapter 5.

13　Cordiant of Montreal and Actis of London (UK).

14　For a discussion of Canada's efforts in support of African peace-and-security capacity building, see Akuffo (2012, esp. chapters 4 and 5).

15　Though, as noted above, the trade liberalization commitments, in particular, proved illusory.

16　Harper's first trip to Africa was for the Commonwealth Heads of Government Meeting in Kampala in November 2007.

17　Canada's combat role in Kandahar Province became the country's costliest since the Korean War, in both human and material terms. Similarly, CIDA's bilateral aid program in Afghanistan quickly became its largest ever. On the "integrated" character of the mission, see Travers and Owen (2008).

18　In keeping with the theme of consistent inconsistency, the Conservatives revised the list of development focus countries again in June 2014. Among other changes, the government restored African countries Benin and Burkina Faso—both dropped in 2009—to the priority list (see Chapter 5; also Shane 2014).

19　These reductions were exacerbated by the "stealth cuts" resulting from C$290 million in "lapsed" (unspent) commitments in 2013, resulting in an overall decline in aid spending of more than 11 percent (see S. Brown 2014).

20　Reducing under-five mortality by two-thirds; and reducing maternal mortality by three-quarters and achieving universal access to reproductive health. For the text of the Muskoka Initiative, see "G8 Muskoka Declaration Recovery and New Beginnings," 25–26 June 2010, http:// g8.gc.ca/g8-summit/summit-documents/g8-muskoka-declaration -recovery-and-new-beginnings/.

21　These countries were Mozambique, Mali, Malawi, Nigeria, southern Sudan, Ethiopia, and Tanzania. Other focus countries for the initiative were Afghanistan, Haiti, and Bangladesh.

22　The result of the commitment made at the Gleneagles G8 Summit in 2005 to double total aid spending between 2001 and 2009–10.

23 The final decision was contraception yes, but abortion no (see Gavai 2010).

24 This may explain in part why one year later, at the 2011 Deauville Summit in France, implementation of the Muskoka commitments by other G8 governments was so desultory (see Clark and Saunders 2011).

25 See CIDA, 1/11/2010. http://www.acdi-cida.gc.ca/acdi-cida/ACDI -CIDA.nsf/eng/FRA-103117396-TE2.

26 Albeit with less than 40 percent of the popular vote—a result made possible by Canada's first-past-the-post electoral system.

27 The historic third party—the social democratic New Democrats— became the official opposition with over 30 percent of the popular vote.

28 Grant Dawson cites personal testimony that Jean Chrétien received "thousands of congratulatory messages on two issues: staying out of the 2003 Iraq war, and emphasizing African development" (2013, 6).

Notes to Chapter 3

1 Both narrative strands can be seen to grow out of the "humane internationalist" tradition in Canadian political culture, conceptualized by Cranford Pratt as "an acceptance by the citizens of industrialized states that they have ethical obligations toward those beyond their borders and that these impose obligations upon their governments" (1989a, 13). A more recent effort to conceptualize the ethical framing of Canada's role in Africa can be found in Edward Akuffo's (2012) constructivist idea that the continent serves as a key vehicle for this country's "moral identity."

2 The critical scholarly commentary, much of it coming from a materialist perspective, took a different view on this, arguing that the "natural" Canadian role was to act in conformity with the interests of capitalism in this country and beyond, and in consonance with our major Western allies. Hence Canada's moment of leadership was either aberrant or best understood as a reflection of "enlightened capitalist" thinking. See Saul (1988) and L. Freeman (1997).

3 In fact, the seeds of this narrative were first sown in the context of Canada's involvement in the (first) Congo crisis in 1960–64. See Spooner (2009).

4 In May 2014, Dallaire resigned from the Senate at the age of 67—well before the mandatory retirement age of 75—in order to devote more time to the international advocacy and training work that has grown out of his experiences in, and subsequent to, Rwanda. See Galloway (2014).

5 Sherene Razack (2004 and 2007) has gone furthest in doing so. See also Whitworth (2004).

6 It is also noteworthy that an eminent internationalist Canadian, Stephen Lewis, was one of seven members of the Organization of African Unity's "Panel of Eminent Personalities to Investigate the 1994 Genocide in Rwanda," and another, Gerald Caplan, was its senior writer. Both have continued to be prominent voices in Canadian public discourse, particularly concerning Africa. See also Chapter 4.

7 For elaboration on some of these points, see Black (2010a).

Notes to Chapter 4

1 According to Sabourin (1976, 138), there were more than 2,000 French Canadian Catholic missionaries in Africa by 1960, and hundreds of missionaries from other denominations. Paradoxically, however, a substantial majority of them were based in current and former British colonial territories. See Gendron (2006, 64–65).

2 Africa's economic marginality should not be overstated however. It has often weighed disproportionately in the strategic interests of Canadian capitalists, while its growth as a market for Canadian extractive-industry trade and investment over the past decade-and-a-half has been striking. See L. Freeman (1985); and Chapter 7.

3 This is not to suggest that either has been without prominent critics in Canada. However, it is fair to say that they enjoy the respect and admiration of most, including many who would oppose specific aspects of their politics and policy positions. Thus, it has become unseemly to attack them too vigorously or publicly in light of the stature they hold.

4 For a more forthright instance of this, see MacKenzie (2008, 209–30).

5 Although his criticism might be more muted and the potential for co-optation higher, as reflected in his being named in 2005 as one of former Prime Minister Paul Martin's three high-level representatives on the issue of Darfur, along with Robert Fowler and Senator Mobina Jaffer. The January 2014 decision of Liberal leader Justin Trudeau to remove all Liberal Senators from the party's caucus is unlikely to alter the perception of Dallaire and his Liberal-appointed colleagues as partisan Liberals, particularly in the eyes of the hyper-partisan Harper Conservatives—though Dallaire's May 2014 decision to resign from the Senate may mitigate this perception.

6 Famously pronounced by Bono, the celebrity-activist, at the November 2003 Liberal leadership convention that anointed Paul Martin as leader, and thus Prime Minister.

7 Notably AIDS orphans and the grandmothers who have been compelled to take on extraordinary caregiving roles as a result of the pandemic. This is one of the major focuses of Lewis's own foundation, the Stephen Lewis Foundation (www.stephenlewisfoundation.org/index.cfm).

8 It is worth noting that this objective was ultimately fulfilled, with the creation by the UN General Assembly of UN Women in 2010. See http://www.unwomen.org.

Notes to Chapter 5

1 The literature on Canadian aid policy, the Canadian International Development Agency (CIDA), and their respective travails is extensive. For an excellent contemporary summary and analysis, see Brown (2012b). For classic analyses, see Morrison (1998) and C. Pratt (2004). At the time this book was being completed, the federal government had recently taken its surprise (though not altogether unanticipated) decision to merge CIDA with DFAIT into the reconstituted Department of Foreign Affairs, Trade, and Development. While the prospective ramifications of this restructuring for the focus and effectiveness of Canadian aid policy have generated considerable debate, some substantial transitional trials are inevitable.

2 The fact that sub-Saharan Africa experienced a period of prolonged relative decline, or "crisis," even as it received the largest share of global aid spending has fuelled the critiques of aid skeptics. See SSCFAIT (2007) and, for a highly publicized and polemical attack on the effects of aid in Africa, Moyo (2009).

3 It is useful to put these Canadian trends in comparative perspective. Among its most highly valued peer group in the G8, Canada's cuts were not exceptional. For example, French ODA declined from 0.6 percent of GNI in 1990 to 0.3 percent in 2000; German aid declined from 0.42 percent of GNI in 1990 to 0.27 percent in 2000; and US ODA dropped from 0.21 percent of GNI in 1990 to 0.1 percent in 2000. The fact that these peers were also making dramatic aid cuts doubtless made the decision easier for the Canadian government. On the other hand, governments from what had traditionally been regarded as "like-minded" middle powers, like Norway, Denmark, and the Netherlands, retained high and consistent levels of aid spending, never declining below 0.8 percent of GNI in Norway and Denmark, or 0.73 percent of GNI in the Netherlands. (All figures are drawn from the OECD DAC: http://stats.oecd.org.)

4 Stephen Brown (2013) argues that these figures significantly underestimate the decline in aid to Africa during the 1990s, though measuring this trend is complicated by the rapid rise in aid spending not allocated by region during this same period.

5 For an early and influential articulation of the debate concerning the mixed motives underpinning Canadian aid see Spicer (1966), who emphasized humanitarian, economic, and political motivations.

6 Morrison quotes Prime Minister John Diefenbaker—the most

enthusiastic proponent of the Commonwealth among postwar Canadian leaders—as declaring: "Our first consideration in external aid programs should be to raise living standards within the Commonwealth, for I consider the Commonwealth the greatest instrument of freedom that the world has ever seen" (1998, 34).

7 Pratt's full definition of humane internationalism is: "an acceptance of an obligation to alleviate global poverty and to promote development in the [Less Developed Countries]; a conviction that a more equitable world would be in their (developed countries') real long-term interests; and an assumption that the meeting of these international responsibilities is compatible with the maintenance of socially responsible national economic and social welfare policies" (1989a, 16).

8 My argument here is similar to Julia Gallagher's (2011) analysis of the way in which Africa policy became the crucial manifestation of the desire of Britain's New Labour government to "locate" and give political expression to the "good state."

9 For a contemporary articulation of the good that can and has been done through Canadian aid, see McArthur (2013).

10 The argument about the weaknesses of excessive diffusion needs to be carefully made. There has been a strong tendency toward the "fetishization of focus" by many analysts and organizations, in this country and elsewhere in the "donor community." These arguments have not taken sufficient account of what *kinds of* focus make sense, and the *risks of* excessively narrow focus, whether thematic or geographic. I am indebted to Stephen Brown for highlighting this point. See also Munro (2005) for a balanced assessment of the costs, benefits, and uncertainties of increased focus.

11 Carrier-Sabourin and Tiessen (2012) highlight how the seemingly innocuous shift in policy language under the Harper government from "gender equality" to "equality of men and women" reflected a regressive turn in the Canadian government's approach to gender issues in what should have been a flagship gender initiative—the Muskoka Initiative on Maternal, Newborn, and Child Health.

12 Reflected, even more intensively, in the growing phenomenon of both "aid darlings," seen as strong performers in relation to the shared agenda of Western donors, and "aid orphans," widely perceived as weak performers.

13 For excellent summaries of this intensifying process, see de Renzio and Mulley (2007), and Lalonde (2009, esp. 25–69).

14 This reinvestment only succeeded in elevating Canada to a level of comparative mediocrity among OECD donors however. By 2007, Canada's ODA was 9th in terms of total volume and 15th as a percentage of GNI

in the 22-member Development Assistance Committee of the OECD (Brown and Jackson 2009).

15 Portions of the following discussion are adapted from Black (2012a).

16 It is noteworthy, in terms of Canada's historic multilateral commitments to the Commonwealth and la Francophonie, that seven of the newly designated core development partners were Commonwealth member states and seven were Francophonie members. One (Cameroon) was a member of both and only one (Ethiopia) was a member of neither.

17 Outlined in the IPS as: good governance, health (with a focus on HIV/AIDS), basic education, private sector development, and environmental sustainability, with gender equality as a cross-cutting theme.

18 The drafters of the platform seem to have been unaware that the widely used acronym for aid, ODA, in fact stands for "Official Development Assistance."

19 Some close to the government argue that the attitude of at least some Conservative parliamentarians was closer to disparagement or disdain. See Black (2009).

20 Interviews with aid officials and non-governmental representatives, Addis Ababa, Ethiopia, February 2010.

21 Specifically Benin, Burkina Faso, Cameroon, Kenya, Malawi, Niger, Rwanda, and Zambia. For an insightful account of the impact in one of these—Malawi—see York (2009b).

22 As Swiss (2014) notes, for example, several of the new focus countries (Mongolia, Benin, and Burkina Faso) are identified in the government's 2013 *Global Markets Action Plan* as "emerging markets with specific opportunities for Canadian businesses" (DFATD 2013a, 8), while others (Philippines and Jordan) are middle-income countries that have recently become foreign policy priorities as a consequence of humanitarian emergencies (Typhoon Haiyan and the Syrian refugee crisis).

23 See http://www.acdi-cida.gc.ca/acdi-cida/acdi-cida.nsf/eng/NAT-5208 469-GYW.

24 See http://www.acdi-cida.gc.ca/acdi-cida/ACDI-CIDA.nsf/eng/FRA-82 5105226-KFT. See also Brown and Jackson (2009).

Notes to Chapter 6

1 Terminology concerning the spectrum of peace operations can be confusing. The UN's "capstone document" (United Nations 2008) on Peacekeeping Operations specifies the following specific stages along the spectrum: conflict prevention; peacemaking; peacekeeping; peace enforcement; and peacebuilding. In this chapter, the encompassing term "peace operations" is used, except with reference to UN-sanctioned

operations that meet the specific definition of peacekeeping: "a technique designed to preserve the peace, however fragile, where fighting has been halted, and to assist in implementing agreements achieved by the peacemakers."

2　As discussed in the next chapter, the rapid growth of investments in Africa by Canadian extractive companies during the latter part of the 1990s and the new millennium is an important development, with potentially contradictory implications for Canada's professed objectives of promoting African peace and security. However, it arguably had little to do with the deployment of Canadian defence-and-security resources for most of the post-colonial period in Africa, since the bulk of these deployments predated the recent growth of Canadian economic interests there.

3　For a full exploration of these ideas, see Linklater and Suganami (2006). For an application of these ideas to the crisis in Darfur, see Williams and Black (2010).

4　As discussed in Chapter 1, "hegemonic" is used in the (neo-)Gramscian sense, in which an order is fostered that masks persistent inequalities and disparities through the fostering of a "common sense" arrangement enjoying a relatively high level of consent from subordinate groups.

5　Although Canada's role in "contributing to international peace and security" (DND 2008, 8–9) through multilateral deployments persisted primarily through its long and costly deployment in the NATO-led war in Afghanistan.

6　There were others, including those in Mozambique, Angola, and Western Sahara, where Canada contributed small numbers of military observers (UNMOs), and still others, such as Namibia and Côte d'Ivoire, where RCMP officers were deployed to the policing dimensions of operations and/or to aid with Security Sector Reform. Indeed there have been few UN PSOs in Africa since 1990 without a Canadian presence of some type.

7　I am indebted to Bob Edwards for highlighting this dynamic.

8　The UN-mandated Standby High Readiness Brigade (SHIRBRIG) headquartered in Denmark that became operationally available in January 2000 (see Armstrong-Whitworth 2007; Koops and Varwick 2008). Its membership was composed of twelve core countries: Argentina, Austria, Canada, Denmark, Finland, Italy, the Netherlands, Norway, Poland, Romania, Spain, and Sweden. SHIRBRIG was disbanded on 30 June 2009.

9　In the revised 2014 list of countries of focus, South Sudan was retained but Sudan dropped.

10　Historically, beyond longstanding Commonwealth links, Sierra Leone's capital of Freetown was settled in 1792 by more than a thousand freed slaves from Nova Scotia. With regard to Canada's medium-term involvement in peacebuilding, it should be noted that, since 2009, Canada has been the chair of the UN Peace-Building Commission's Sierra Leone Country Configuration. This role underscores the continued salience of multilateral venues and modalities in Canada's Africa policies, notwithstanding the Harper government's skepticism toward inclusive multilateralism and the UN. See http://www.canadainternational.gc.ca/ghana/bilateral_relations_bilaterales/bilateral_canada_sierra_leone.aspx. For a telling critique of Canada's performance in this role, see Gberie and Swillie 2014.

11 The UN Mission in Sudan and in South Sudan, respectively.

12 For in-depth analyses of Canada's role in Darfur and Sudan, see Black (2010a), Nossal (2005), and Matthews (2005).

13 Though note the Secretary-General's caveat that, "in seeking to promote 'African solutions to African problems', the international community must be careful to avoid a segregated environment in which Member States only contribute to peacekeeping within their own region" (UNSG 2004, 3–4).

14 For a fuller discussion of recent Canadian support for African peace-and-security capacity building, on which this analysis draws, see Powell (2005), and Akuffo (2012, esp. chaps. 4 and 5).

15 These included programs at the *École de maintien de la paix* in Bamako, Mali—though this training role was suspended following the March 2012 Malian coup. Moreover, the Pearson Centre closed its doors in October 2013 after losing core federal funding in 2012. And as of late 2013, the Global Peace and Security Fund was slated to expire with no clear decision on how (or whether) work in its area of focus would be carried forward.

16 See the website of the Global Peace and Security Program, and in particular its "Conflict Prevention and Peacebuilding Group": http://www.international.gc.ca/START-GTSR/gpsp-ppsm.aspx.

17 Of course, this tendency and the problems associated with it are widespread, and have long been recognized internationally. They reflect the profound difficulty of mobilizing political support for a sustained, comprehensive approach to peacebuilding. See for example the *Report of the Panel on United Nations Peace Operations* (Brahimi Report) (UN 2000).

18 Those associated with the Canadian Airborne Regiment in Somalia being by far the best-known example.

19 Although it should be noted that this trend is from the post–Cold War baseline of the 1990s when there was a dramatic upsurge in UN-mandated peacekeeping operations globally, accompanied by a qualitative shift to more complex operations.

20 A jarring trend in a country that long celebrated its "leadership" in international peacekeeping. For example, as of August 2012 Canada ranked 56th among military and police contributors to UN operations, with 152 people deployed. See United Nations Peacekeeping: http://www .un.org/en/peacekeeping/resources/statistics/contributors.shtml.

21 For example, by underwriting earlier efforts of international experts and military professionals to think through how the Responsibility to Protect could actually be operationalized in the face of large-scale atrocity crimes (see Holt and Berkman 2006). This effort has been constrained, however, by the Harper government's obvious lack of enthusiasm for R2P (see Boucher 2012).

22 As of 2014, for example, DFATD's Stabilization and Reconstruction Task Force has designated eight priority "countries": Colombia, Guatemala, and Haiti in the Americas; Afghanistan in Asia; Sudan, South Sudan, and the Democratic Republic of the Congo in Africa; and the Middle East peace process.

23 As reported on the then CIDA's website. This point should be qualified in light of Canada's role as chair of the UN Peace-Building Commission's Sierra Leone Country Configuration since 2009 (see note 10 above).

Notes to Chapter 7

1 Much of this chapter draws on Black and Savage (2010).

2 Figures from Natural Resources Canada show that the C$31.6 billion of Canadian investment in African mining by 2011 was spread across 39 countries (Lupick 2013).

3 For a discussion of alternative views of human security, distinguishing more mainstream and "official" versions with more critical understandings, see Black (2006b) and Grayson (2004).

4 China gets the lion's share of attention in this regard, but many other countries have become active in pursuit of African market share, including India, Brazil, South Korea, and Turkey, along with "established" investors and traders like the US and EU.

5 As discussed briefly in Chapter 2, Structural Adjustment refers to a set of economic policies advocated and imposed by the International Monetary Fund and World Bank based on neoclassical economic principles. These policies called for free markets and required the downsizing of state bureaucracies and the removal of government regulations on and intrusions into economic activity. While the approach to Structural Adjustment conditions by International Financial Institutions and other Western donors softened in the first decade of the new millennium,

the core consensus on the importance of "market-friendly" reforms has remained firm.

6   While such forward and backward linkages are smaller in the mineral sector compared with other economic activities such as manufacturing due to the capital-intensive and enclave nature of resource extraction, Di Boscio and Humphreys point out that the real contribution of mining activities lies in its ability to "add value with relatively low pre-existing economic conditions" (2005, 589). Thus, mining activities may provide a trigger for economic development where few other prospects exist.

7   The EITI is a multi-stakeholder initiative whose objective is to "ensure full disclosure of taxes and other payments made by oil, gas and mining companies to governments ... (allowing) citizens to see for themselves how much their government is receiving from their country's natural resources" and thus create the conditions for improved resource governance. See http://www.eiti.org/eiti. More recently, the British hosts of the 2013 Lough Earne G8 Summit made transparency one of its hallmark themes, and the Canadian government committed to a consultative process leading to a mandatory reporting regime for Canadian companies in the extractive sector. (See "G8 Lough Earne Communqué" 2013; and Gallinger 2013.)

8   For instance, Canada's positive image in Africa resulted in its gaining the support of all African member states in its successful bid for a non-permanent seat on the Security Council in 1999–2000. Conversely, Canada's almost unprecedented failure to win a non-permanent seat in 2010 was partly a consequence of its diminished interest in, and engagement with, African governments.

9   Generally speaking, mining companies operating internationally can be divided into three categories. The first two consist of large and small companies, with the former spending more than US$3 million on exploration and the later spending more than US$100,000 but less than US$3 million (Lemieux 2005). Companies in both of these categories are engaged in the production of minerals (mining, smelting, and processing) as well as in exploration. The final category comprises junior exploration companies that engage only in exploration, not production (Ericsson 2005).

10 An additional C$3.9 billion was invested in oil and gas (CCA 2007).

11 Lupick (2013) cites a December 2012 report drafted by the Toronto Stock Exchange stating that in the first nine months of 2012, 89 percent of all global mining equity financings happened on the TSX and TSX Venture exchanges. (See also Campbell 1999; and Bhushan 2014.)

12 For example, Canadian companies retain the largest share of exploration markets in Latin America and the Caribbean by a significant

margin, with 32 percent of the larger company market in 2009 (see Natural Resources Canada 2011, 5.9). This activity has been, if anything, *more* controversial and contested than Canadian extractive investments in Africa. For a critical materialist perspective, see Gordon (2010).

13 See http://www19.edc.ca/publications/2012/2011csr/english/1.shtml.

14 Although it should be noted that ongoing research and monitoring by Canadian civil society organizations and networks like the CNCA and Mining Watch Canada, collaborating with developing country partner organizations, have added considerably to the depth of knowledge on the prevalence of these problems. For a broader analysis of the problems associated with mining-centred development in Africa, not limited to Canadian corporate conduct, see Campbell (2009b).

15 The other departments and agencies represented were: Natural Resources Canada, Industry Canada, Environment Canada, CIDA, Indian and Northern Affairs, the Department of Justice, the EDC, and the Privy Council Office.

16 Interview, Ottawa, 30 March 2007. The Canadian government provided an up-front contribution to the EITI Multi-Donor Trust Fund of C$750,000, with a commitment to provide a further C$100,000 annually. This bought it a "seat at the table" with other major supporters, including France, Germany, the Netherlands, Norway, and the UK.

17 Another useful way to think about the process, and its nascent outcomes, is as an emergent form of "governmentality," in which both corporate representatives and civil society groups are subjects as well as objects of governmental practices. See Sending and Neumann (2006).

18 A point highlighted by participants in the process.

19 The extent to which corporate representatives on the Advisory Group were "out in front of" the more recalcitrant attitudes in much of the private sector is revealed by the responses to the Advisory Group report from umbrella organizations like the Canadian Chamber of Commerce (2007). These intra-private sector differences, which are echoed by intra-state differences (see below), seem to be a major reason why the government took so long to respond to the Report. See also Evans (2007).

Notes to Chapter 8

1 The other two being Tanzania and Ghana. See http://cidpnsi.ca/blog/portfolio/canadas-foreign-aid.

2 The Muskoka Initiative is Africa-centric because 80 percent of the funds committed to it for the 2011–2015 period were to be spent in Africa,

and seven of ten priority countries under the initiative are African. For details, see Carrier-Sabourin and Tiessen (2012), and Black (2013).

3   The commitment was renewed in a carefully stage-managed MNCH "Summit" at the end of May 2014, during which the Canadian government committed a further C$3.5 billion to MNCH issues between 2015 and 2020. The significance of this commitment must, however, be discounted against the sharp overall decline in real aid spending since 2010. See PMO (2014).

4   These goals are: to reduce by two-thirds under-five mortality between 1990 and 2015 (MDG 4); to reduce by three-quarters the maternal mortality ratio in the same period (MDG 5a); and to achieve universal access to reproductive health by 2015 (MDG 5b).

5   These arguments are elaborated in Black (2013).

6   Fantino succeeded Bev Oda as Minister, serving in the portfolio from July 2012 to July 2013.

7   As reflected in Minister Fantino's apparent lack of knowledge of the Paris Principles, four months after his appointment (see Mackrael 2012).

8   Admittedly Fowler is a deeply interested party, given his incarceration at the hands of Al-Qaeda in the Islamic Maghreb (AQIM) in northern Mali for 130 days in 2009.

References

Adam, Heribert, and Kogila Moodley. 1992. *Democratizing Southern Africa: Challenges for Canadian Policy.* Ottawa: Canadian Institute for International Peace and Security.

Advisory Group Report. 2007. "National Roundtables on Corporate Social Responsibility (CSR) and the Canadian Extractive Industry in Developing Countries." Ottawa: Department of Foreign Affairs and International Trade, 29 March.

Africa Action Plan (AAP). 2002. "Kananaskis Summit: G8 Africa Action Plan." http://www.g8.fr/evian/english/navigation/g8_documents/archives_from_previous_summits/kananaskis_summit_-_2002/g8_africa_action_plan.html.

Africa-Canada Forum. 2007. "Where Is Africa in Canada's Priorities?" http://www.ccic.ca/_files/en/working_groups/003_acf_2007-11_africa_briefing_note.pdf.

Akabzaa, Thomas. 2009. "Mining in Ghana: Implications for National Economic Development and Poverty Reduction." In *Mining in Africa: Regulation and Development,* edited by Bonnie Campbell, 25–65. Ottawa: International Development Research Centre.

Akuffo, Edward. 2012. *Canadian Foreign Policy in Africa: Regional Approaches to Peace, Security, and Development.* Farnham, Surrey: Ashgate.

Amevor, Selorm. 2007. "Ghana: Mining Has Not Helped Alleviate Poverty." *Public Agenda* (Accra), 9 April.

Anglin, Douglas. 2000–01. "Rwanda Revisited: Search for the Truth." *International Journal* 56 (1): 149–69.

Appathurai, James, and Ralph Lysyshyn. 1998. "Lessons Learned from the Zaire Mission." *Canadian Foreign Policy* 5 (2): 93–105.

Arimatsu, Louise, and Hemi Mistry. 2012. "Conflict Minerals: The Search for a Normative Framework." International Law Programme Paper 2012/01, September. London: Chatham House.

Armstrong-Whitworth, Peter. 2007. "SHIRBRIG: The Future of Canada's Contribution to UN Peace Operations?" *Canadian Military Journal* Summer:25–34.

Arthur, Peter, and David Black. 2007. "The Benefits of an Indirect Approach: The Case of Ghana." In *Exporting Good Governance: Temptations and Challenges in Canada's Aid Program*, edited by Jennifer Welsh and Ngaire Woods, 119–42. Waterloo, ON: Wilfrid Laurier University Press.

Ascher, William. 2005. "The 'Resource Curse.'" In *International and Comparative Mineral Law Policy*, edited by Elizabeth Bastida, Thomas Wälde, and Janeth Warden-Fernández, 569–89. The Hague: Kluwer Law International.

Auditor General of Canada. 2009. "Report to the House of Commons. Chapter 8: Strengthening Aid Effectiveness—Canadian International Development Agency." Ottawa: Office of the Auditor General of Canada.

Axworthy, Lloyd. 2004. *Navigating a New World: Canada's Global Future*. Toronto: Vintage Canada.

Bain, William. 1999. "Against Crusading: The Ethic of Human Security and Canadian Foreign Policy." *Canadian Foreign Policy Journal* 6 (3): 85–98.

Baird, John. 2012. "Address by Minister Baird at Montreal Council on Foreign Relations Luncheon." 14 September.

Barry-Shaw, Nikolas, and Dru Oja Jay. 2012. *Paved with Good Intentions: Canada's Development NGOs from Idealism to Imperialism*. Halifax: Fernwood Publishing.

Bayart, Jean-François. 2004. "Commentary: Towards a New Start for Africa and Europe." *African Affairs* 103/412:453–58.

Bayne, Nicholas. 2003. "The New Partnership for Africa's Development and the G8's Africa Action Plan: A Marshall Plan for Africa?" In *Sustaining Global Growth and Development: G7 and IMF Governance*, edited by Michele Fratianni, Paolo Savona, and John Kirton, 117–30. Farnham, Surrey: Ashgate.

Beardsley, Brent. 2005a. "Learning from the Rwandan Genocide of 1994 to Stop the Genocide in Darfur—Part I." *Canadian Military Journal* Spring:41–50.

———. 2005b. "Learning from the Rwandan Genocide of 1994 to Stop the Genocide in Darfur—Part II." *Canadian Military Journal* Summer:41–48.

Bellamy, Alex. 2009. *Responsibility to Protect*. Cambridge: Polity Press.

Bellamy, Alex, and Paul Williams. 2012. "Broadening the Base of United Nations Troop—and Police—Contributing Countries." Providing for Peacekeeping No. 1, August. New York: International Peace Institute.

Bhushan, Aniket. 2014. "Canada and Africa's Natural Resources: Key Features 2013." In *The Canadian International Development Report*. Ottawa: North-South Institute. http://www.nsi-ins.ca/wp-content/uploads/2014/01/Report-Canada-and-Africa%E2%80%99s

-Natural-Resources.pdf?utm_source=Canadian+International+
Development+Report+2013&utm_campaign=CIDR&utm_medium=
email.

Bieler, Andreas, and Adam David Morton. 2004. "A Critical Theory Route
to Hegemony, World Order, and Historical Change." *Capital and Class*
82:85–113.

Biersteker, Thomas. 1992. "The 'Triumph' of Neoclassical Economics in
the Developing World: Policy Convergence and Bases of Governance
in the International Economic Order." In *Governance without Government: Order and Change in World Politics*, edited by James Rosenau and
Ernst-Otto Czempiel, 102–31. Cambridge: Cambridge University Press.

Black, David. 1997. "Addressing Apartheid: Lessons from Australian,
Canadian, and Swedish Policies in Southern Africa." In *Niche Diplomacy:
Middle Power Diplomacy after the Cold War*, edited by Andrew F. Cooper,
100–28. London: Macmillan.

———. 2001a. "Echoes of Apartheid? Canada, Nigeria, and the Politics of
Norms." In *Ethics and Security in Canadian Foreign Policy*, edited by Rosa-
lind Irwin, 138–59. Vancouver: University of British Columbia Press.

———. 2001b. "How Exceptional? Reassessing the Mulroney Government's Anti-Apartheid 'Crusade.'" In *Diplomatic Departures: The Conservative Era in Canadian Foreign Policy*, edited by Nelson Michaud and Kim
Nossal, 173–93. Vancouver: University of British Columbia Press.

———. 2001c. "Pivots of Peace: UN Transitional Operations." In *Adapt-
ing the United Nations to a Post-Modern Era*, edited by W. Andy Knight,
163–77. New York: Palgrave.

———. 2004. "Canada and Africa: Activist Aspirations in Straitened Circumstances." In *Africa in International Politics*, edited by Ian Taylor and
Paul Williams, 136–54. London: Routledge.

———. 2006a. "Canadian Aid to Africa: Assessing 'Reform.'" In *Canada
among Nations 2006: Minorities and Priorities*, edited by Andrew Cooper
and Dane Rowlands, 319–38. Montreal and Kingston: McGill-Queen's
University Press.

———. 2006b. "Mapping the Interplay of Human Security Practice and
Debates: The Canadian Experience." In *A Decade of Human Security:
Global Governance and New Multilateralisms*, edited by Sandra MacLean,
David Black, and Timothy Shaw, 53–62. Farnham, Surrey: Ashgate.

———. 2009. "Out of Africa? The Harper Government's New 'Tilt' in the
Developing World." *Canadian Foreign Policy* 15 (2): 41–56.

———. 2010a. "Canada." In *The International Politics of Mass Atrocities: The
Case of Darfur*, edited by David Black and Paul Williams, 232–48. London: Routledge.

———. 2010b. "Canada and the Commonwealth: The Multilateral Politics
of a 'Wasting Asset.'" *Canadian Foreign Policy* 16 (2): 61–77.

————. 2011. "Canada, the G8, and Africa: The Rise and Decline of a Hegemonic Project?" In *Readings in Canadian Foreign Policy: Classic Debates and New Ideas*, edited by Duane Bratt and Christopher Kukucha, 487-502. 2nd ed. Don Mills, ON: Oxford University Press.

————. 2012a. "Between Indifference and Idiosyncracy: The Conservatives and Canada Aid to Africa." In *Struggling for Effectiveness: CIDA and Canadian Foreign Aid*, edited by Stephen Brown, 246–68. Montreal and Kingston: McGill-Queen's University Press.

————. 2012b. "The Harper Government, Africa Policy, and the Relative Decline of Humane Internationalism." In *Canada in the World: Internationalism in Canadian Foreign Policy*, edited by Heather Smith and Claire Turenne Sjolander, 217–38. Don Mills, ON: Oxford University Press.

————. 2013. "The Muskoka Initiative and the Politics of Fence-Mending with Africa." In *Canada among Nations 2013. Canada and Africa: From Investment to Engagement—Looking Back, Looking Ahead*, edited by Rohinton Medhora and Yiagadeesen Samy, 239-251. Montreal and Kingston: McGill-Queen's University Press.

Black, David, and Malcolm Savage. 2010. "Mainstreaming Investment: Developmental and Security Implications of Canadian Extractive Industries in Africa." In *Locating Global Order: American Power and Canadian Security After 9/11*, edited by Bruno Charbonneau and Wayne Cox, 235–69. Vancouver: University of British Columbia Press.

Black, David, and Claire Turenne Sjolander. 1996. "Multilateralism Reconstituted and the Discourse of Canadian Foreign Policy." *Studies in Political Economy* 49:7–36.

Black, David, and Jean-Phillipe Thérien, with Andrew Clark. 1996. "Moving with the Crowd: Canadian Aid to Africa." *International Journal* 51 (2): 259–86.

Black, David, and Rebecca Tiessen. 2007. "The Canadian International Development Agency: New Policies, Old Problems." *Canadian Journal of Development Studies* 28 (2): 191–212.

Black, David, and Paul Williams. 2008. "Darfur's Challenge to International Society." *Behind the Headlines* 65 (6): 1–23.

————. 2010. "Conclusion: Darfur's Challenge to International Society." In *The International Politics of Mass Atrocities: The Case of Darfur*, edited by David Black and Paul Williams, 249–62. London: Routledge.

Blackwood, Elizabeth. 2006. "Human Security and Corporate Governance: A Critical Assessment of Canada's Human Security Agenda." In *A Decade of Human Security: Global Governance and New Multilateralisms*, edited by Sandra Maclean, David Black, and Timothy Shaw, 85–100. Farnham, Surrey: Ashgate.

Blackwood, Elizabeth, and Veronika Stewart. 2012. "CIDA and the Mining Sector: Extractive Industries As an Overseas Development Strategy." In *Struggling for Effectiveness: CIDA and Canadian Foreign Aid*, edited by Stephen Brown, 217–45. Montreal and Kingston: McGill-Queen's University Press.

Böge, Volker, Christopher Fitzpatrick, Willem Jaspers, and Wolf-Christian Paes. 2006. *Who's Minding the Store? The Business of Private, Public, and Civil Actors in Zones of Conflict*. Bonn International Centre for Conversion (BICC) Brief 32.

Bond, Patrick. 2006. "Resource Extraction and African Underdevelopment." *Capitalism Nature Socialism* 17 (2): 5–25.

Boucher, Jean-Christophe. 2012. "The Responsibility to Think Clearly about Interests: Stephen Harper's Realist Internationalism, 2006–2011." In *Canada in the World: Internationalism in Canadian Foreign Policy*, edited by Heather Smith and Claire Turenne Sjolander, 53–71. Don Mills, ON: Oxford University Press.

Bradbury, Adrian, Alexa McDonough, and Paul Dewar. 2007. "Quiet Diplomacy or Lost Opportunity?" *Chronicle-Herald*, 18 November.

Brouwer, Ruth Compton. 2014. *Canada's Global Villagers: CUSO in Development, 1961–86*. Vancouver: University of British Columbia Press.

Brown, Chris. 2001. "Africa in Canadian Foreign Policy 2000: The Human Security Agenda." In *Canada among Nations 2001: The Axworthy Legacy*, edited by Fen Osler Hampson, Norman Hillmer, and Maureen Molot, 192–212. Don Mills, ON: Oxford University Press.

Brown, Chris, and Edward Jackson. 2009. "Could the Senate Be Right? Should CIDA Be Abolished?" In *How Ottawa Spends, 2009–10*, edited by Alan Maslove, 151–74. Montreal and Kingston: McGill-Queen's University Press.

Brown, Stephen. 2008. "CIDA under the Gun." In *Canada among Nations 2007: What Room for Manoeuvre?*, edited by Jean Daudelin and Daniel Schwanen, 91–107. Montreal and Kingston: McGill-Queen's University Press.

———. 2009. "CIDA Under Attack (from Its Own Minister)." *The Mark*, 24 June.

———. 2012a. "CIDA's New Partnership with Canadian NGOs: Modernizing for Greater Effectiveness?" In *Struggling for Effectiveness: CIDA and Canadian Foreign Aid*, edited by Stephen Brown, 287–304. Montreal and Kingston: McGill-Queen's University Press.

———, ed. 2012b. *Struggling for Effectiveness: CIDA and Canadian Foreign Aid*. Montreal and Kingston: McGill-Queen's University Press.

———. 2013. "Canadian Aid to Africa." In *Canada Among Nations 2013. Canada and Africa: From Investment to Engagement—Looking Back, Looking*

Ahead, edited by Rohinton Medhora and Yiagadeesen Samy, 181–94. Montreal and Kingston: McGill-Queen's University Press.

———. 2014. "CIDA's Underspending: The Minister's Explanations Don't Add Up." CIPS Blog, 28 April. http://cips.uottawa.ca/cidas-under spending-the-ministers-explanations-dont-add-up/.

———. Forthcoming. "Undermining Foreign Aid: The Extractive Sector and the Recommercialization of Canadian Development Assistance." In *Rethinking Canadian Aid*, edited by Stephen Brown, Molly den Heyer, and David Black. Ottawa: University of Ottawa Press.

Brown, William. 2006. "The Commission for Africa: Results and Prospects for the West's Africa Policy." *Journal of Modern African Studies* 44 (3): 349–74.

Browning, Christopher. 2002. "Coming Home or Moving Home? 'Western-izing' Narratives in Finnish Foreign Policy and the Reinterpretation of Past Identities." *Cooperation and Conflict* 37 (1): 37–72.

Brysk, Alison. 2009. *Global Good Samaritans: Human Rights as Foreign Policy*. New York: Oxford University Press.

Bull, Hedley. 1977. *The Anarchical Society*. London: Macmillan.

Bunting, Madeleine. 2005. "Humiliated Once More." *Guardian Weekly*, 8–14 July.

Burdette, Marcia. 1994. "Structural Adjustment and Canadian Aid Policy." In *Canadian International Development Assistance Policies: An Appraisal*, edited by Cranford Pratt, 210–39. Montreal and Kingston: McGill-Queen's University Press.

Buzan, Barry. 2004. *From International to World Society? English School Theory and the Social Structure of Globalisation*. Cambridge: Cambridge University Press.

Campbell, Bonnie. 1999. *Canadian Mining Interests and Human Rights in Africa in the Context of Globalization*. Montreal: International Centre for Human Rights and Democratic Development (ICHRDD).

———. 2003. "Factoring in Governance in Not Enough. Mining Codes in Africa, Policy Reform and Corporate Responsibility." *Minerals and Energy* 18 (1): 2–13.

———. 2006. "Good Governance, Security and Mining in Africa." *Minerals and Energy* 21 (1): 31–44.

———. 2009a. "Introduction." In *Mining in Africa: Regulation and Development*, edited by Bonnie Campbell, 1–24. Ottawa: International Development Research Centre.

———, ed. 2009b. *Mining in Africa: Regulation and Development*. Ottawa: International Development Research Centre.

———. 2011. "Canadian Mining in Africa: 'Do As You Please' Approach Comes at High Cost." *Canadian Dimension*, 24 May.

Canadian Broadcasting Corporation (CBC) News. 2011. "Analysis: Is Harper Trying to Increase Canada's Military Might?" 24 November. http://www.cbc.ca/news/politics/story/2011/11/24/f-military -canada.html.

Canadian Chamber of Commerce. 2007. *Response to the Federal Government on the Advisory Group Report of the National Roundtables on CSR and the Canadian Extractive Industry in Developing Countries.* 26 July.

Canadian Council for International Cooperation (CCIC). 2009. "A Review of CIDA's Countries of Priorities: A CCIC Briefing Note," February.

———. 2012. *CCIC Analysis of Budget 2012.*

Canadian Council for International Cooperation (CCIC) and Inter-Council Network of Provincial/Regional Councils for International Cooperation (ICN). 2012. *Putting Partnership Back at the Heart of Development: Canadian Civil Society Experience with CIDA's Call-for-Proposal Mechanism, Partnerships with Canadians Branch.* Ottawa: Canadian Council for International Cooperation.

Canadian Council on Africa (CCA). 2009. "Presentation to the Standing Committee on Foreign Affairs and International Development of the Parliament of Canada," 3 June.

———. 2013. *The Rising Africa* 3, Winter.

Canadian International Development Agency (CIDA). 1987. *Sharing Our Future.* Gatineau, QC: Canadian International Development Agency.

———. 2002. *Canada Making a Difference in the World: A Policy Statement on Strengthening Aid Effectiveness.* Gatineau, QC: Canadian International Development Agency.

———. 2003. *New Vision, New Partnership: Canada Fund for Africa.* Gatineau, QC: Canadian International Development Agency.

———. 2004. *Canada and the G8 Africa Action Plan: Maintaining the Momentum.* Gatineau, QC: Canadian International Development Agency.

———. 2005. *A Role of Pride and Influence in the World: Development—International Policy Statement.* Ottawa: Government of Canada.

———. 2009. *CIDA's Aid Effectiveness Action Plan (2009–12).* http://www.acdi -cida.gc.ca/acdi-cida/ACDI-CIDA.nsf/eng/FRA-825105226-KFT.

———. 2010. "Minister Oda Announces Global Health, Nutrition and Disease Prevention".

———. 2011a. *Canada Fund for Africa: Summative Evaluation Executive Report.* Prepared by Evaluation Directorate, Strategic Policy and Performance Branch, Canadian International Development Agency, January.

———. 2011b. "Minister Oda Announces Initiatives to Increase the Benefits of Natural Resource Management for People in Africa and South America." Toronto, 29 September. http://www.acdi-cida.gc.ca/acdi -cida/ACDI-CIDA.nsf/eng/CAR-929105317-KGD.

———. 2011c. "The Official Development Assistance Accountability Act." http://www.acdi-cida.gc.ca/acdi-cida/ACDI-CIDA.nsf/eng/ FRA-121185349-JB8.

———. 2011d. *Statistical Report on International Assistance 2010/11.* Gatineau, QC: Canadian International Development Agency. http://www .acdi-cida.gc.ca/acdi-cida/ACDI-CIDA.nsf/eng/ANN-321112057-KZN.

———. n.d. "Sudan and South Sudan." Foreign Affairs, Trade, and Development. http://www.acdi-cida.gc.ca/acdi-cida/ACDI-CIDA.nsf/ Eng/JUD-217124359-NT2#a2.

Canadian International Development Platform (CIDP). 2014. Ottawa: North-South Institute. http://www.cidpnsi.ca.

Canadian Journal of Development Studies (*CJDS*). 2010. Special Issue on "Rethinking Extractive Industry: Regulation, Dispossession, and Emerging Claims." 30 (1–2).

Canadian Network on Corporate Accountability (CNCA). 2007. *An Important Step Forward: The Final Report of the National Roundtables on Corporate Social Responsibility and the Canadian Industry in Developing Countries.* 30 March.

———. 2009. "Government Squanders Opportunity to Hold Extractive Companies to Account." News release. 26 March.

Caplan, Gerald. 2009. "Abandoning Our Responsibility." *Globe and Mail,* 25 September.

Cargill, Tom. 2010. *Our Common Strategic Interests: Africa's Role in the Post-G8 World.* London: Chatham House.

Carin, Barry, and Gordon Smith. 2010. *Reinventing CIDA.* Calgary: Canadian Defence and Foreign Affairs Institute.

Carment, David. 2013. "It's about Ethnic Votes, Not Church and State." *Globe and Mail,* 21 February.

Carment, David, Milana Nikolko, and Dacia Douhaibi. 2013. "Canadian Foreign Policy and Africa's Diaspora: Slippery Slope or Opportunity Unrealised?" In *Canada among Nations 2013. Canada and Africa: From Investment to Engagement—Looking Back, Looking Ahead,* edited by Rohinton Medhora and Yiagadeesen Samy, 61–78. Montreal and Kingston: McGill-Queen's University Press.

Carrier-Sabourin, Krystel, and Rebecca Tiessen. 2012. "Women and Children First: Maternal Health and the Silencing of Gender in Canadian Foreign Policy." In *Canada in the World: Internationalism in Canadian Foreign Policy,* edited by Heather Smith and Claire Turenne Sjolander, 183–200. Don Mills, ON: Oxford University Press.

Cerny, Philip. 1997. "Paradoxes of the Competition State: The Dynamics of Political Globalization." *Government and Opposition* 32 (2): 251–74.

Chalk, Frank, Roméo Dallaire, Kyle Matthews, Carla Barqueiro, and Simon Doyle. 2010. *Mobilizing the Will to Intervene: Leadership to Prevent Mass Atrocities.* Montreal and Kingston: McGill-Queen's University Press.

Chapnick, Adam. 2011–12. "A Diplomatic Counter-Revolution: Conservative Foreign Policy, 2006–11." *International Journal* 67 (1): 137–54.

Charbonneau, Bruno, and Wayne S. Cox. 2011. *Locating Global Order: American Power and Canadian Security after 9/11.* Vancouver: UBC Press.

Charlton, Mark. 1994. "Continuity and Change in Canadian Food Aid." In *Canadian International Development Assistance Policies: An Appraisal,* edited by Cranford Pratt, 210–39. Montreal and Kingston: McGill-Queen's University Press.

Chrétien, Jean. 1996. Press conference by the Prime Minister. Transcript. CBC Newsworld, 12 November.

———. 2002. "Address by Prime Minister Chrétien to the World Economic Forum Plenary Session." New York, 1 February.

———. 2007. *My Years as Prime Minister.* Toronto: Alfred A. Knopf.

Clark, Andrew. 1991. *Mosaic or Patchwork? Canadian Policy toward Sub-Saharan Africa in the 1980s.* Ottawa: North-South Institute.

Clark, Campbell. 2010. "Canada Rejects UN Request to Lead Congo Mission." *Globe and Mail,* 30 April.

———. 2013a. "From Odd to Surreal, Ottawa's Mali Message." *Globe and Mail,* 31 January.

———. 2013b. "Baird Warns Mali Involvement Invites 'Another Afghanistan.'" *Globe and Mail,* 13 February.

Clark, Campbell, and Doug Saunders. 2011. "Europe Debt Crunch Delays Harper's G8 Initiatives on Maternal Health." *Globe and Mail,* 26 May.

Clark, Joe. 2007. "Is Africa Falling Off Canada's Map? Remarks to the National Capital Branch of the Canadian Institute of International Affairs." Ottawa, 6 November.

———. 2013. *How We Lead: Canada in a Century of Change.* Toronto: Random House.

Commission for Africa. 2005. *Our Common Future.* London: UK Government.

Conservative Party of Canada. 2006. *Stand Up for Canada: Federal Election Platform,* 13 January.

Cooper, Andrew. 2000. "Between Will and Capabilities: Canada and the Zaire/Great Lakes Initiative." In *Worthwhile Initiatives? Canada and Mission-Oriented Diplomacy,* edited by Andrew Cooper and Geoffrey Hayes, 64–78. Toronto: Irwin.

Cornut, Jérémie. 2012. "Progress in the Discipline. The history of IR from a Pragmatic Perspective." Paper presented to the annual meeting of the International Studies Association, San Diego, CA, April.

Cornwall, Andrea, and Karen Brock. 2005. "What Do Buzzwords Do for Development Policy? A Critical Look at 'Participation', 'Empowerment' and 'Poverty Reduction.'" *Third World Quarterly* 26 (7): 1043–60.

Coulter, Kendra. 2009. "Deep Neoliberal Integration: The Production of Third Way Politics in Ontario." *Studies in Political Economy* 83:191–208.

Coumans, Catherine. 2012. "The Back Story to the CIDA-Mining Partnerships." *Embassy*, 8 February.

Courtemanche, Gil. 2005. "The Nightmare Diaries. Romeo Dallaire Gives His Account of a Disastrous UN Command in *Shake Hands with the Devil.* Gil Courtemanche Tries to Be Sympathetic." *Guardian*, 23 April.

Cousineau, Sophie, and Kim Mackrael. 2013. "Mali and the Quebec Connection." *Globe and Mail*, 9 February.

Cox, Robert. 1989. "Middlepowermanship, Japan, and Future World Order." *International Journal* 44 (4): 823–62.

Cox, Robert, with Timothy Sinclair. 1996. *Approaches to World Order.* Cambridge: Cambridge University Press.

Crowson, Philip. 2005. "Old Wine in New Bottles: Policy Issues for the Mining Industry." In *International and Comparative Mineral Law Policy*, edited by Elizabeth Bastida, Thomas Wälde, and Janeth Warden-Fernández, 607–20. The Hague: Kluwer Law International.

Dallaire, Roméo. 2003. *Shake Hands with the Devil: The Failure of Humanity in Rwanda.* Toronto: Random House.

———. 2006a. "Are All Humans Human or Are Some More Human Than Others?" Holocaust Memorial Day national commemoration 2006. http://www.hmd.org.uk.

———. 2006b. "History Will Judge Canada, Not Sudan, on the Fate of Darfur." *Globe and Mail*, 14 September.

———. 2007. "Speech to the US Congressional Subcommittee on Human Rights and the Law." http://sandubc.blogspot.com/2007/02/team-this-is-speech-senator-dallaire.html.

———. 2008. "Speech by Senator Roméo Dallaire to the Parliamentary Network for Nuclear Disarmament." Physicians for Global Survival Canada, April 29. http://pgs.ca/?page_id=384.

Darimani, A. 2005. *Impacts of Activities of Canadian Mining Companies in Africa.* Background document prepared for Mining Watch Canada roundtable on "Regulating Canadian Mining Companies Operating Internationally," 31 October. http://www.miningwatch.ca/sites/www.miningwatch.ca/files/Africa_case_study_0.pdf.

Dashwood, Hevina. 2005. "Canadian Mining Companies and the Shaping of Global Norms of Corporate Social Responsibility." *International Journal* 60 (4): 977–98.

———. 2007. "Canadian Mining Companies and Corporate Social Responsibility: Weighing the Impact of Global Norms." *Canadian Journal of Political Science* 40 (1): 129–56.

———. 2012. *The Rise of Global Corporate Social Responsbility: Mining and the Spread of Global Norms.* Cambridge: Cambridge University Press.

DATA Report. 2009. http://www.one.org/c/international/hottopic/2816.

———. 2013. http://one-org.s3.amazonaws.com/us/wp-content/uploads/2013/06/ONE_2013DataReport.pdf.

Dawson, Grant. 2007. *"Here Is Hell": Canada's Engagement in Somalia.* Vancouver: University of British Columbia Press.

———. 2009. "Contact Africa: Canadian Foreign Policy, the Contact Group, and Southern Africa." *International Journal* 64 (2): 521–36.

———. 2012. "Who Wants a Mission? Canadian Forces' Resistance to a Role in the UN Transition Assistance Group for Namibia, 1978." *International Peacekeeping* 19 (1): 114–27.

———. 2013. "Player, Partner, and Friend: Canada's Africa Policy since 1945." *International Politics* 50, online version.

De Renzio, Paolo, and Sarah Mulley. 2007. "Donor Coordination and Good Governance: Donor-Led and Recipient-Led Approaches." In *Exporting Good Governance: Temptations and Challenges in Canada's Aid Program,* edited by Jennifer Welsh and Ngaire Woods, 253–78. Waterloo, ON: Wilfrid Laurier University Press.

Den Heyer, Molly. 2012. "Untangling Canadian Aid Policy: International Agreements, CIDA's Policies and Micro-policy Negotiations in Tanzania." In *Struggling for Effectiveness: CIDA and Canadian Foreign Aid,* edited by Stephen Brown, 186–216. Montreal and Kingston: McGill-Queen's University Press.

Department of Finance. 2010. *Budget 2010: Leading the Way on Jobs and Growth.* 4 March. http://www.budget.gc.ca/2010/plan/chap3e-eng.html.

Department of Foreign Affairs and International Trade (DFAIT). 2008. "Canada Announces Important Contributions to Strengthen Peacekeeping in Africa." News Release no. 90, 16 April.

———. 2009. "Building the Canadian Advantage: A Corporate Social Responsibility (CSR) Strategy for the Canadian International Extractive Sector." March. http://www.international.gc.ca/trade-agreements-accords-commerciaux/topics-domaines/other-autre/csr-strat-rse.aspx.

Department of Foreign Affairs, Trade, and Development (DFATD). 2013a. *Global Markets Action Plan: The Blueprint for Creating Jobs and Opportunities for Canadians through Trade.* http://international.gc.ca/global-markets-marches-mondiaux/index.aspx?lang=eng.

———. 2013b. News Release: "Minister Fast Concludes Successful Trade Mission to Africa." 1 February. http://www.international.gc.ca/media_commerce/comm/news-communiques/2013/02/01a.aspx?lang=eng.

———. 2014a. "Canada Enhances Focus in Global Fight Against Poverty." News Release, 27 June. http://www.international.gc.ca/media/dev/news-communiques/2014/06/27a.aspx?lang=eng.

———. 2014b. "Statistical Report on International Assistance—by Country

Spending." http://www.acdi-cida.gc.ca/acdi-cida/acdi-cida.nsf/eng/
CAR-616135752-P3Q.

Department of National Defence (DND). 2004. "Backgrounder: Canadian
Forces Contribution to Bosnia-Herzegovina." 30 August. http://www
.forces.gc.ca/en/news/article.page?doc=canadian-forces-contribution
-to-bosnia-herzegovina/hnocfnnp.

———. 2008. *Canada First Defence Strategy.* Ottawa.

Di Boscio, Nicolas, and David Humphreys. 2005. "Mining and Regional
Economic Development." In *International and Comparative Mineral Law
Policy,* edited by Elizabeth Bastida, Thomas Wälde, and Janeth Warden-
Fernández, 589–606. The Hague: Kluwer Law International.

Directorate of Military Training Assistance Programme (DMTAP). 2007.
Annual Report, 2006/07. Ottawa: Department of National Defence.

Directorate of Military Training and Cooperation (DMTC). 2010. *Annual
Report, 2009/10.* Ottawa: Department of National Defence.

Donaghy, Greg. 1995. "The Rise and Fall of Canadian Military Assistance
in the Developing World, 1952–1971." *Canadian Military History* 4 (1):
75–84.

Drimmer, Jonathan, and Michael Liberman. 2010. "Talisman Energy and
the Alien Tort Statute: The Continuing Threat of Secondary Liability."
Lexis-Nexis Emerging Issues Analysis 5182, July.

Drohan, Madeleine. 2003. *Making a Killing: How and Why Corporations Use
Armed Force to Do Business.* Toronto: Random House.

Dunne, Tim. 1998. *Inventing International Society: A History of the English
School.* London: Macmillan.

Dunne, Tim, and Nicholas J. Wheeler. 2001. "Blair's Britain: A Force for
Good in the World?" In *Ethics and Foreign Policy,* edited by Karen E.
Smith and Margot Light, 167–84. Cambridge: Cambridge University
Press.

Earthworks and Oxfam America. 2004. *Dirty Metals: Mining, Communities
and the Environment.* http://www.nodirtygold.org/pubs/DirtyMetals_
HR.pdf.

Economic Commission for Africa (ECA). 2012. *Economic Report on Africa
2012: Unleashing Africa's Potential as a Pole of Growth.* http://new.uneca
.org/era/era2012.aspx.

Elder, David C. 2013. "Canada's Diplomacy in Africa." In *Canada among
Nations 2013. Canada and Africa: From Investment to Engagement—Look-
ing Back, Looking Ahead,* edited by Rohinton Medhora and Yiagadeesen
Samy, 23–41. Montreal and Kingston: McGill-Queen's University Press.

Elliott, Larry. 2003. "Do Us All a Favour—Pull the Plug on G8." *Guardian
Weekly,* 5–11 June.

———. 2005. "No Marshall Plan—But a Start." *Guardian Weekly,* 15–21 July.

Engler, Yves. 2012. *The Ugly Canadian: Stephen Harper's Foreign Policy*. Halifax: Fernwood Publishing.

Ericsson, M. 2005. "Structural Changes in the Minerals Industry." In *International and Comparative Mineral Law Policy*, edited by Elizabeth Bastida, Thomas Wälde, and Janeth Warden-Fernandez, 469–92. The Hague: Kluwer Law International.

Evans, Marketa. 2007. "New Collaborations for International Development: Corporate Social Responsibility and Beyond." *International Journal* 62 (2): 311–25.

Fantino, Julian. 2012. "Speaking Notes for the Honourable Julian Fantino Minister of International Cooperation for the Economic Club of Canada 'Reducing Poverty—Building Tomorrow's Markets.'" Toronto, 23 November.

———. 2013. "Government of Canada and World Economic Forum Conference: Maximizing the Value of Extractives for Development—Introduction." Toronto, 2 March.

Fast, Ed. 2012. "Address by Minister Fast at Canadian Council on Africa 10th Anniversary Symposium." Ottawa, 16 October.

Fédération Internationale des Ligues des Droits de l'Homme (FIDH). 2007. *Mali: Mining and Human Rights. International Fact-Finding Mission Report*, September.

Ferguson, James. 2006. *Global Shadows: Africa in the Neoliberal World Order*. Durham: Duke University Press.

Flanagan, Tom. 2009. "Do We Have the Means to Match Our Will?" *Globe and Mail*, 22 September.

Forcese, Craig. 2001. "'Militarized Commerce' in Sudan's Oilfields: Lessons for Canadian Foreign Policy." *Canadian Foreign Policy* 8 (3): 37–56.

Foster, Ally. 2013. "How France Pulled Diplomatic Strings to Get Canada's Aircraft." *Embassy*, 16 January.

Fowler, Robert. 2003. "Canadian Leadership and the Kananaskis G-8 Summit: Towards a Less Self-Centred Foreign Policy." In *Canada among Nations 2003: Coping with the American Colossus*, edited by David Carment, Fen Osler Hampson, and Norman Hillmer, 219–41. Don Mills, ON: Oxford University Press.

———. 2011. *A Season in Hell*. Toronto: HarperCollins Canada.

———. 2013. "Robert Fowler: Why Canada Must Intervene in Mali." *Globe and Mail*, 8 January.

Freedman, Jim. 2006–07. "International Remedies for Resource-Based Conflict." *International Journal* 62 (1): 108–19.

Freeman, Alan. 2007. "Harper Signals Shift from Africa to Americas." *Globe and Mail*, 8 June.

Freeman, Linda. 1980. "Canada and Africa in the 1970s." *International Journal* 35 (4): 794–820.

———. 1982. "CIDA, Wheat, and Rural Development in Tanzania." *Canadian Journal of African Studies* 16 (3): 479–504.

———. 1985. "The Effect of the World Crisis on Canada's Involvement in Africa." *Studies in Political Economy* 17:107–39.

———. 1997. *The Ambiguous Champion: Canada and South Africa in the Trudeau and Mulroney Years.* Toronto: University of Toronto Press.

Gallagher, Julia. 2009. "Healing the Scar? Idealizing Britain in Africa, 1997–2007." *African Affairs* 108 (432): 435–51.

———. 2011. *Britain and Africa under Blair: In Pursuit of the Good State.* Manchester: Manchester University Press.

Gallinger, Ross. 2013. "A Made-in-Canada Solution." *Embassy,* 19 June.

Galloway, Gloria. 2014. "Roméo Dallaire Resigns from Senate." *Globe and Mail,* 28 May.

Gavai, Avinash. 2010. "How the Rest of the G8 Stacks Up on Contraceptives, Abortion." *Embassy,* 31 March.

Gberie, Lansana, and Ian Smillie. 2014. "Ebola is Canada's Responsibility in Sierra Leone." *Embassy,* 17 September.

Gecelovsky, Paul, and Tom Keating. 2001. "Liberal Internationalism for Conservatives." In *Diplomatic Departures: The Conservative Era in Canadian Foreign Policy,* edited by Nelson Michaud and Kim Nossal, 194–210. Vancouver: University of British Columbia Press.

"G8 Agreement on Africa." 2005. G8 Information Centre. Gleneagles, Scotland, 8 July. http://www.g8.utoronto.ca/summit/2005gleneagles/africa.html.

"G8 Lough Earne Communiqué." 2013. G8 Information Centre. 18 June. http://www.g8.utoronto.ca.

Gendron, Robin S. 2006. *Towards a Francophone Community: Canada's Relations with France and French Africa, 1945–1968.* Montreal and Kingston: McGill-Queen's University Press.

Gillies, David. 1994. "Export Promotion and Canadian Development Assistance." In *Canadian International Development Assistance Policies: An Appraisal,* edited by Cranford Pratt, 210–39. Montreal and Kingston: McGill-Queen's University Press.

Global Peace and Security Program. 2009. Department of Foreign Affairs and International Trade, Canada. http://www.international.gc.ca/START-GTSR/gpsp-ppsm.aspx.

Globe and Mail. 1996. "Punishing Nigeria." Editorial, 28 June.

———. 2002a. "Man of Action Aims to Make a Difference in Africa." 12 April.

———. 2002b. "G8 Snubs PM's Vision for Africa." 28 June.

———. 2005. "What the G8 Leaders Were Able to Achieve." Editorial, 9 July.

———. 2007. "Geldof Calls Canada Obstructionist." 5 June.

———. 2010. "Canada Rejects UN Call to Lead in Congo." 1 May.

Gordon, Todd. 2010. *Imperialist Canada.* Winnipeg: Arbeiter Ring.

Government of Canada. 2005. *International Policy Statement—A Role of Pride and Influence in the World: Development.* Ottawa: Canadian International Development Agency.

———. 2009. *Canada and the Americas: Priorities and Progress.* http://www.international.gc.ca/americas-ameriques/assets/pdfs/Report2009-eng.pdf.

Goyette, Gabriel. Forthcoming. "Charity Begins at Home: The Extractive Sector As an Illustration of Changes and Continuities in the New *de facto* Canadian Aid Policy." In *Rethinking Canadian Aid,* edited by Stephen Brown, Molly den Heyer, and David Black. Ottawa: University of Ottawa Press.

Granatstein, J.L. 2010. "Defining Canada's Role in Congo." *Globe and Mail,* 6 April. http://www.theglobeandmail.com/globe-debate/defining-canadas-role-in-congo/article4189359.

Grayson, Kyle. 2004. "Branding 'Transformation' in Canadian Foreign Policy: Human Security." *Canadian Foreign Policy* 11 (2): 41–68.

———. 2006. "Promoting Responsibility and Accountability: Human Security and Canadian Corporate Conduct." *International Journal* 61 (1): 479–94.

Green, Reginald, and Mike Faber. 1994. "The Structural Adjustment of Structural Adjustment: Sub-Saharan Africa 1980–1993." *IDS Bulletin* 25 (3): 1–8.

Guardian Weekly. 2002a. "Africa Betrayed: The Aid Workers' Verdict." 4–10 July.

———. 2002b. "Africa Let Down by the Rich." 4–10 July.

Gulrajani, Nilima. 2010. *Re-imagining Canadian Aid: A Comparative Examination of Norway and the UK.* Toronto: Walter and Duncan Gordon Foundation.

Gurzu, Anca. 2011. "Democracy Promotion Falling Off Radar Even as Experts See More Need." *Embassy,* 27 April.

Halifax Initiative. 2006. Mining Map. http://halifaxinitiative.org/content/mining-map-referenced.

Halliday, Anthony. 2009. "Canada Is Turning Its Back on the Poorest of Africa." Globe and Mail, 3 April.

Harper, Stephen. 2010. "Statement by the Prime Minister of Canada." World Economic Forum, Davos, Switzerland, 28 January.

Harker, John. 2000. *Human Security in Sudan: The Report of a Canadian Assessment Mission/Prepared for the Minister of Foreign Affairs.* Ottawa: Department of Foreign Affairs and International Trade.

Haussman, Melissa, and Lisa Mills. 2012. "Doing the North American
  Two-Step on Global Stage: Canada, Its G8 Muskoka Initiative and Safe
  Abortion Spending." In *How Ottawa Spends 2012/2013: The Harper
  Majority, Budget Cuts, and the New Opposition*, edited by G. Bruce Doern
  and Christopher Stoney, 242–60. Montreal and Kingston: McGill-
  Queen's University Press.

Hayes, Frank. 1982. "Canada, the Commonwealth, and the Rhodesian
  Issue." In *An Acceptance of Paradox: Essays on Canadian Diplomacy in
  Honour of John W. Holmes*, edited by Kim Nossal, 141–73. Toronto: Can-
  adian Institute of International Affairs.

Healy, Teresa, and Sheila Katz. 2008. "Big and Little Brother Bilateralism:
  Security, Prosperity, and Canada's Deal with Colombia." *Studies in Political Economy* 82:35–60.

Helleiner, Gerald. 1994–95. "Globalization and Fragmentation in the International Economy." *Canadian Foreign Policy* 2 (3): 101–8.

Hennessy, Michael. 2001. "Operation 'Assurance': Planning a Multi-
  National Force for Rwanda/Zaire." *Canadian Military Journal*, Spring:
  11–20.

Herold, R.A. 2004–05. "Future Leadership and the Road to Somalia." *Canadian Military Journal*, Winter: 88–89.

Holt, Victoria, and Tobias Berkman. 2006. *The Impossible Mandate? Military
  Preparedness, the Responsibility to Protect and Modern Peace Operations.*
  Washington: Henry L. Stimson Centre.

Humphreys, David. 2005. "Corporate Strategies in the Global Mining
  Industry." In *International and Comparative Mineral Law Policy*, edited
  by Elizabeth Bastida, Thomas Wälde, and Janeth Warden-Fernández,
  451–67. The Hague: Kluwer Law International.

Ignatieff, Michael. 2009. "Speech to the Canadian Club of Ottawa: Canada's Place in a Changing World." Ottawa, 14 September.

———. 2010. "Rebuilding Canada's Leadership on the World Stage."
  Speech to the Montreal Council on Foreign Relations, 2 November.

International Commission on Intervention and State Sovereignty (ICISS).
  2001. *The Responsibility to Protect.* Ottawa: International Development
  Research Centre.

Jackson, Robert H. 2000. *The Global Covenant: Human Conduct in a World of
  States.* Oxford: Oxford University Press.

Johnston, Patrick. 2010. "Canadian Generosity Tumbles." *Globe and Mail*,
  23 September.

Katzenstein, Peter, and Rudra Sil. 2008. "Eclectic Theorizing in the Study
  and Practice of International Relations." In *The Oxford Handbook of
  International Relations*, edited by Christian Reus-Smit and Duncan
  Snidal, 109–30. New York: Oxford University Press.

Keating, Tom. 2013. *Canada and World Order*. 3rd ed. Don Mills, ON: Oxford University Press.

———. 2014. "The transition in Canadian Foreign Policy through an English School Lens." *International Journal*, online version, 2 April.

Keenan, Karyn. 2013. "Commentary: Desperately Seeking Sanction: Canadian Extractive Companies and Their Public Partners." *Canadian Journal of Development Studies* 34 (1): 111–21.

Kennedy, Mark. 2013. "How Brian Mulroney Spearheaded Canadian Push to End Apartheid in South Africa and Free Nelson Mandela." *National Post*, 5 December. http://news.nationalpost.com/2013/12/05/how-brian-mulroney-spearheaded-canadian-push-to-end-apartheid-in-south-africa-and-free-nelson-mandela/.

Kirton, John. 2002. "Canada As a Principal Summit Power: G-7/8 Concert Diplomacy from Halifax 1995 to Kananaskis 2002". In *Canada Among Nations 2002: A Fading Power*, edited by Norman Hillmer and Maureen Molot, 209–32. Don Mills, ON: Oxford University Press.

———. 2007. *Canadian Foreign Policy in a Changing World*. Toronto: Nelson.

Koops, Joachim, and Johannes Varwick. 2008. "Ten Years of SHIRBRIG: Lessons Learned, Development Prospects and Strategic Opportunities for Germany." GPPI Research Paper Series No. 11. Berlin: Global Public Policy Institute.

Lalonde, Jennifer. 2009. "Harmony and Discord: International Aid Harmonization and Donor State Domestic Influence. The Case of Canada and the Canadian International Development Agency." Unpublished doctoral dissertation, Johns Hopkins University.

Lawson, Guy. 2005. "Sorrows of a Hero." *New York Review of Books* 52 (9), 26 May.

Le Billon, Phillipe. 2006–07. "Securing Transparency: Armed Conflicts and the Management of Natural Resource Revenues." *International Journal* 62 (1): 93–107.

Leblanc, Daniel. 2012. "Miners Show New Way for CIDA." *Globe and Mail*, 30 January.

Lemieux, André. 2005. "Canada's Global Mining Presence." *Canadian Mineral Yearbook, 2005*.

Lewis, Stephen. 2005. *Race Against Time: Searching for Hope in AIDS Ravaged Africa*. Toronto: House of Anansi.

Linklater, Andrew, and Hidemi Suganami. 2006. *The English School of International Relations*. Cambridge: Cambridge University Press.

Lisk, Franklyn, Hany Besada, and Philip Martin. 2013. "Regulating Extraction in the Global South: Towards a Framework for Accountability." Background Research Paper submitted to the High Level Panel on the Post-2015 Development Agenda, May.

Lupick, Trevor. 2013. "Canada at the Forefront of a Controversial Mining Boom in Africa." *Straight.com* (Vancouver), 13 April.

Lyon, Peyton. 1976. "Introduction." In *Canada and the Third World*, edited by Peyton Lyon and Tareq Ismael, x–l. Toronto: Macmillan.

MacDonald, David. 1986. "No More Famine: A Decade for Africa: Report for the Period Ending March 31, 1986." Canadian Emergency Coordinator/African Famine.

MacDonald, Laura. 1995. "Unequal Partnerships: The Politics of Canada's Relations with the Third World." *Studies in Political Economy* 47: 111–41.

MacKenzie, Lewis. 2008. *Soldiers Made Me Look Good.* Vancouver: Douglas and McIntyre.

———. 2009. "Has Uncle Sam Run Out of Patience?" *Globe and Mail,* 3 February.

Mackrael, Kim. 2012. "Fantino Under Fire to Explain CIDA Direction." *Globe and Mail,* 4 December. http://www.theglobeandmail.com/news/politics/fantino-under-fire-to-explain-cida-direction/article5958392.

———. 2013. "Canada Scraps Sudan Task Force as Darfur Conflict Resurges." *Globe and Mail,* 10 October. http://www.theglobeandmail.com/news/politics/canada-scraps-sudan-task-force-as-darfur-conflict-resurges/article14793442/.

Maclean, Sandra, and Timothy Shaw. 2001. "Canada and New 'Global' Strategic Alliances." *Canadian Foreign Policy* 8 (3): 17–36.

Martin, Paul. 2004. "Address by Prime Minister Paul Martin at the United Nations." New York, 22 September.

Martineau, Michael. 2005. "Rebirth of Gold Mining in Sub-Saharan Africa." *Mining Journal* 4 February: 3–5.

Massie, Justin. 2009. "Making Sense of Canada's 'Irrational' International Security Policy: A Tale of Three Strategic Cultures." *International Journal* 64 (3): 625–45.

Matthews, Robert. 1976. "Canada and Anglophone Africa." In *Canada and the Third World*, edited by Peyton Lyon and Tareq Ismael, 60–132. Toronto: Macmillan.

———. 2005. "Sudan's Humanitarian Disaster: Will Canada Live Up to Its Responsibility to Protect?" *International Journal* 60 (4): 1049–64.

Mbembe, Achilla. 2001. *On the Postcolony.* Berkeley: University of California Press.

McArthur, John. 2013. "Starting a New Canadian Aid Conversation." Canadian International Council, *OpenCanada.org, Canada's Hub for International Affairs.* http://opencanada.org/indepth/starting-a-new-conversation-about-aid/.

McRae, Rob, and Don Hubert, eds. 2001. *Human Security and the New Diplomacy.* Montreal and Kingston: McGill-Queen's University Press.

Medhora, Rohinton, and Yiagadeesen Samy. 2013. "Introduction." In *Canada among Nations 2013. Canada and Africa: From Investment to Engagement—Looking Back, Looking Ahead*, edited by Medhora and Samy, 1–19. Montreal and Kingston: McGill-Queen's University Press.

Metals Economics Group (MEG). 2012. *World Explorations Trends 2012*. Halifax.

Meyer, Paul. n.d. "Case study #7: Canada's Response to the Humanitarian Crisis in Eastern Zaire: Operation Assurance 1996." Centre for Dialogue International Security, Simon Fraser University, Vancouver, BC.

Mittelman, James. 1998. "Coxian Historicism as an Alternative Perspective in International Studies." *Alternatives* 23 (1): 63–92.

Möllander, Anders. 2009. "UN Angola Sanctions—A Committee Success Revisited." Uppsala: Department of Peace and Conflict Research, Uppsala University.

Morrison, David. 1998. *Aid and Ebb Tide: A History of CIDA and Canadian Development Assistance*. Waterloo, ON: Wilfrid Laurier University Press.

Moyo, Dambisa. 2009. *Dead Aid: Why Aid Is Not Working and How There Is a Better Way for Africa*. Vancouver: Douglas and McIntyre.

Mulcair, Tom. 2013. "Rethinking Canada's Approach to International and Trade Relations." Address to the Montreal Council on Foreign Relations, 7 February. http://www.ndp.ca/news/rethinking-canadas-approach-to -international-and-trade-relations.

Mulroney, Brian. 2007. *Memoirs, 1939–1993*. Toronto: McClelland and Stewart.

Munro, Lachlan. 2005. "Focus Pocus? Thinking Critically about Whether Aid Organizations Should Do Fewer Things in Fewer Countries." *Development and Change* 36 (3): 425–47.

Munton, Don. 2002–03. "Whither Internationalism?" *International Journal* 58 (1): 155–80.

Murray, Robert W. 2013. *System, Society and the World: Exploring the English School of International Relations*. e-International Relations, April. http:// www.e-IR.info.

Natural Resources Canada. 2011. *Overview of Trends in Canadian Mineral Exploration 2009*. Ottawa: Natural Resources Canada.

Neufeld, Mark. 1995. "Hegemony and Foreign Policy Analysis: The Case of Canada as a Middle Power." *Studies in Political Economy* 48:7–29.

Noël, Alain, Jean-Philippe Thérien, and Sébastien Dallaire. 2004. "Divided over Internationalism: The Canadian Public and Development Assistance." *Canadian Public Policy* 30 (1): 29–46.

North-South Institute (NSI). 2003. *Canadian Development Report 2003*. Ottawa: North-South Institute.

———. 2014. *Canadian International Development Report 2013: Governing*

Natural Resources for Africa's Development. Ottawa. http://www.nsi-ins.ca/publications/canadian-international-development-report-2013.

Nossal, Kim. 1988. "Mixed Motives Revisited: Canada's Interest in Development Assistance." *Canadian Journal of Political Science* 21 (1): 35–56.

———. 1998–99. "Pinchpenny Diplomacy: The Decline of 'Good International Citizenship' in Canadian Foreign Policy?" *International Journal* 54 (1): 88–105.

———. 2000. "Mission Diplomacy and the 'Cult of the Initiative' in Canadian Foreign Policy." In *Worthwhile Initiatives? Canadian Mission-Oriented Diplomacy*, edited by Andrew Cooper and Geoffrey Hayes, 1–12. Toronto: Irwin Publishing and the Canadian Institute of International Affairs.

———. 2005. "Ear Candy: Canadian Policy toward Humanitarian Intervention and Atrocity Crimes in Darfur." *International Journal* 60 (4): 1017–32.

———. 2012. "The Liberal Past in the Conservative Present: Internationalism in the Harper Era." In *Canada in the World: Internationalism in Canadian Foreign Policy*, edited by Claire Sjolander and Heather Smith, 21–36. Don Mills, ON: Oxford University Press.

Nossal, Kim, Stéphane Roussel, and Stéphane Paquin. 2010. *International Policy and Politics in Canada*. Toronto: Pearson.

Nutt, Samantha. 2011. *Damned Nations: Guns, Greed, Armies, and Aid*. Toronto: McClelland and Stewart.

Oda, Bev. 2009a. "Speaking Notes for the Honourable Beverley J. Oda Minister of International Cooperation at the Munk Centre for International Studies." Toronto, 20 May.

———. 2009b. "Speaking Notes for the Honourable Beverley J. Oda Minister of International Cooperation for a meeting with African Ambassadors to Canada." Ottawa, 26 October.

Off, Carol. 2000. *The Lion, the Fox, and the Eagle*. Toronto: Random House.

O'Neill, Juliet. 2010. "Funds Earmarked for Maternal and Child Health in 10 Impoverished Countries." *Ottawa Citizen*, 1 November.

Orbinski, James. 2008. *An Imperfect Offering: Humanitarian Action in the 21st Century*. Toronto: Anchor.

Organization for Economic Cooperation and Development (OECD)'s Development Assistance Committee (DAC). 1996. *Shaping the 21st Century: The Contribution of Development Cooperation*. Paris.

Owen, Taylor, and David Eaves. 2007. "Africa Is Not a Liberal Idea." *Embassy*, 3 October.

Oxfam America. 2006. *Tarnished Gold: Mining and the Unmet Promise of Development*. Report. http://www.bicusa.org/wp-content/uploads/2013/01/Tarnished+Gold_Mining.pdf.

Panetta, Alexander. 2010. "Michaëlle Jean and Entourage Challenge Idea of Africa as 'Aid Receptacle.'" *Canadian Press*, 24 April.

Paras, Andrea. 2012. "CIDA's Secular Fiction and Canadian Faith-Based Organizations." *Canadian Journal of Development Studies* 33 (2): 231–49.

Paris, Roland. Forthcoming. "Are Canadians Still Liberal Internationalists? Foreign Policy and Public Opinion in the Harper Era." *International Journal*, September.

Payne, Anthony. 2006. "Blair, Brown and the Gleneagles Agenda: Making Poverty History, or Confronting the Global Politics of Unequal Development?" *International Affairs* 82 (5): 917–35.

Payne, Elizabeth. 2012. "Foreign Policy Is Mining Policy." *Ottawa Citizen*, 7 March.

Pearson, Glen. 2010. "Maternal Health Pledge Sows Confusion." *Embassy*, 3 February.

Pedro, Antonio. 2006. "Mainstreaming Mineral Wealth in Growth and Poverty Reduction Strategies." *Minerals and Energy* 21 (1): 2–16.

Piiparinen, Touko. 2007. "The Lessons of Darfur for the Future of Humanitarian Intervention." *Global Governance* 13 (3): 365–90.

Potter, Mitch. 2009. "What Next for G8 … and Canada?" *Toronto Star*, 26 September.

Powell, Kristiana. 2005. "The African Union's Emerging Peace and Security Regime: Opportunities and Challenges for Delivering on *The Responsibility to Protect*." Ottawa: the North-South Institute, May.

Pratt, Cranford. 1983–84. "Dominant Class Theory and Canadian Foreign Policy: The Case of the Counter-Consensus." *International Journal* 39 (1): 99–135.

———. 1989a. "Canada: A Limited and Eroding Internationalism." In *The North-South Policies of Canada, the Netherlands, Norway, and Sweden*, edited by Cranford Pratt, 24–69. Toronto: University of Toronto Press.

———, ed. 1989b. *Internationalism Under Strain: The North-South Policies of Canada, the Netherlands, Norway, and Sweden*. Toronto: University of Toronto Press.

———, ed. 1994. *Canadian International Development Assistance Policies: An Appraisal*. Montreal and Kingston: McGill-Queen's University Press.

———. 2003. "Ethical Values and Canadian Foreign Aid Policies." *Canadian Journal of African Studies* 37 (1): 84–101.

Pratt, Renate. 1997. *In Good Faith: Canadian Churches against Apartheid*. Waterloo, ON: Wilfrid Laurier University Press.

Prime Minister's Office (PMO), Canada. 2014. "Canada's Forward Strategy Saving Every Woman, Every Child: Within Arm's Reach." 29 May. http://pm.gc.ca/eng/news/2014/05/29/canadas-forward-strategy -saving-every-woman-every-child-within-arms-reach.

Pring, George, and Linda Siegle. 2005."International Law and Mineral Resource Development." In *International and Comparative Mineral Law Policy*, edited by Elizabeth Bastida, Thomas Wälde, and Janeth Warden-Fernández, 127–48. The Hague: Kluwer Law International.

Razack, Sherene. 2004. *Dark Threats and White Knights*. Toronto: University of Toronto Press.

———. 2007. "Stealing the Pain of Others: Reflections on Canadian Humanitarian Responses." *Review of Education, Pedagogy, and Cultural Studies* 29 (4): 375–94.

Redekop, Clarence. 1982. "Trudeau at Singapore: The Commonwealth and Arms Sales to South Africa." In *An Acceptance of Paradox: Essays on Canadian Diplomacy in Honour of John W. Holmes*, edited by Kim Nossal, 174–96. Toronto: Canadian Institute of International Affairs.

Reid, Richard. 2014. "Horror, Hubris, and Humanity: The International Engagement with Africa, 1914–2014." *International Affairs* 90: 142–65.

Rempel, Roy. 2006. *Dreamland: How Canada's Pretend Foreign Policy Has Undermined Sovereignty*. Montreal and Kingston: McGill-Queen's University Press.

Riddell-Dixon, Elizabeth. 2005. "Canada's Human Security Agenda: Walking the Talk?" *International Journal* 60 (4): 1067–92.

Roberts, Chris. 2013a. "West African Canaries in the Gold Mine: Investment Outlook and Challenges for Burkina Faso and Mali." Calgary: Canadian Defence and Foreign Affairs Institute, April.

———. 2013b. "Mali's Post-crisis Crisis." *Embassy*, 29 May.

Roe, Emery. 1991. "Development Narratives, or Making the Best of Blueprint Development." *World Development* 19 (4): 287–300.

Ruggie, John. 2004. "Reconstituting the Global Public Domain—Issues, Actors, and Practices." *European Journal of International Relations* 10 (4): 499–531.

Sabourin, Louis. 1976. "Canada and Francophone Africa." In *Canada and the Third World*, edited by Peyton Lyon and Tareq Ismael, 133–61. Toronto: Macmillan.

Said, Edward. 1991. *Culture and Imperialism*. New York: Alfred A. Knopf.

Sandbrook, Richard. 2005. "Africa's Great Transformation?" *Journal of Development Studies* 41 (6): 1118–25.

Saul, John. 1988. "Militant Mulroney? The Tories and South Africa." Paper prepared for the Annual Meeting of the Canadian Association of African Studies, Queen's University, Kingston, ON, May.

Schlegel, John P. 1978. *The Deceptive Ash: Bilingualism and Canadian Foreign Policy in Africa: 1957–1971*. Washington, DC: University Press of America.

Schmitz, Gerald. 1996. "The Verdict on Aid Effectiveness: Why the Jury Stays Out." *International Journal* 51 (2): 287–313.

Schorr, Victoria, and Paul Hitschfeld. 2013. "Canadian Trade and Investment in Africa." In *Canada among Nations 2013. Canada and Africa: From Investment to Engagement—Looking Back, Looking Ahead*, edited by Rohinton Medhora and Yiagadeesen Samy, 133–52. Montreal and Kingston: McGill-Queen's University Press.

Sears, Jonathan. 2010. "Peacebuilding between Canadian Values and Local Knowledge: Some Lessons from Timbuktu." In *Locating Global Order: American Power and Canadian Security after 9/11*, edited by Bruno Charbonneau and Wayne S. Cox, 260–75. Vancouver: University of British Columbia Press.

Senate Standing Committee on Foreign Affairs and International Trade (SSCFAIT). 2007. *Overcoming Forty Years of Failure: A New Road Map for Sub-Saharan Africa*. Ottawa: SSCFAIT.

Sending, Ole, and Iver Neumann. 2006. "Governance to Governmentality: Analyzing NGOs, States, and Power." *International Studies Quarterly* 50: 651–72.

Shane, Kristen. 2014. "Expanded Aid Priority-Country List Overlaps with Trade Interests." *Embassy*, 27 June.

Sharma, Serena. 2010. "Towards a Global Responsibility to Protect: Setbacks on the Path to Implementation." *Global Governance* 16 (1): 121–38.

Siebert, John. 2013. "Principles for a Mali-first Security Strategy for Canada." *Project Ploughshares Briefing*, January. http://www.ploughshares.ca.

Siegel, Shefa. 2013. "The Missing Ethics of Mining." *Ethics and International Affairs* 27 (1). http://www.ethicsandinternationalaffairs.org/2013/the-missing-ethics-of-mining-full-text.

Sil, Rudra. 2009. "Simplifying Pragmatism: From Social Theory to Problem-Driven Eclecticism." *International Studies Review* 11:648–52.

Simons, Penelope, and Audrey Macklin. 2010. "Defeat of Responsible Mining Bill Is Missed Opportunity." *Globe and Mail*, 3 November.

Simpson, Jeffrey. 2013. "Slice-and-Dice Politics, Conservative Style." *Globe and Mail*, 23 February.

Small, Michael. 2001. "Peacebuilding in Post-Conflict Societies." In *Human Security and the New Diplomacy: Protecting People, Promoting Peace*, edited by Rob McRae and Don Hubert, 75–87. Montreal and Kingston: McGill-Queen's University Press.

Smillie, Ian. 1985. *The Land of Lost Content, A History of CUSO*. Toronto: Deneau.

———. 2006. "Whose Security? Innovation and Responsibility, Perception and Reality." In *A Decade of Human Security: Global Governance and New Multilateralisms*, edited by Sandra MacLean, David Black, and Timothy Shaw, 19–30. Farnham, Surrey: Ashgate.

———. 2010. "High Time for a Minister Who Understands the Role of Aid." *Globe and Mail*, 7 January.

———. 2012. "Tying Up the Cow: CIDA, Advocacy, and Public Engagement." In *Struggling for Effectiveness: CIDA and Canadian Foreign Aid*, edited by Stephen Brown, 269–86. Montreal and Kingston: McGill-Queen's University Press.

———. 2013. "Blood Diamonds: Canada, Africa and Some Object Lessons in Global Governance." In *Canada among Nations 2013. Canada and Africa: From Investment to Engagement—Looking Back, Looking Ahead*, edited by Rohinton Medhora and Yiagadeesen Samy, 169–78. Montreal and Kingston: McGill-Queen's University Press.

Smith, Malinda. 2005. "The Constitution of Africa as a Security Threat." *Review of Constitutional Studies* 10 (1–2): 163–206.

Smythe, Elizabeth. 2007. "Don't You Know That Tears Are Not Enough? Transnational Campaigns, Canadian Foreign Aid and the Politics of Shame." Paper presented to the annual meeting of the Canadian Political Science Association, Saskatoon, SK, May.

Spicer, Keith. 1966. *A Samaritan State? External Aid in Canada's Foreign Policy*. Toronto: University of Toronto Press.

Spooner, Kevin. 2009. *Canada, the Congo Crisis, and UN Peacekeeping, 1960–64*. Vancouver: University of British Columbia Press.

Stairs, Denis. 1982. "The Political Culture of Canadian Foreign Policy." *Canadian Journal of Political Science* 15 (4): 667–90.

———. 2005. "Confusing the Innocent with Numbers and Categories: The International Policy Statement and the Concentration of Development Assistance." Calgary: Canadian Defence and Foreign Affairs Institute. http://www.cdfai.org/PDF/Confusing%20the%20Innocent.pdf.

Standing Committee on Foreign Affairs and International Trade (SCFAIT). 2005. *Fourteenth Report: Mining in Developing Countries: Corporate Social Responsibility*. 38th Parliament, 1st Session, June.

Stopford, John, and Susan Strange, with John Henley. 1991. *Rival States, Rival Firms: Competition for World Market Shares*. Cambridge: Cambridge University Press.

Swiss, Liam. 2014. "New Focus Countries Not About Effective Aid." Blogpost, 14 July. http://blog.liamswiss.com.

Taylor, Ian. 2005a. "Advice Is Judged by Results, Not by Intentions: Why Gordon Brown Is Wrong about Africa." *International Affairs* 81 (2): 299–310.

———. 2005b. *NEPAD: Towards Africa's Development or Another False Start?* Boulder, CO: Lynne Rienner.

Tettey, W., and K. Puplampu. 2005. *The African Diaspora in Canada: Negotiating Identity and Belonging*. Calgary: University of Calgary Press.

Thomas, David P. 2013. "Bombardier and the Gautrain Project in South

Africa: The Political Economy of Canadian Investment in a Rapid Rail Megaproject." *Studies in Political Economy* 91: 137–57.

Tienhaara, Kyla. 2006. "Mineral Investments and the Regulation of the Environment in Developing Countries: Lessons from Ghana." *International Environmental Agreements* 6 (4): 371–94.

Tomlinson, Brian. 2008. "Canada: Overview: Unmet Promises and No Plans to Increase Canadian ODA." In *The Reality of Aid 2008*, edited by Reality of Aid Management Committee, 179–83. Quezon City, Philippines: IBON Books.

Tomlinson, Brian, and Pam Foster. 2004. "At the Table or in the Kitchen? CIDA's New Aid Strategies, Developing Country Ownership and Donor Conditionality." Canadian Council for International Cooperation/ Halifax Initiative Briefing Paper, September. http://www.ccic.ca/_ files/en/what_we_do/002_aid_2004-09_at_the_table.pdf.

Toycen, Dave. 2010. "Maternal, Child Health Go Beyond Politics." *Embassy*, 22 September.

Travers, Patrick, and Taylor Owen. 2008. "Between Metaphor and Strategy: Canada's Integrated Approach to Peacebuilding in Afghanistan." *International Journal* 63 (3): 685–702.

United Nations. 2000. *Report of the Panel on United Nations Peace Operations (The Brahimi Report).* http://unrol.org/doc.aspx?n=brahimi+report+ peacekeeping.pdf.

———. 2008. *United Nations Peacekeeping Operations: Principles and Guidelines.* New York: Department of Peacekeeping Operations. http://pbpu .unlb.org/pbps/library/capstone_doctrine_eNg.pdf.

United Nations Conference on Trade and Development (UNCTAD). 2005. "Economic Development in Africa: Rethinking the Role of Foreign Direct Investment." UNCTAD/GDS/AFRICA/2005/1. Geneva: United Nations.

United Nations Secretary General (UNSG). 2004. *Enhancement of African Peacekeeping Capacity.* Report to the United Nations General Assembly, A/59/591, 30 November. http://www.un.org/ga/search/view_doc .asp?symbol=A/59/591.

Valpy, Michael. 1987. "Mulroney in Africa: Superb Fluff and a Stunning Revelation." *Globe and Mail*, 31 January.

———. 1988. "An Interview with Stephen Lewis." *Southern Africa Report*, 4 (3): 13–15.

Van Ameringen, Marc. 2013. "Nelson Mandela and Canada's Outsized Role in the New South Africa." *Embassy*, 11 December.

van Ham, Peter. 2001. "The Rise of the Brand State: The Postmodern Politics of Image and Reputation." *Foreign Affairs* 80 (5): 2–6.

Van Loan, Peter. 2011. "Address by Minister Van Loan at Africa Rising:

Entrepreneurship and Innovation Frontiers." DFAIT No. 2011/14, Toronto, 15 March.

Vervaeke, Alison. 2013. "'It's Not My Story': The Development Disconnect between Corporate Social Responsibility and the Narratives of Communities Impacted by Mining in Peru's Andes.' MA thesis, Dalhousie University, Halifax, NS.

Vines, Alex, and Thomas Cargill. 2006. "'The World Must Judge Us on Africa'—Prime Minister Blair's Africa Legacy." *Politique Africaine*, April, 132–47.

Wallace, Tina. 2003. "NGO Dilemmas: Trojan Horses for Global Neoliberalism?" In *Socialist Register 2004: The New Imperial Challenge*, edited by Leo Panitch and Colin Leys, 203–19. London: Merlin Press.

Wheeler, Nicholas J. 2000. *Saving Strangers: Humanitarian Intervention in International Society*. Oxford: Oxford University Press.

Wheeler, Nicholas J., and Tim Dunne. 1998. "Good International Citizenship: A Third Way for British Foreign Policy." *International Affairs* 74 (4): 847–70.

Whitworth, Sandra. 2004. *Men, Militarism, and UN Peacekeeping: A Gendered Analysis*. Boulder, CO: Lynne Rienner.

WHO and UNICEF. 2012. "Countdown 2015: Maternal, Newborn and Child Survival: Building a Future for Women and Children: The 2012 Report." Washington, DC: Communications Development.

Wight, Martin. 1991. *International Theory: The Three Traditions*. Edited by G. White and B. Porter. Leicester: Leicester University Press.

Williams, Paul. 2005. "Blair's Commission for Africa: Problems and Prospects for UK Policy." *Political Quarterly* 76 (4): 529–39.

———. 2008. "Keeping the Peace in Africa: Why 'African' Solutions Are Not Enough." *Ethics and International Affairs* 22 (3): 309–29.

———. 2009. "The 'Responsibility to Protect', Norm Localisation, and African International Society." *Global Responsibility to Protect* 1 (3): 392–416.

Williams, Paul D., and Alex J. Bellamy. 2012. "Principles, Politics, Prudence: Libya, the Responsibility to Protect, and the Use of Military Force." *Global Governance* 18 (3): 273–97.

Williams, Paul, and David Black. 2010. "Introduction: International Society and the Crisis in Darfur." In *The International Politics of Mass Atrocities: The Case of Darfur*, edited by David Black and Paul Williams, 1–24. London: Routledge.

Wood, Bernard. 2007. "Managing Canada's Growing Development Cooperation: Out of the Labyrinth." In *Exporting Good Governance: Temptations and Challenges in Canada's Aid Program*, edited by Jennifer Welsh and Ngaire Woods, 225–51. Waterloo, ON: Wilfrid Laurier University Press.

Wood, Bernard, Dorte Kabell, Francisco Sagasti, and Nansozi Muwanga. 2008. *Synthesis Report on the First Phase of the Evaluation of the*

Implementation of the Paris Declaration. Copenhagen: Ministry of Foreign Affairs of Denmark, July.

Wright, Robert. 1991. *A World Mission: Canadian Protestantism and the Quest for a New International Order, 1918–1939.* Montreal and Kingston: McGill-Queen's University Press.

Yamashita, Hikaru. 2013. "The Group of 8 and Global Peacekeeping, 2004–2010." *Global Governance* 19 (3): 333–52.

York, Geoffrey. 2009a. "Why Has It Taken So Long?" *Globe and Mail,* 30 January.

———. 2009b. "Banned Aid." *Globe and Mail,* 29 May.

———. 2011. "19 Villagers Dead/$155 Million Profit." *Report on Business Magazine, Globe and Mail,* November.

———. 2012a. "Canada Reduces Support for Zimbabwe on Cusp of Critical Election." *Globe and Mail,* 16 July.

———. 2012b. "Africa Next: With Investment Outpacing Aid, Is This a New Golden Age for the Poorest Continent?" *Globe and Mail,* 22 September.

———. 2012c. "Trade, Not Aid, the Theme of Harper's Visit to Africa." *Globe and Mail,* 9 October.

Index

Tables indicated by italic page numbers

Abacha, Sani, 72, 73
Abyei: UNIFSA, 216
Accra Agenda for Action, 110, 121
activist engagement, 2. *See also*
 good international citizenship
Advisory Group, 174, 177–78,
 258n19
Advisory Group Consensus Report,
 154, 174–75, 177, 178–79, 180
AE. *See* Analytical Eclecticism
 framework
Afghanistan: aid to, 52, *115*, 118,
 183, 248n17; Canadian contributions to war in, 136, 143,
 248n17, 254n5; Canadian
 troops in, 52, 142; and Harper
 government, 51, 57, 118, 124;
 and Muskoka Initiative, 248n21;
 Roméo Dallaire support for
 Canada in, 88; and START,
 256n22; and UNAMID, 77
AFISMA (African-led International
 Support Mission to Mali), 193,
 217
Africa: in 1950s and 1960s, 86;
 "Africa rising" narrative, 10, 81,
 198–99; Canada in, approach
 to, 3–4; economic marginality
 of, 250n2; Ethiopian famine,

and framing, 65; GDP growth
 of, 246n2; and Liberal governments, 113; lost decade of, 5; as
 marginal to Canada, 3, 4–5, 58;
 objectification of, 9, 29–30, 61;
 scholarship on Canada in, 7–8,
 245n2. *See also* Canada; commercial links; diplomatic links;
 investment links; morality tale;
 trans-societal links
Africa Action Plan (AAP): *vs.* "Africa rising" narrative, 199; and
 Canadian moral identity, 6, 75;
 and Chrétien government, 2,
 11, 15, 27, 37, 40–41, 74; evaluation of, 44–45, 56, 59, 75–76;
 goals and effects of, 37, 40, 44,
 55–56, 130; and Harper government, 29; as hegemonic project,
 27, 35, 130, 192; post–Washington Consensus of, 40; security
 capacity-building in, 130–31,
 137, 144
Africa Day celebration, 1
African Barrick Gold, 171–72
African Mineral Development Centre, 191
African Peace and Security Architecture (APSA), 137

African Police for Peace program, 139

African Union (AU): African Peace and Security Architecture, 137; AMISOM (Somalia), 139; Canadian contributions for capacity building, 47, 137, 138, 139, 140, 143, 144; DITF (Darfur), 139; Lawrence Cannon visit to, 53. *See also* AMIS (AU Mission in Sudan [Darfur]); UNAMID (Darfur)

Africa Partnership Forum (APF), 45, 113

aid darlings, 252n12

aid effectiveness: Chrétien and Martin governments' commitment to, 47, 112; and CIDA, 112, 120–21, 122–23; debates over, 6, 251n2; of Harper government, 107, 119–20, 122–23; as hegemonic, 190; in *International Policy Statement*, 113–14; and post–Washington Consensus, 40. *See also* Aid Effectiveness Agenda; Paris Declaration on Aid Effectiveness

Aid Effectiveness Agenda, 110–11, 112, 114, 192. *See also* aid effectiveness; Paris Declaration on Aid Effectiveness

aid orphans, 252n12

aid policies: as basis for Canadian links with Africa, 97; and commercial interests, 102, 192; Conservative platform on, 116–17; consistent inconsistency of, 2, 5–6, 12; ethical argument for, 103–4; as good international citizenship, 104–8; and hegemonic middlepowermanship, 107–14; introduction to, 98;

ODA Accountability Act (Bill C-293), 107; political motives for, 101–2; public attitudes toward, 116; scholarship on, 8; statist analysis of, 102–3; tied, 100, 102, 107, 118, 192; trends in, 100; and weak links with Africa, 97; weaknesses of, 101, 103, 106–7. *See also* aid effectiveness; Aid Effectiveness Agenda; CIDA; foreign aid

Air Task Force Mali, 243

Akuffo, Edward: on Canada's moral identity in Africa, 21, 26, 196, 249n1; *Canadian Foreign Policy in Africa*, 8; on Canadian policy in Africa, 15, 21; on idealization of Canadian activism, 23

Alcan, 162. *See also* Rio Tinto Alcan

Alien Torts Claims Act (US), 169

AMIS (AU Mission in Sudan [Darfur]): and Canada's reputation, 190; Canadian contributions to, 47, 57, 77, 84–85, 136, 139; end of, 233; and Robert Fowler, 21; support of as good international citizenship, 35, 141. *See also* Darfur

AMISOM (AU Mission in Somalia), 139

Analytical Eclecticism framework, 10, 16–17

Anglin, Douglas, 87

AngloGold Ashanti, 172

Angola: and Africa Action Plan, 130; and aid policies, 102; Canada in peace operations in, 254n6; and extractive industries, 158; MONUA, 210; and Robert Fowler, 21, 84; UNAVEM II, 205; UNAVEM III, 209

Aouzou Strip: UNASOG, 209

apartheid. *See* South Africa apartheid
APF (Africa Partnership Forum),
    45, 113
APRs (Personal Representatives of
    Heads of Government for Af-
    rica), 45
APSA (African Peace and Security
    Architecture), 137
arms, small, 22, 134
Arone, Shidane, 68
Aruush, Ahmad, 68
Asia: aid to, 100, 101
AU. *See* African Union
Axworthy, Lloyd: and Abacha re-
    gime, Nigeria, 84; as foreign
    minister, 73, 134, 185; Harker
    Commission, 168; Human Se-
    curity Agenda, 15, 22, 73, 130;
    and northern Uganda conflict,
    136; soft power agenda, 188

Baird, John, 1, 186, 187, 194, 198
Balkans, 142, 143
Bangladesh, *115*, 248n21
Baranja: UNTAES, 209
Baranyi, Stephen, 142–43
Barrick Gold Corp., 160, 171–72,
    179, 190–91
Bayne, Nicholas, 40
Benin, *115*, 248n12, 248n18,
    253nn21–22
Better Aid Bill (Bill C-293), 107,
    167
Biafran War, 31
Bill C-293 (ODA Accountability
    Act), 107, 167
Bill C-300 (on CSR), 179, 180
Blair, Tony, 43, 48, 76
Blair government: African policy
    of, 9, 30, 64, 252n8; and Glen-
    eagles Summit, 48, 49, 50, 93;
    "Year of Africa," 48

Bolivia, *115*
Bono, 48, 51, 91, 250n6
Bonte Gold Mines, 171
Bosnia and Herzegovina: UNMIBH,
    209; UNPROFOR, 206
Botswana, 157
Bouchard, Charles, 194
Boucher, Jean-Christophe, 64
Brazil, 256n4
Bre-X, 163
Britain. *See* Blair government
Brown, Chris, 113
Brown, Gordon, 48, 49
Brown, Stephen, 8, 251n4, 252n10
Browning, Christopher, 64
Brysk, Alison: Global Good Samari-
    tans, 185–86
"Building the Canadian Advan-
    tage" (DFAIT), 178–79
Bull, Hedley, 17
Bulyanhulu Gold Mine, 171
Burkina Faso: aid for, *115*, 161,
    248n12, 248n18, 253nn21–22;
    CSR pilot project in, 179, 190–
    91; investments in, 161
Burma, *115*
Burundi: ONUB, 215

Cambodia: aid for, *115*; UNAMIC,
    206; UNTAC, 206
Cameroon, 52, *115*, 201–3,
    248n12, 253n16, 253n21
Campbell, Bonnie, 158
Camp David Summit (2012), 45
Canada: in Africa, approach to,
    3–4; brand, 159, 160, 167;
    consistent inconsistency of,
    1–2, 4, 5–6, 41, 58–59, 84,
    183, 200; and international
    middlepowermanship, 41–42;
    international society concep-
    tions in, 21; as non-imperial, 31,

245n6; scholarship of in Africa,
7–8, 245n2; statements on relationship with Africa, 1; view
of Africa, 9, 61, 79–80. *See also*
Africa; aid policies; Canadian
Forces; Canadians; Chrétien
government; commercial links;
counter-narratives; Dept. of Foreign Affairs and International
Trade (DFAIT); diplomatic links;
ethical mission; extractive industries; foreign aid; foreign policy;
G8; good international citizenship; Harper government; hegemonic middlepowermanship;
iconic internationalists; identity,
Canadian; Martin government;
morality tale; Mulroney government; post-colonial framework;
security policies

Canada Among Nations (2013 edition), 8

Canada Fund for Africa, 46, 47, 52,
56, 138, 165

Canada Investment Fund for Africa
(CIFA), 47, 165–66

Canada Making a Difference in
the World (CIDA), 112, 113–14,
122–23

Canada Pension Plan (CPP), 166,
171, 172

Canada's Access to Medicines Regime, 53

Canadian Airborne Regiment, 32,
68, 133, 255n18

Canadian Council for International
Cooperation (CCIC), 100, 123

Canadian Council on Africa, 155,
166, 198

Canadian Election Survey, 116

Canadian Forces (CF): Air Task
Force Mali, 243; Canadian
Airborne Regiment, 32, 68, 133,
255n18; Conservative platform
on, 117; counter-narrative from,
78–79; in DRC, 71, 72, 133; and
good enough international citizenship, 186; in Libya, 142, 194;
in Mali, 172; and NATO, 142,
146; realist internationalism of,
146–47, 197; in Somalia, 67–68,
133; and UN, 91; view of Africa,
136, 137–38, 143, 146. *See also*
task forces

Canadian Foreign Policy in Africa
(Akuffo), 8

Canadian International Development Agency. *See* CIDA

Canadian International Development Platform, 183

Canadian International Institute
for Extractive Industries and
Development (CIIEID), 191–92

Canadian Network on Corporate
Accountability (CNCA), 169,
174, 175, 258n14

Canadian Peacebuilding Initiative,
134–35

Canadians: Africa-affected, 86–87;
iconic internationalists, 85;
peacekeeping ideal held by,
128–29, 131, 147–48; self-image
of, 84; and trends in policy, 200.
See also identity, Canadian

Canadian University Service Overseas (CUSO), 87, 100

Cannon, Lawrence, 53

capacity building: analysis of efforts
for, 140–41; Canadian contributions to, 47, 138–39, 143;
emphasis on, 13, 127, 137, 138,
144; G8 commitment to, 45;
Stephen Lewis on, 94

Caplan, Gerald, 86, 250n6

CAR. *See* Central African Republic
CARE, 100
Caribbean, *115*, 118, 119, 256n12
Carrier-Sabourin, Krystel, 189, 252n11
CCIC (Canadian Council for International Cooperation), 100, 123
Central African Republic (CAR): extractive industries in, 157; MINURCA, 132, 211, 227–28; MINURCAT, 216
Centre d'information et de documentation sur le Mozambique et l'Afrique australe (CIDMAA), 63
CF. *See* Canadian Forces
CFA (Commission for Africa), 40, 48, 49, 50
Chad: MINURCAT, 216; UNASOG, 209
Chapnick, Adam, 187
Chévrier, Lionel, 99
child soldiers, 90
China, 164, 256n4
Chirac, Jacques, 39, 43
Chrétien, Aline, 71
Chrétien, Jean, 42, 43, 75, 249n28. *See also* Chrétien government
Chrétien, Raymond, 71
Chrétien government: on Abacha regime, Nigeria, 72–73; activism of, 185; and Africa Action Plan, 2, 11, 15, 27, 37, 40–41, 44, 45, 55–56, 74; and aid effectiveness, 112; cuts to aid, 12, 29, 58, 75, 101, 106; in DRC, 71–72, 133, 195; and good international citizenship, 130, 134; Kananaskis Summit, 43–44; Pinchpenny Diplomacy, 23; reinvestment in CIDA, 12, 98, 112. *See also* Chrétien, Jean

CIDA (Canadian International Development Agency): and Advisory Group report, 174; in Afghanistan, 118, 248n17; and aid effectiveness, 112, 120–21, 122–23; aid partners of, 80, 114, 184, 196; on Canada Fund for Africa, 46; *Canada Making a Difference in the World*, 112, 113–14, 122–23; Chrétien reinvestment in, 12, 112, 252n14; creation of, 100; and CSR, 166; CSR pilot projects, 179, 181, 190–91, 192; and extractive industries, 165; in Ghana, 105; and Harper government, 118–19, 121–22; health initiatives through, 53; as hegemonic, 125; industrial cooperation programs, 102, 192; in Inter-Departmental Steering Committee, 258n15; in Liberia, 224; merge with DFAIT, 12–13, 103, 184, 192–93, 246n10, 251n1; and Muskoka Initiative, 56; and NGOs and CSOs, 106, 123, 186; partnerships focus of, 143–44; responsive programming of, 112; and Sierra Leone, 144; Stephen Brown on, 8; and Structural Adjustment Programs, 109; and Sudan and South Sudan, 135; weaknesses of, 97, 103, 122–23; in West Africa, 224; and women's development, 105. *See also* aid policies; foreign aid
CIDMAA (Centre d'information et de documentation sur le Mozambique et l'Afrique australe), 63
CIFA (Canada Investment Fund for Africa), 47, 165–66

CIIEID (Canadian International Institute for Extractive Industries
and Development), 191–92
civil society organizations (CSOs):
and CIDA, 106, 123, 179; and
governmentality, 258n17; and
Harper government, 186, 189,
191; power of, and extractive
industries, 152, 153, 168, 169;
in Roundtable process, 176
Clark, Campbell, 194
Clark, Joe, 53, 66, 117, 187, 197
CNCA (Canadian Network on Corporate Accountability), 169,
174, 175, 258n14
Colombo Plan, 99
Colombia, 115, 119, 256n22
commercial links: and "Africa rising" narrative, 81; and aid, 102,
192; British, 30; and extractive
industries, 26; growth of, 97–98,
196; under Harper government,
120, 161, 167, 200; to Latin
America, 57; as marginal, 4–5,
154; overshadowed by ethical
narrative, 31, 97; overview of,
155–56; trade, amount of, 4–5,
15, 155; types of, 9–10. See also
extractive industries
Commission for Africa (CFA), 40,
48, 49, 50
Commonwealth: and Abacha regime, Nigeria, 72, 73; and Canadian engagement with Africa, 41,
73, 99, 102, 138, 186, 253n16;
centrality of for Canada, 246n7;
Colombo Plan, 99; and Harper
government, 57, 117; John
Diefenbaker on, 252n6
Congo: ONUC, 127, 249n3. See also
Democratic Republic of the
Congo (DRC)

Conservative government. See
Harper government
Convention on Genocide, 129
Corporate Social Responsibility. See
CSR
corporations, 167, 169, 176. See
also CSR (Corporate Social
Responsibility)
Côte d'Ivoire: aid for, 201–2;
UNOCI, 134, 214, 241–42, 254n6
counter-consensus, 63
counter-narratives, 58, 63–64, 66,
78–79, 116, 197. See also realist
internationalism
Cox, Robert, 24, 25, 41
Coxian historicism, 24. See also he-
gemonic middlepowermanship
CPP (Canada Pension Plan), 166,
171, 172
Croatia: UNCRO, 209; UNMOP, 210;
UNPROFOR, 206; UNTAES, 209
Crowson, Philip, 180
CSOs. See civil society organizations
CSR (Corporate Social Responsibil-
ity): Advisory Group Consensus
Report and Roundtables, 174–
78; and Alien Torts Claims Act
(US), 169; Bill C-300 on, 179,
180; Canadian government on,
154, 166–67; critiques of imple-
mentation, 169
CUSO (Canadian University Service
Overseas), 87, 100

Daigle, J.R.P., 208
Dallaire, Roméo: belief in UN, 91;
causes supported by, 89–90; and
Darfur, 90–91, 250n5; as iconic
internationalist, 12, 22, 69, 89,
91–92, 250n3; introduction to,
85–86, 88; as patriot, 90–91;
and Rwandan genocide, 2,

68–69, 88–89, 133; and senate, 249n4, 250n5; in UNAMIR, 208, 232; in UNOMUR, 207
Dallaire, Sébastien, 116
Darfur: and Canadian counter-narrative, 79; DITF, 139; and Harper government, 196; Martin government on, 77, 194; and R2P, 15; Roméo Dallaire on, 90–91. *See also* AMIS (AU Mission in Sudan [Darfur]); UNAMID (Darfur)
Darfur Integrated Task Force (DITF), 139
Darimani, Adbulai, 172
Dashwood, Hevina, 175–76
Dawson, Grant, 4–5, 7, 245n3, 249n28
Deauville Summit (2011), 249n24
defence policies. *See* security policies
de Gaulle, Charles, 99
Democratic Republic of the Congo (DRC): aid for, *115, 202*; in *Global Markets Action Plan*, 161; Great Lakes crisis, 70; investments in, 161; Ituri region crisis, 195; mining industry in, 157; MNF, 70–72, 79, 132, 133, 141; MONUC, 80, 81, 135, 193, 213, 238–39, 241; MONUSCO, 135, 217, 238, 240–41; ONUC, 127, 249n3; peacekeeping failure in, 13; and START, 256n22; Stephen Harper visit to, 198; UN panel on resource exploitation in, 169–70
Denmark: ODA, 251n3
Dept. of Foreign Affairs, Trade, and Development (DFATD). *See* Dept. of Foreign Affairs and International Trade (DFAIT)

Dept. of Foreign Affairs and International Trade (DFAIT): and Advisory Group report, 174; and aid as hegemonic, 125; and capacity building, 143, 146; and extractive industries, 166; Global Issues Bureau, 134, 143, 177; Inter-Departmental Steering Committee, 174; merge with CIDA, 8, 12–13, 103, 184, 192–93, 246n10, 251n1; and NGOs and CSOs, 186; and R2P, 256n21; renaming of, 246n10; Stabilization and Reconstruction Task Force, 135, 143, 256n22; view of Africa, 32
Dept. of National Defence (DND), 58, 137, 140, 146
DFAIT. *See* Dept. of Foreign Affairs and International Trade
DFATD. *See* Dept. of Foreign Affairs and International Trade (DFAIT)
Diamond Development Initiative (DDI), 106
diamonds, conflict, 22, 105–6, 134, 177
diasporas, African, 5, 10
Di Boscio, Nicolas, 257n6
Diefenbaker, John, 2, 15, 251n6
diplomatic links, 31, 52, 53, 97
DITF (Darfur Integrated Task Force), 139
DND. *See* Dept. of National Defence
Dominicans, French Canadian, 87. *See also* missionaries
DRC. *See* Democratic Republic of the Congo
Duggal, Sneh, 1
Dunne, Tim, 17, 19

ear candy impulse, 77, 78
Eastern Slavonia: UNTAES, 209

East Timor: UNMISET, 213; UNMIT, 215; UNTAET, 212

ECOMIL (ECOWAS Mission in Liberia), 214, 221–22

economic links. *See* commercial links

ECOWAS: Canadian contribution to, 138; ECOMIL (Liberia), 214, 221–22

EDC (Export Development Canada), 47, 165, 166, 171, 177, 258n15

EITI (Extractive Industries Transparency Initiative), 158, 174–75, 257n7, 258n16

El Salvador: ONUSAL, 206

English School of International Relations theory, 17–18, 19, 20, 129. *See also* good international citizenship

entrepreneurial leadership, 21–22, 23, 28, 35, 186. *See also* norm entrepreneurship

Ericsson, Magnus, 157, 160, 162

Eritrea: UNMEE, 132, 133–34, 141, 213, 225–27; UNMEE-SHIRBRIG, 132, 133, 213, 225

ethical mission, 2–3, 11, 83, 152, 192. *See also* identity, Canadian; morality tale

Ethiopia: aid for, 99, *115*, 183, *201–3*, 248n12, 253n16; and CIDA, 119, 122; famine in, 2, 15, 31, 65, 105; and Muskoka Initiative, 248n21; UNMEE, 132, 133–34, 141, 213, 225–27; UNMEE-SHIRBRIG, 132, 133, 213, 225

EU. *See* European Union

European Union (EU), 256n4

Evian Summit (2003), 45, 113

Export Development Corporation (EDC), 47, 165, 166, 171, 177, 258n15

extractive industries: Advisory Group and Roundtables process, 174–79, 180–81; in Africa, 156–57, 161–62; Canada's support for, 152; Canadian companies, 151–52, 160–61, 162–63, 164, 171; Canadian companies as political actors, 169; Canadian companies in DRC, 169–70; and Canadian self-image, 160; competition in Africa, 164; consolidation of companies, 162; controversies in, 167–68, 170–71, 172–73; critiques of, 157–58; debate over, 180–81; decline in exploration, 163; and economic development, 257n6; fast track for, 124; and Harper government, 28, 153–54; hegemonic interests in, 180; importance of in Africa, 13–14, 97–98, 154; investments in, and security resources, 254n2; investments in Africa, 151–52, 161, 256n2; junior exploration companies, 162, 163–64, 165, 257n9; in Latin America, 257n12; limitations of focus on, 9; and morality tale, 152, 153–55, 181; support for, 157; and sustainable development, 164, 176; and trade, 5; types of companies, 257n9

Extractive Industries Transparency Initiative (EITI), 158, 174–75, 257n7, 258n16

faith-based organizations, 99

Falconbridge, 162

Fantino, Julian, 191, 359nn6–7

Fast, Ed, 1, 198

fire brigade internationalism, 141

Forcese, Craig, 168

foreign aid: 1990-2010 to Sub-Saharan Africa, 100–101, 201–3; claim of doubling, 50, 51, 52, 54; and commercial aims, 161; Countries of Focus, 115, 248n12, 248n18, 253n16, 253n21, 254n9; cuts to, 23, 29, 248n19, 251nn3–4; diffusion of, 106, 252n10; under Harper government, 52, 83, 119, 120, 144, 183, 196; history of, 99; as largest link to Africa, 5, 31; under Martin government, 114; and Structural Adjustment Programs, 109. See also aid policies; CIDA

foreign policy, 15, 21, 26–27. See also counter-narratives; good international citizenship; hegemonic middlepowermanship; morality tale; post-colonial framework

Fowler, Robert: and Africa Action Plan, 43, 44, 56, 74, 130; and Angola conflict, 21, 84, 247n8; career, 247n8; and Darfur, 250n5; Mali abduction of, 87, 247n8, 359n8; on Mali crisis, 193

France: and Africa Action Plan, 39; desire to burden share, 132; and Ituri crisis, 195; and Mali, 172, 193, 194; and MNF, 70; ODA cuts, 251n3; and peace operations, 136

francophone Africa: aid to, 99, 102, 119; and Canada, further study needed on, 9; capacity building in, 139; Quebec and Canada and, 15, 26, 87, 246n7

Francophonie, la, 41, 57, 65, 102, 186, 253n16

Freeman, Linda, 87, 246n8

Free the Children, 85

Freetown, Sierra Leone, 254n10

G8: African focus as hegemonic project, 39, 59; African focus of, 30, 39–40, 45–46; and anti-globalization protests, 39, 246n3; Canada in, 11, 37, 42, 46–48, 49–50, 59, 131; and capacity building, 131, 136, 145; failure to meet commitments, 46, 247n9. See also Africa Action Plan; Gleneagles Summit (2005); Heiligendamm Summit (2007); Kananaskis Summit (2002); Muskoka Initiative on Maternal, Newborn and Child Health; other summits

GAD (Gender and Development), 110

Gallagher, Julia, 9, 30, 64, 67, 188, 252n8

Gaza, 115

Geldof, Bob, 48, 51

Gender and Development (GAD), 110

Genoa Summit (2001), 39

Georgia: UNOMIG, 208

Germany: ODA, 251n3

Ghana: aid for, 99, 110, 115, 161, 201–3, 248n12, 258n1; and CIDA, 105, 109, 179, 190–91; Ed Fast visit to, 198; military training assistance for, 137, 138; mining controversies in, 171; mining industry, 157, 161, 162

Gleneagles Summit (2005): African focus of, 48–49, 76; aid commitments, 93, 248n22; and

Canadian commitments, 37, 38, 49–50, 51, 113; Commission for Africa report, 40, 48, 49; politics of, and hegemonic interests, 59

Global Good Samaritans (Brysk), 185–86

Global Issues Bureau, 134, 143, 177

globalization, 38, 39, 42

Global Markets Action Plan (2013), 161, 248n22

Global Peace and Security Fund, 139, 143, 255n15

Global Peace Operations Initiative, 137, 139

Global Peace Operations Program (GPOP), 139

Global Reporting Initiative (GRI), 177

Goodale, Ralph, 48

good international citizenship: and aid policy, 98, 104–8, 125; Alison Brysk on, 185; approach to, 10, 16; basis of, 17–19, 129; and Canada, 2, 21–23, 129–30; and Edward Akuffo, 8; and extractive industries, 14, 154; good enough, 47–48, 128, 146, 186; and Harper government, 186–90; and hegemonic middlepowermanship, 27–28, 42; influence of, 20; Kim Nossal on, 20–21; overview, 34–35; and peace operations, 128, 141; and positive self-image, 84; and post-colonial framework, 32; principles of, 19–20; resilience of, 11–12

governmentality, 258n17

Gramsci, Antonio, 24

Grayson, Kyle, 159

Great Britain. See Blair government

Greater Nile Petroleum Operating Company (GNPOC), 168

Great Lakes crisis. See Democratic Republic of the Congo

GRI (Global Reporting Initiative), 177

Guatemala: MINUGUA, 210; and START, 256n22

Guay, Louis, 87

Guinea, 157

Guyana, 115

Haiti: aid for, 52, 115, 119, 183; MINUSTAH, 214; MIPONUH, 211; and Muskoka Initiative, 248n21; and START, 256n22; UNSMIH, 210; UNTMIH, 210

Halliday, Anthony, 83

Harker Commission, 168

Harper, Stephen, 50–51, 80, 198, 248n16

Harper government: and "Africa rising" narrative, 81; and aid effectiveness, 119–20; aid policy, 54–55, 83, 98, 116–17, 118–20, 121, 122–23, 124–25, 144, 161; and Canadian brand, 159; critiques of from opposition, 184, 200; differentiation efforts of, 57, 124, 184; distancing from Africa, 2, 3, 12, 14, 15, 23, 29, 76, 80, 83, 117, 147, 151, 196–97, 199; and economic opportunities in Africa, 155, 156; and extractive industries, 179, 190–91; focus on accountability, 248n11; foreign policy of, 57, 58, 63–64, 186, 187–88, 192–93; foundations for African claims of, 53–54; and good international citizenship, 186–90;

as hegemonic middlepowerman-ship, 190–95; in Libya, 194; as majority, 58, 81; and Mali, 190, 193–94, 199; Michael Ignatieff on, 1; as minority, 50–51; and MONUC, 80, 81; national narrative of, 142; and NGOs, 123; and northern Uganda, 136; peacekeeping under, 13, 131, 135, 148; policy drift on Africa, 51, 117, 118–19; policy process of, 184; and post-colonial framework, 32–33; and R2P, 256n21; realist internationalism of, 98, 116, 147, 187, 197, 199; reengagement with Africa, 183, 197–98, 200; response to Advisory Group report and Roundtables, 178–79, 184, 258n19; and tied aid, 107; tilt toward Latin America, 37, 51, 57–58, 80, 83, 118, 119, 124, 196; and UN Security Council seat, 38, 53, 120, 197, 257n8. *See also* Muskoka Initiative on Maternal, Newborn and Child Health

hegemonic: Africa Action Plan as, 130; definition of, 254n4; extractive industries as, 154, 180

hegemonic middlepowermanship: and accountability, 248n11; and aid policy, 98, 107–14, 125; approach to, 10, 14, 16; basis for, 24–26; Canada as, 2, 23, 25–26, 38, 190, 246n9; critique of, 29, 43; and G8 activism, 11; and good international citizenship, 27–28, 42; and Harper government, 190–95, 200; overview, 34–35; and peace operations, 128, 144–45. *See also* hegemonic

Heiligendamm Summit (2007): African focus of, 45, 76; and Harper government's commitments shift, 37, 50, 51, 80, 118

Hennessy, Michael, 71

Hitschfeld, Paul, 155

Holmes, John, 25, 41

Honduras, *115*

humane internationalism: Alison Brysk on, 185; as Canadian self-image, 42, 104; definition of, 249n1, 252n7; and Harper government, 81, 123, 124; and Jean Chrétien, 71; *vs.* realist internationalism, 116; Roméo Dallaire as, 69, 88, 91, 95–96; Stephen Lewis as, 88, 95–96

humanitarian emergencies, 18, 19, 28, 31, 67, 148

human rights: and aid policy, 98, 110; and Canada, 21, 185–86; and extractive industries, 153, 168, 172, 181; Roméo Dallaire on, 89–90; in solidarist view of international society, 18, 129. *See also* CSR (Corporate Social Responsibility); human security; Responsibility to Protect (R2P)

human security, 2, 6, 21, 159, 173. *See also* human rights; Human Security Agenda; peace operations; Responsibility to Protect (R2P)

Human Security Agenda, 15, 22, 28, 73, 130, 194

Humphreys, David, 163, 257n6

Huntsville Summit (2010). *See* Muskoka Initiative on Maternal, Newborn and Child Health; Muskoka Summit (2010)

hypocritical internationalism, 189

IAMGOLD Corp., 172, 179, 190–91
ICISS (International Commission
    on Intervention and State Sover-
    eignty), 73–74, 134
iconic internationalists, 12, 22, 85,
    95–96, 187. *See also* Axworthy,
    Lloyd; Dallaire, Roméo; Fowler,
    Robert; Lewis, Stephen; Pear-
    son, Lester
identity, Canadian: African policy
    for positive self-, 59, 77, 200;
    basis of, 1–2; bilingual, 9; brand-
    ing of, 159, 160, 167; Edward
    Akuffo on, 21, 26, 196, 249n1;
    ethically oriented, 2–3, 28,
    249n1; and extractive industries,
    160; factors for positive self-,
    84–85; and Great Lakes crisis,
    71; and Harper government, 33,
    116, 147; and hegemonic work,
    42; and iconic internationalists,
    84–86, 95–96; importance of
    initiatives for, 79; and la Fran-
    cophonie, 65, 102; moral, 8;
    non-imperial, 31, 245n6; peace-
    keeping, 135; and post-colonial
    framework, 10–11, 16, 78, 154,
    195–96. *See also* ethical mission
IFI (International Financial Institu-
    tion), 110, 112
Ignatieff, Michael, 1, 184
IMATT (International Military Assis-
    tance Training Team), 219
IMF (International Monetary
    Fund), 102, 109, 256n5
INCO, 162
India, 101, 164, 256n4
Indonesia, *115*
Inter-Departmental Steering Com-
    mittee, 174, 177–78, 258n15
International Assistance Envelope,
    196

International Commission on In-
    tervention and State Sovereignty
    (ICISS), 73–74, 134
International Criminal Court, 28,
    130, 134, 186
International Finance Corporation
    (IFC) Performance Standards,
    177
International Financial Institution
    (IFI), 110, 112
internationalist middlepowerman-
    ship, 41
International Military Assistance
    Training Team (IMATT), 219
International Monetary Fund
    (IMF), 102, 109, 256n5
International Policy Statement (2005),
    1, 46, 113–14, 165, 196,
    253n17
international society, 17–21, 129.
    See also good international
    citizenship
international system (system of
    states), 17–18
investment links, 151, 155–56, 161,
    196. *See also* commercial links
IPS. *See* International Policy State-
    ment (2005)
Iran, 188
Iraq: aid for, *115*; UNIKOM, 205
Israel, 187, 188
Ituri region, DRC, 195

Jackson, Robert, 18
Jackson, Ted, 113
Jaffer, Mobina, 250n5
Japan, 52
Jean, Michaëlle, 53, 81
Jordan, *115*, 253n22

KAIROS, 123
Kananaskis Summit (2002), 43–44,

74–75, 75–76. *See also* Africa Action Plan
Kent, Peter, 52
Kenya: aid for, 52, *115, 201,* 248n12, 253n21; capacity building in, 137, 139
Kielburger, Craig and Marc, 85
Kimberley Process, 105–6, 134, 177
Kosovo: UNMIK, 211
Kuwait, 205

Landmine Treaty, 130, 134
Langdon, Steven, 86–87
l'Aquila Summit (2009), 45, 50, 52
Latin America: aid to, 100; Canadian diplomatic missions in, 52; Canadian mineral exploration in, 257n12; CIDA and extractive sector in, 165; Harper government tilt toward, 37, 51, 57–58, 80, 83, 118, 119, 124, 196; mining companies from, 164
Lemay, Jean-Jacques, 208
Lemieux, André, 160, 161
Leslie, Andrew, 80, 135
Lewis, Stephen: on Africa in 1950s and 1960s, 86; and apartheid in South Africa, 66; as "Canadian of the Year," 92; critical stance of, 92–94; as iconic internationalist, 12, 22, 95, 250n3; introduction to, 85–86, 88; Massey Lectures, 92–93; public service of, 88, 92; on Rwanda panel, 250n6; Stephen Lewis Foundation, 250n7; and UN, 94
Liberal Party of Canada, 58, 250n5. *See also* Chrétien government; Martin government
Liberia: aid for, 99; mining industry in, 157, 158; UNMIL, 134, 214, 222, 223–24; UNMIL-SHIRBRIG, 135, 214, 221, 223; UNOMIL, 208, 221, 222, 224
Libya: Harper government in, 136, 142, 194; UNASOG, 209
Linklater, Andrew, 18–19
Live 8 concerts, 48
Lough Earne Summit (2013), 257n7
Lyon, Peyton, 103

MacDonald, David, 87
MacDonald, Flora, 187
MacDonald, Laura, 31
Macedonia: UNPREDEP, 209
MacKenzie, Lewis, 206
Madagascar, 161
Make Poverty History (MPH) campaign, 48
Malawi: aid for, 52, *115, 202,* 248n12, 253n21; and Muskoka Initiative, 248n21
Mali: AFISMA, 217, 243; aid for, 110, *115, 201–3,* 248n12; capacity building in, 139, 193, 255n15; crisis, and Harper government, 81, 147, 190, 193–94, 199; mining industry in, 172; and Muskoka Initiative, 248n21
Mandela, Nelson, 67
Martin, Paul, 76–77, 113, 250n6
Martin government: aid policy, 98, 112; commitment to Africa, 113; end of, 50; *International Policy Statement* (2005), 46, 113–14; and R2P, 74, 76–77; and SCFAIT report, 174; transition to, 76
Massie, Justin, 142
materialist (neo-Marxist) framework, 26–27, 249n2
Matthews, Robert, 138
Mauritania, 157, 161

Mbeki, Thabo, 39
Mbembe, Achille, 29–30
McKay, John, 179
McLean, Walter, 87
Médecins sans frontières (MSF), 85, 100
Merkel, Angela, 45, 76
MI. See Muskoka Initiative on Maternal, Newborn and Child Health
middle powers, 25, 41, 45, 131, 190. See also hegemonic middlepowermanship
migration links, 97
Military Training and Cooperation Program (MTCP), 47, 139. See also Military Training Assistance Program
Military Training Assistance Program (MTAP), 139, 140, 143. See also Military Training and Cooperation Program
Millennium Development Goals (MDGs), 46, 49, 110, 120, 188–89, 359n4
Mining Association of Canada, 174
mining companies. See extractive industries
Mining in Developing Countries—Corporate Social Responsibility (SCFAIT), 173–74
Mining Watch Canada, 258n14
MINUGUA (Guatemala), 210
MINURCA (CAR), 132, 211, 227–28
MINURCAT (CAR and Chad), 216
MINURSO (Western Sahara), 205
MINUSTAH (Haiti), 214
MIPONUH (Haiti), 211
missionaries, 31, 87, 250n1
Mitchell, Gregory, 215
Mittelman, James, 24
MNCH. See Muskoka Initiative on

Maternal, Newborn and Child Health
MNF. See Multinational Force (MNF), DCR
Mongolia, 115, 253n22
Monterrey Consensus on Financing for Development, 110, 120
MONUA (Angola), 210
MONUC (DRC): and Harper government, 80, 81, 135, 193; overview of, 213, 238–39, 241
MONUSCO (DRC), 135, 217, 238, 240–41
morality tale: and African marginality, 79–80, 195; and Chrétien government, 134; counter-narratives to, 63–64; and extractive industries, 152, 159; introduction to, 61–62; policy implications of, 78–80, 114, 116, 195–96; redemption in, 72–73; self-serving nature of, 76. See also ethical mission; identity, Canadian
Morrison, David, 251n6
Mozambique: aid for, 102, 115, 201–3, 248n12; Canadian military observers in, 254n6; and Muskoka Initiative, 248n21; ONUMOZ, 207
MSF (Médecins sans Frontières), 85, 100
MTAP (Military Training Assistance Program), 139, 140, 143. See also MTCP
MTCP (Military Training and Cooperation Program), 47, 139. See also MTAP
Mugabe, Robert, 66
Mulcair, Thomas, 184
Mulroney, Brian, 65, 187, 197
Mulroney government: African

engagement of, 65; apartheid South Africa and, 2, 15, 27, 65–66, 67, 75; and good international citizenship, 130

multilateralism, 20, 117, 186, 187

Multinational Force (MNF), DCR, 70–72, 79, 132, 133, 141

Muskoka Initiative on Maternal, Newborn and Child Health (MI): and abortion, 56, 189, 249n23; as Africa-centric, 258n2; announcement of, 56; and Canadian identity, 6; and gender issues, 252n11; goals of, 248n20; and good international citizenship, 125, 188–89; overview of, 54–55; renewed at 2014 "Summit," 259n3

Muskoka Summit (2010), 54, 56. *See also* Muskoka Initiative on Maternal, Newborn and Child Health

Namibia: aid for, 102; Canada in peace operations in, 254n6; mining industry in, 157; UNTAG, 132, 205

narratives, purpose of, 64

National Roundtables on CSR and the Canadian Extractive Industry in Developing Countries, 154, 174, 175–77, 177–78, 180, 181, 184

National University of Rwanda, 87

NATO: in Afghanistan, 51, 57, 136, 142; and Canada, 4, 101, 130, 136, 142, 143, 146, 194; in Libya, 136, 194; and Mali crisis, 193; realist internationalism of, 87

Natural Resources Canada (NRCan), 166, 174, 175, 177, 258n15

neo-Gramscian framework. *See* hegemonic middlepowermanship

neo-Marxist (materialist) framework, 26–27

NEPAD (New Partnership for Africa's Development), 37, 39, 40, 44, 74, 110

Netherlands: ODA, 251n3

Neufeld, Mark, 26

New Democratic Party, 249n27

new global public domain, 153, 167, 173, 180

New Labour government. *See* Blair government

New Partnership for Africa's Development (NEPAD), 37, 39, 40, 44, 74, 110

NGDOs (non-governmental development organizations), 99–100, 107, 112. *See also* civil society organizations

NGOs (non-governmental organizations), 99–100, 105, 106, 123. *See also* civil society organizations

Nicaragua, *115*

Niger, 52, *115*, 157, 248n12, 253n21

Nigeria, 72–73, 137, 198, *202*, 248n21

Noël, Alain, 116

norm entrepreneurship, 41, 70, 73, 134. *See also* entrepreneurial leadership

North Mara Gold Mine, 171–72

North–South Institute, 183

Norway: ODA, 251n3

Nossal, Kim, 20–21, 23, 77, 102–3, 184

NRCan (Natural Resources Canada), 166, 174, 175, 177, 258n15

nuclear disarmament, 90
Nutt, Samantha, 22, 85

Obasanjo, Olusegun, 39
ODA (Official Development Assis-
    tance), 101, 113, 161, 201–3,
    253n18
Oda, Bev, 52, 83, 107, 118, 120,
    179
ODA Accountability Act (Bill
    C-293), 107, 167
OECD Guidelines for Multinational
    Enterprises, 166, 170
Office for Democratic Governance,
    118
Office of Religious Freedom, 188
Official Development Assistance
    Accountability Act (Bill C-293),
    107, 167
ONUB (Burundi), 215
ONUC (Congo), 127, 249n3
ONUMOZ (Mozambique), 207
ONUSAL (El Salvador), 206
Operation Addition (UNMEE, Ethio-
    pia and Eritrea), 226–27
Operation Augural (AMIS, Sudan),
    233
Operation Chaperon (UNMOP, Pre-
    vlaka), 210
Operation Consonance (ONUMOZ,
    Mozambique), 207
Operation Constable (UNTMIH,
    Haiti), 210
Operation Crocodile (MONUC,
    DRC), 213, 238–39
Operation Crocodile (MONUSCO,
    DRC), 217
Operation Deliverance (UNOSOM I
    and II, Somalia), 207, 229
Operation Eclipse (UNMEE-
    SHIRBRIG, Ethiopia and Eritrea),
    213, 225–26

Operation Halo (MINUSTAH,
    Haiti), 214
Operation Harmony (UNPROFOR,
    Croatia and Bosnia Herzegov-
    ina), 206
Operation Liane (UNMIL-SHIRBRIG,
    Liberia), 214, 222
Operation Matador (UNTAG, Na-
    mibia), 205
Operation Passage (UNAMIR,
    Rwanda), 208, 231
Operation Prudence (MINURCA,
    CAR), 211, 227–28
Operation Record (UNIKOM, Iraq-
    Kuwait), 205
Operation Safari (UNMIS, Sudan),
    215, 235–36
Operation Saturn (UNAMID, Dar-
    fur), 216, 233–34
Operation Scotch (UNAMIR,
    Rwanda), 208, 231
Operation Sculpture (UNAMSIL,
    Sierra Leone), 212, 219–21
Opération Serval (AFISMA, Mali),
    243
Operation Soprano (UNMISS,
    South Sudan), 216, 237
Operation Toucan (UNTAET, East
    Timor), 212
Operation Vision (MINUGUA, Gua-
    temala), 210
Orbinski, James, 22, 85
Organization of African Unity, 225,
    250n6
Our Common Future (CFA), 48
Oxfam, 100

Pakistan, 115
Paris, Roland, 148
Paris Club, 109
Paris Declaration on Aid Effective-
    ness: in Aid Effectiveness Agenda,

110; and Canadian aid policy, 12, 27, 113; and CIDA aid effectiveness plan, 120; and Harper government, 192; principles of, 110–11. *See also* aid effectiveness; Aid Effectiveness Agenda
Partnership Africa Canada, 22, 105
partnerships, 110, 143–44, 152
Pax Americana, 24, 25
Pax Britannica, 25
peacebuilding, 6, 22, 28, 73, 138, 144
peacekeeping, 148, 254n1, 255n13, 255n19
peace operations: in Africa Action Plan, 130–31; Canada in, 13, 52, 135–36, 141–44, 254nn5–6, 256n20; and Canadian self-image, 148; capacity-building, 47, 137–39, 137–41, 140–41, 143; consistent inconsistency of, 6; French-speaking personnel, 131–32; as good enough international citizenship, 145–46; regionalization of, 127, 136, 144; terminology for, 253n1; trends among West, 136; UN *vs.* NATO, 136, 142, 143. *See also* Canadian Forces; peacebuilding; peacekeeping; security policies
Pearson, Lester, 15, 26, 87
Pearson Commission on International Development, 49
Pearsonian internationalism, 66
Pearson Peacekeeping Centre, 139, 143, 255n15
Personal Representatives of Heads of Government for Africa (APRS), 45
Peru, *115*, 119, 179, 190–91
Philippines, *115*, 253n22
Pinchpenny Diplomacy, 23

Plan Canada, 179
post-colonial framework: and "Africa rising" narrative, 199; and Blair government, 30–31; and Canada, 31–32; and Canada's self-image, 152, 154, 159, 160; and good international citizenship, 32; and Harper government, 32–33, 125; and initiative-manship, 156; introduction to, 10–11, 16, 29–30; and morality tale, 195; overview, *34–35*; and peace operations, 128, 148; Somalia and Rwanda in, 70
post-Washington Consensus, 40
Pouliot, Neil, 208
Poverty Reduction Strategy Papers (PRSPS), 110, 111–12
Powell, Kristiana, 140, 141
Pratt, Cranford, 63, 87, 104, 246n8, 249n1, 252n7
Prevlaka: UNMOP, 210
Pring, George, 164
Project Ploughshares, 22
Prospectors and Developers Association of Canada, 174
PRSPS (Poverty Reduction Strategy Papers), 110, 111–12

Quebec: on aid to francophone Africa, 99; and francophone Africa, 15, 26, 65, 87, 246n7; and Mali, 193

R2P. *See* Responsibility to Protect
radical internationalism, 87
Razack, Sherene, 7, 89
RCAF (Royal Canadian Air Force), 172. *See also* Canadian Forces
Reagan government, 109
realist internationalism: of Canadian Forces, 146–47; definition

of, 6–7; of Harper government, 64, 98, 116, 197; of NATO, 87
Red Cross, 100
Regehr, Ernie, 22
regionalization. *See* capacity building
Reid, Richard, 61
resource nationalism, 176
Responsibility to Protect (R2P): and Darfur, 15; debate over, 74; and DFAIT, 256n21; as good international citizenship, 22, 130; and Harper government, 53, 142; as hegemonic, 28; as norm entrepreneurship, 134, 186; and Paul Martin, 76–77; and Roméo Dallaire, 90
responsive programming, 112. *See also* aid effectiveness
Rhodesia, 15, 26, 102. *See also* Zimbabwe
Rio Tinto Alcan, 162, 179, 190–91
"rising Africa" narrative, 10, 81, 198–99
Rock, Allan, 136
Roe, Emery, 64
Rome Declaration on Harmonization, 110
Roméo Dallaire Child Soldiers Initiative, 90
Rome Treaty, 130, 134
Roundtable process. *See* National Roundtables on CSR and the Canadian Extractive Industry in Developing Countries
Royal Canadian Air Force (RCAF), 172. *See also* Canadian Forces
Ruggie, John, 152–53, 167, 177
Rwanda: aid for, 52, *115*, *201–2*, 248n12, 253n21; as Canadian moral dereliction, 6, 13, 15, 70; genocide in, 2, 68–69, 88–89; National University of Rwanda, 87; Organization of African Unity panel on genocide in, 250n6; and R2P, 74; and SHIRBRIG, 134; UNAMIR, 68–69, 88–89, 91, 132, 133, 208, 231–32; UNOMUR, 207
Rwanda effect, 70

Sabourin, Louis, 250n1
Sadiola Gold Mine, 172
Said, Edward, 29
Saro-Wiwa, Ken, 72
Saul, John, 27, 87
SCFAIT (Standing Committee on Foreign Affairs and International Trade), 173–74
Schorr, Victoria, 155
Sea Island Summit (2004), 45
security policies: Canadian priorities, 4; and extractive industries, 254n2; failure of, 2; growth of, 97–98; of Harper government, 190, 193, 195; of Liberal governments, 195. *See also* Canadian Forces; capacity building; peace operations
self-image. *See* identity, Canadian
SEMA (Special Economic Measures Act), 169
Senegal, *115*, 157, 198, *201–2*, 248n12
Sharp, Mitchell, 103
SHIRBRIG (Standing High Readiness Brigade): overview of, 133–34, 254n8; UNAMIS- (Sudan), 215; UNMEE- (Ethiopia and Eritrea), 132, 133, 213, 225; UNMIL- (Liberia), 135, 214, 221, 223; UNMIS- (Sudan), 134, 215

Siegel, Shefa, 192
Siegle, Linda, 164
Sierra Leone: and Canada,
    254n10, 256n23; and CIDA,
    144; mining industry in, 157,
    158; UNAMSIL, 132, 135, 212,
    219–21; UNOMSIL, 211
Smillie, Ian, 22, 105
social licence, 176. *See also*
    CSR (Corporate Social
    Responsibility)
society of states, 18, 129
Somalia: AMISOM, 139; Canadian
    Airborne Regiment in, 32,
    67–68, 133; as Canadian moral
    dereliction, 6, 13, 15, 21, 67–
    68, 70; UNITAF, 67; UNOSOM I,
    67–68, 132, 141, 207, 229–30;
    UNOSOM II, 207, 229, 230
Somalia syndrome, 67–68
South Africa, 155, 161
South Africa apartheid: and aid
    policy, 102; and British arms
    sales to, 26; Canada against,
    2; and Canadian identity, 6;
    counter-consensus on, 66; and
    Mulroney government, 15, 27,
    65–66, 197; sanctions against,
    and Canada, 26
South Asia: aid to, 99
South Korea, 256n4
South Sudan: aid for, *115*, 135,
    144, 196, 254n9; and Canada,
    77; and Muskoka Initiative,
    248n21; and START, 256n22;
    UNMISS, 135–36, 216, 237–38
SPA (Special Program of Assistance
    for Low-Income Countries in
    Sub-Saharan Africa), 109–10
Special Economic Measures Act
    (SEMA), 169

Special Program of Assistance for
    Low-Income Countries in Sub-
    Saharan Africa (SPA), 109–10
Sri Lanka, *115*
Stabilization and Reconstruction
    Task Force (START), 135, 143,
    256n22
Stairs, Denis, 114
Standing Committee on Foreign
    Affairs and International Trade
    (SCFAIT), 173–74
START (Stabilization and Recon-
    struction Task Force), 135, 143,
    256n22
Stephen Lewis Foundation, 250n7
stock exchanges, Canadian, 161,
    163, 257n11
St. Petersburg Summit (2006), 45
Structural Adjustment policies:
    Canadian requirement for, 102;
    definition of, 256n5; effects of,
    109; and extractive industries,
    158, 161–62, 164; as hege-
    monic, 27, 190
Struggling for Effectiveness
    (Brown), 8
Sudan: aid for, 77, 114, *115*, 135,
    144, 196, *203*, 254n9; and ca-
    pacity building, 145; mining
    industry in, 158; and START,
    256n22; Talisman Energy con-
    troversy, 168; UNAMID, 233–34;
    UNAMIS-SHIRBRIG, 215; UNIFSA,
    216; UNMIS, 135–36, 215, 235–
    36; UNMIS-SHIRBRIG, 134, 215.
    See also AMIS (AU Mission in Su-
    dan [Darfur]); Darfur
Sudan Inter-Agency Reference
    Group, 169
Sudan Task Force, 144, *237*
Suganami, Hidemi, 18–19

sustainable development, 164.
   See also CSR (Corporate Social
   Responsibility)
Sutton Resources, 171
system of states (international sys-
   tem), 17–18

Tajikistan: UNMOT, 209
Talisman Energy, 168–69, 174, 176
Tanzania: aid for, *115, 201–3*,
   248n12, 258n1; investments in,
   161; military training assistance
   for, 137, 138; mining industry
   in, 171; and Muskoka Initiative,
   248n21
Task Force Darfur, 234
Task Force DRC, 239
Task Force South Sudan, 237
Task Force Sudan, 144, 215, 235
TAT (Theatre Activation Team),
   226–27
Taylor, Ian, 30
TCLSAC (Toronto Committee for
   the Liberation of Southern Af-
   rica), 63
Thatcher, Margaret, 65, 109
Theatre Activation Team (TAT),
   226–27
Thérien, Jean-Philippe, 116
Third World Network–Africa Secre-
   tariat, 171, 172
tied aid, 100, 102, 107, 118, 192
Tiessen, Rebecca, 189, 252n11
Timor-Leste. *See* East Timor
Toronto Committee for the Libera-
   tion of Southern Africa (TCL-
   SAC), 63
Toronto Stock Exchange, 257n11.
   See also stock exchanges,
   Canadian
Tousignant, Guy, 208, 232

Tokyo Summit (2008), 45
trade links. *See* commercial links
transparency, 257n7. *See also* CSR
   (Corporate Social Responsibility); Extractive Industries Transparency Initiative
trans-societal links, 5, 10, 97
Trudeau, Justin, 250n5
Trudeau, Pierre, 26
Turkey, 256n4

Uganda: conflict in northern, 136;
   military training assistance for,
   137; UNOMUR, 207
UNAMIC (Cambodia), 206
UNAMID (Darfur), 77, 136, 139,
   216, 233–34
UNAMIR (Rwanda): Canadian
   contribution to, 132, 133; and
   genocide, 68–69; overview of,
   208, 231–32; and Roméo Dal-
   laire, 88–89; and UN Security
   Council, 91
UNAMIS (Sudan), 134, 235
UNAMIS-SHIRBRIG (Sudan), 215
UNAMSIL (Sierra Leone), 132, 135,
   144, 212, 219–21
UNASOG (Aouzou Strip), 209
UNAVEM II (Angola), 205
UNAVEM III (Angola), 209
UNCRO (Croatia), 209
UNDP (UN Development Pro-
   gramme), 109
UNIFSA (Abyei), 216
UNIKOM (Iraq-Kuwait), 205
UNITAF (Somalia), 67
United Kingdom. *See* Blair
   government
United Nations: and Canada, 186;
   Charter, 129; peace operations
   of, 67, 142; Roméo Dallaire

belief in, 91; Stephen Lewis on, 94; Women, 251n8; World Summit document, 74. *See also* UN Security Council

United States of America: Camp David Summit, 45; and capacity building, 138; foreign aid by, 99, 251n3; investments in Africa, 256n4; Sea Island Summit, 45; in Somalia, 67; and UN peace operations, 67

Universal Declaration of Human Rights, 129

University of Dar es Salaam, 87

University of Zambia, 87

UNMEE (Ethiopia and Eritrea), 132, 133–34, 141, 213, 225–27

UNMEE-SHIRBRIG (Ethiopia and Eritrea), 132, 133, 213, 225

UNMIBH (Bosnia and Herzegovina), 209

UNMIH (Haiti), 208

UNMIK (Kosovo), 211

UNMIL (Liberia), 134, 214, 222, 223–24

UNMIL-SHIRBRIG (Liberia), 135, 214, 221, 223

UNMIS (Sudan), 134, 135–36, 215, 235–36

UNMISET (East Timor), 213

UNMISS (UN Mission in South Sudan), 135–36, 216, 237–38

UNMIS-SHIRBRIG (Sudan), 134, 215

UNMIT (Timor-Leste), 215

UN Monterrey Conference on Financing for Development (2002), 44

UNMOP (Prevlaka), 210

UNMOT (Tajikistan), 209

UNOCI (Côte d'Ivoire), 134, 214, 241–42

UNOMIG (Georgia), 208

UNOMIL (Liberia), 135, 208, 221, 222

UNOMSIL (Sierra Leone), 211

UNOMUR (Uganda-Rwanda), 207

UNOSOM I (Somalia), 67, 132, 133, 141, 207, 229–30

UNOSOM II (Somalia), 207, 229, 230

UNPREDEP (Macedonia), 209

UNPROFOR (Croatia and Bosnia Herzegovina), 206

UN Security Council: and Angola conflict, 21, 84, 247n8; Canadian seats on, 38, 53, 120, 197, 257n8; and MNF for DRC, 70–71; panel on resource exploitation in DRC, 169–70; and Rwandan genocide, 68–69. *See also* United Nations

UNSMIH (Haiti), 210

UNTAC (Cambodia), 206

UNTAES (Eastern Slavonia, Baranja, Western Sirmium), 209

UNTAET (East Timor), 212

UNTAG (Namibia), 132, 205

UNTMIH (Haiti), 210

UN Women, 251n8

van Ham, Peter, 160

Van Loan, Peter, 53, 198

Vietnam, *115*

Voluntary Principles on Security and Human Rights, 177

Wade, Abdoulaye, 39

War Child Canada, 85

weapons, light, 22

West Africa Peace and Security initiative, 138

West Bank, *115*

Western Sahara: MINURSO, 205,
    254n6
Western Sirmium: UNTAES, 209
Wheeler, Nicholas, 18, 19
WID (Women in Development),
    110
Wight, Martin, 19
Winsor, Hugh, 87
Women in Development (WID),
    110
World Bank, 102, 109, 256n5
World University Service of Canada
    (WUSC), 100, 179
World Vision, 179
WUSC (World University Service of
    Canada), 100, 179

Yamashita, Hikaru, 145
"Year of Africa" (2005), 30, 48

Zaire. See Democratic Republic of
    the Congo (DRC)
Zambia: aid for, 52, 109, *115*, *201*–
    3, 248n12, 253n21; military
    training assistance for, 137; min-
    ing industry in, 157, 161, 165
Zimbabwe: aid for, 102, 106, *201*;
    and capacity building, 145; min-
    ing industry in, 157, 165. *See also*
    Rhodesia